SHORTCAKE CAKE

STORY AND ART BY

suu Morishita

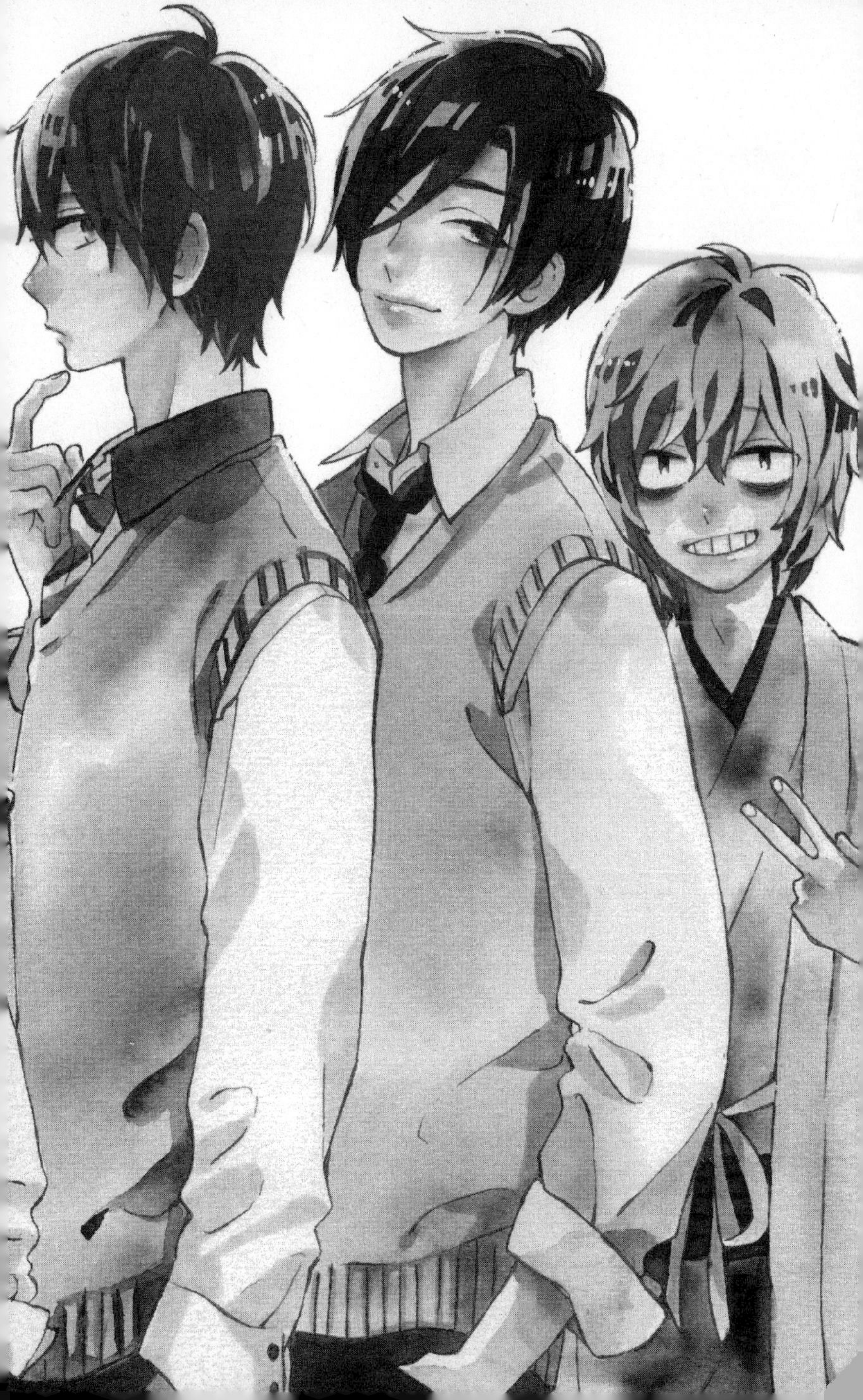

SHORTCAKE CAKE

1

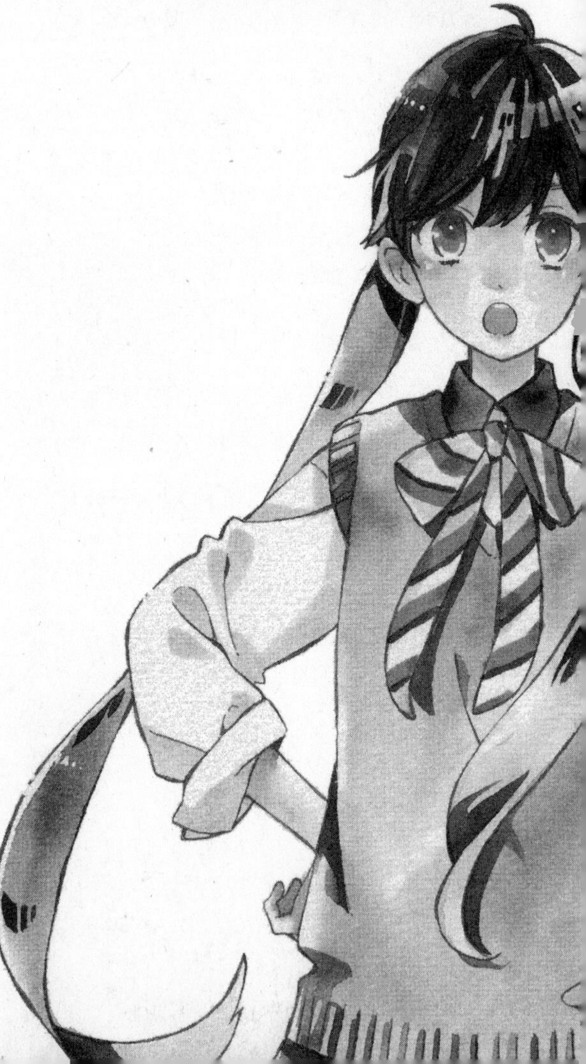

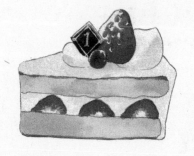

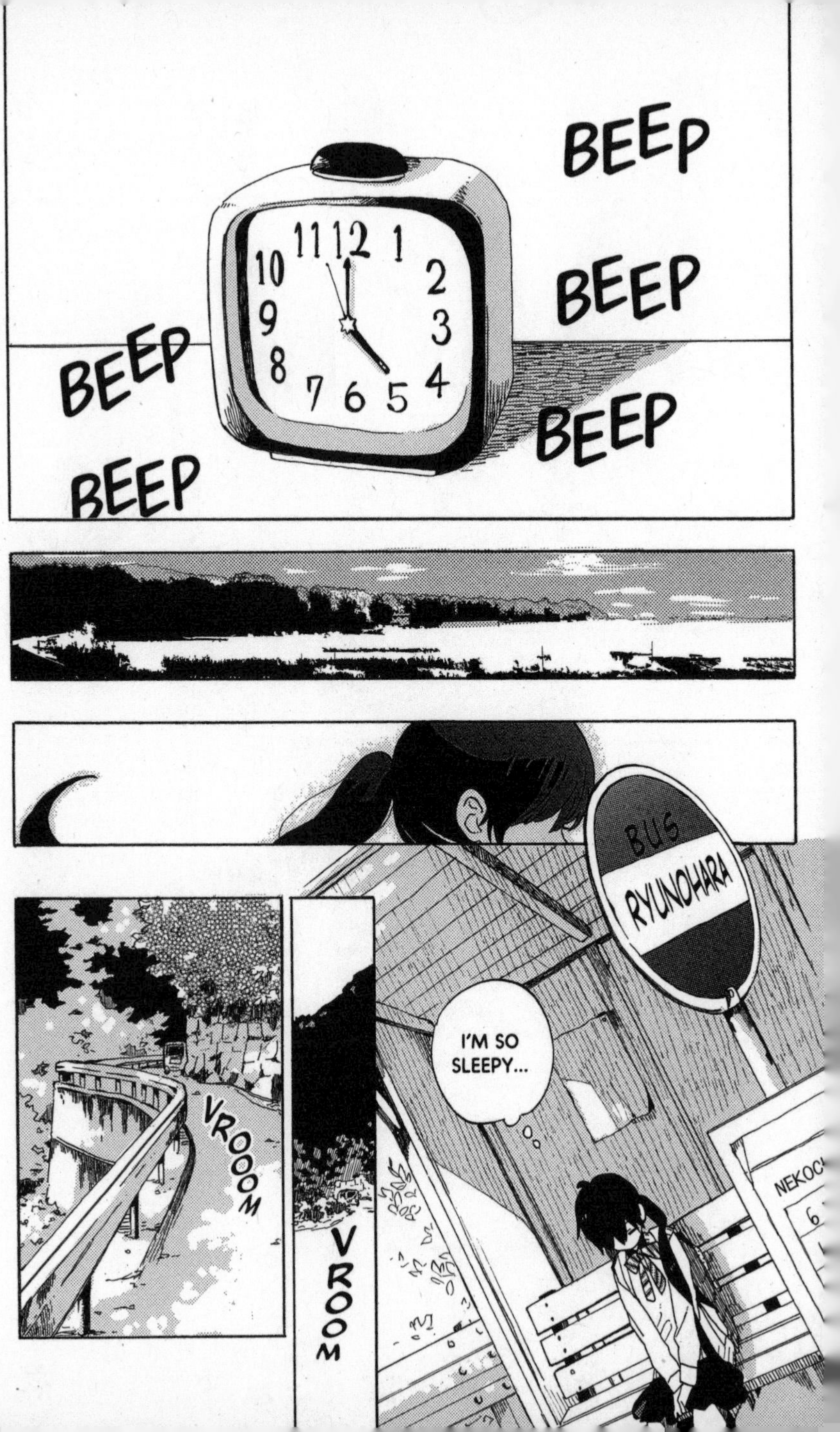
BEEP
BEEP
BEEP
BEEP
BEEP
BUS
RYUNOHARA
I'M SO SLEEPY...
VROOM
VROOOOM

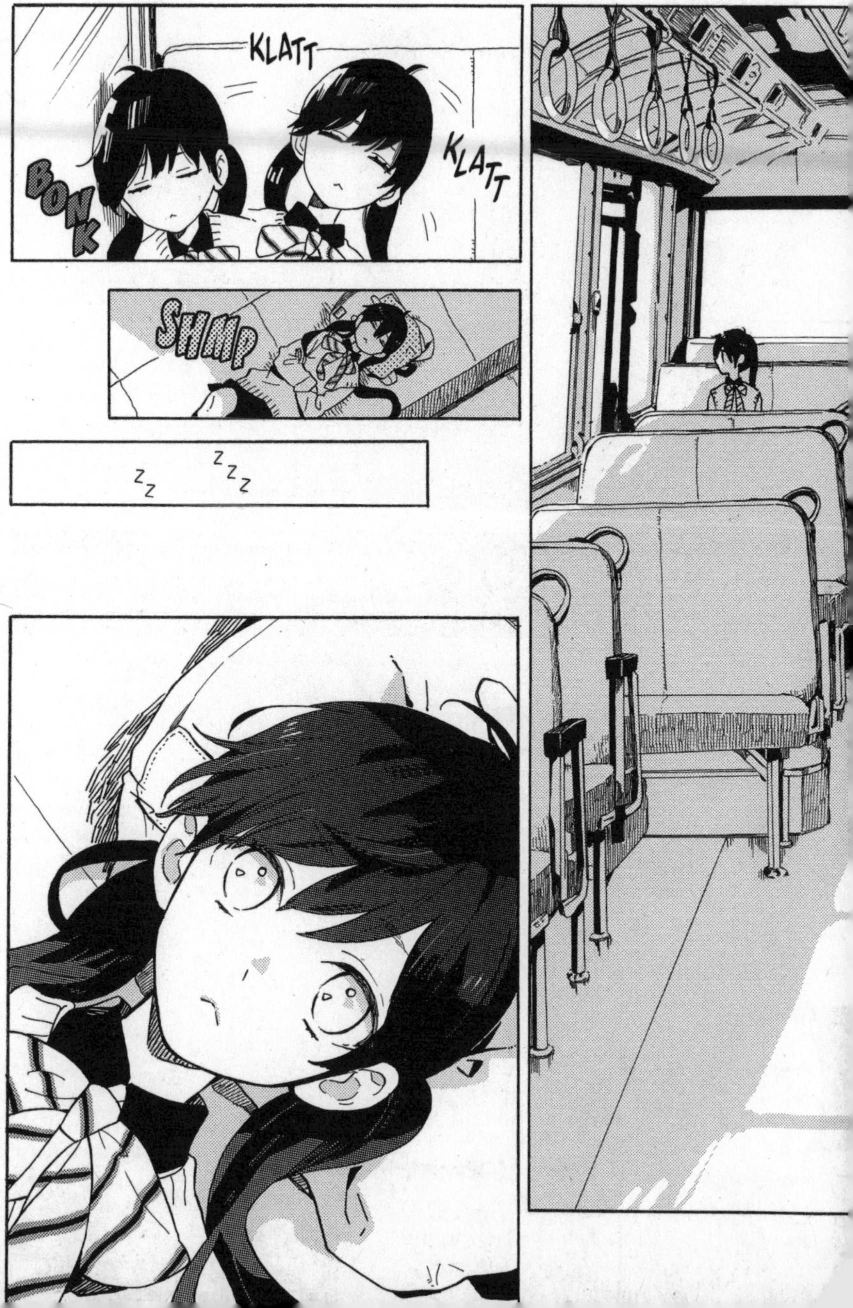
KLATT
KLATT
BONK
SHMP
ZZ
ZZZ

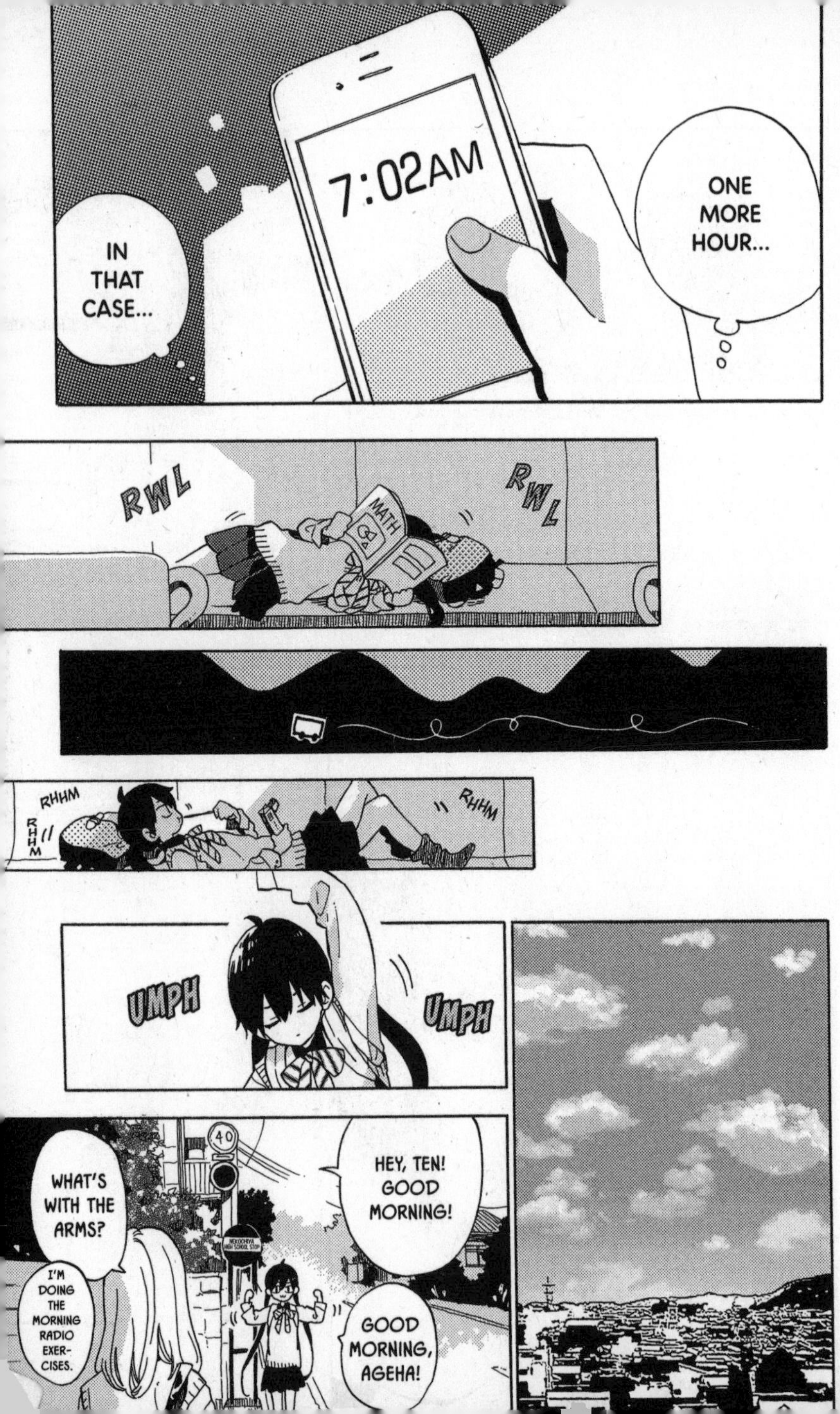
ONE MORE HOUR...
7:02AM
IN THAT CASE...
RWL
RWL
MATH
RHHM
RHHM
RHHM
UMPH
UMPH
HEY, TEN! GOOD MORNING!
40
WHAT'S WITH THE ARMS?
GOOD MORNING, AGEHA!
I'M DOING THE MORNING RADIO EXERCISES.

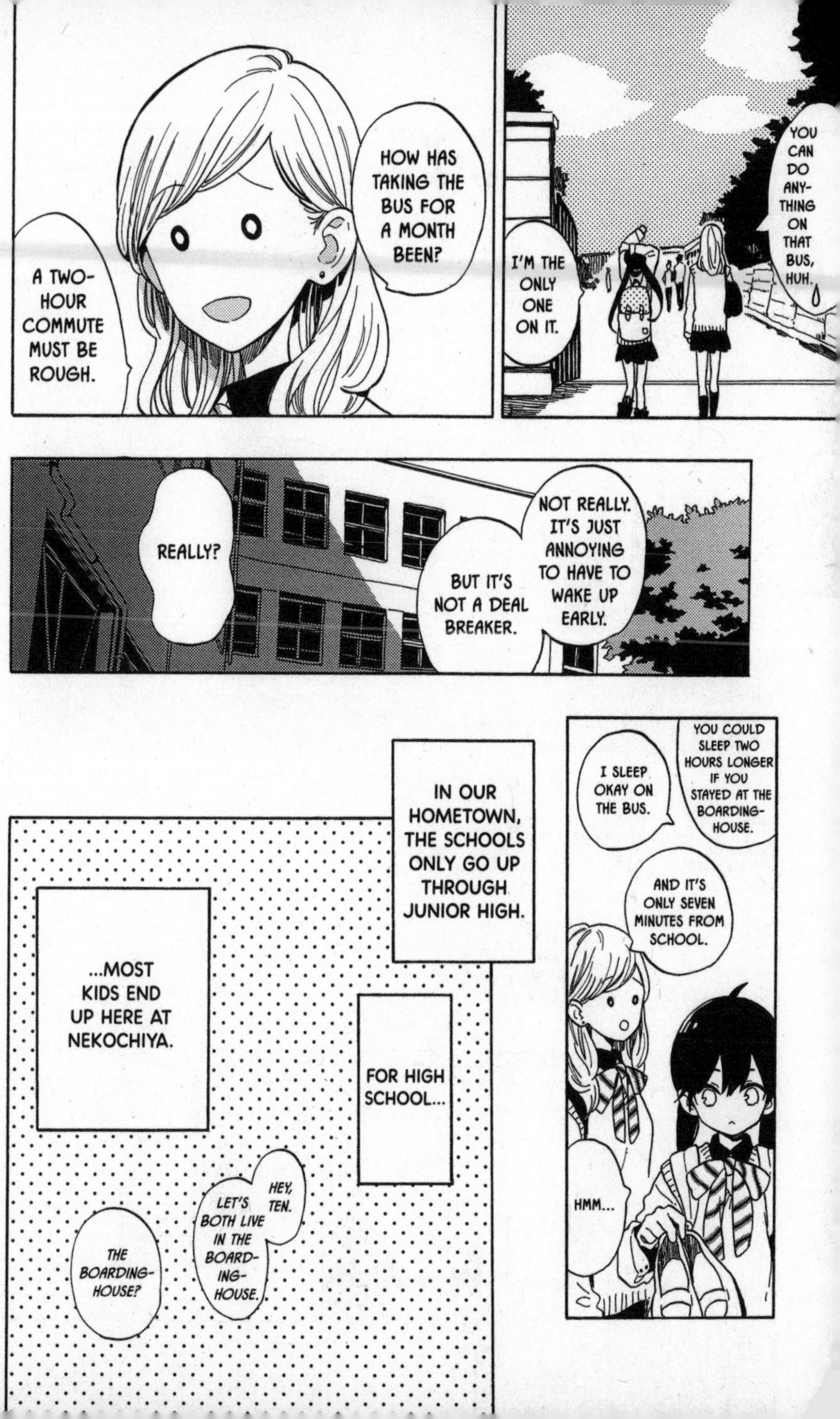
YOU CAN DO ANYTHING ON THAT BUS, HUH.
I'M THE ONLY ONE ON IT.
HOW HAS TAKING THE BUS FOR A MONTH BEEN?
A TWO-HOUR COMMUTE MUST BE ROUGH.
NOT REALLY. IT'S JUST ANNOYING TO HAVE TO WAKE UP EARLY.
BUT IT'S NOT A DEAL BREAKER.
REALLY?
YOU COULD SLEEP TWO HOURS LONGER IF YOU STAYED AT THE BOARDING-HOUSE.
I SLEEP OKAY ON THE BUS.
AND IT'S ONLY SEVEN MINUTES FROM SCHOOL.
HMM...
IN OUR HOMETOWN, THE SCHOOLS ONLY GO UP THROUGH JUNIOR HIGH.
FOR HIGH SCHOOL...
...MOST KIDS END UP HERE AT NEKOCHIYA.
HEY, TEN.
LET'S BOTH LIVE IN THE BOARDING-HOUSE.
THE BOARDING-HOUSE?

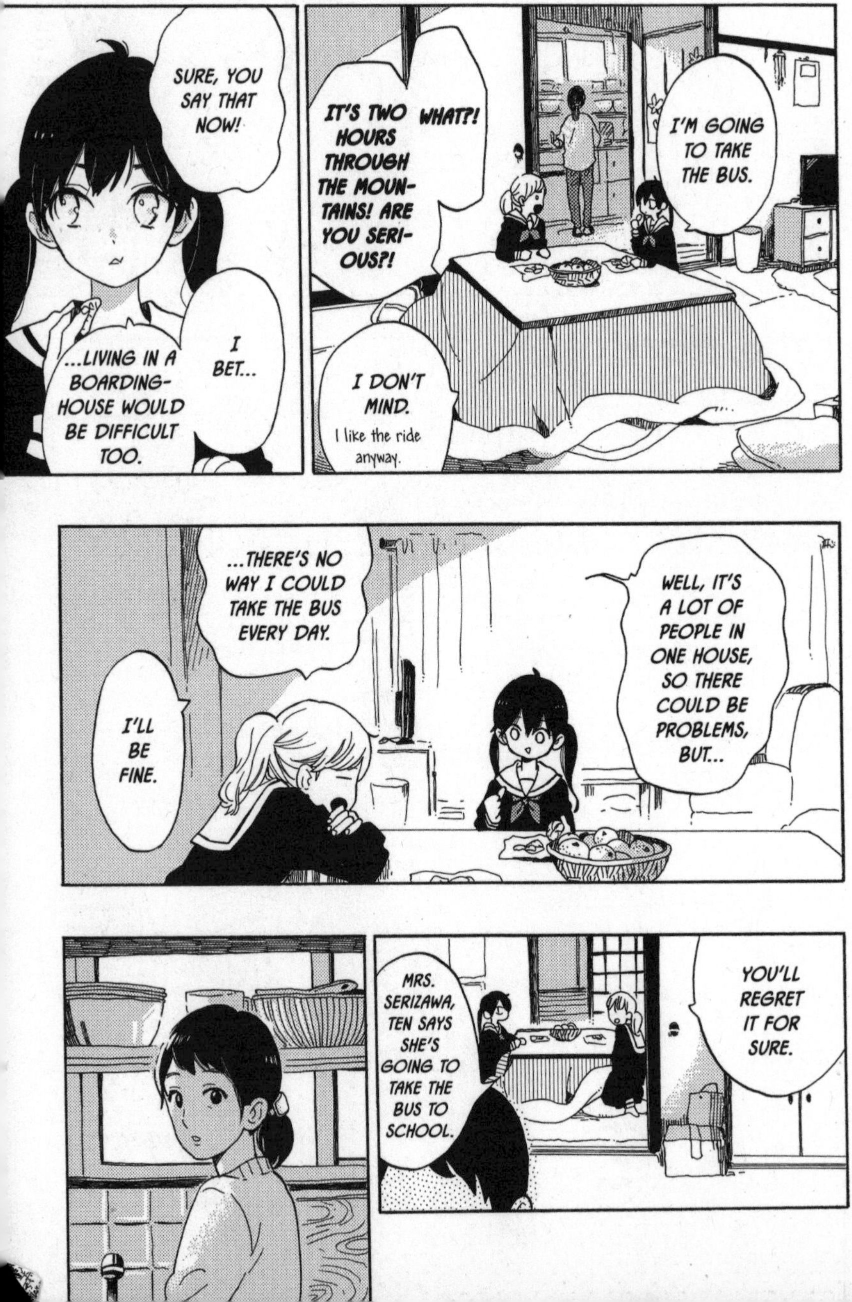
I'M GOING TO TAKE THE BUS.
WHAT?!
IT'S TWO HOURS THROUGH THE MOUNTAINS! ARE YOU SERIOUS?!
I DON'T MIND. I like the ride anyway.
SURE, YOU SAY THAT NOW!
I BET...
...LIVING IN A BOARDING-HOUSE WOULD BE DIFFICULT TOO.
WELL, IT'S A LOT OF PEOPLE IN ONE HOUSE, SO THERE COULD BE PROBLEMS, BUT...
...THERE'S NO WAY I COULD TAKE THE BUS EVERY DAY.
I'LL BE FINE.
YOU'LL REGRET IT FOR SURE.
MRS. SERIZAWA, TEN SAYS SHE'S GOING TO TAKE THE BUS TO SCHOOL.

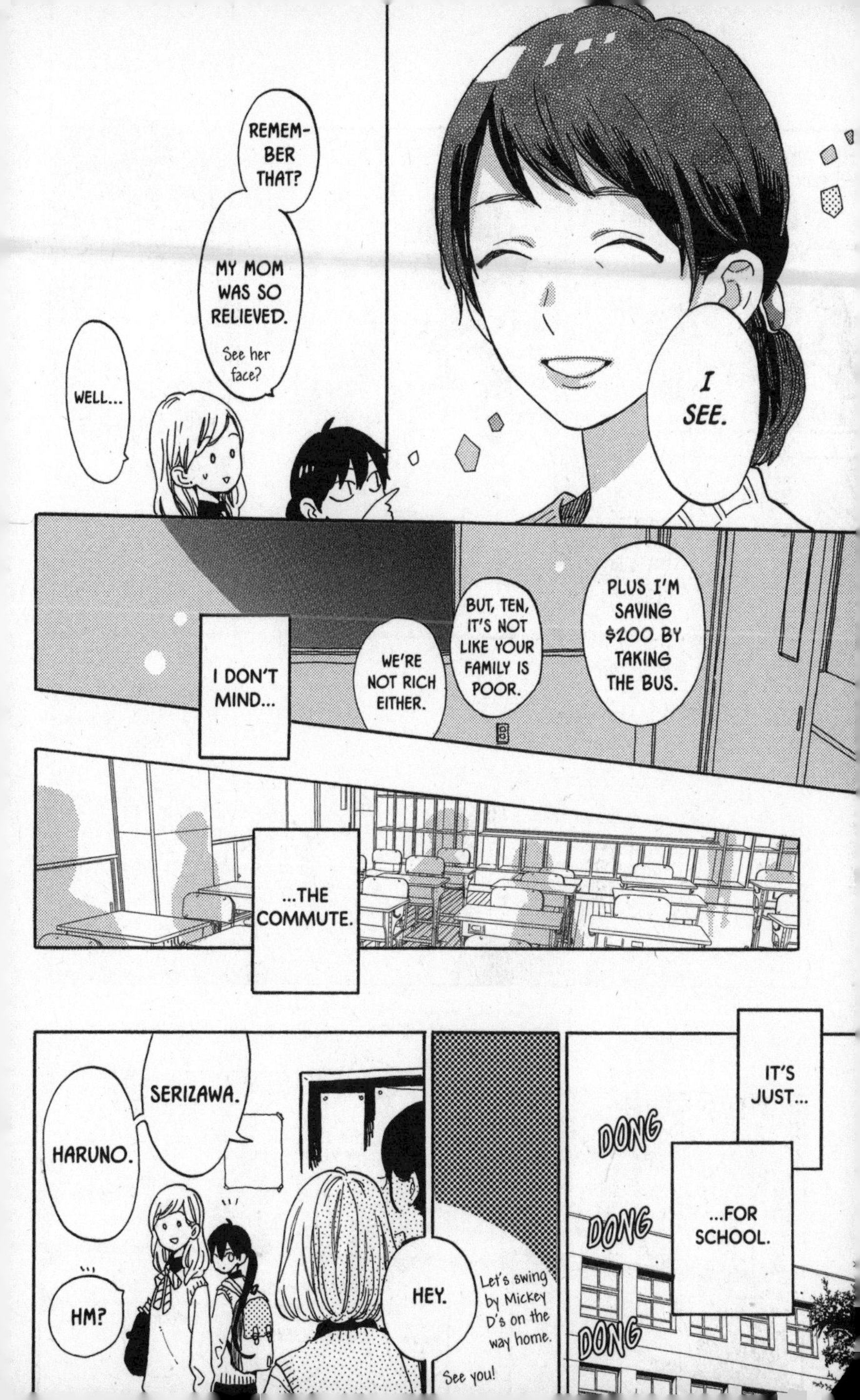
I SEE.
REMEMBER THAT?
MY MOM WAS SO RELIEVED.
See her face?
WELL...
PLUS I'M SAVING $200 BY TAKING THE BUS.
BUT, TEN, IT'S NOT LIKE YOUR FAMILY IS POOR.
WE'RE NOT RICH EITHER.
I DON'T MIND...
...THE COMMUTE.
IT'S JUST...
DONG
DONG
DONG
...FOR SCHOOL.
SERIZAWA.
HARUNO.
HEY.
Let's swing by Mickey D's on the way home.
See you!
HM?

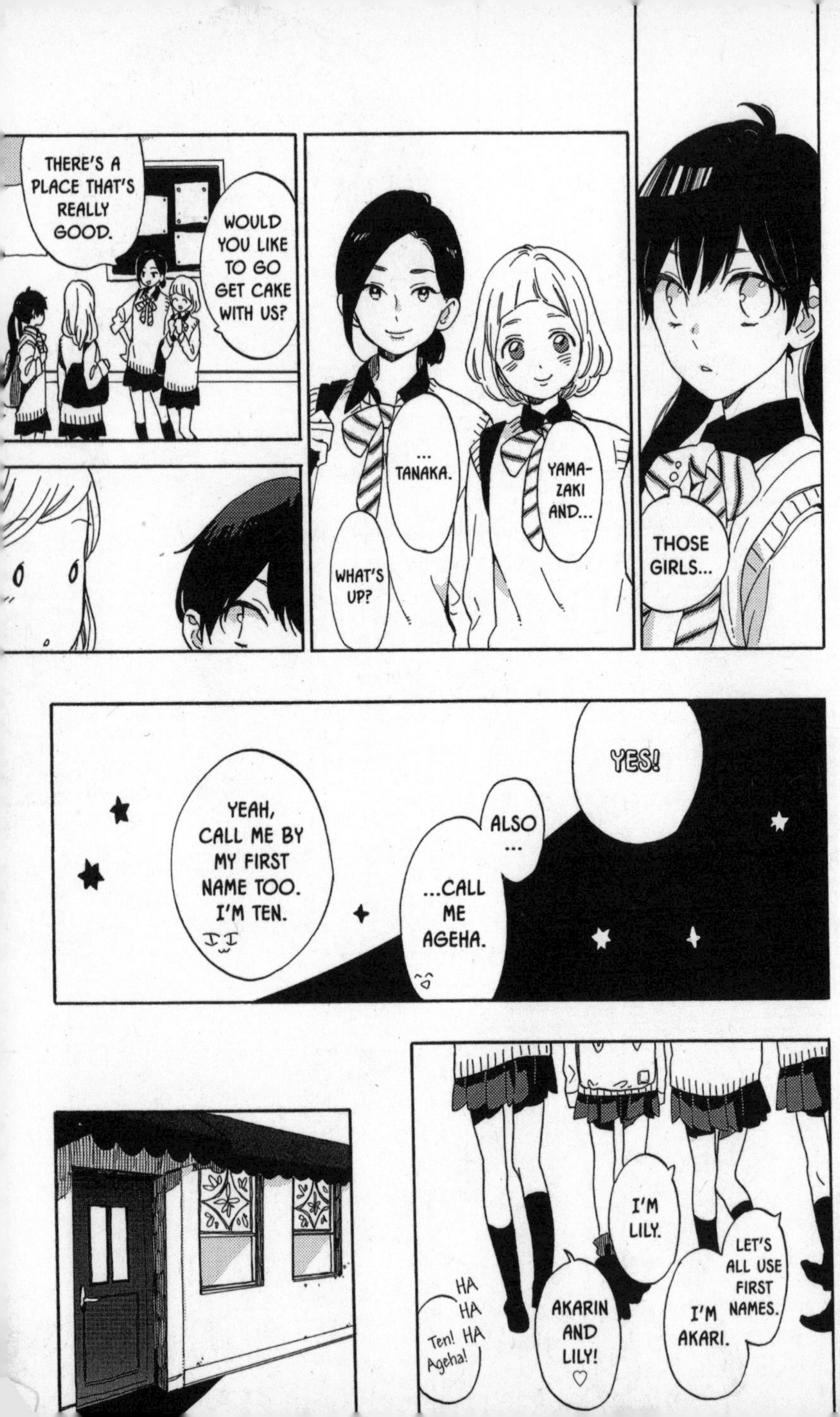
THOSE GIRLS...
YAMA-ZAKI AND...
...TANAKA.
WHAT'S UP?
THERE'S A PLACE THAT'S REALLY GOOD.
WOULD YOU LIKE TO GO GET CAKE WITH US?
YES!
ALSO...
...CALL ME AGEHA.
YEAH, CALL ME BY MY FIRST NAME TOO. I'M TEN.
LET'S ALL USE FIRST NAMES.
I'M AKARI.
I'M LILY.
AKARIN AND LILY! ♡
HA HA HA
Ten! Ageha!

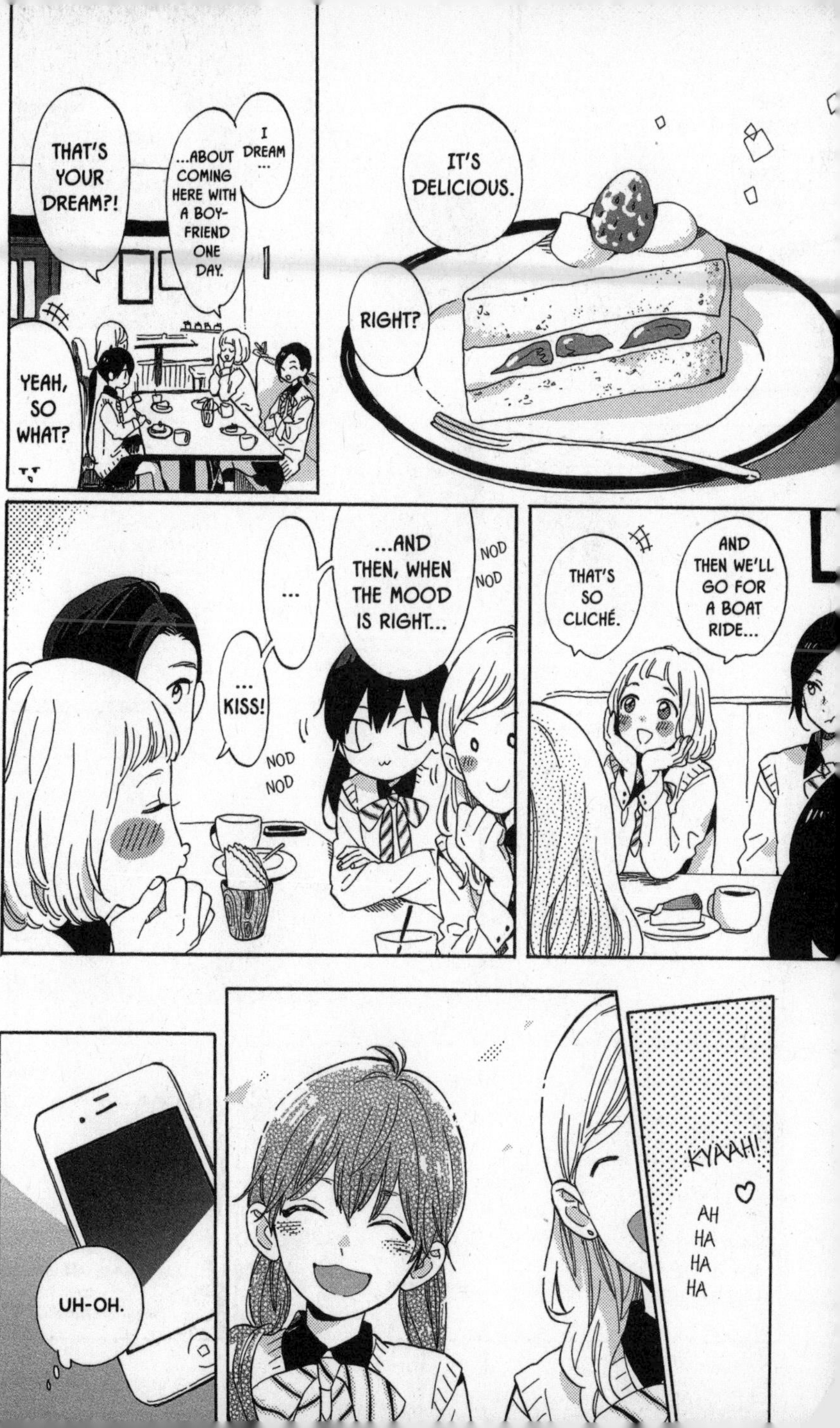
IT'S DELICIOUS.
RIGHT?
I DREAM ...
...ABOUT COMING HERE WITH A BOY-FRIEND ONE DAY.
THAT'S YOUR DREAM?!
YEAH, SO WHAT?
AND THEN WE'LL GO FOR A BOAT RIDE...
THAT'S SO CLICHÉ.
...AND THEN, WHEN THE MOOD IS RIGHT...
NOD NOD
...
... KISS!
NOD NOD
KYAAH! ♡
AH HA HA HA
UH-OH.

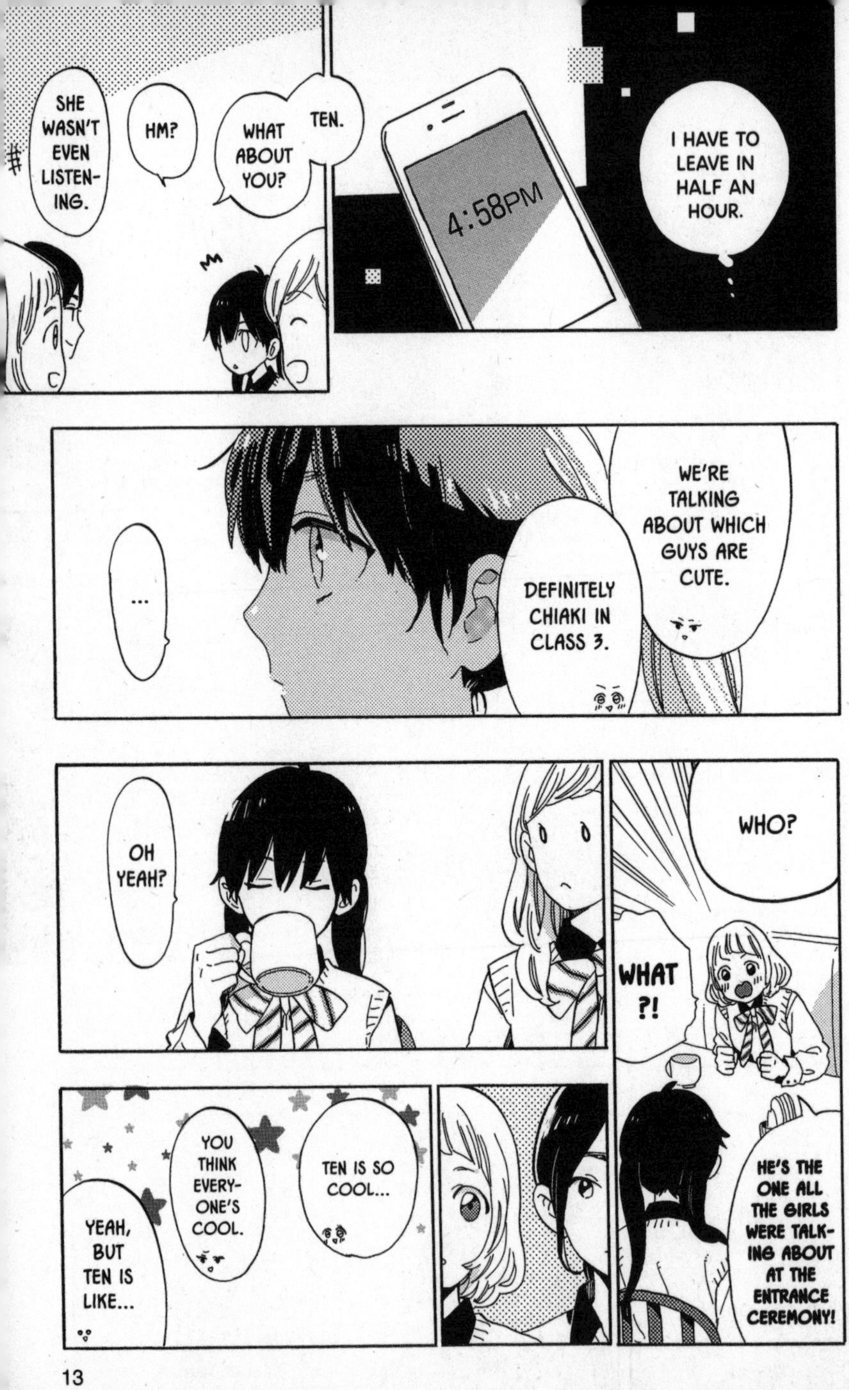
I HAVE TO LEAVE IN HALF AN HOUR.
4:58PM
TEN.
WHAT ABOUT YOU?
HM?
SHE WASN'T EVEN LISTEN-ING.
WE'RE TALKING ABOUT WHICH GUYS ARE CUTE.
DEFINITELY CHIAKI IN CLASS 3.
...
WHO?
WHAT?!
HE'S THE ONE ALL THE GIRLS WERE TALK-ING ABOUT AT THE ENTRANCE CEREMONY!
OH YEAH?
TEN IS SO COOL...
YOU THINK EVERY-ONE'S COOL.
YEAH, BUT TEN IS LIKE...

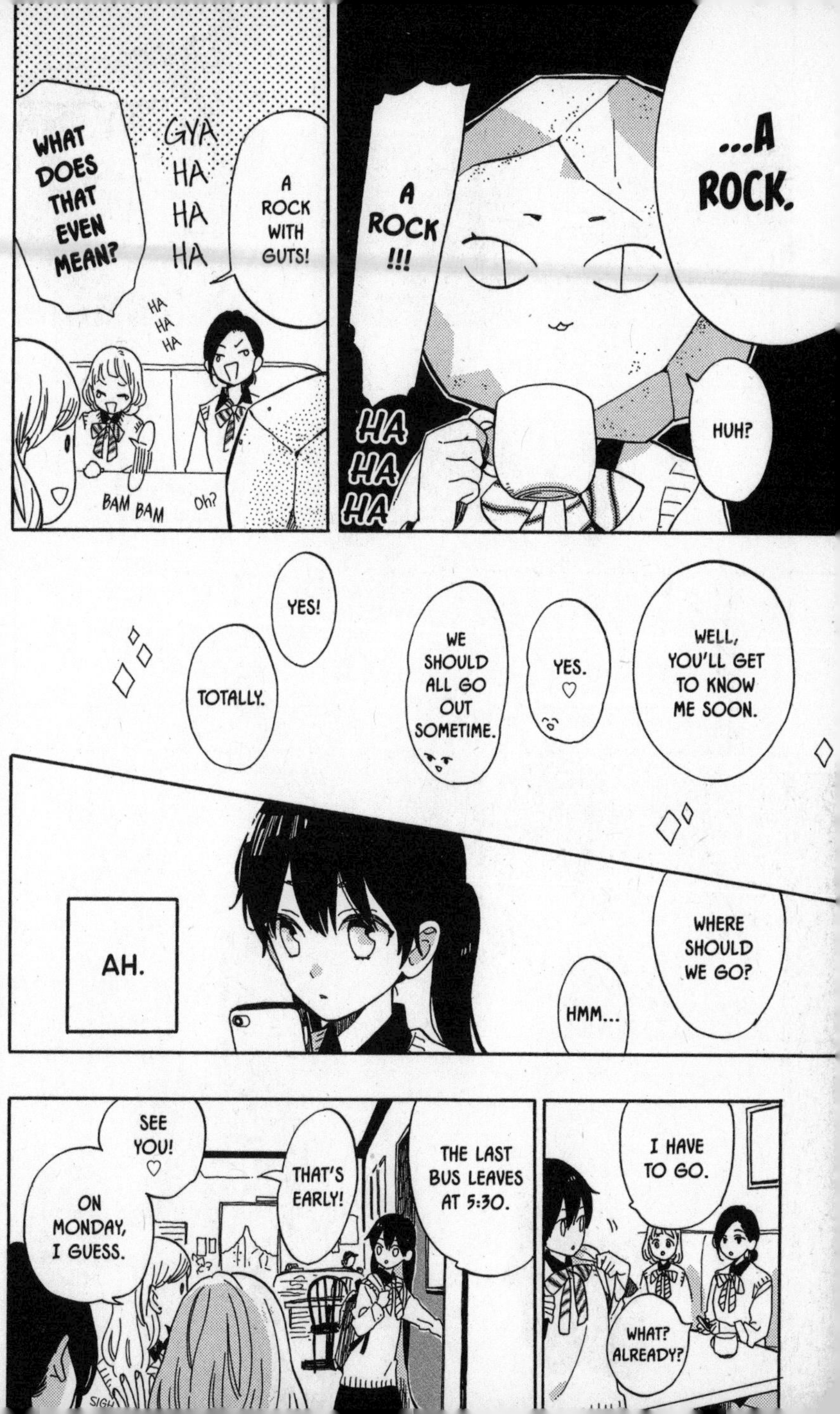
...A ROCK.
HUH?
A ROCK!!!
HA HA HA
A ROCK WITH GUTS!
GYA HA HA HA
WHAT DOES THAT EVEN MEAN?
HA HA HA
Oh?
BAM BAM
WELL, YOU'LL GET TO KNOW ME SOON.
YES. ♡
WE SHOULD ALL GO OUT SOMETIME.
YES!
TOTALLY.
WHERE SHOULD WE GO?
HMM...
AH.
I HAVE TO GO.
WHAT? ALREADY?
THE LAST BUS LEAVES AT 5:30.
THAT'S EARLY!
SEE YOU! ♡
ON MONDAY, I GUESS.
SIGH

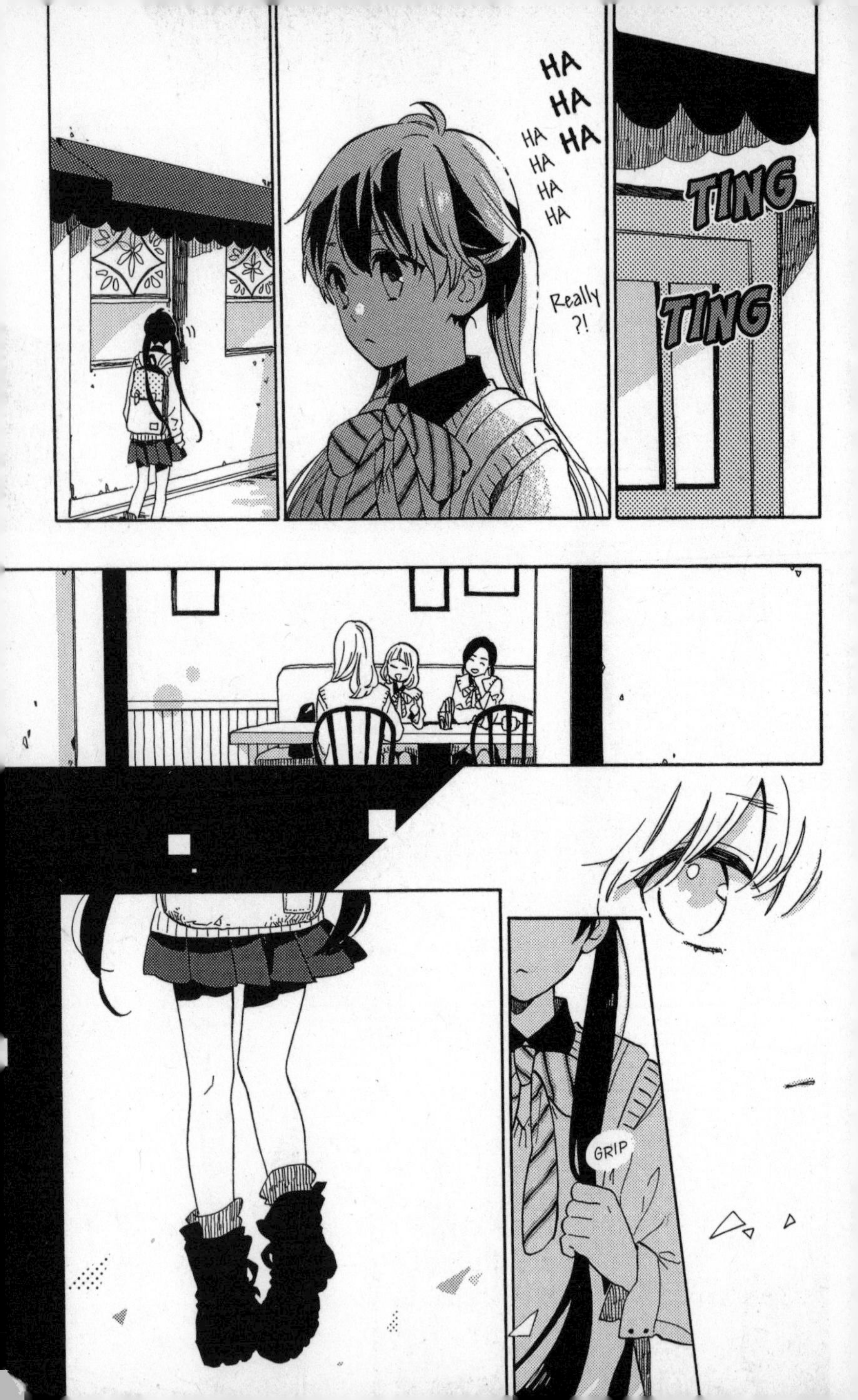
TING
TING
HA
HA
HA
HA
HA
HA
HA
Really ?!
GRIP

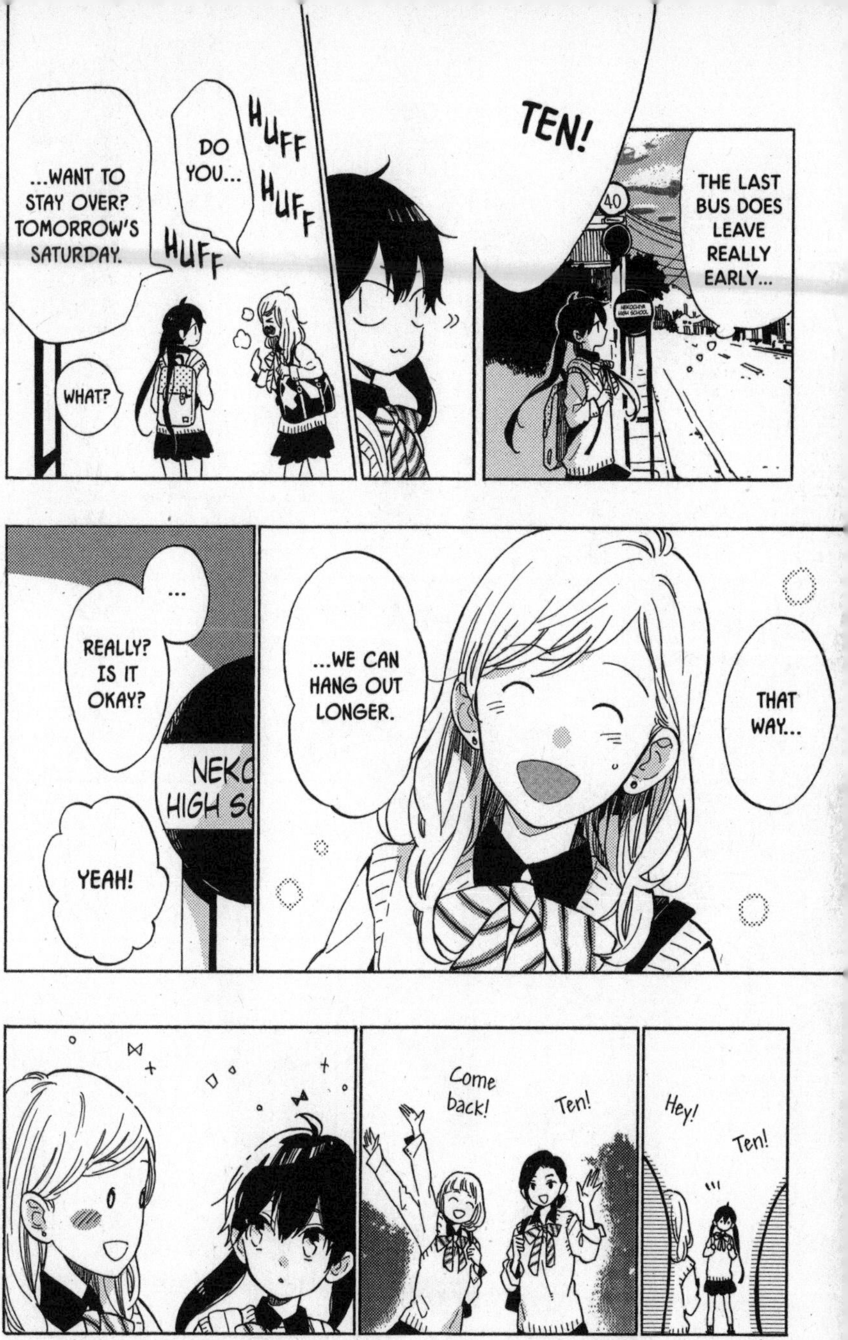
THE LAST BUS DOES LEAVE REALLY EARLY...
40
TEN!
HUFF HUFF
DO YOU...
...WANT TO STAY OVER? TOMORROW'S SATURDAY.
HUFF
WHAT?
THAT WAY...
...WE CAN HANG OUT LONGER.
...
REALLY? IS IT OKAY?
YEAH!
Hey!
Ten!
Ten!
Come back!

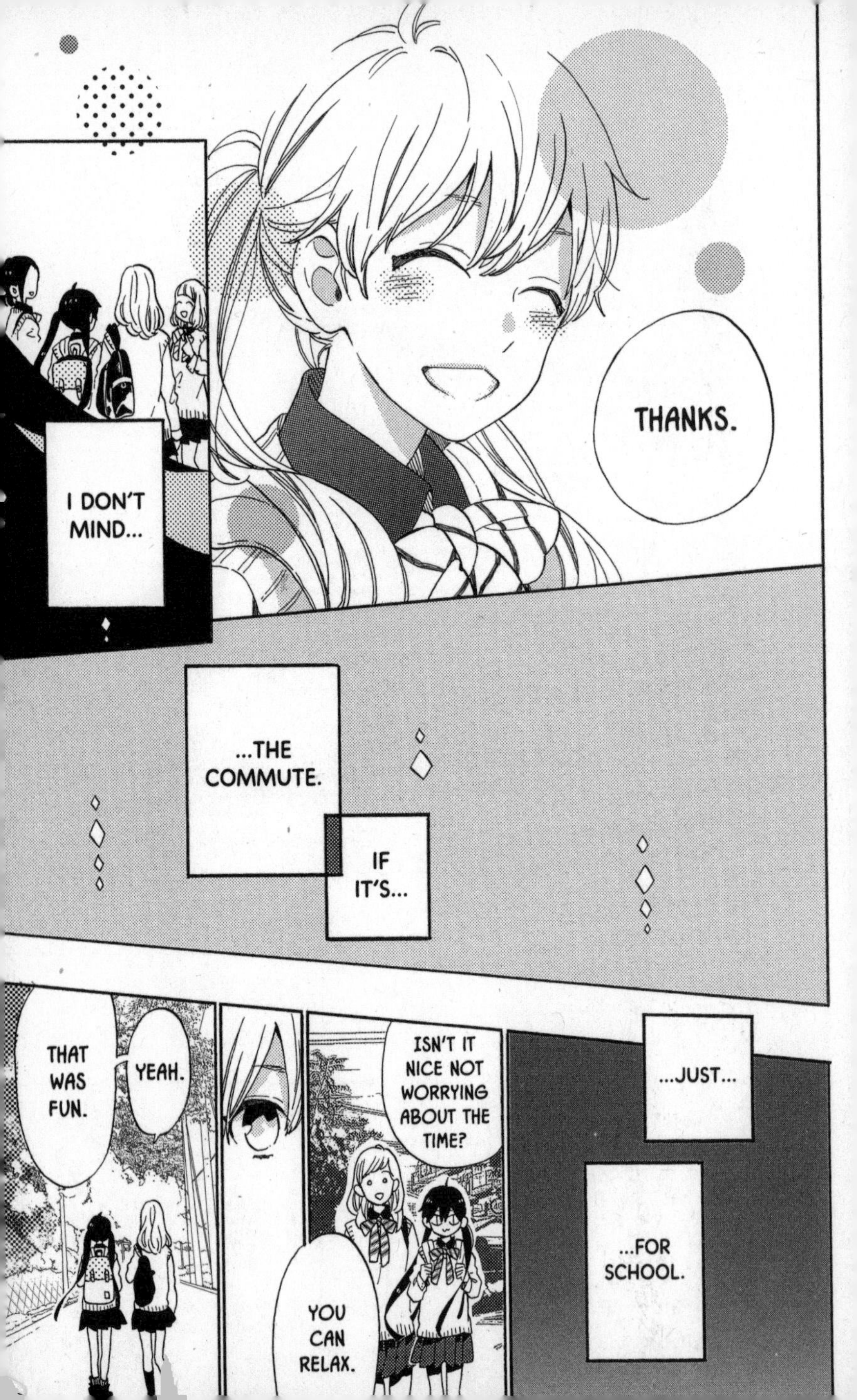
THANKS.
I DON'T MIND...
IF IT'S...
...THE COMMUTE.
...JUST...
...FOR SCHOOL.
ISN'T IT NICE NOT WORRYING ABOUT THE TIME?
YOU CAN RELAX.
YEAH.
THAT WAS FUN.

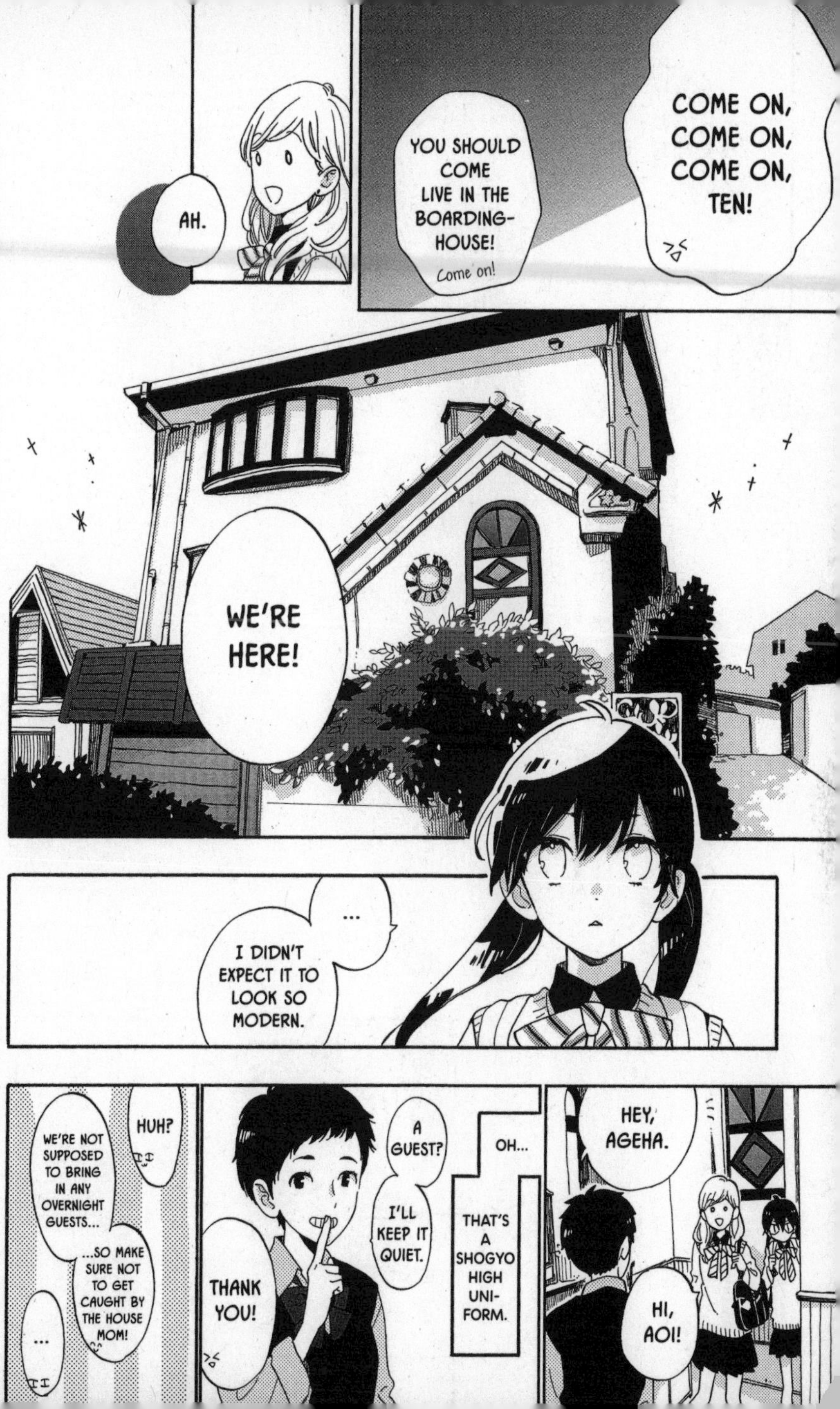
COME ON, COME ON, COME ON, TEN!
YOU SHOULD COME LIVE IN THE BOARDING-HOUSE!
Come on!
AH.
WE'RE HERE!
...
I DIDN'T EXPECT IT TO LOOK SO MODERN.
HEY, AGEHA.
HI, AOI!
OH...
THAT'S A SHOGYO HIGH UNI-FORM.
A GUEST?
I'LL KEEP IT QUIET.
THANK YOU!
HUH?
WE'RE NOT SUPPOSED TO BRING IN ANY OVERNIGHT GUESTS...
...SO MAKE SURE NOT TO GET CAUGHT BY THE HOUSE MOM!
...

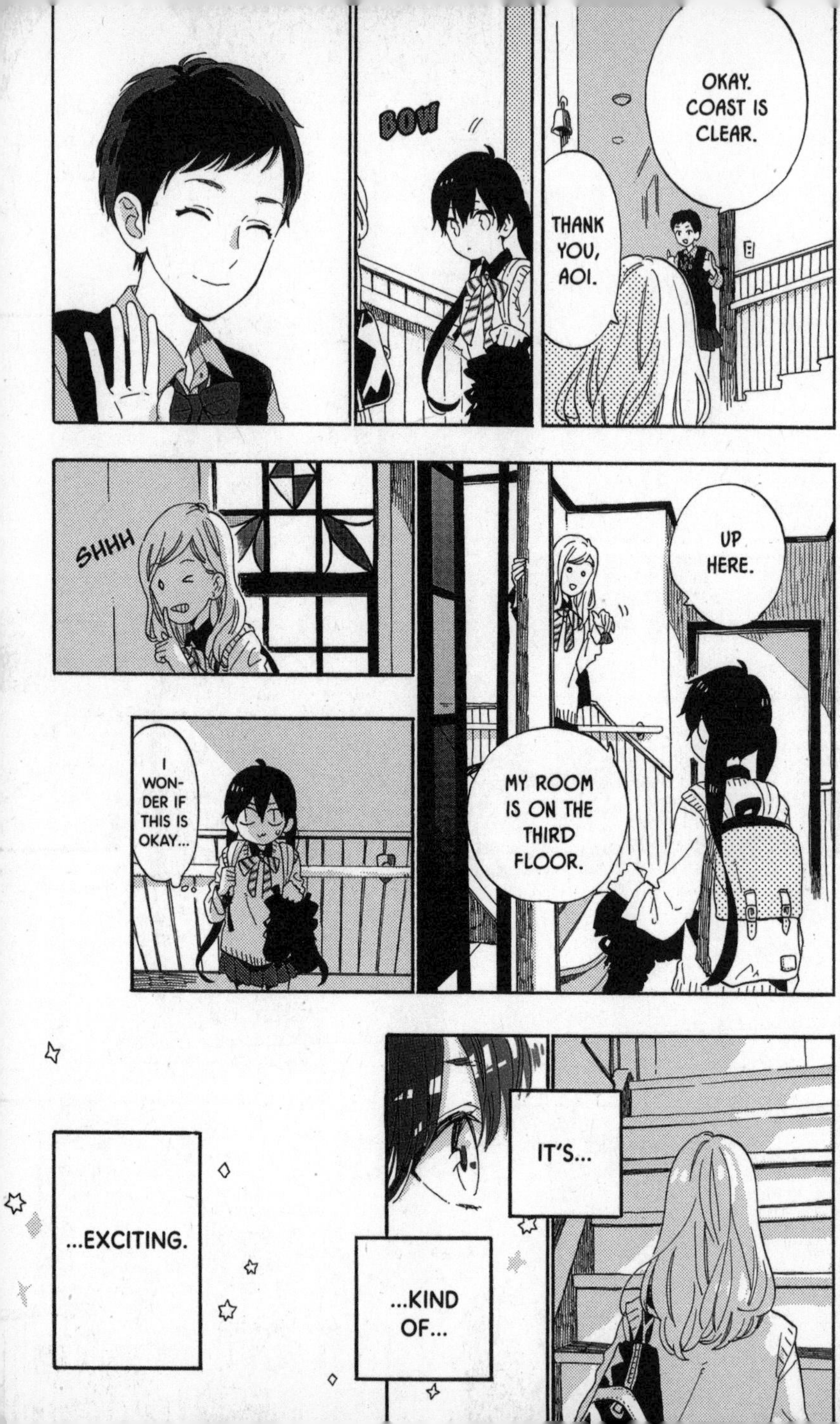
OKAY. COAST IS CLEAR.
THANK YOU, AOI.
BOW
UP HERE.
MY ROOM IS ON THE THIRD FLOOR.
SHHH
I WONDER IF THIS IS OKAY...
IT'S...
...KIND OF...
...EXCITING.

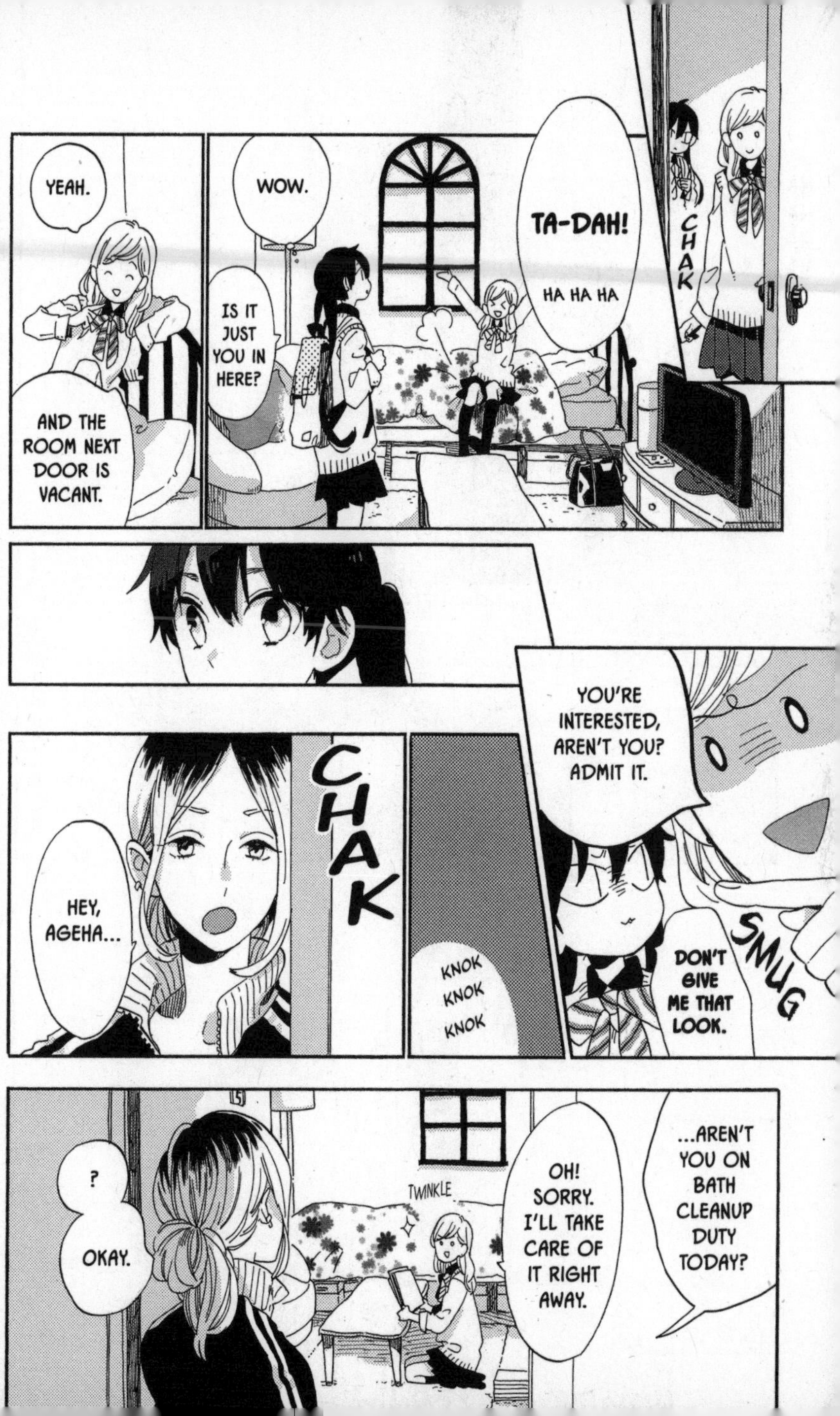
CHAK
TA-DAH!
HA HA HA
WOW.
IS IT JUST YOU IN HERE?
YEAH.
AND THE ROOM NEXT DOOR IS VACANT.
YOU'RE INTERESTED, AREN'T YOU? ADMIT IT.
SMUG
DON'T GIVE ME THAT LOOK.
KNOK KNOK KNOK
CHAK
HEY, AGEHA...
...AREN'T YOU ON BATH CLEANUP DUTY TODAY?
OH! SORRY. I'LL TAKE CARE OF IT RIGHT AWAY.
TWINKLE
?
OKAY.

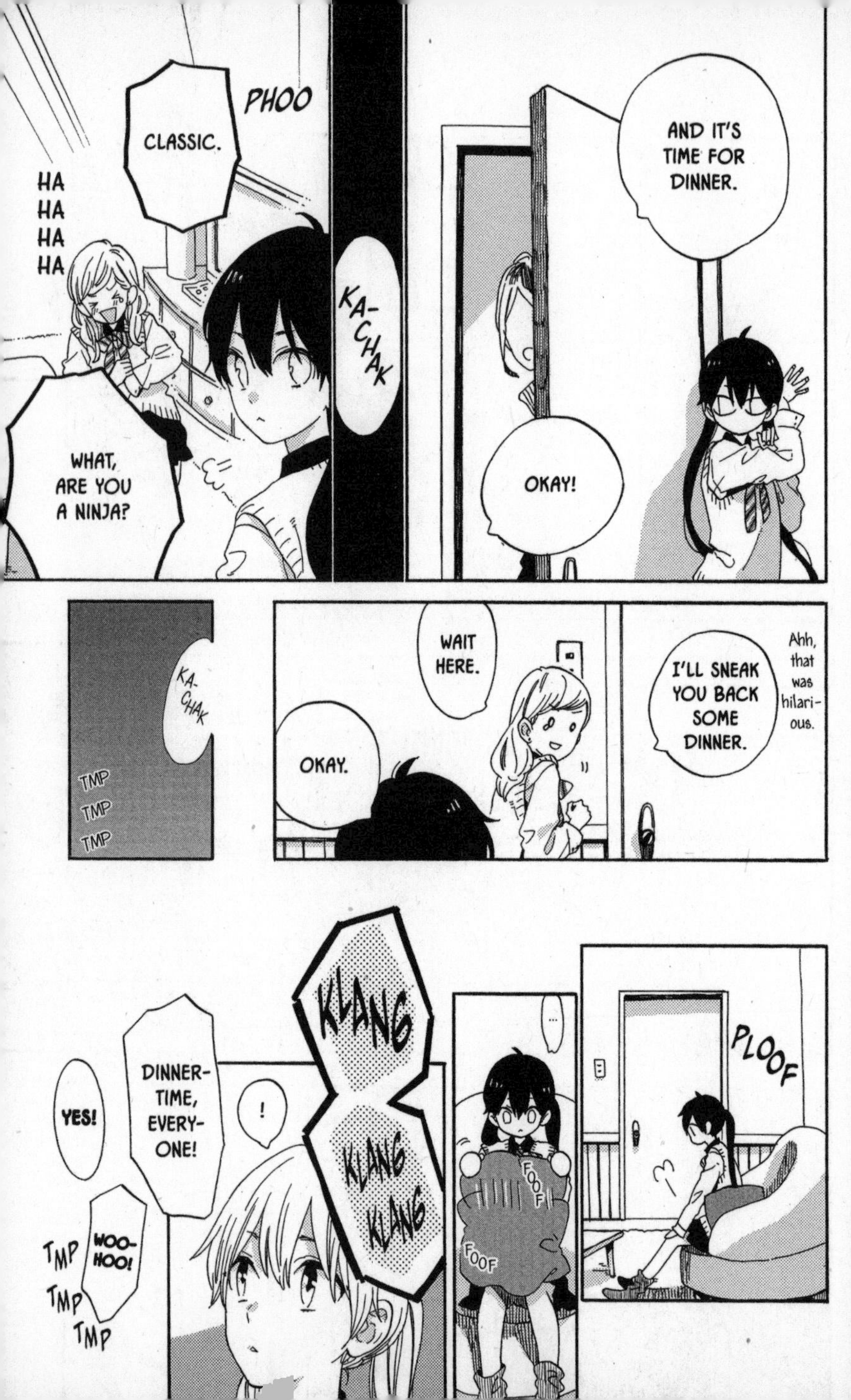
AND IT'S TIME FOR DINNER.
OKAY!
KA-CHAK
PHOO
CLASSIC.
HA HA HA HA
WHAT, ARE YOU A NINJA?
Ahh, that was hilarious.
I'LL SNEAK YOU BACK SOME DINNER.
WAIT HERE.
OKAY.
KA-CHAK
TMP TMP TMP
PLOOF
...
FOOF
FOOF
KLANG
KLANG KLANG
!
DINNER-TIME, EVERYONE!
YES!
WOO-HOO!
TMP TMP TMP

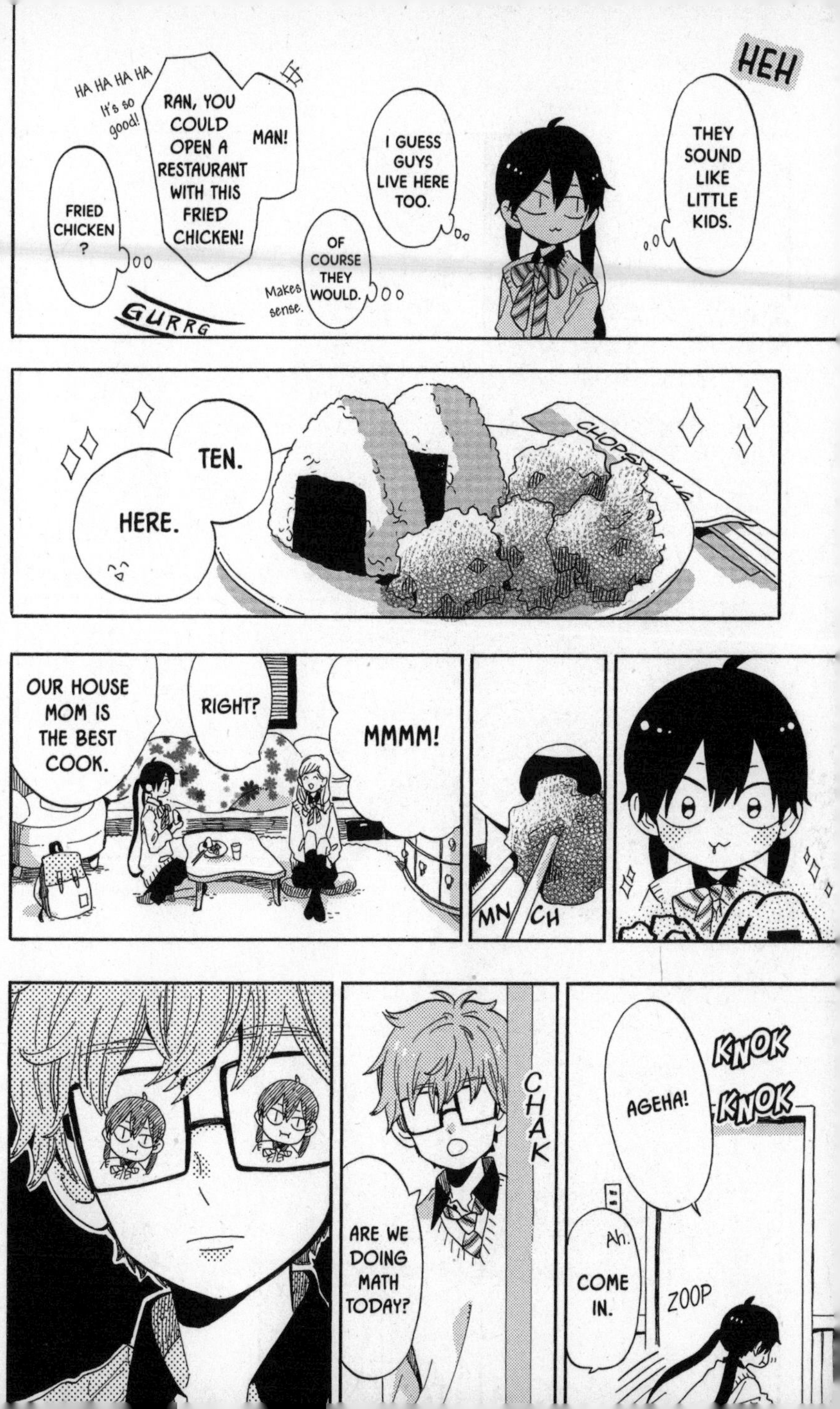
HEH
THEY SOUND LIKE LITTLE KIDS.
I GUESS GUYS LIVE HERE TOO.
OF COURSE THEY WOULD.
Makes sense.
MAN!
RAN, YOU COULD OPEN A RESTAURANT WITH THIS FRIED CHICKEN!
HA HA HA HA
It's so good!
FRIED CHICKEN ?
GURRG
TEN.
HERE.
MN
CH
MMMM!
RIGHT?
OUR HOUSE MOM IS THE BEST COOK.
KNOK
KNOK
AGEHA!
Ah.
COME IN.
ZOOP
CHAK
ARE WE DOING MATH TODAY?

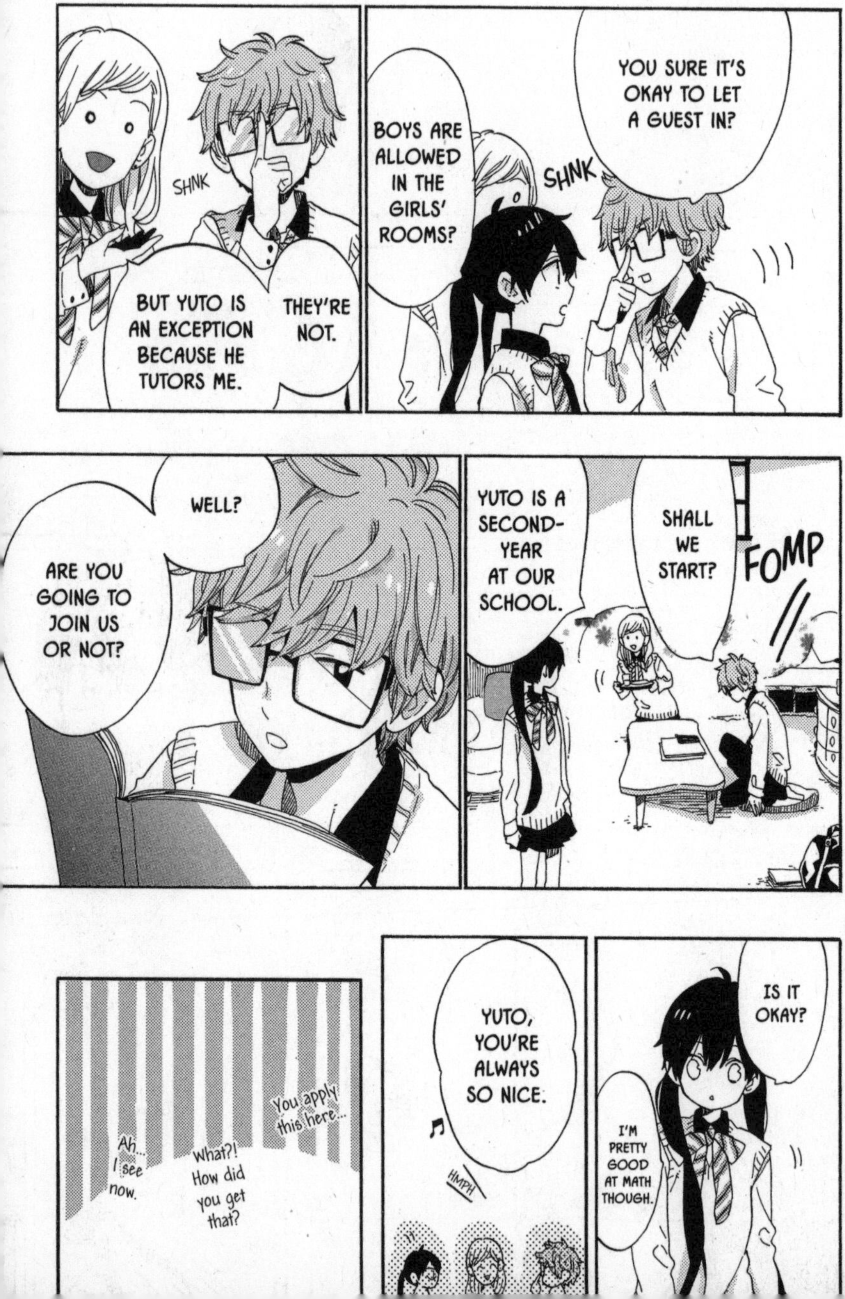
YOU SURE IT'S OKAY TO LET A GUEST IN?
SHNK
BOYS ARE ALLOWED IN THE GIRLS' ROOMS?
SHNK
THEY'RE NOT.
BUT YUTO IS AN EXCEPTION BECAUSE HE TUTORS ME.
FOMP
SHALL WE START?
YUTO IS A SECOND-YEAR AT OUR SCHOOL.
WELL?
ARE YOU GOING TO JOIN US OR NOT?
IS IT OKAY?
I'M PRETTY GOOD AT MATH THOUGH.
YUTO, YOU'RE ALWAYS SO NICE.
HMPH
You apply this here...
What?! How did you get that?
Ah... I see now.

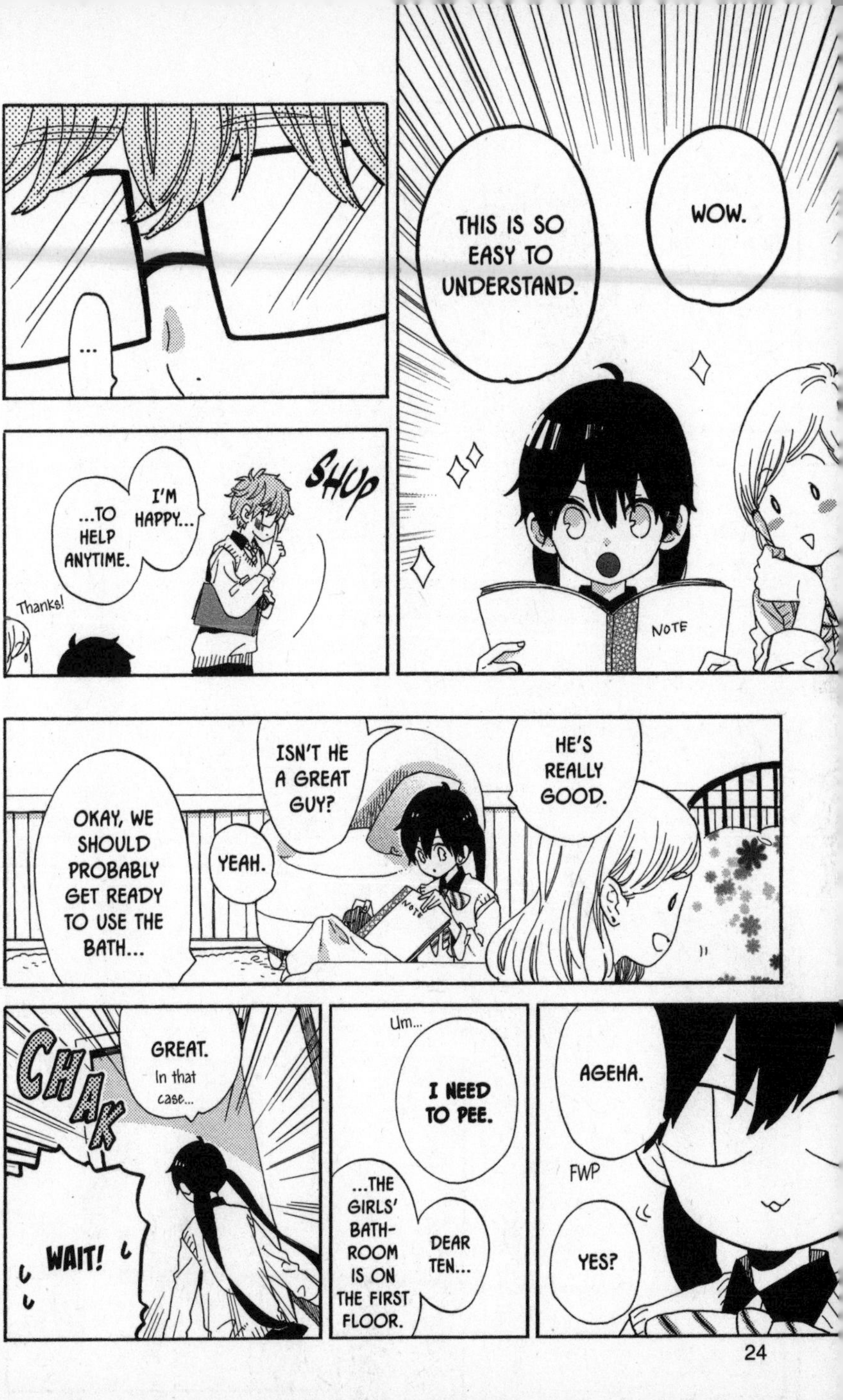
WOW.
THIS IS SO EASY TO UNDERSTAND.
NOTE
...
SHUP
I'M HAPPY...
...TO HELP ANYTIME.
Thanks!
HE'S REALLY GOOD.
ISN'T HE A GREAT GUY?
YEAH.
NOTE
OKAY, WE SHOULD PROBABLY GET READY TO USE THE BATH...
AGEHA.
FWP
YES?
Um...
I NEED TO PEE.
DEAR TEN...
...THE GIRLS' BATHROOM IS ON THE FIRST FLOOR.
GREAT.
In that case...
CHAK
WAIT!

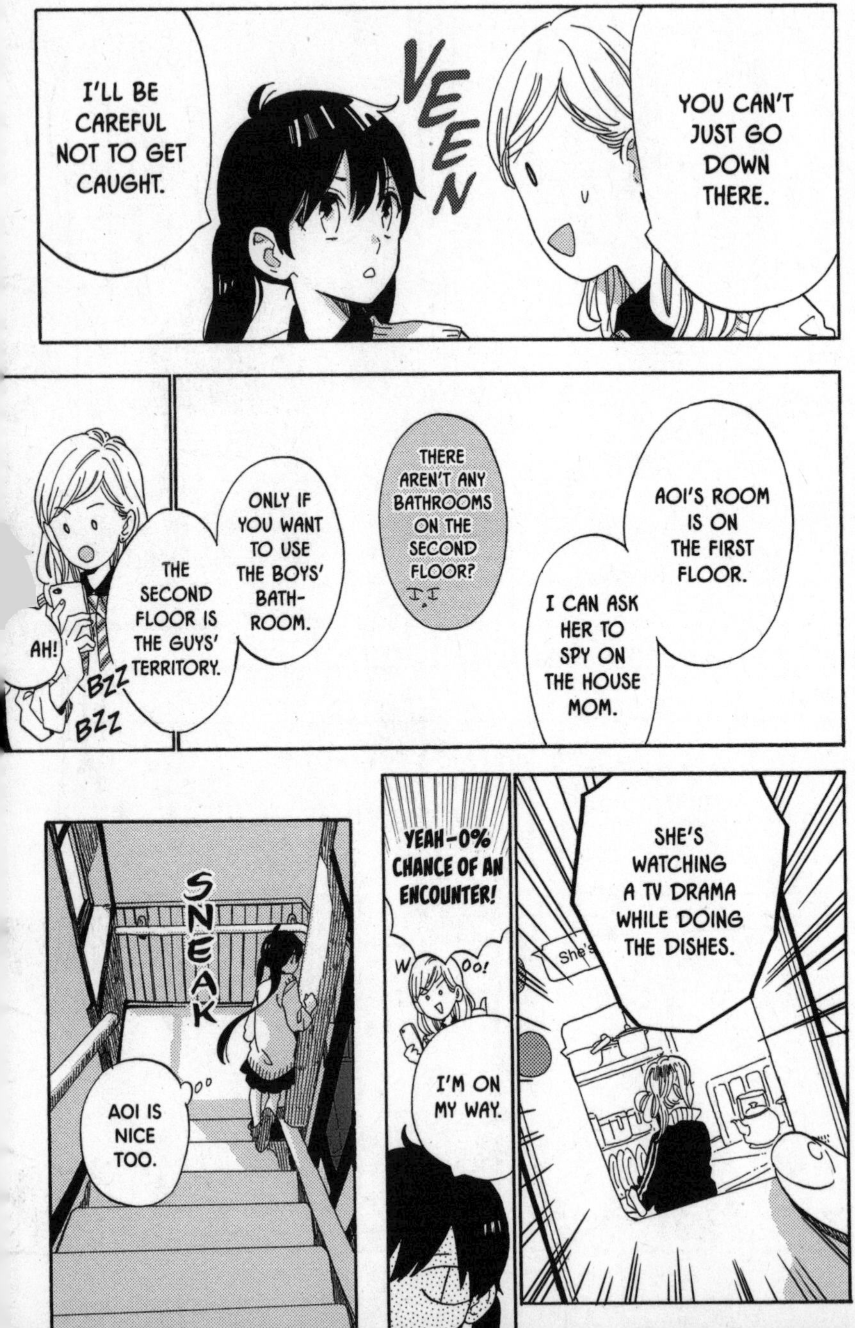
YOU CAN'T JUST GO DOWN THERE.
VEEN
I'LL BE CAREFUL NOT TO GET CAUGHT.
AOI'S ROOM IS ON THE FIRST FLOOR.
I CAN ASK HER TO SPY ON THE HOUSE MOM.
THERE AREN'T ANY BATHROOMS ON THE SECOND FLOOR?
ONLY IF YOU WANT TO USE THE BOYS' BATH-ROOM.
THE SECOND FLOOR IS THE GUYS' TERRITORY.
AH!
BZZ BZZ
She's
SHE'S WATCHING A TV DRAMA WHILE DOING THE DISHES.
YEAH–0% CHANCE OF AN ENCOUNTER!
WOO!
I'M ON MY WAY.
SNEAK
AOI IS NICE TOO.

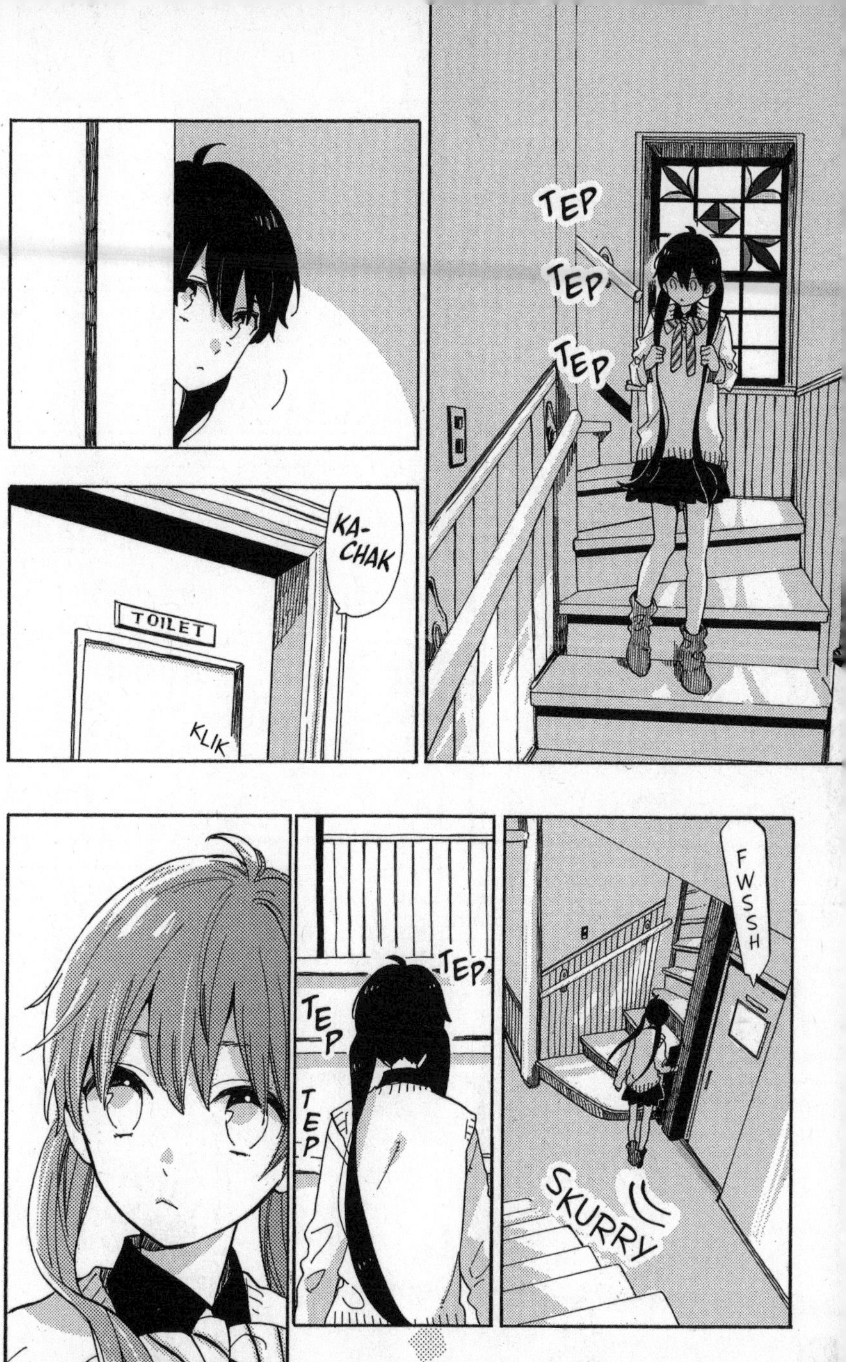
TEP
TEP
TEP
KA-CHAK
KLIK
FWSSH
SKURRY
TEP
TEP
TEP

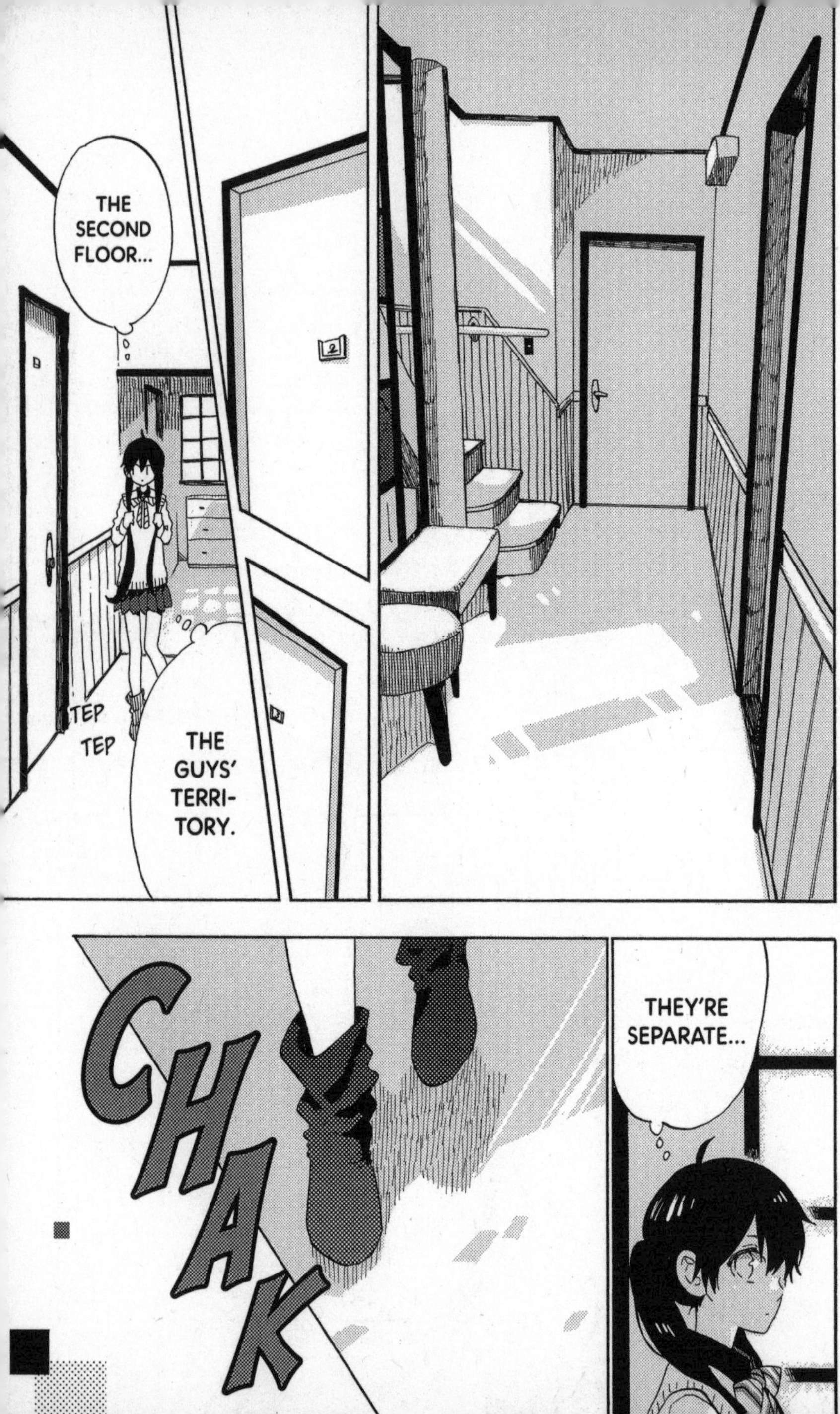
THE SECOND FLOOR...
TEP TEP
THE GUYS' TERRITORY.
THEY'RE SEPARATE...
CHAK

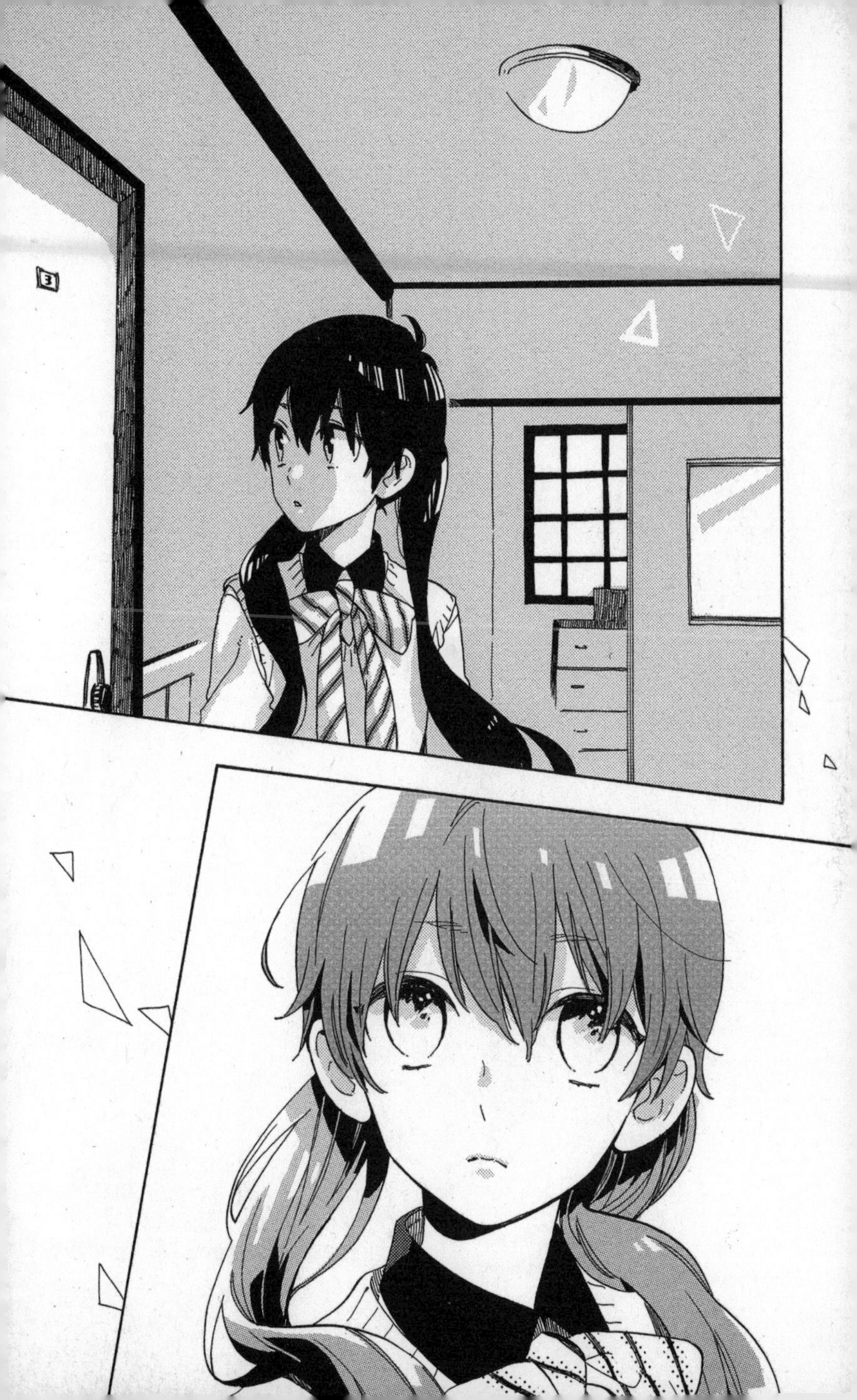
3

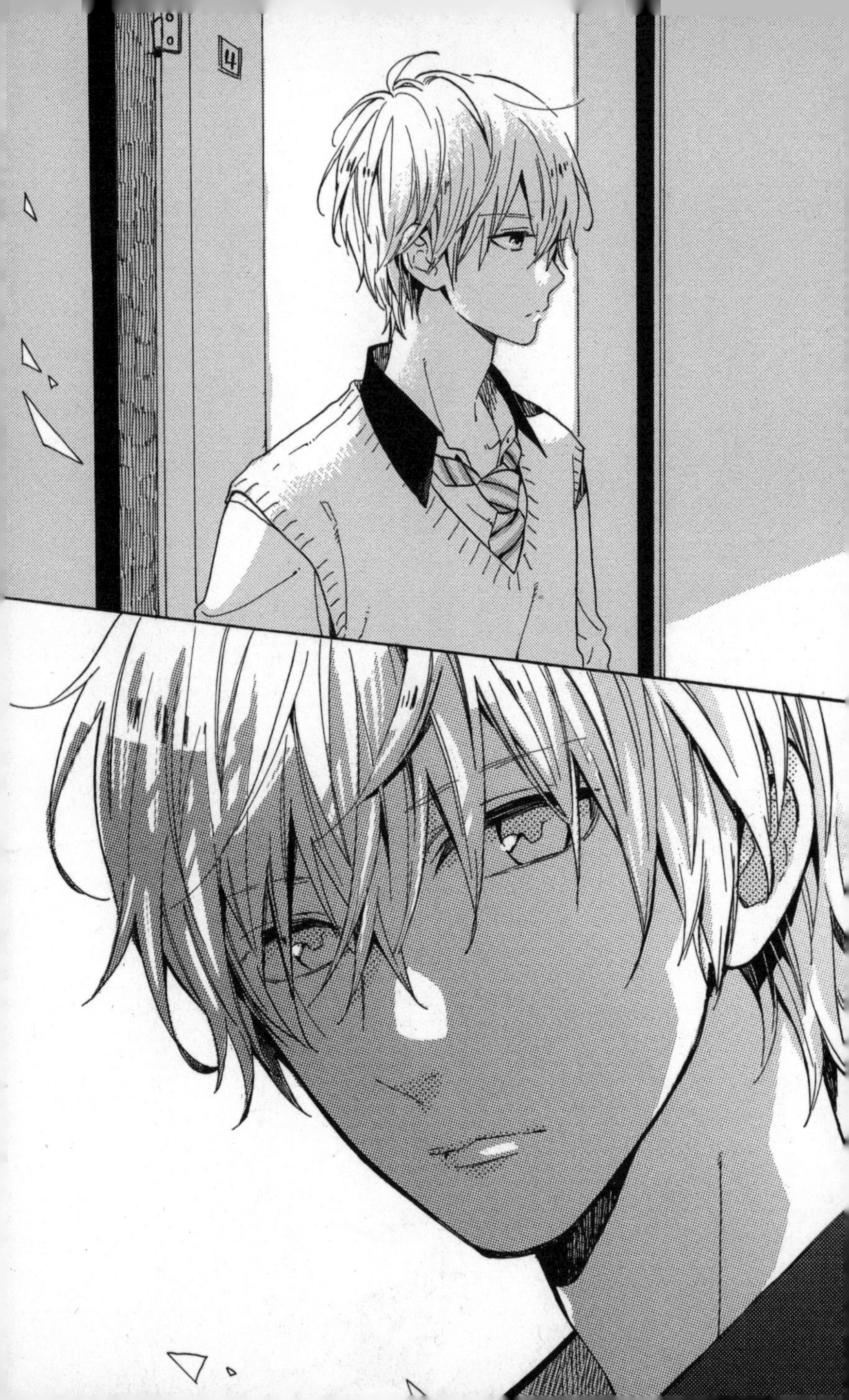

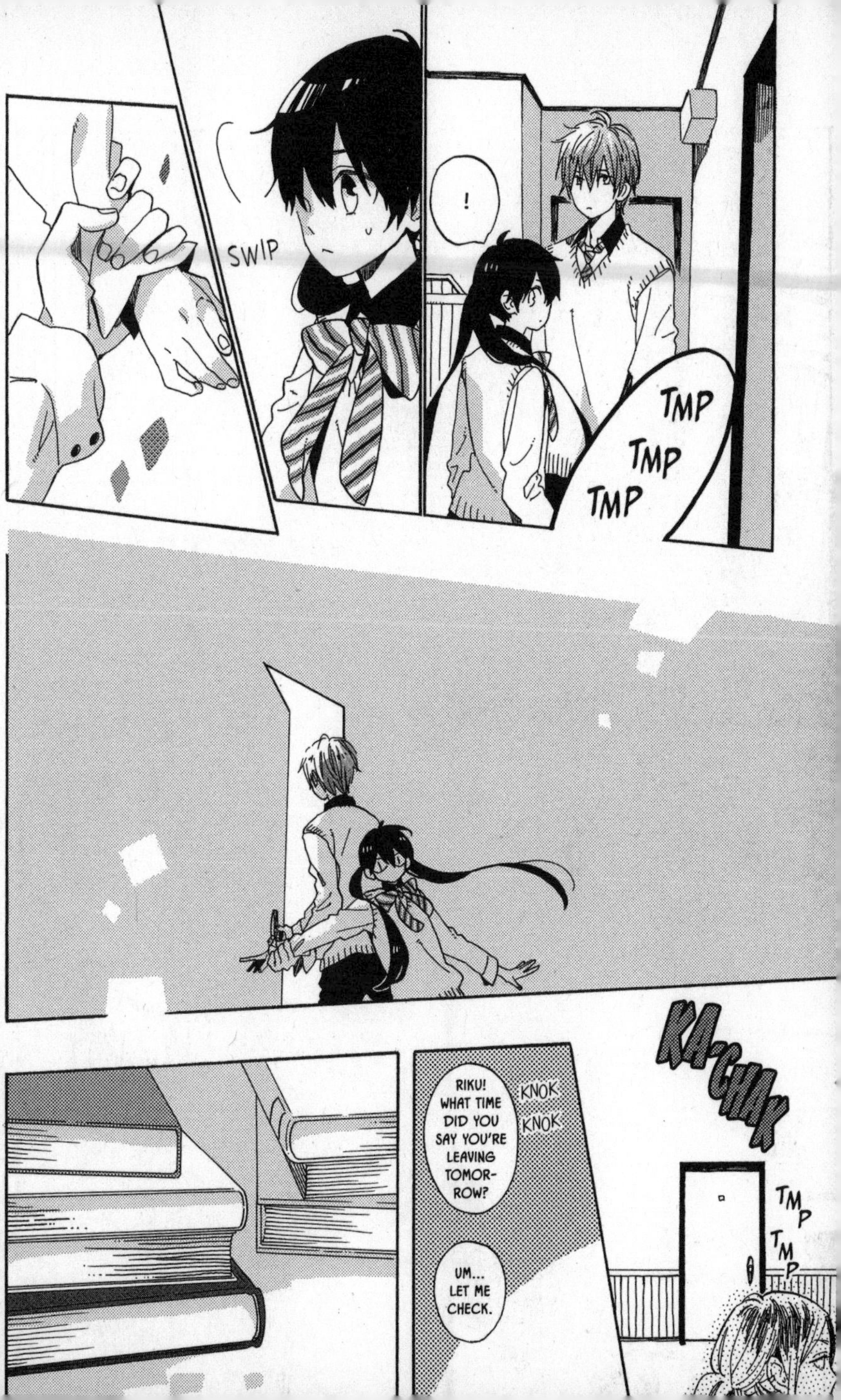
!
TMP TMP TMP
SWIP
KA-CHAK
TMP TMP
KNOK KNOK
RIKU! WHAT TIME DID YOU SAY YOU'RE LEAVING TOMOR-ROW?
UM... LET ME CHECK.

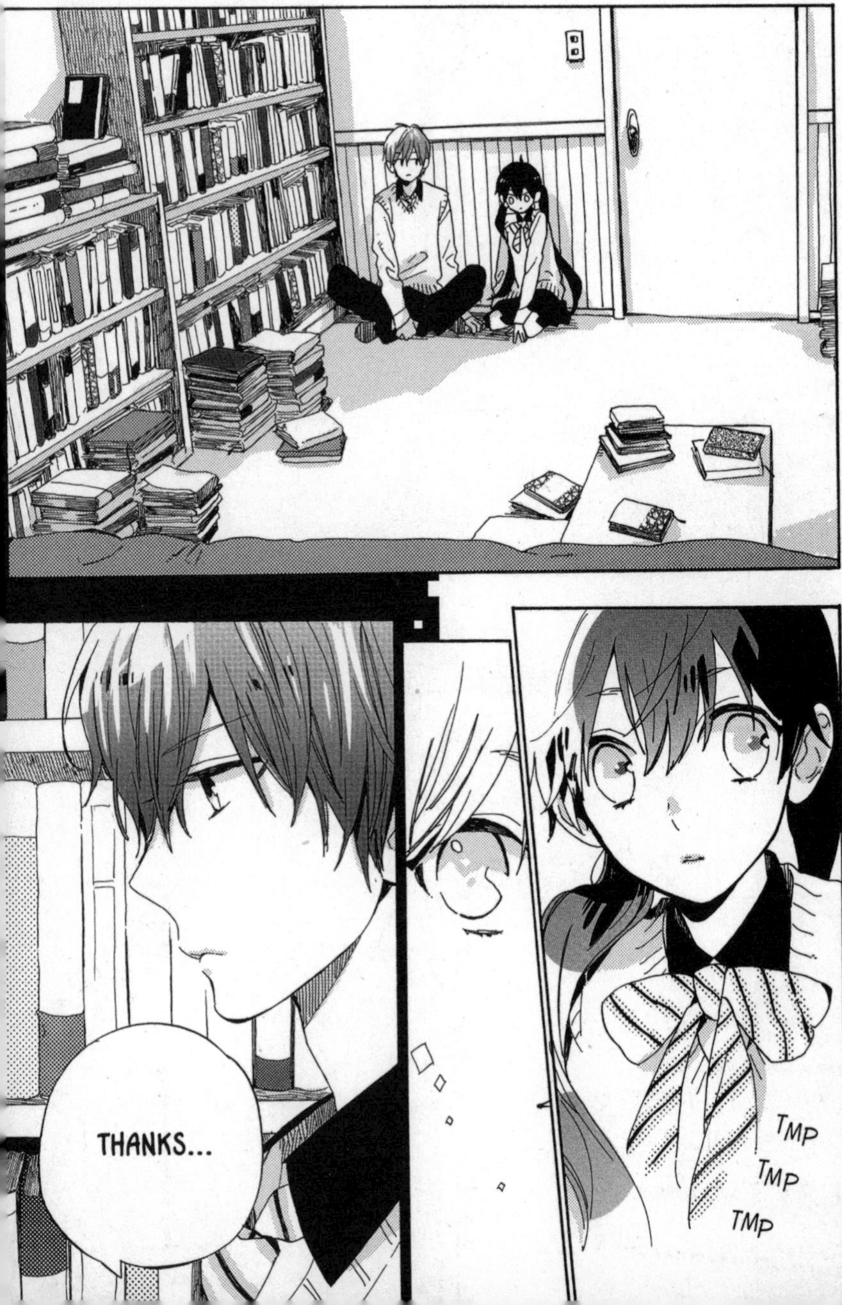
TMP
TMP
TMP
THANKS...

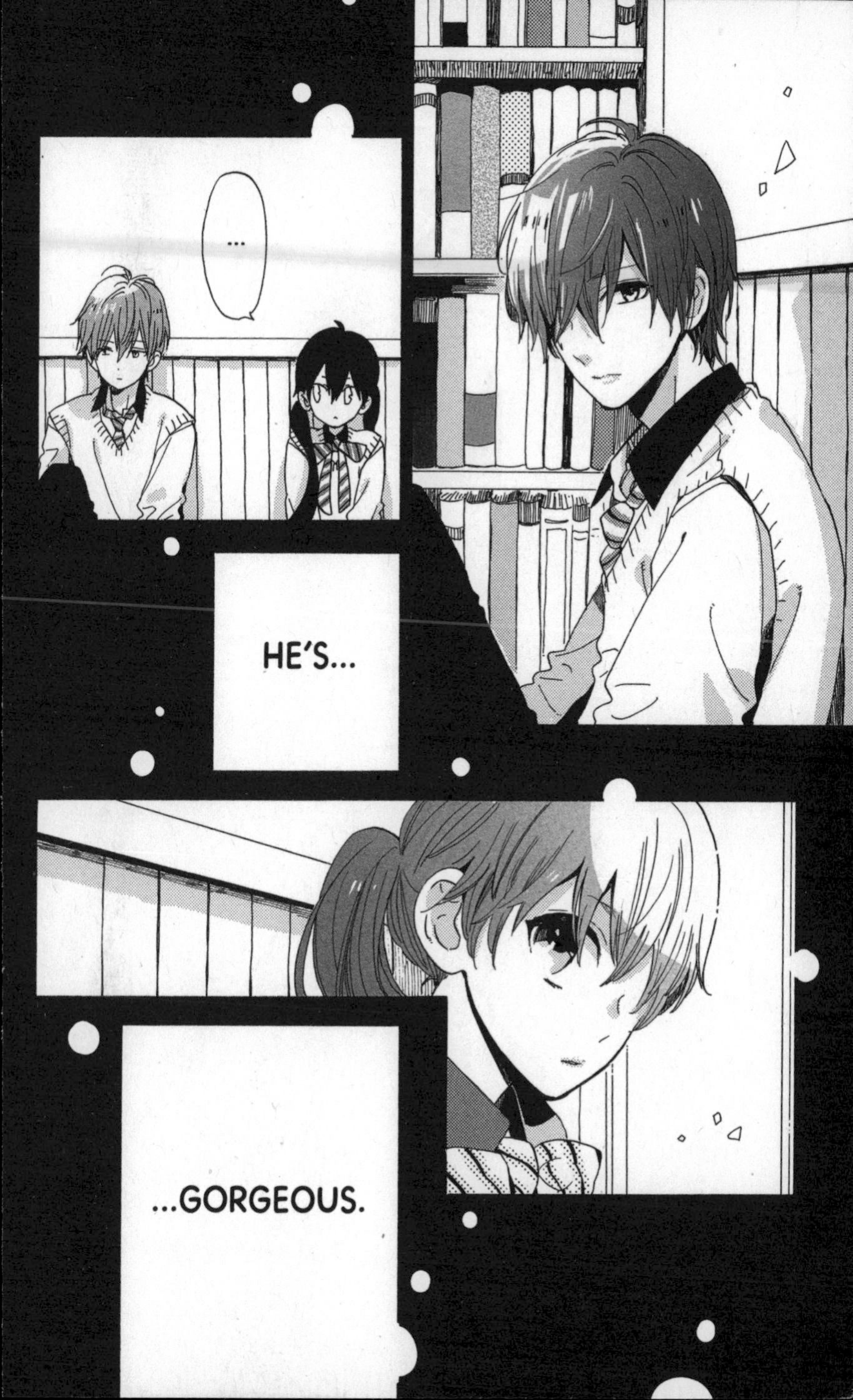
...
HE'S...
...GORGEOUS.

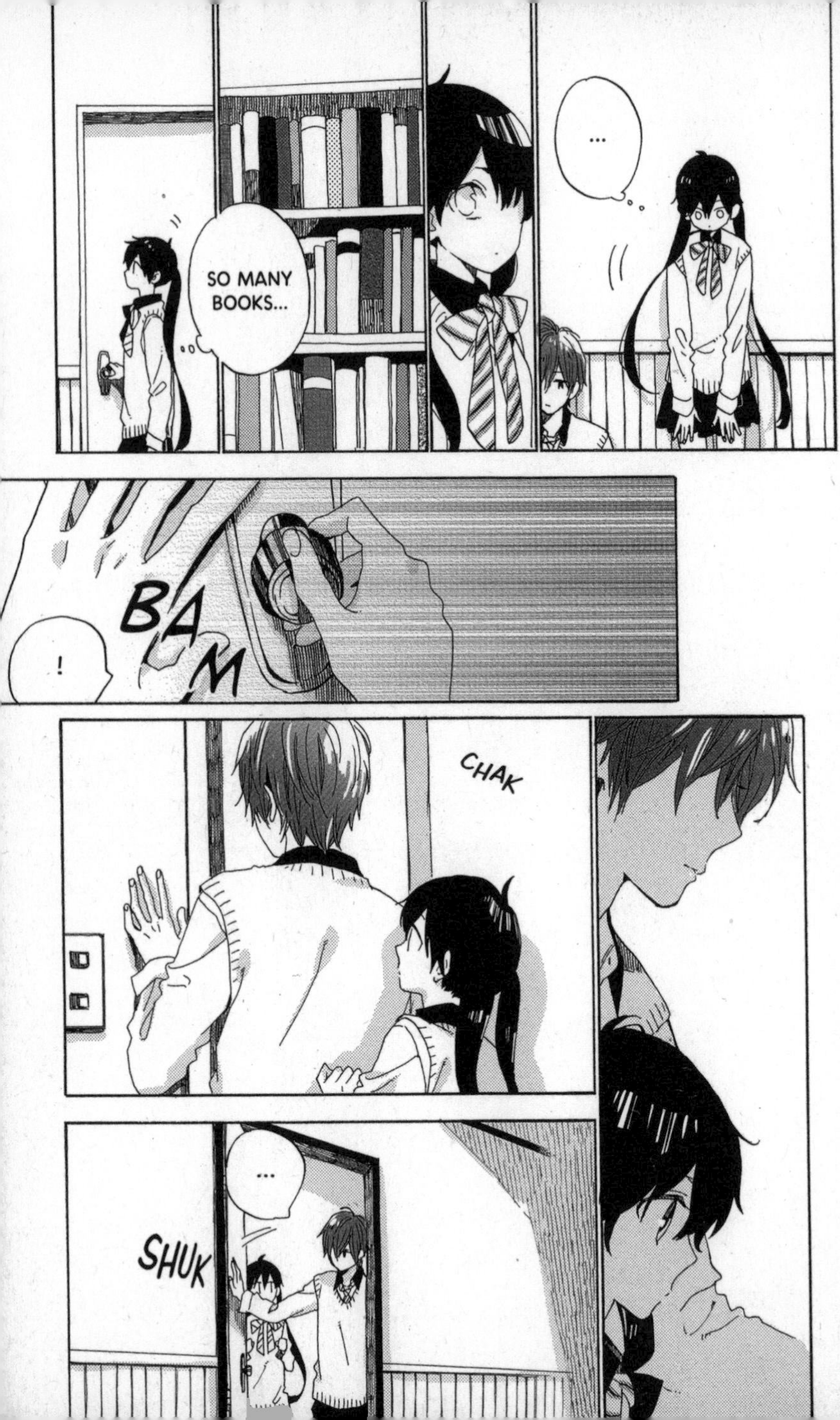
...
SO MANY BOOKS...
BAM
!
CHAK
...
SHUK

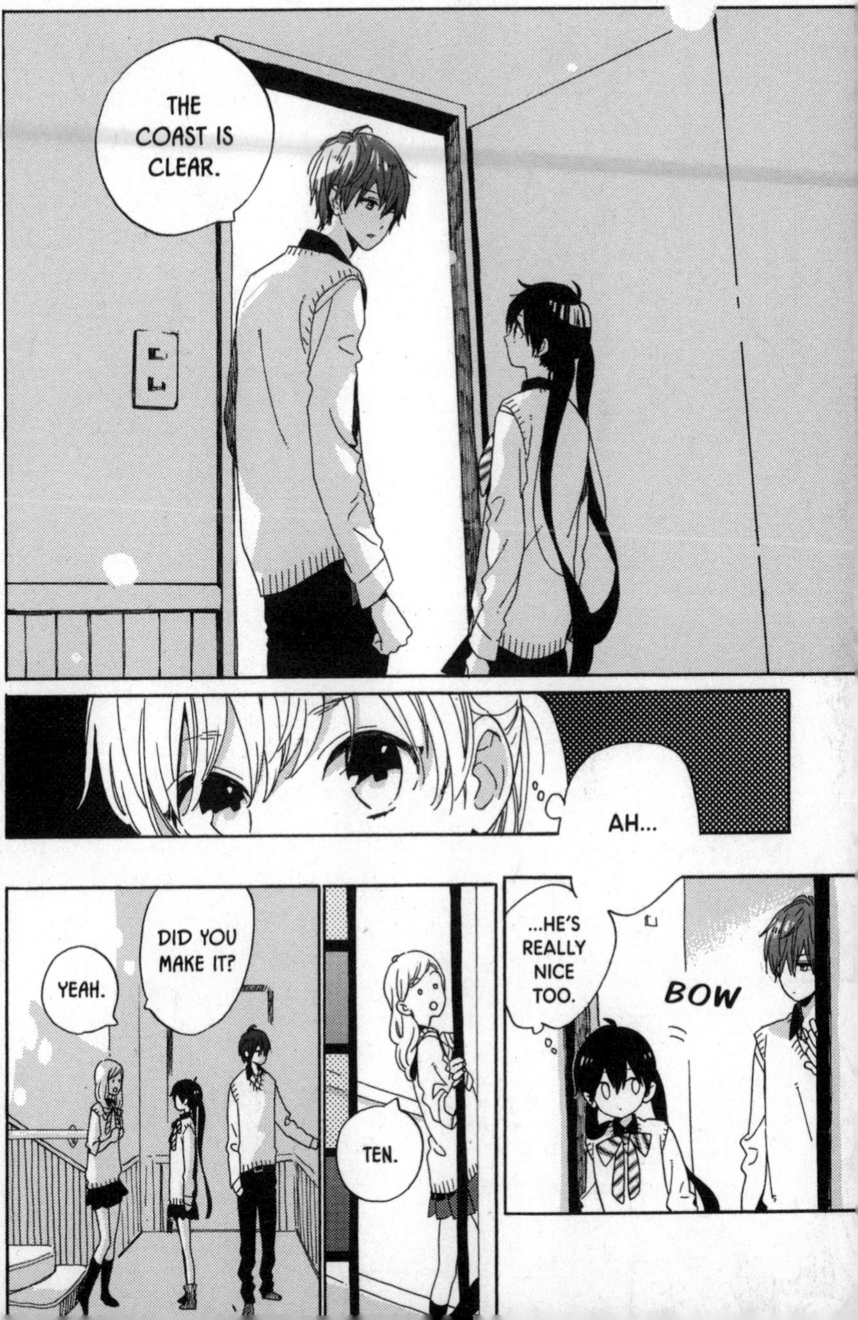
THE COAST IS CLEAR.
AH...
...HE'S REALLY NICE TOO.
BOW
TEN.
DID YOU MAKE IT?
YEAH.

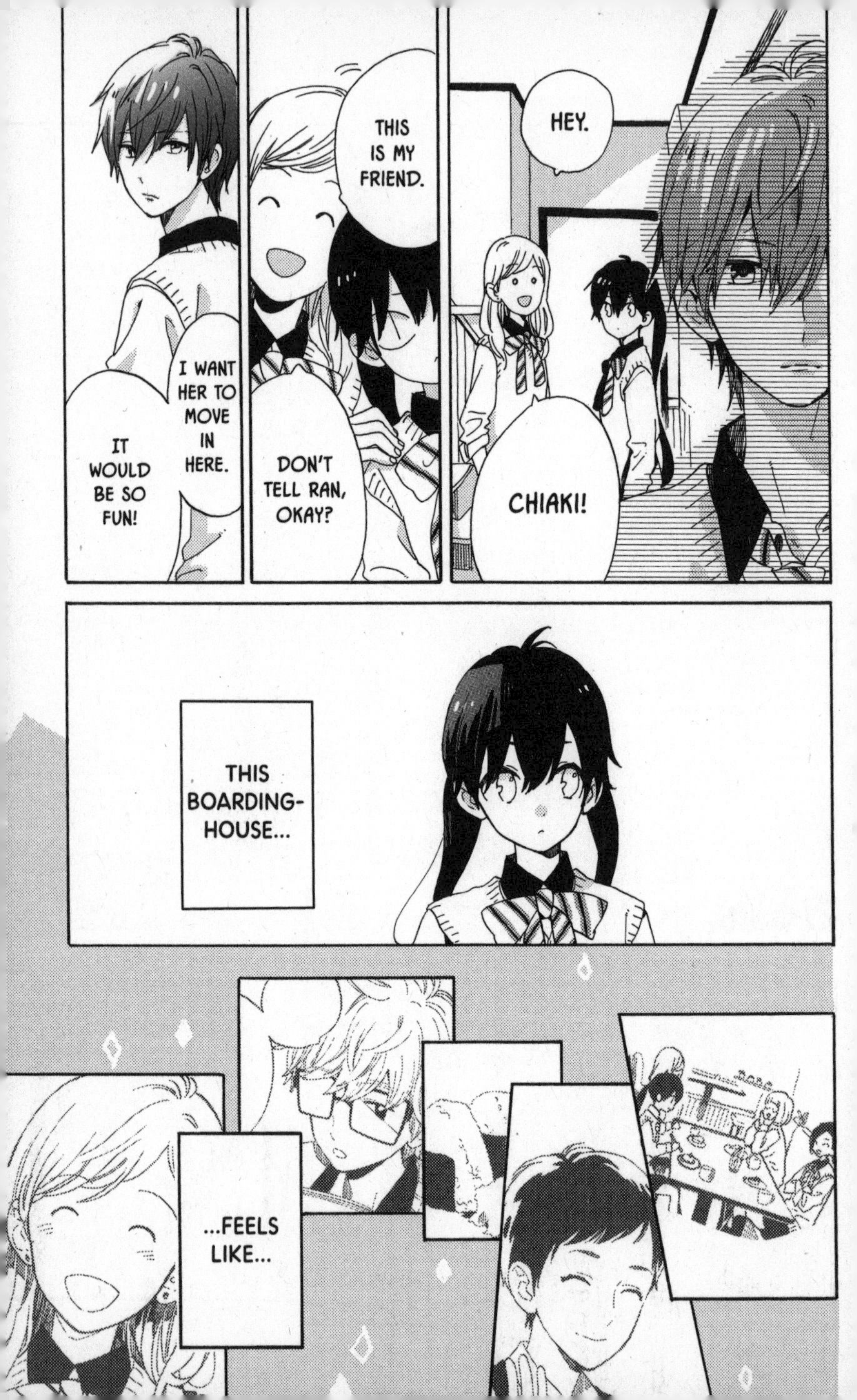
HEY.
CHIAKI!
THIS IS MY FRIEND.
DON'T TELL RAN, OKAY?
I WANT HER TO MOVE IN HERE.
IT WOULD BE SO FUN!
THIS BOARDING-HOUSE...
...FEELS LIKE...

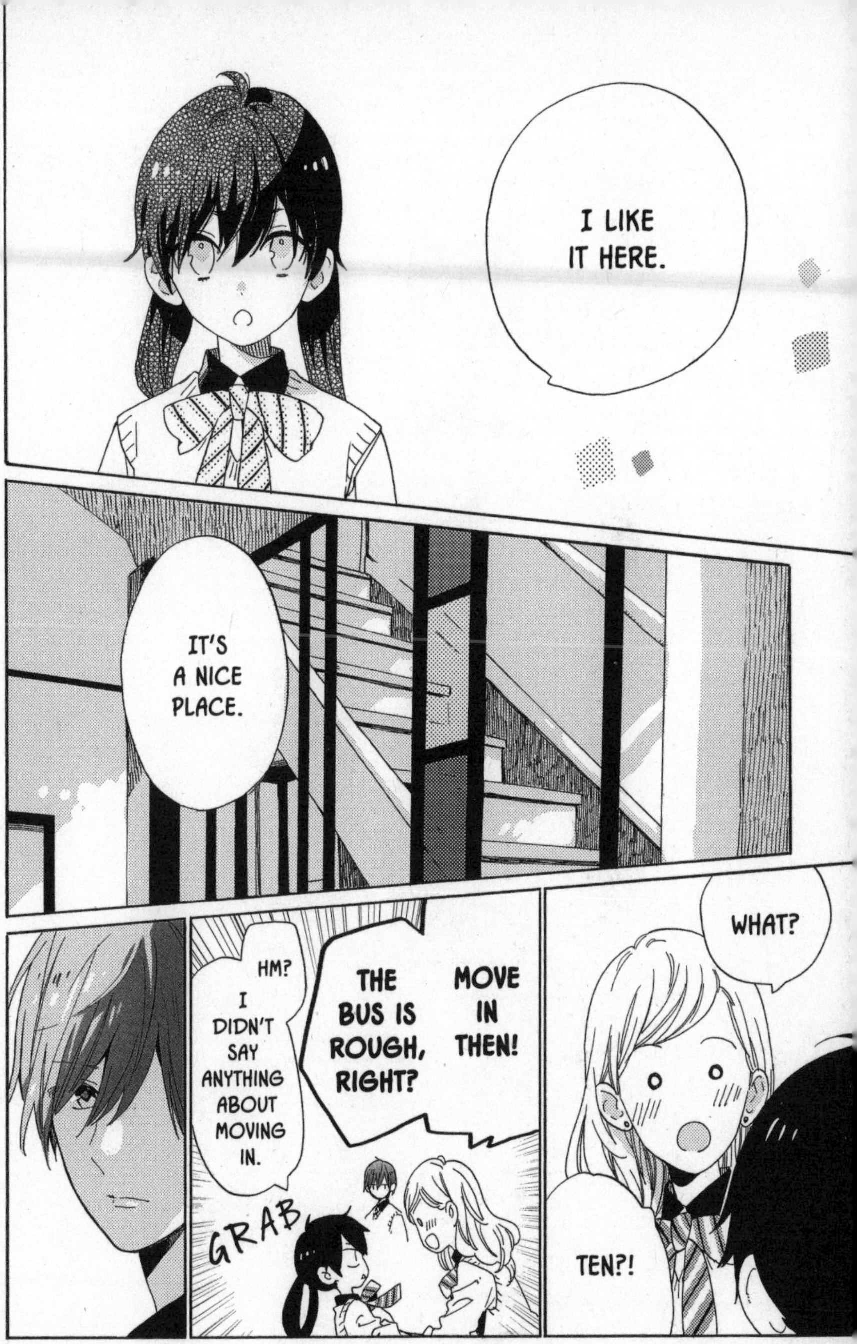
I LIKE IT HERE.
IT'S A NICE PLACE.
WHAT?
TEN?!
MOVE IN THEN!
THE BUS IS ROUGH, RIGHT?
HM? I DIDN'T SAY ANYTHING ABOUT MOVING IN.
GRAB

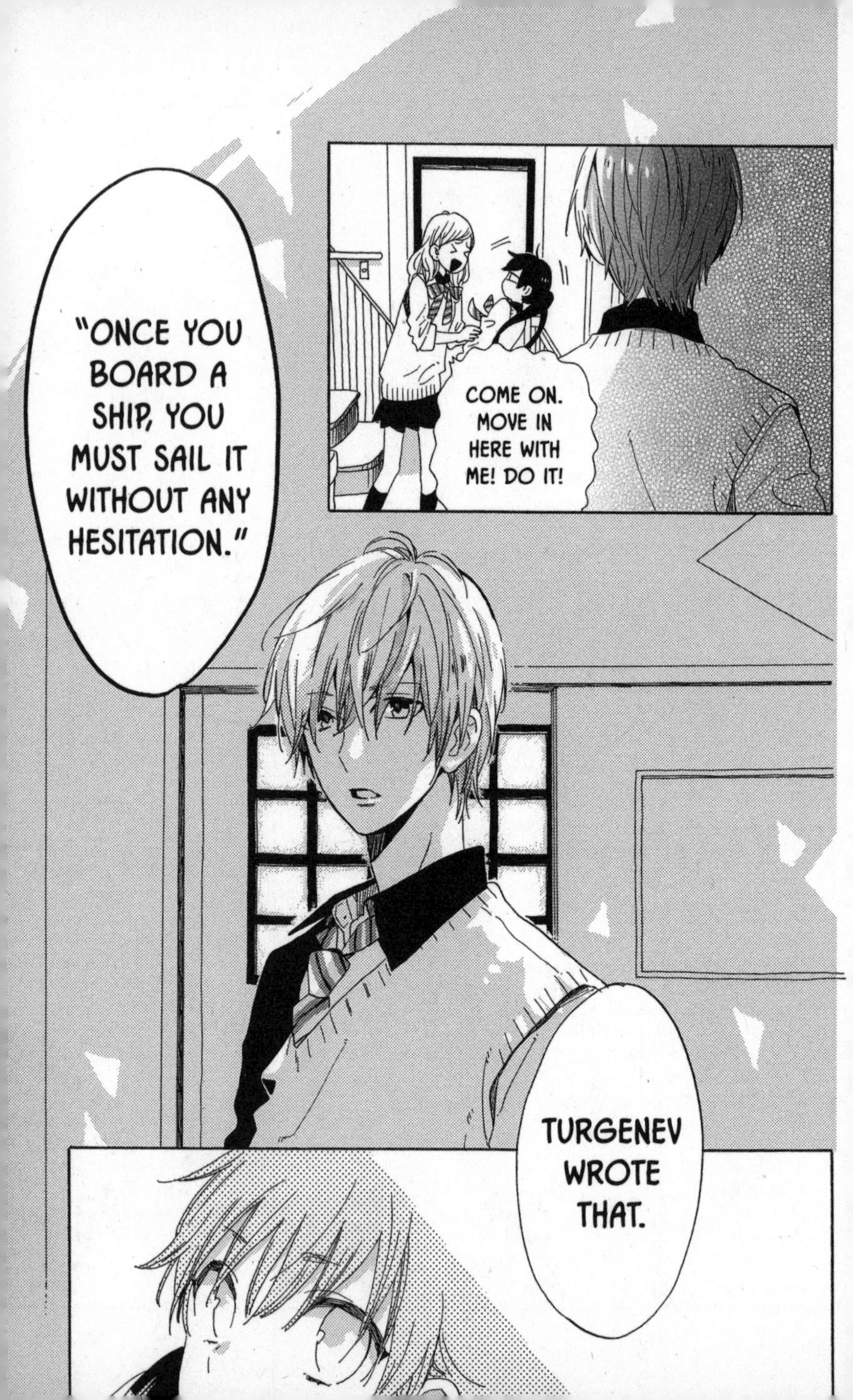
COME ON. MOVE IN HERE WITH ME! DO IT!
"ONCE YOU BOARD A SHIP, YOU MUST SAIL IT WITHOUT ANY HESITATION."
TURGENEV WROTE THAT.

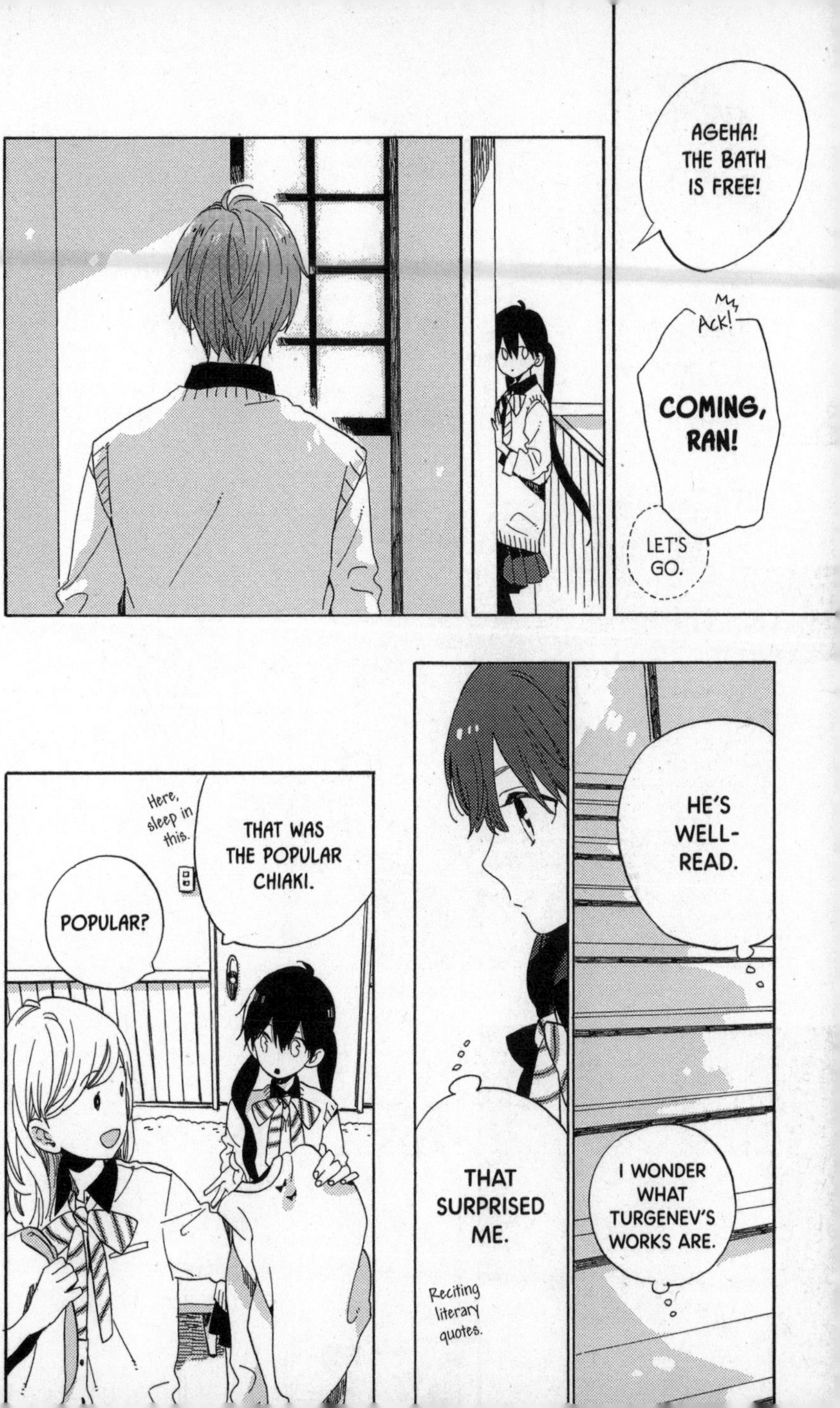
AGEHA! THE BATH IS FREE!
Ack!
COMING, RAN!
LET'S GO.
HE'S WELL-READ.
I WONDER WHAT TURGENEV'S WORKS ARE.
THAT SURPRISED ME.
Reciting literary quotes.
THAT WAS THE POPULAR CHIAKI.
Here, sleep in this.
POPULAR?

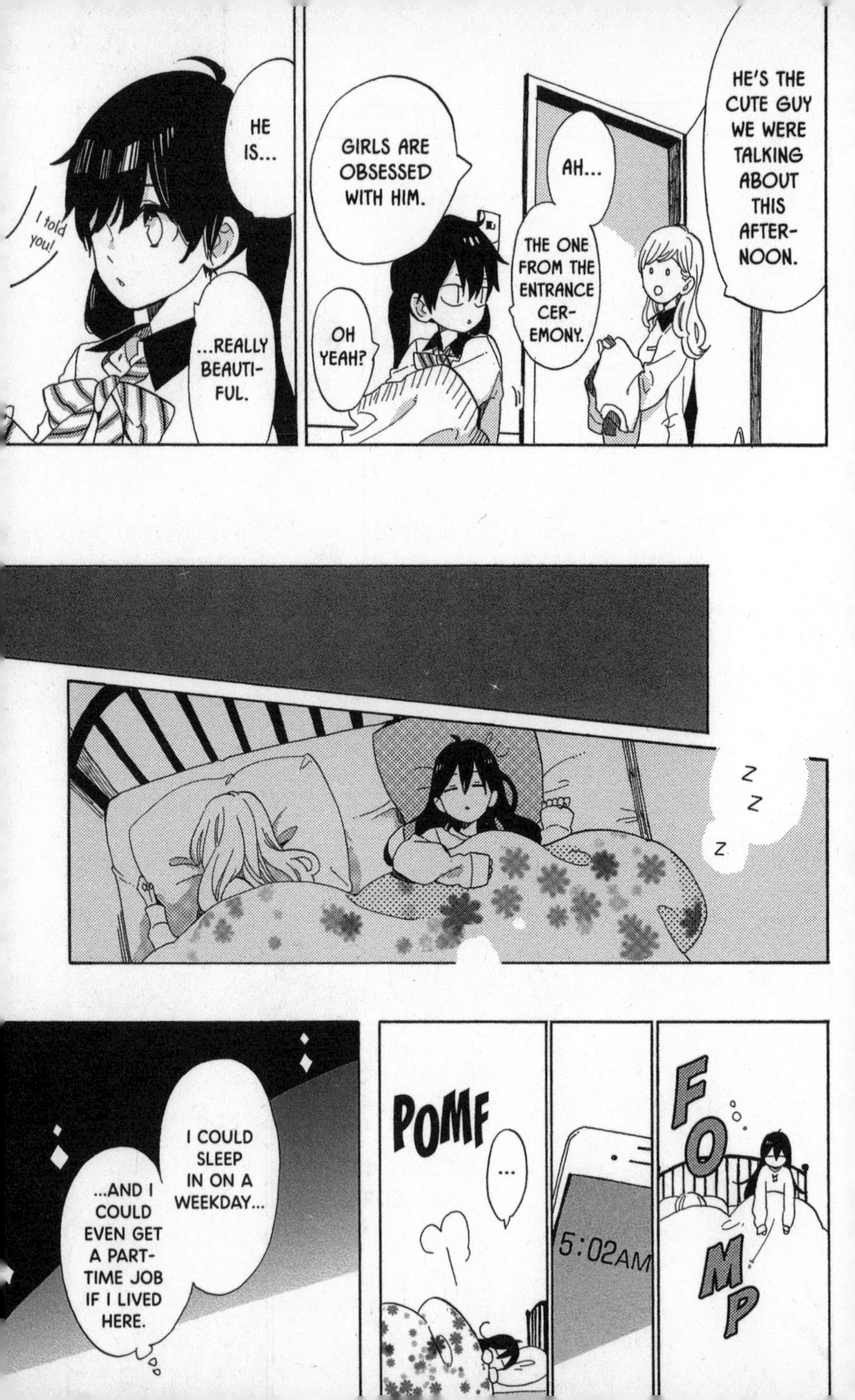
HE'S THE CUTE GUY WE WERE TALKING ABOUT THIS AFTERNOON.
AH...
THE ONE FROM THE ENTRANCE CEREMONY.
GIRLS ARE OBSESSED WITH HIM.
OH YEAH?
HE IS...
I told you!
...REALLY BEAUTIFUL.
Z Z Z
FOMP
5:02AM
POMF
...
I COULD SLEEP IN ON A WEEKDAY...
...AND I COULD EVEN GET A PART-TIME JOB IF I LIVED HERE.

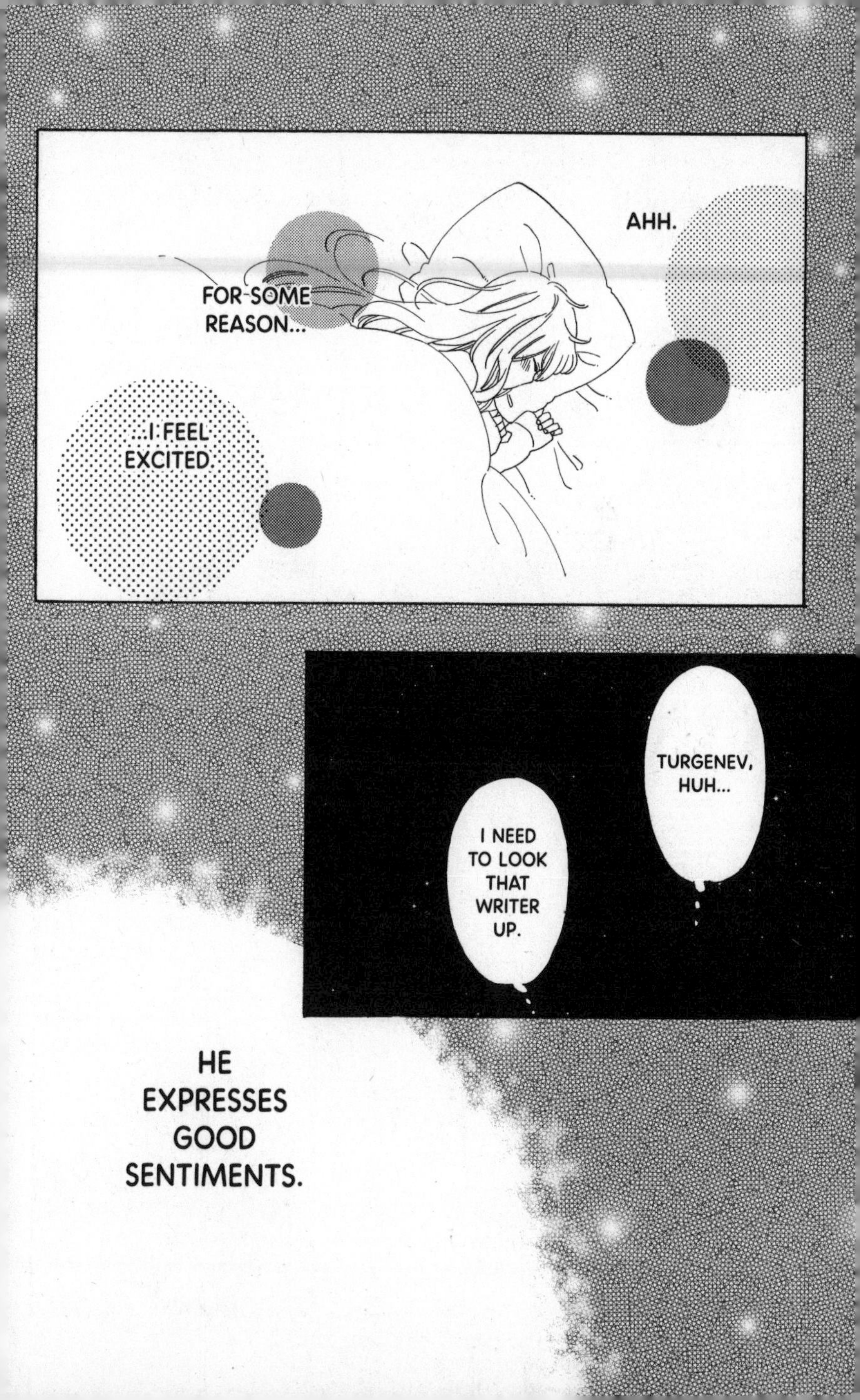
AHH.
FOR SOME REASON...
...I FEEL EXCITED.
TURGENEV, HUH...
I NEED TO LOOK THAT WRITER UP.
HE EXPRESSES GOOD SENTIMENTS.

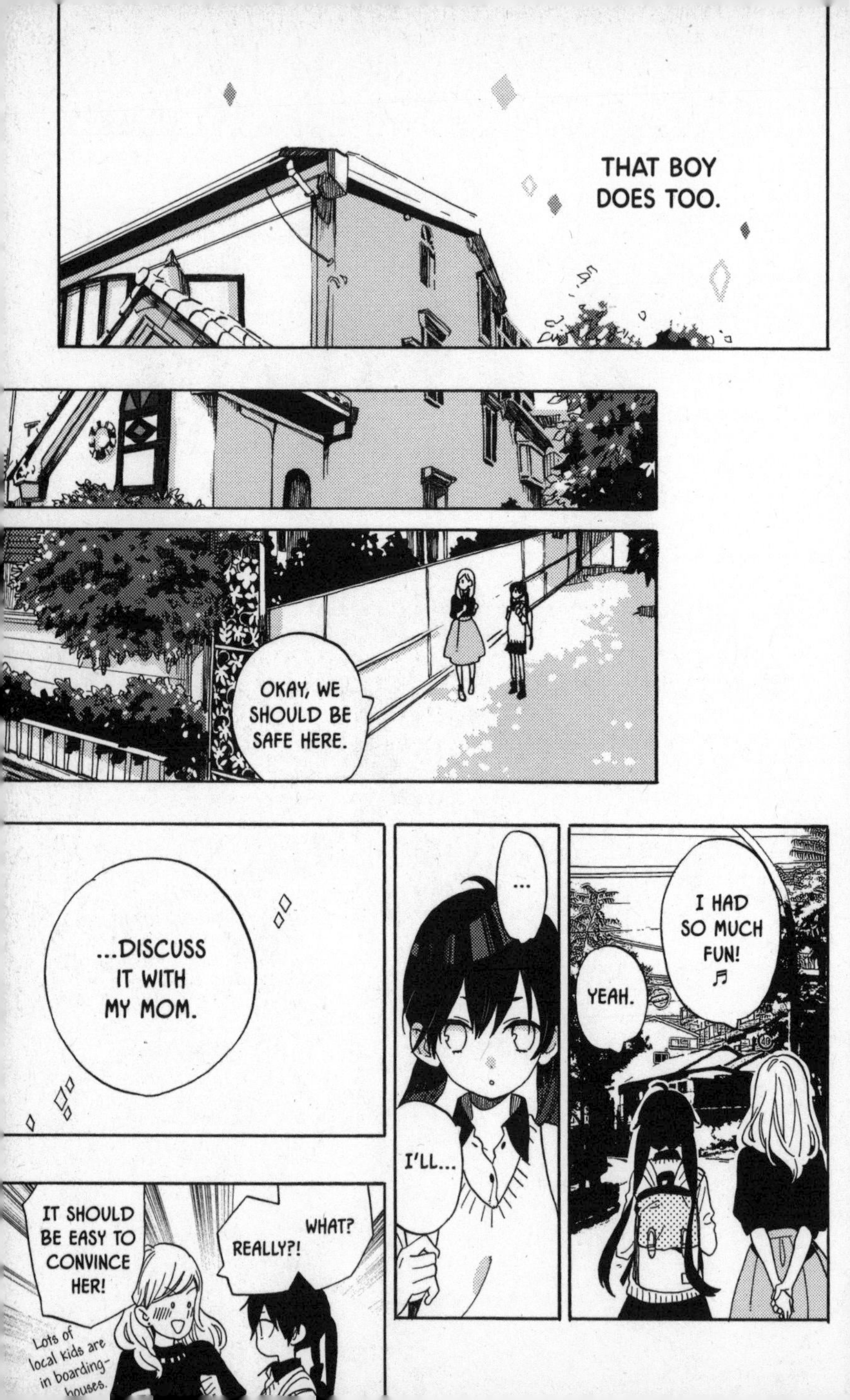
THAT BOY DOES TOO.
OKAY, WE SHOULD BE SAFE HERE.
I HAD SO MUCH FUN! ♫
YEAH.
...
I'LL...
...DISCUSS IT WITH MY MOM.
WHAT? REALLY?!
IT SHOULD BE EASY TO CONVINCE HER!
Lots of local kids are in boarding-houses.

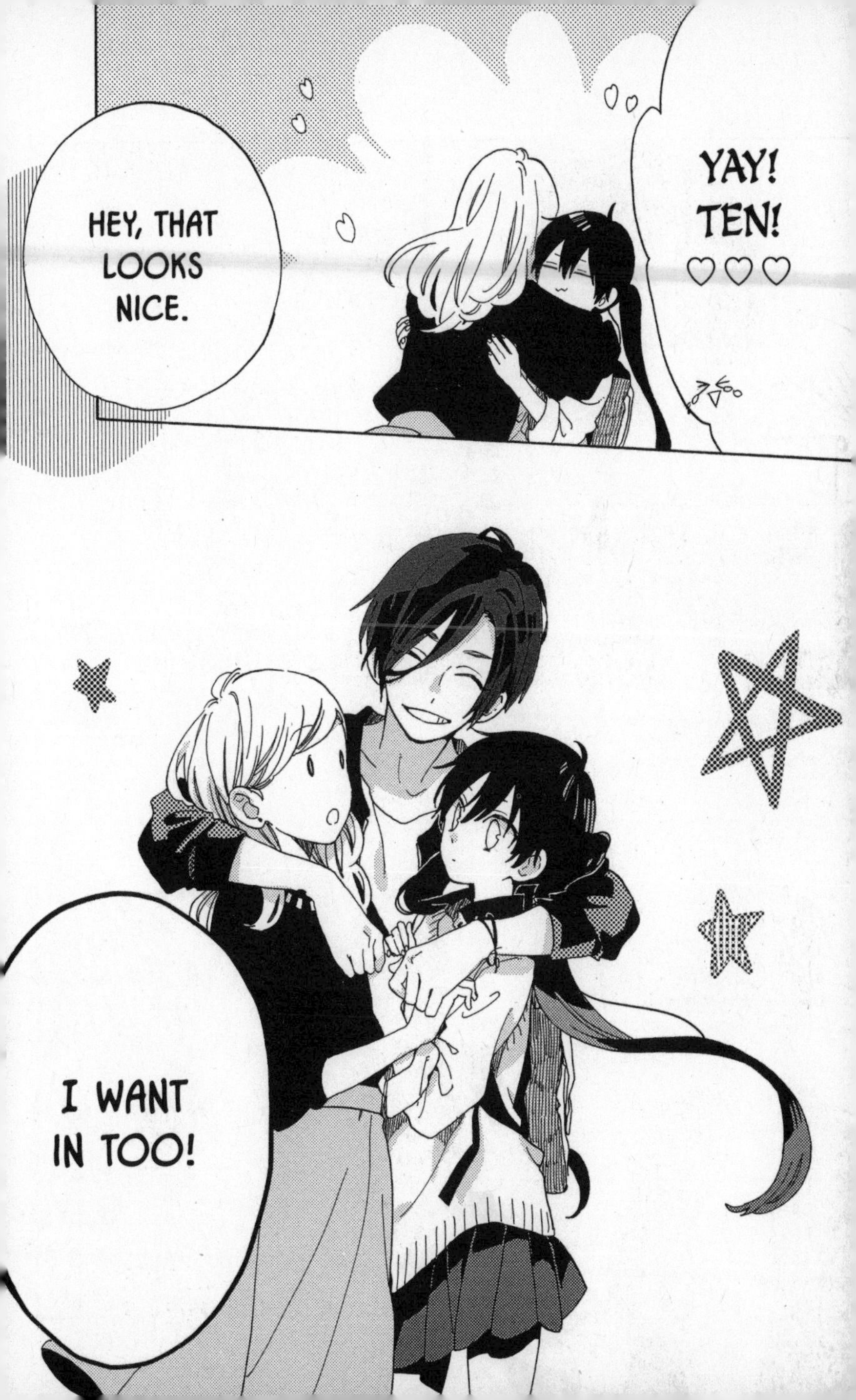
YAY! TEN! ♡♡♡
HEY, THAT LOOKS NICE.
I WANT IN TOO!

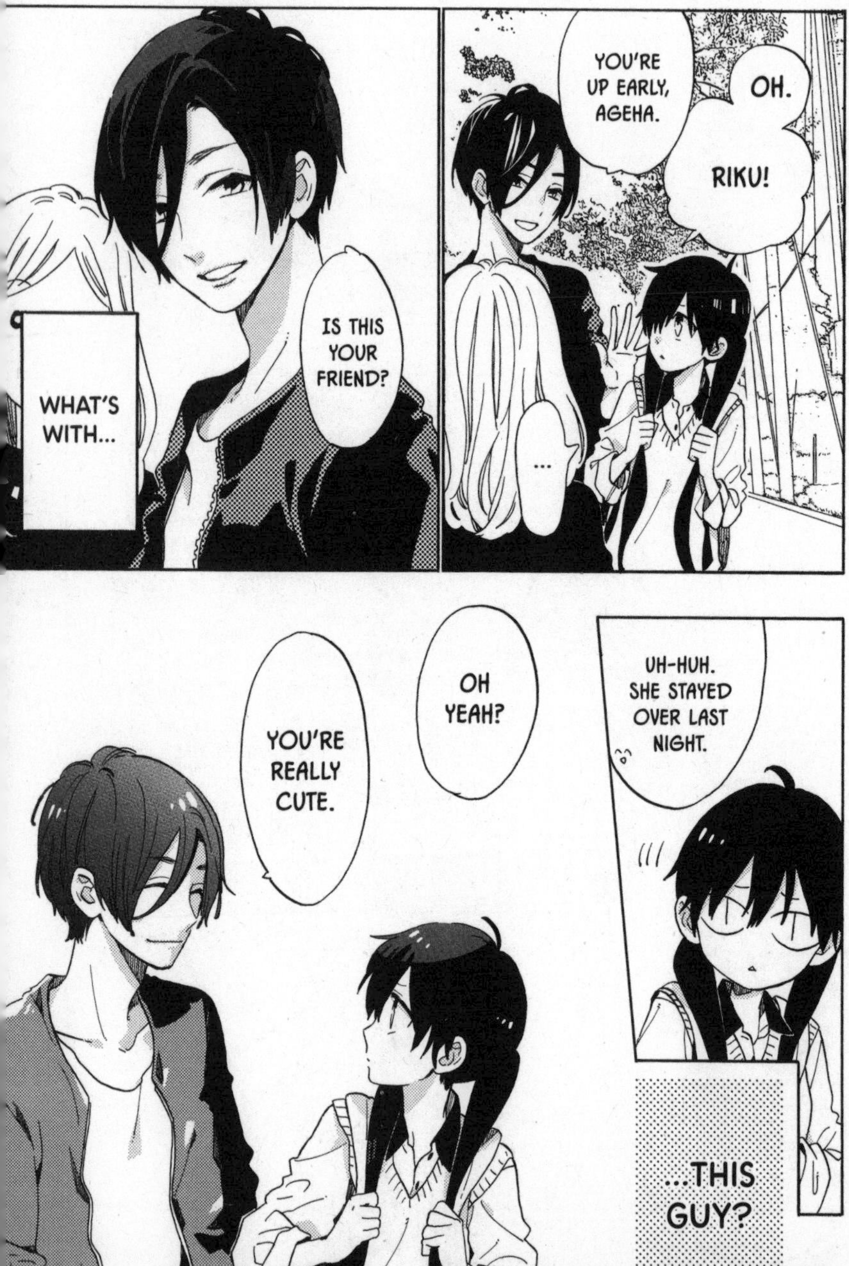
OH. RIKU!
YOU'RE UP EARLY, AGEHA.
...
IS THIS YOUR FRIEND?
WHAT'S WITH...
UH-HUH. SHE STAYED OVER LAST NIGHT.
...THIS GUY?
OH YEAH?
YOU'RE REALLY CUTE.

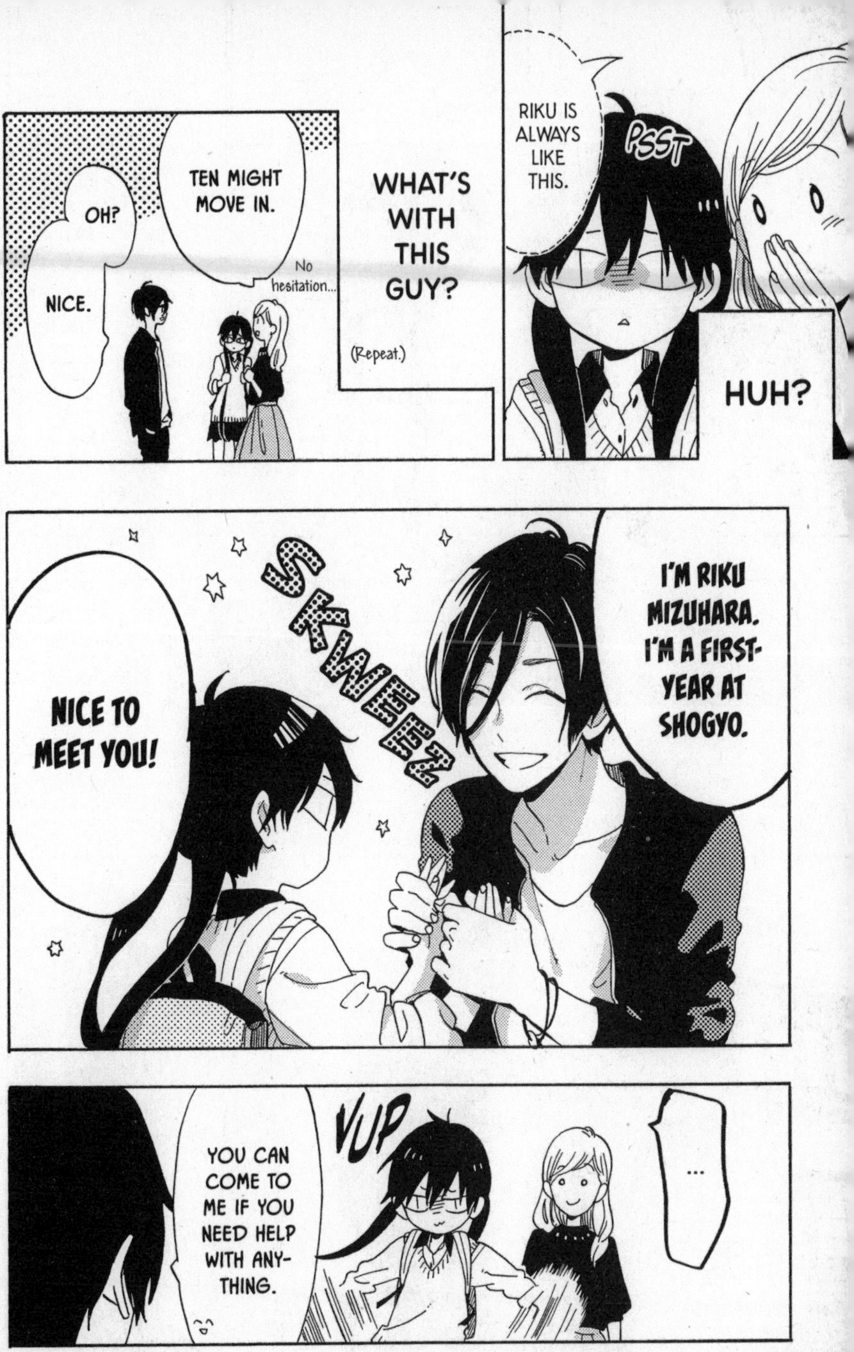
RIKU IS ALWAYS LIKE THIS.
PSST
HUH?
WHAT'S WITH THIS GUY?
(Repeat.)
TEN MIGHT MOVE IN.
OH?
NICE.
No hesitation...
I'M RIKU MIZUHARA. I'M A FIRST-YEAR AT SHOGYO.
SKWEEZ
NICE TO MEET YOU!
...
VUP
YOU CAN COME TO ME IF YOU NEED HELP WITH ANY-THING.

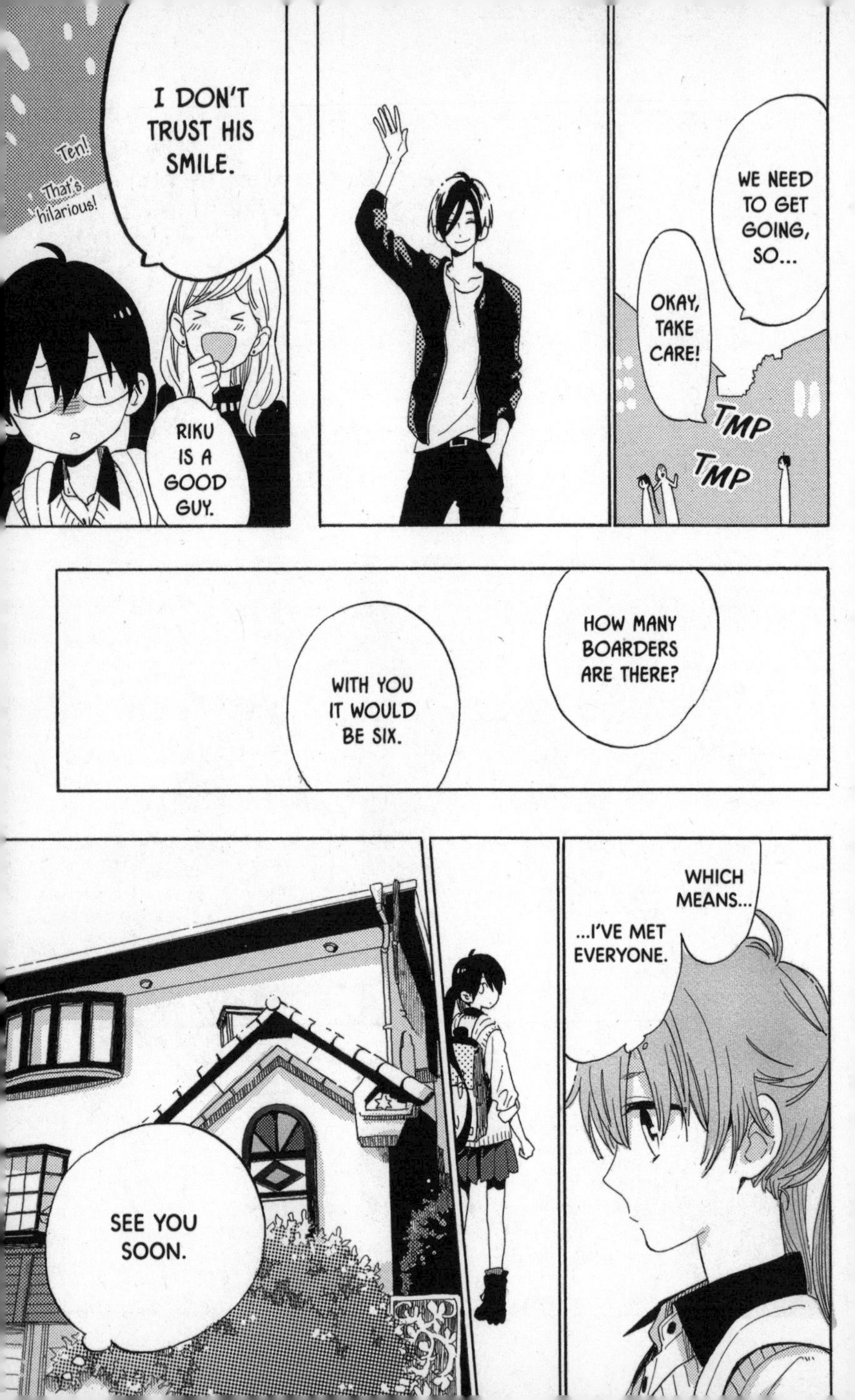
WE NEED TO GET GOING, SO...
OKAY, TAKE CARE!
TMP
TMP
I DON'T TRUST HIS SMILE.
Ten! That's hilarious!
RIKU IS A GOOD GUY.
HOW MANY BOARDERS ARE THERE?
WITH YOU IT WOULD BE SIX.
WHICH MEANS...
...I'VE MET EVERYONE.
SEE YOU SOON.

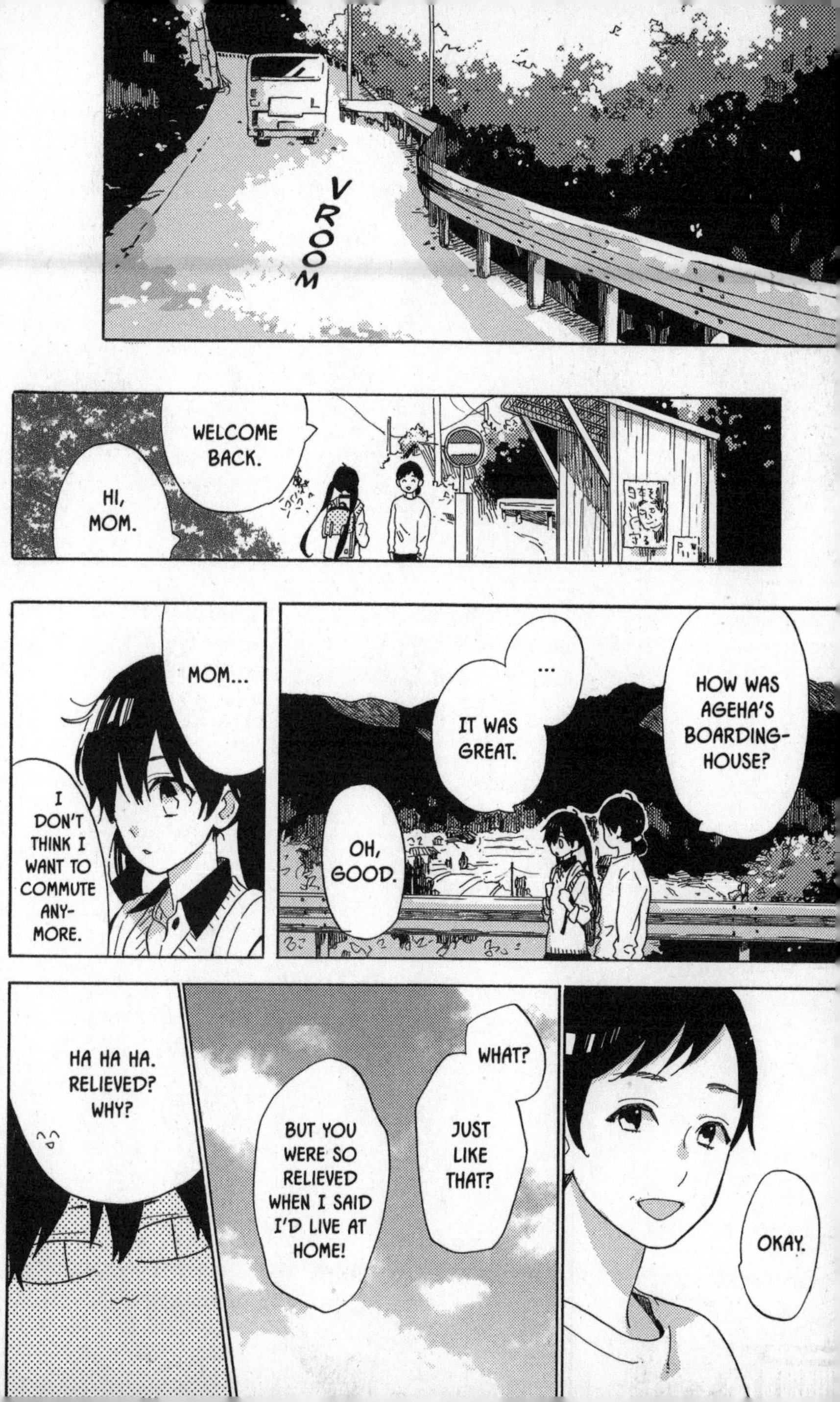
VROOM
WELCOME BACK.
HI, MOM.
HOW WAS AGEHA'S BOARDING-HOUSE?
...
IT WAS GREAT.
OH, GOOD.
MOM...
I DON'T THINK I WANT TO COMMUTE ANYMORE.
OKAY.
WHAT?
JUST LIKE THAT?
BUT YOU WERE SO RELIEVED WHEN I SAID I'D LIVE AT HOME!
HA HA HA. RELIEVED? WHY?

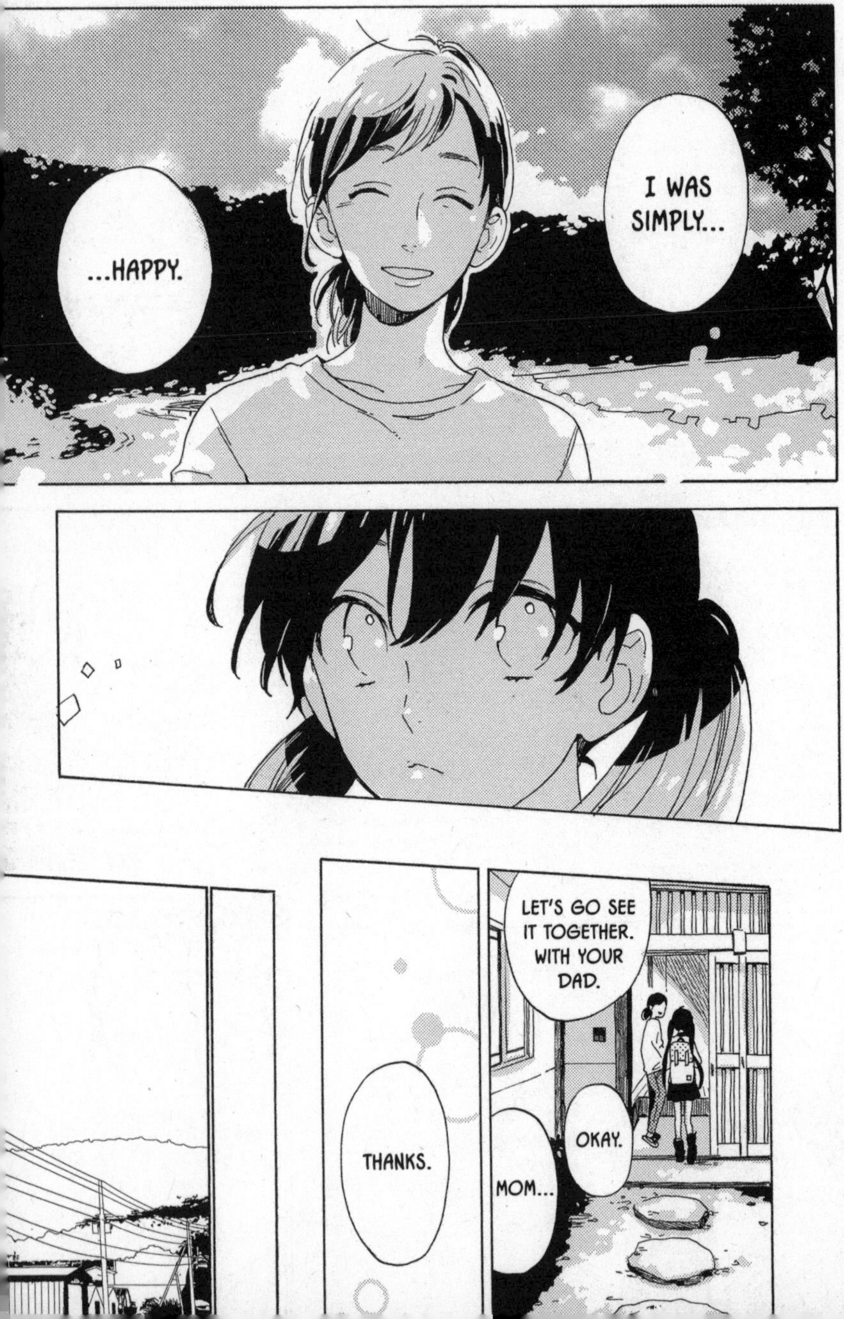
I WAS SIMPLY...
...HAPPY.
LET'S GO SEE IT TOGETHER. WITH YOUR DAD.
OKAY.
MOM...
THANKS.

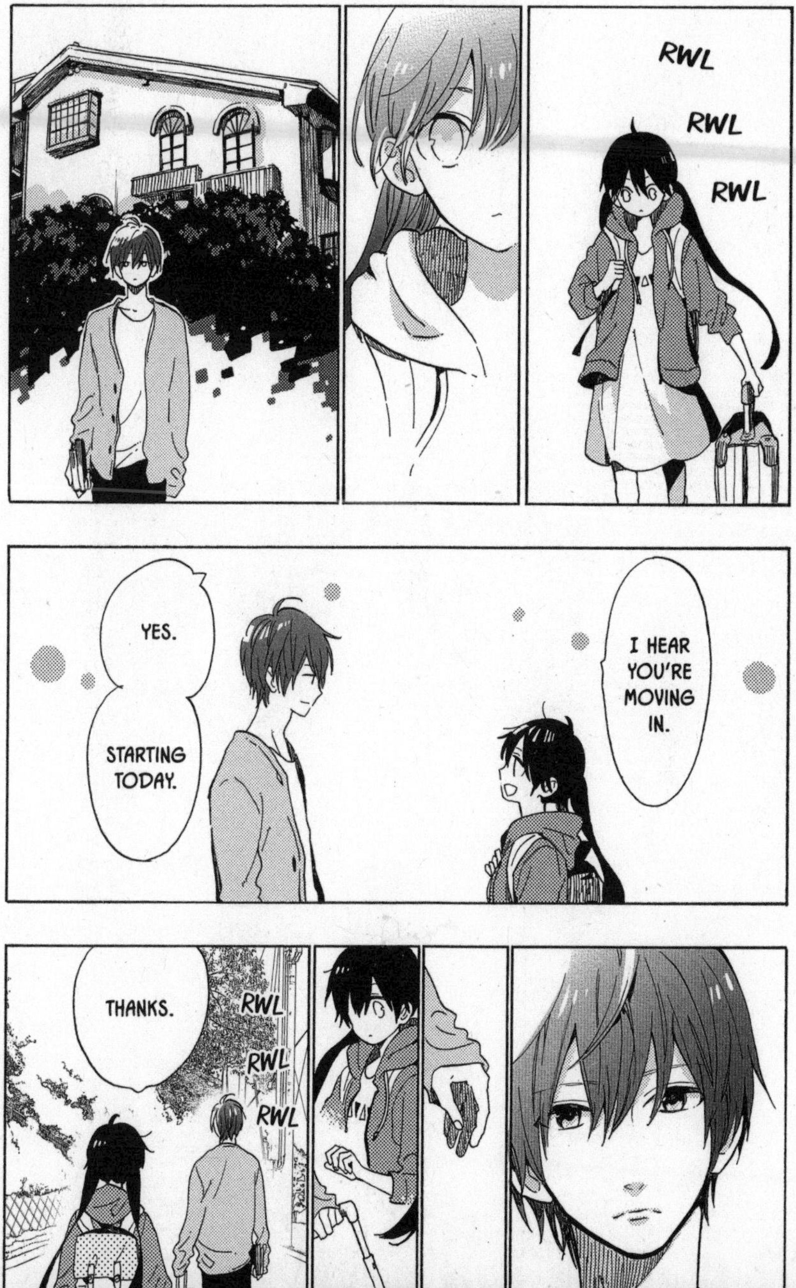
RWL
RWL
RWL
I HEAR YOU'RE MOVING IN.
YES.
STARTING TODAY.
THANKS.
RWL
RWL
RWL

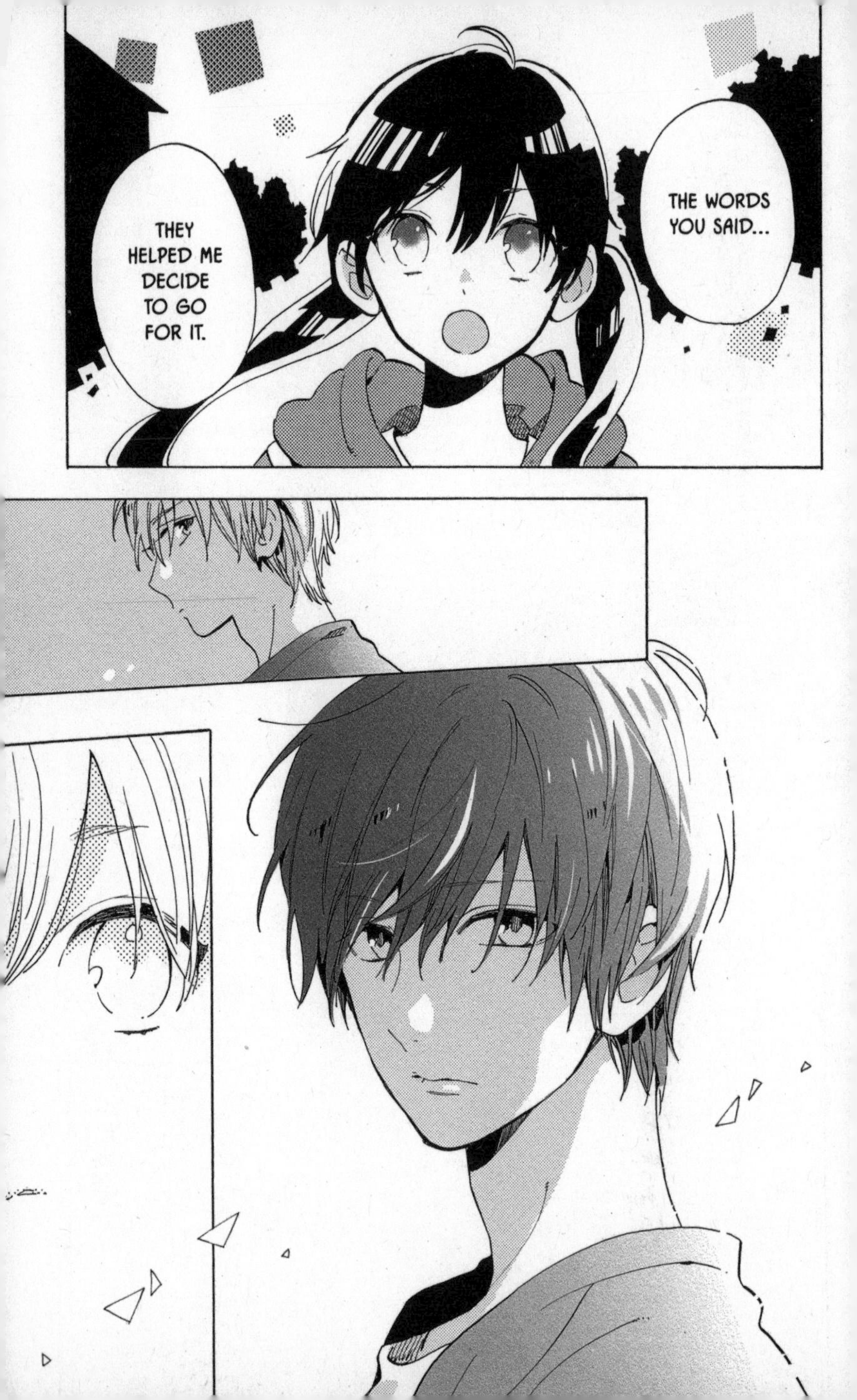
THE WORDS YOU SAID...
THEY HELPED ME DECIDE TO GO FOR IT.

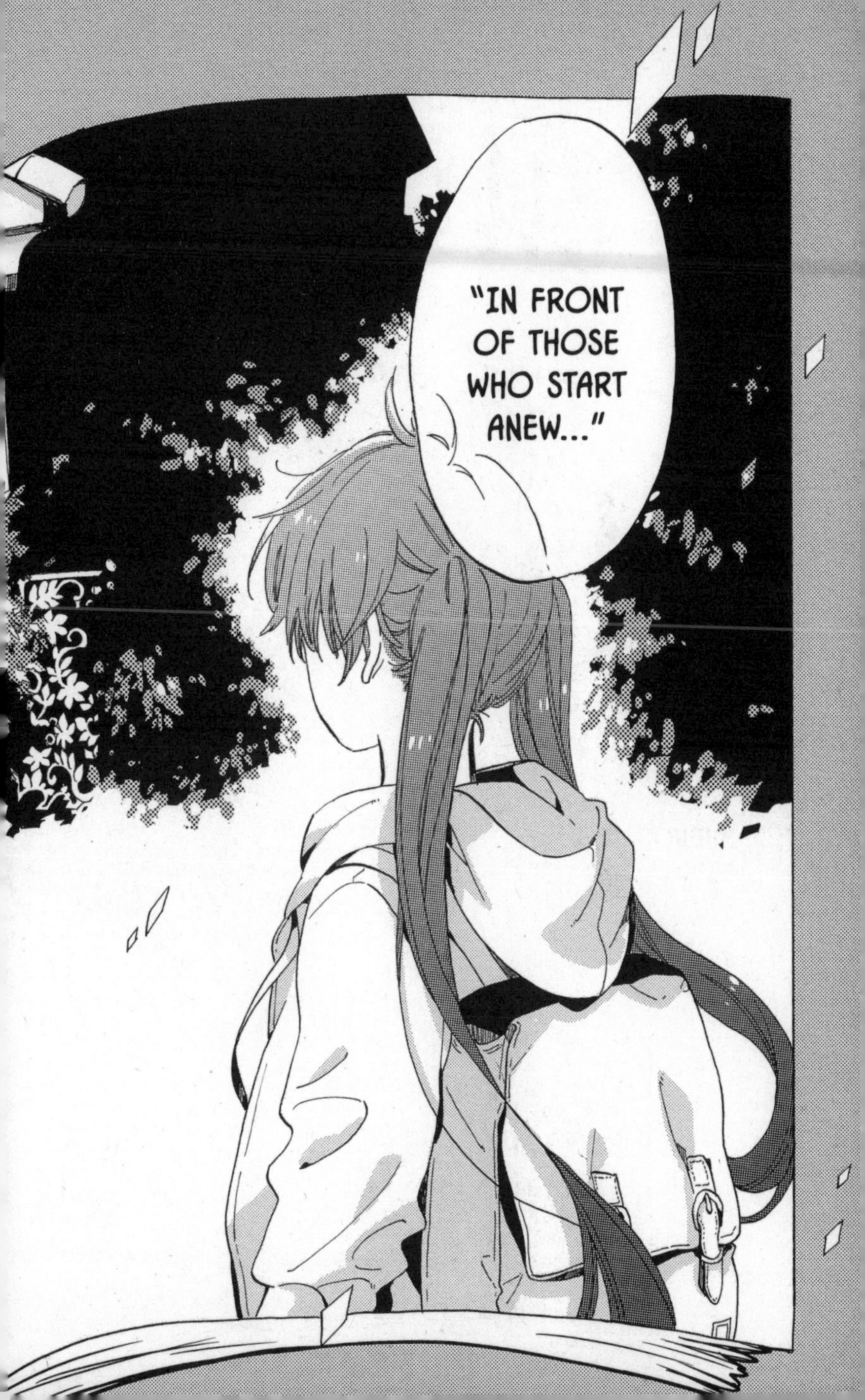
"IN FRONT OF THOSE WHO START ANEW..."

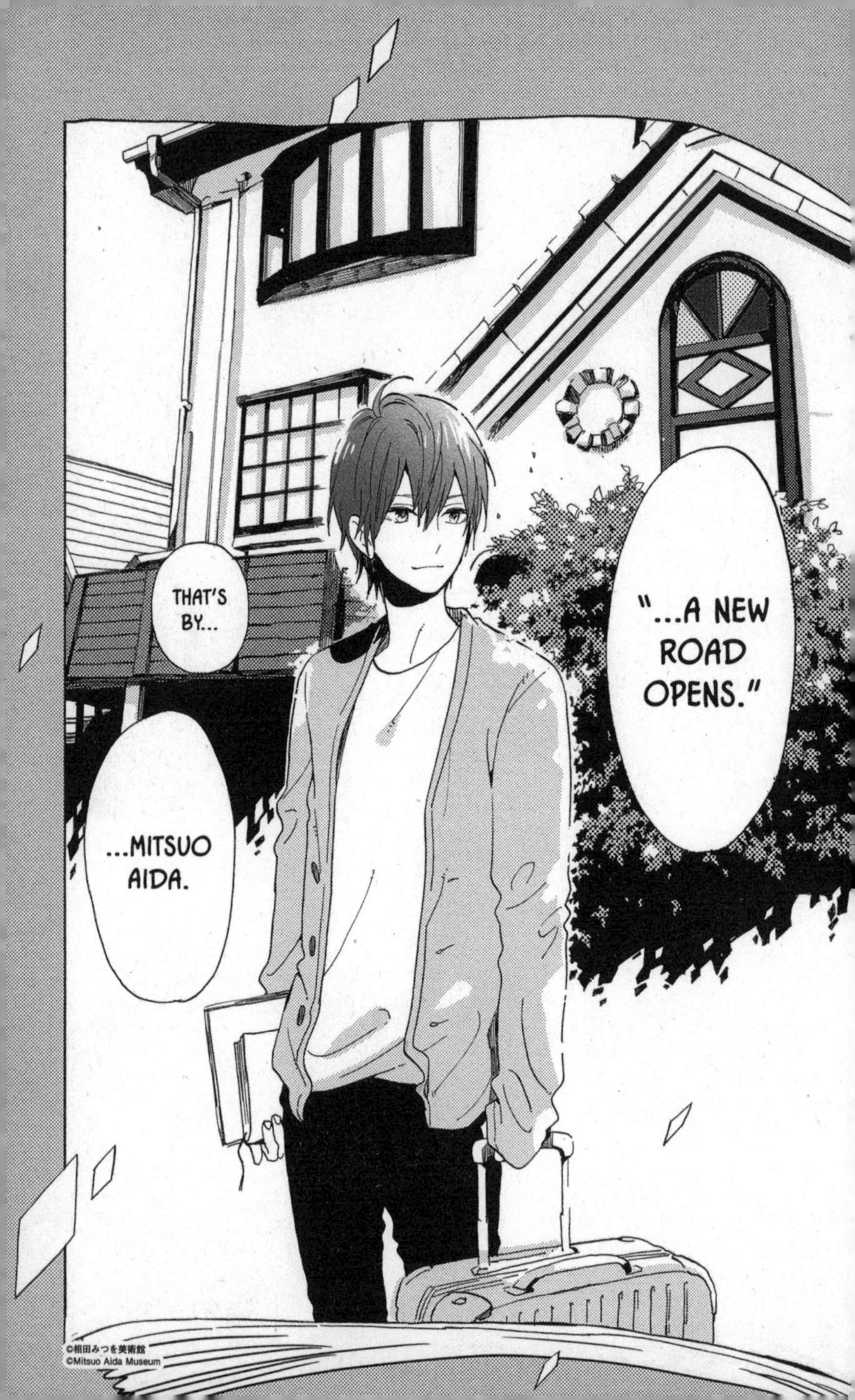
"...A NEW ROAD OPENS."
THAT'S BY...
...MITSUO AIDA.

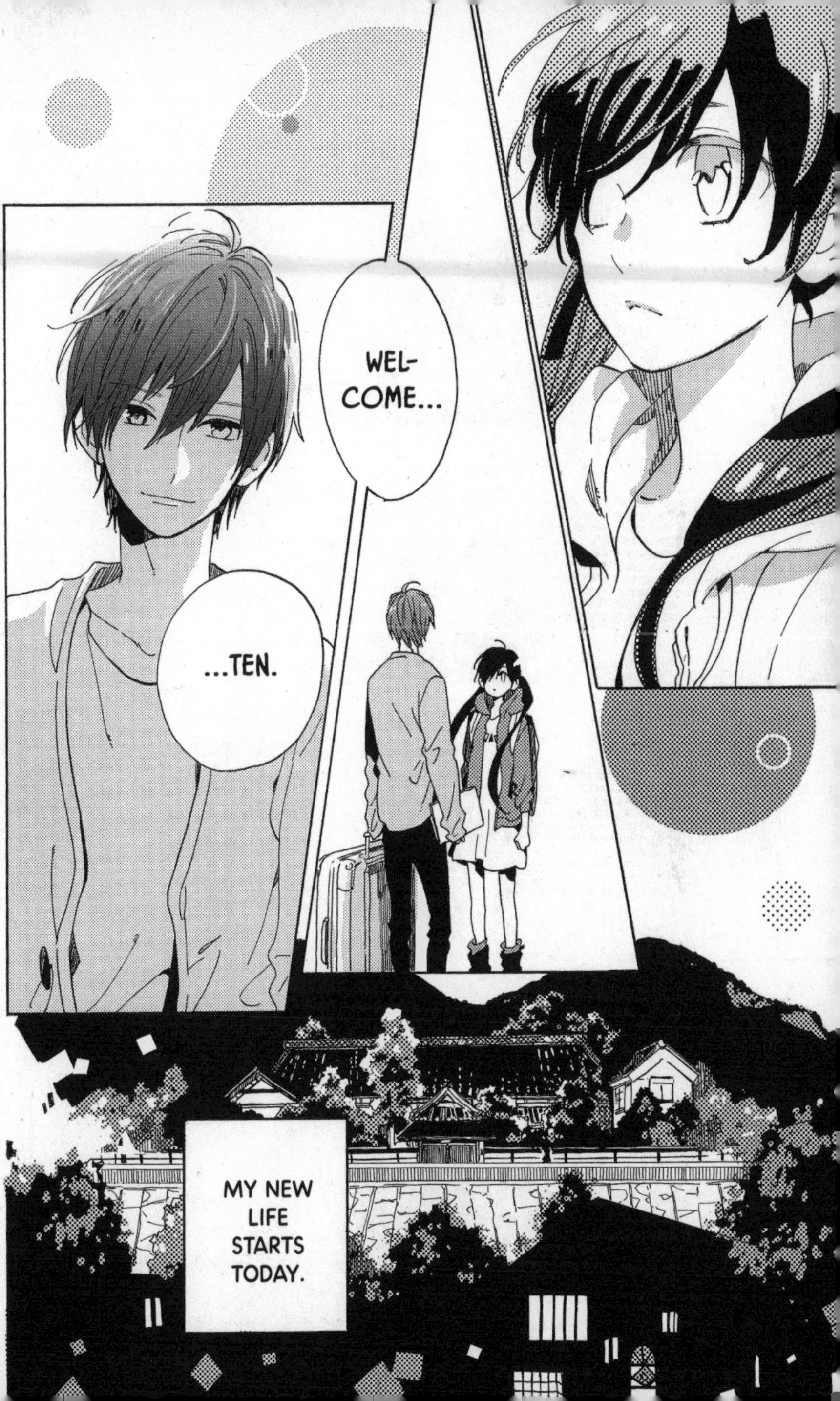
WEL-
COME...
...TEN.
MY NEW LIFE STARTS TODAY.

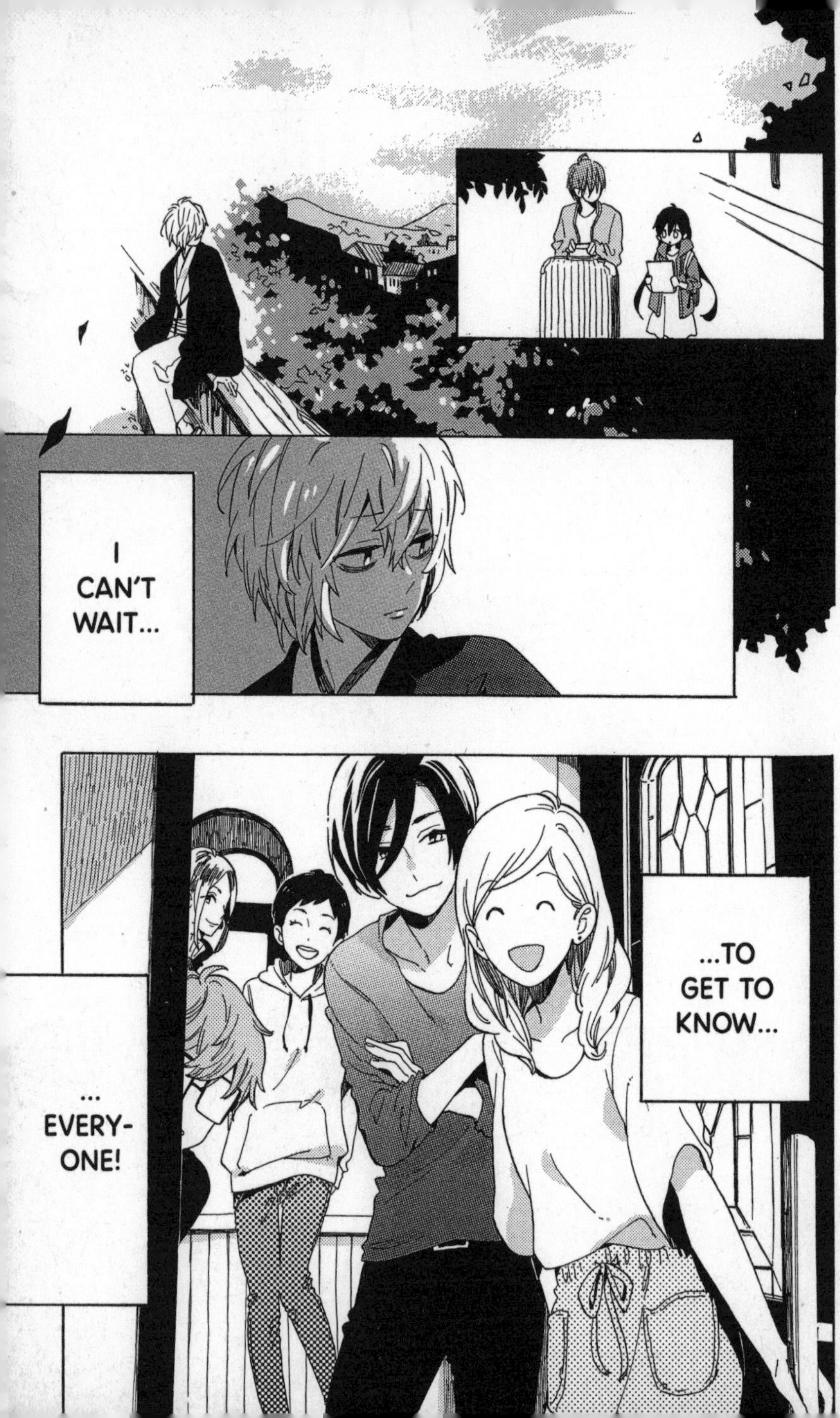
I CAN'T WAIT...
...TO GET TO KNOW...
... EVERY-ONE!

SHORTCAKE
CAKE

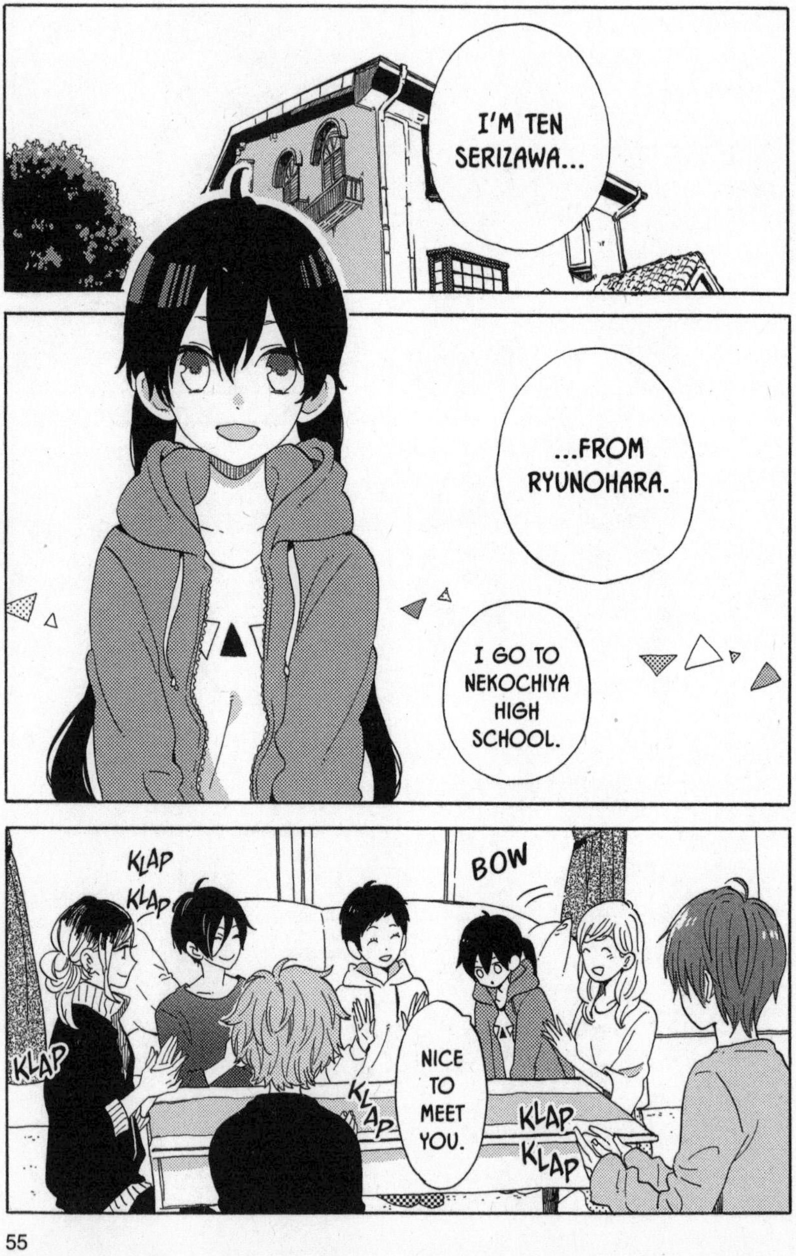
I'M TEN SERIZAWA...
...FROM RYUNOHARA.
I GO TO NEKOCHIYA HIGH SCHOOL.
BOW
KLAP KLAP
NICE TO MEET YOU.
KLAP
KLAP KLAP
KLAP

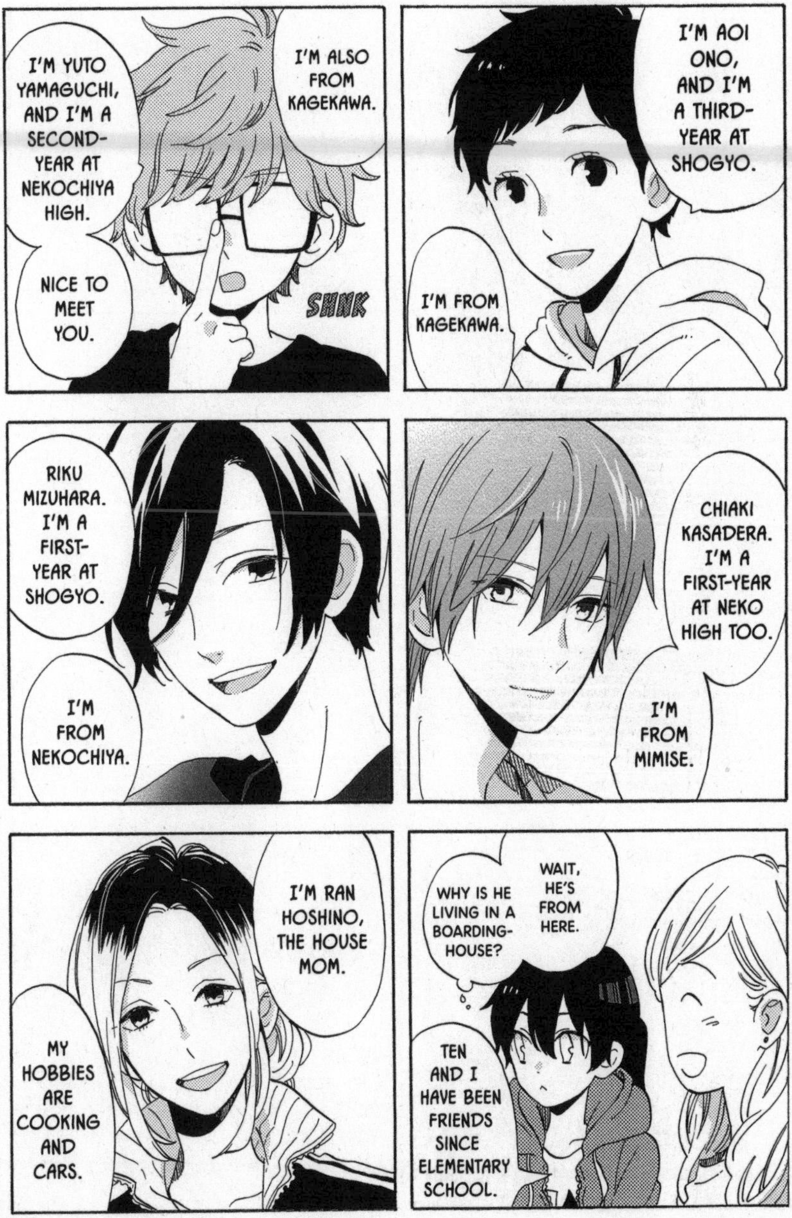
I'M AOI ONO, AND I'M A THIRD-YEAR AT SHOGYO.
I'M FROM KAGEKAWA.
I'M ALSO FROM KAGEKAWA.
I'M YUTO YAMAGUCHI, AND I'M A SECOND-YEAR AT NEKOCHIYA HIGH.
SHNK
NICE TO MEET YOU.
CHIAKI KASADERA. I'M A FIRST-YEAR AT NEKO HIGH TOO.
I'M FROM MIMISE.
RIKU MIZUHARA. I'M A FIRST-YEAR AT SHOGYO.
I'M FROM NEKOCHIYA.
WAIT, HE'S FROM HERE.
WHY IS HE LIVING IN A BOARDING-HOUSE?
TEN AND I HAVE BEEN FRIENDS SINCE ELEMENTARY SCHOOL.
I'M RAN HOSHINO, THE HOUSE MOM.
MY HOBBIES ARE COOKING AND CARS.

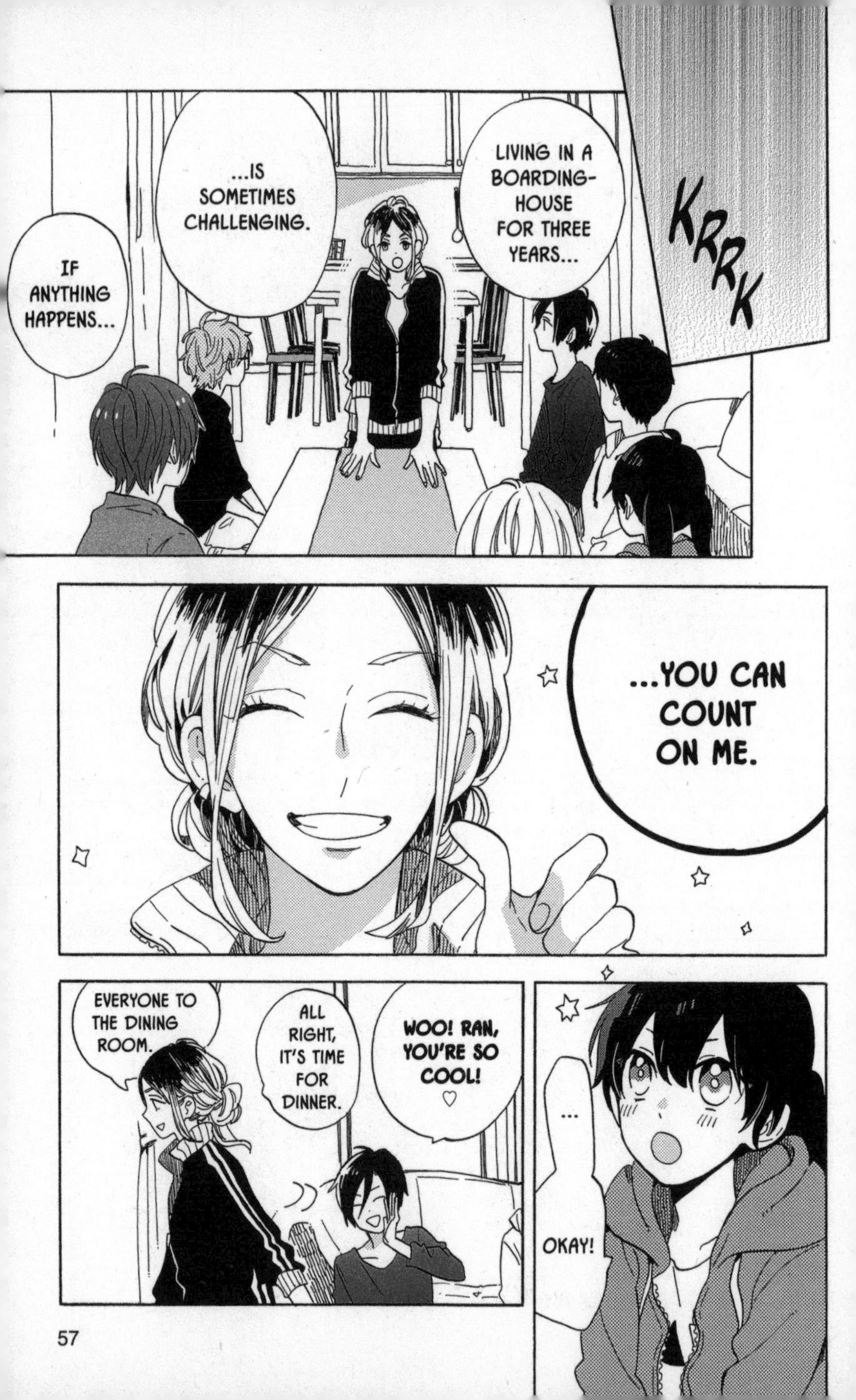
KRRK
LIVING IN A BOARDING-HOUSE FOR THREE YEARS...
...IS SOMETIMES CHALLENGING.
IF ANYTHING HAPPENS...
...YOU CAN COUNT ON ME.
...
OKAY!
WOO! RAN, YOU'RE SO COOL! ♡
ALL RIGHT, IT'S TIME FOR DINNER.
EVERYONE TO THE DINING ROOM.

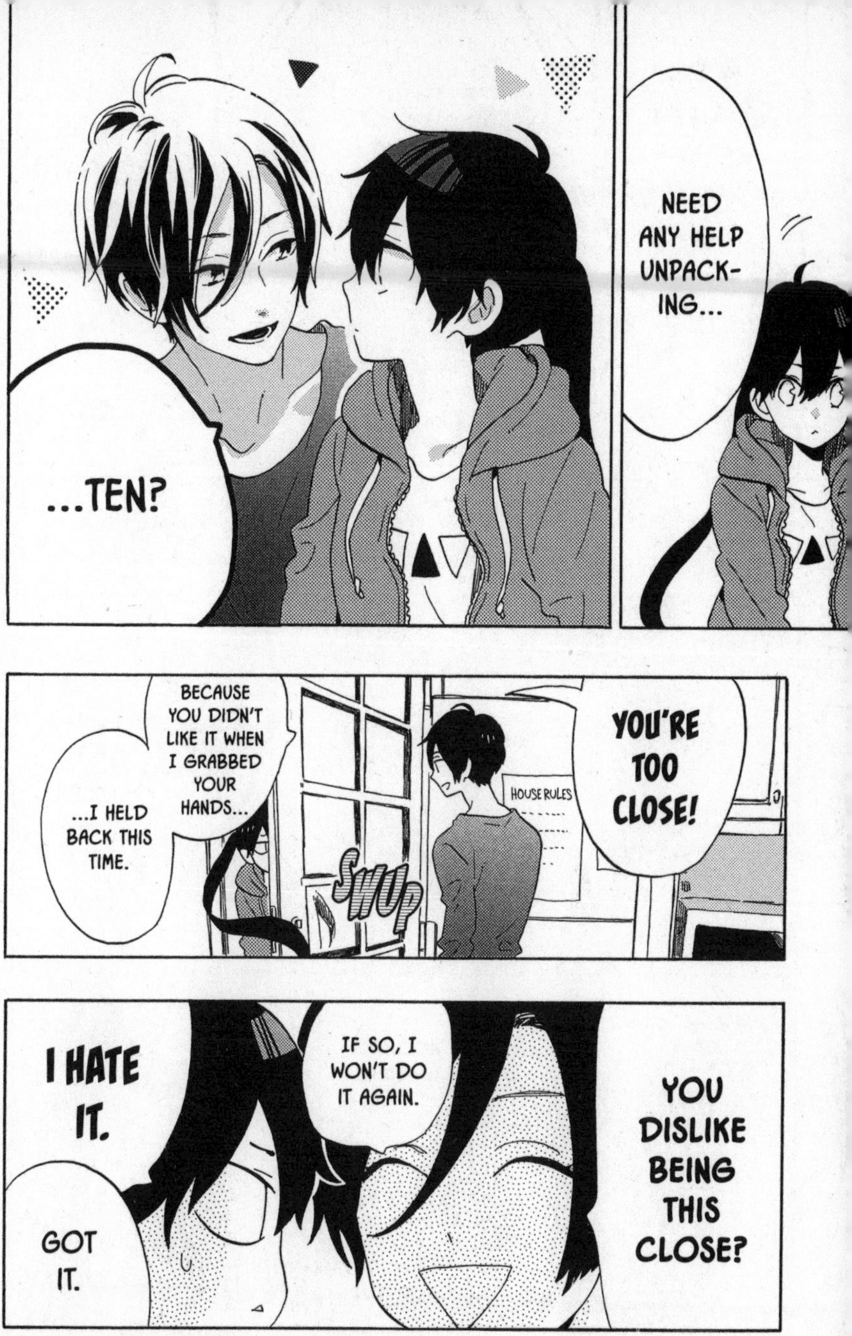
NEED ANY HELP UNPACK-ING...
...TEN?
YOU'RE TOO CLOSE!
BECAUSE YOU DIDN'T LIKE IT WHEN I GRABBED YOUR HANDS...
...I HELD BACK THIS TIME.
HOUSE RULES
SWUP
YOU DISLIKE BEING THIS CLOSE?
IF SO, I WON'T DO IT AGAIN.
I HATE IT.
GOT IT.

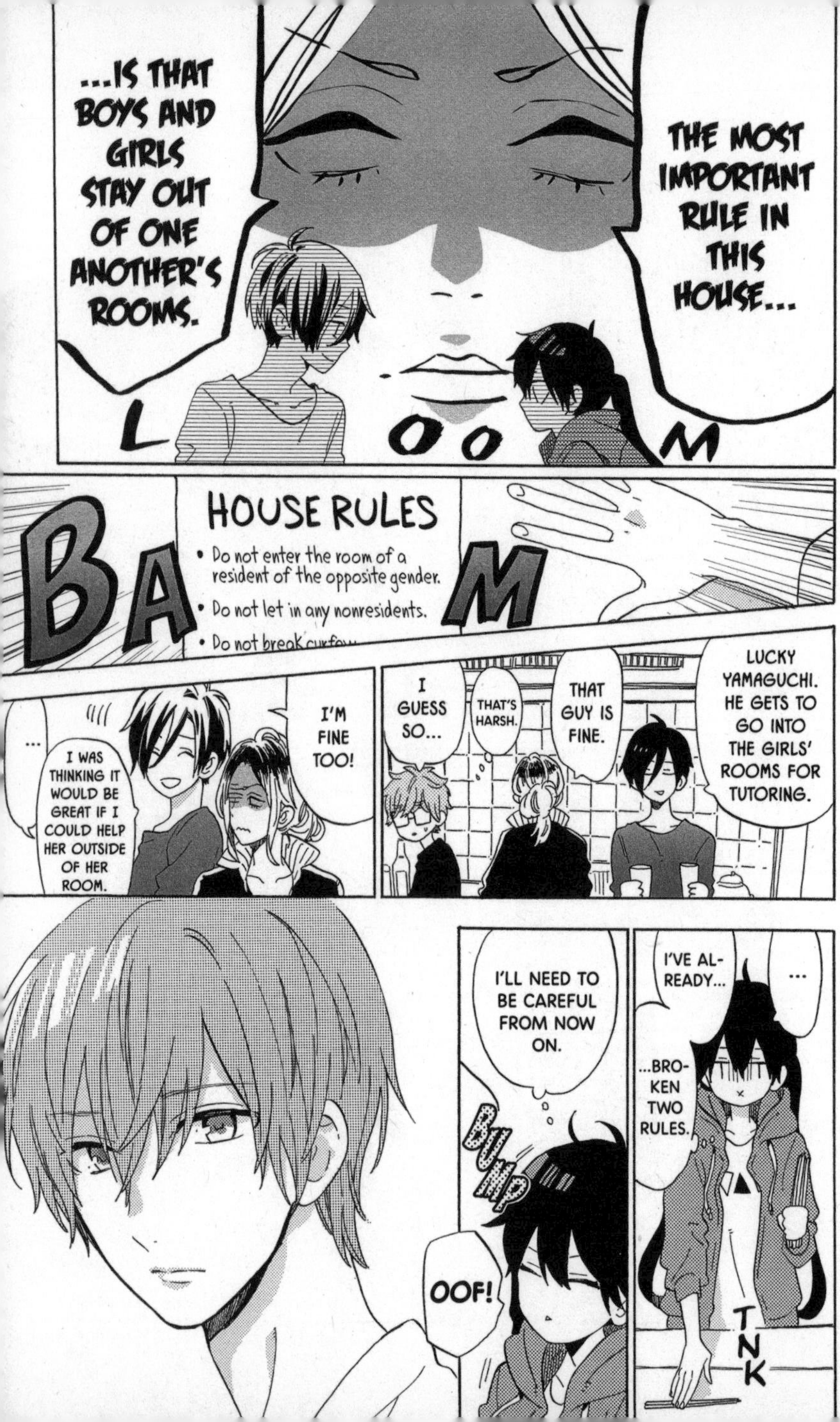
THE MOST IMPORTANT RULE IN THIS HOUSE...
...IS THAT BOYS AND GIRLS STAY OUT OF ONE ANOTHER'S ROOMS.
LOOOM
BAM
HOUSE RULES
• Do not enter the room of a resident of the opposite gender.
• Do not let in any nonresidents.
LUCKY YAMAGUCHI. HE GETS TO GO INTO THE GIRLS' ROOMS FOR TUTORING.
THAT GUY IS FINE.
THAT'S HARSH.
I GUESS SO...
I'M FINE TOO!
...
I WAS THINKING IT WOULD BE GREAT IF I COULD HELP HER OUTSIDE OF HER ROOM.
...
I'VE AL-READY...
...BRO-KEN TWO RULES.
TNK
I'LL NEED TO BE CAREFUL FROM NOW ON.
BUMP
OOF!

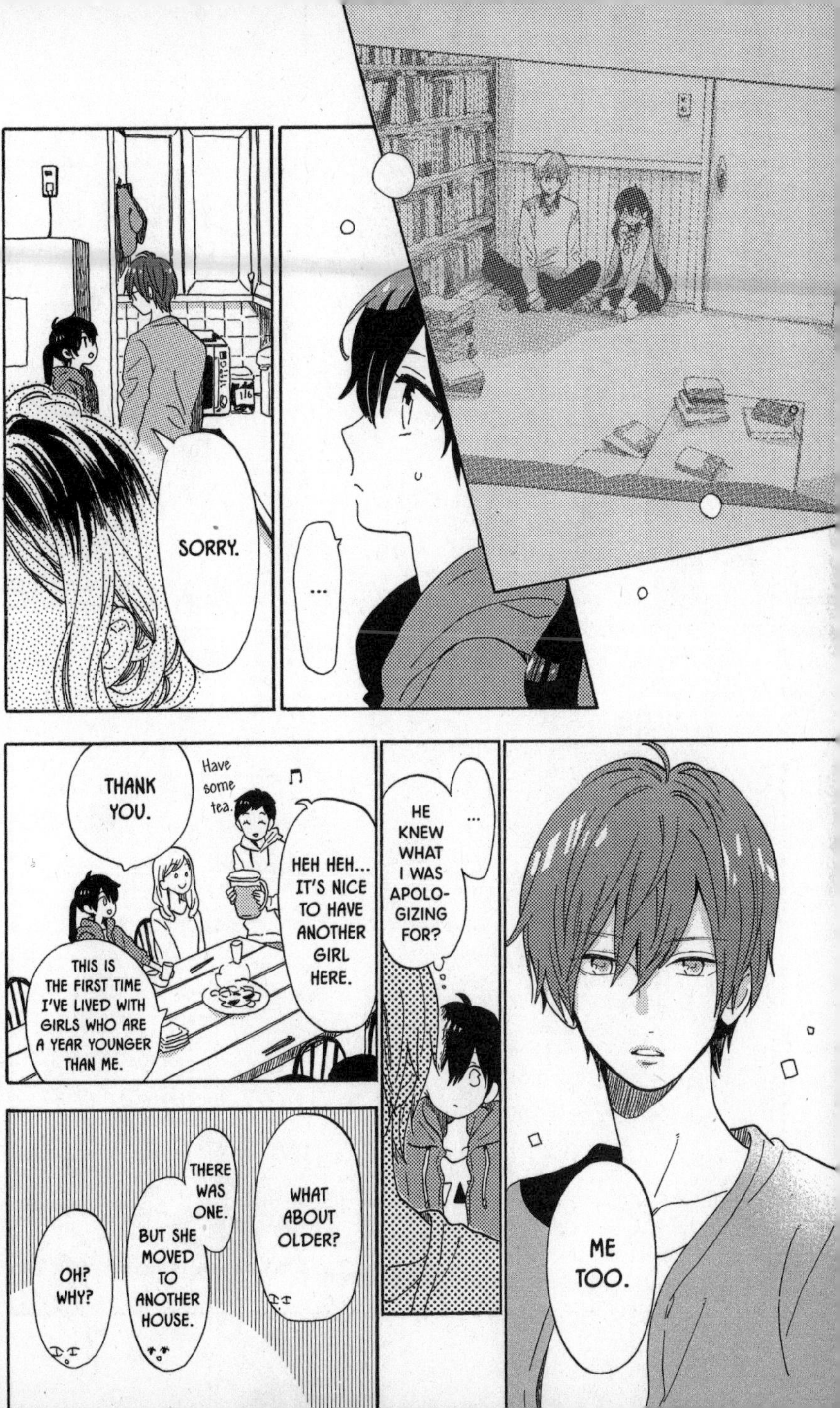

...
SORRY.
ME TOO.
...
HE KNEW WHAT I WAS APOLOGIZING FOR?
Have some tea.
THANK YOU.
HEH HEH... IT'S NICE TO HAVE ANOTHER GIRL HERE.
THIS IS THE FIRST TIME I'VE LIVED WITH GIRLS WHO ARE A YEAR YOUNGER THAN ME.
WHAT ABOUT OLDER?
THERE WAS ONE.
BUT SHE MOVED TO ANOTHER HOUSE.
OH? WHY?

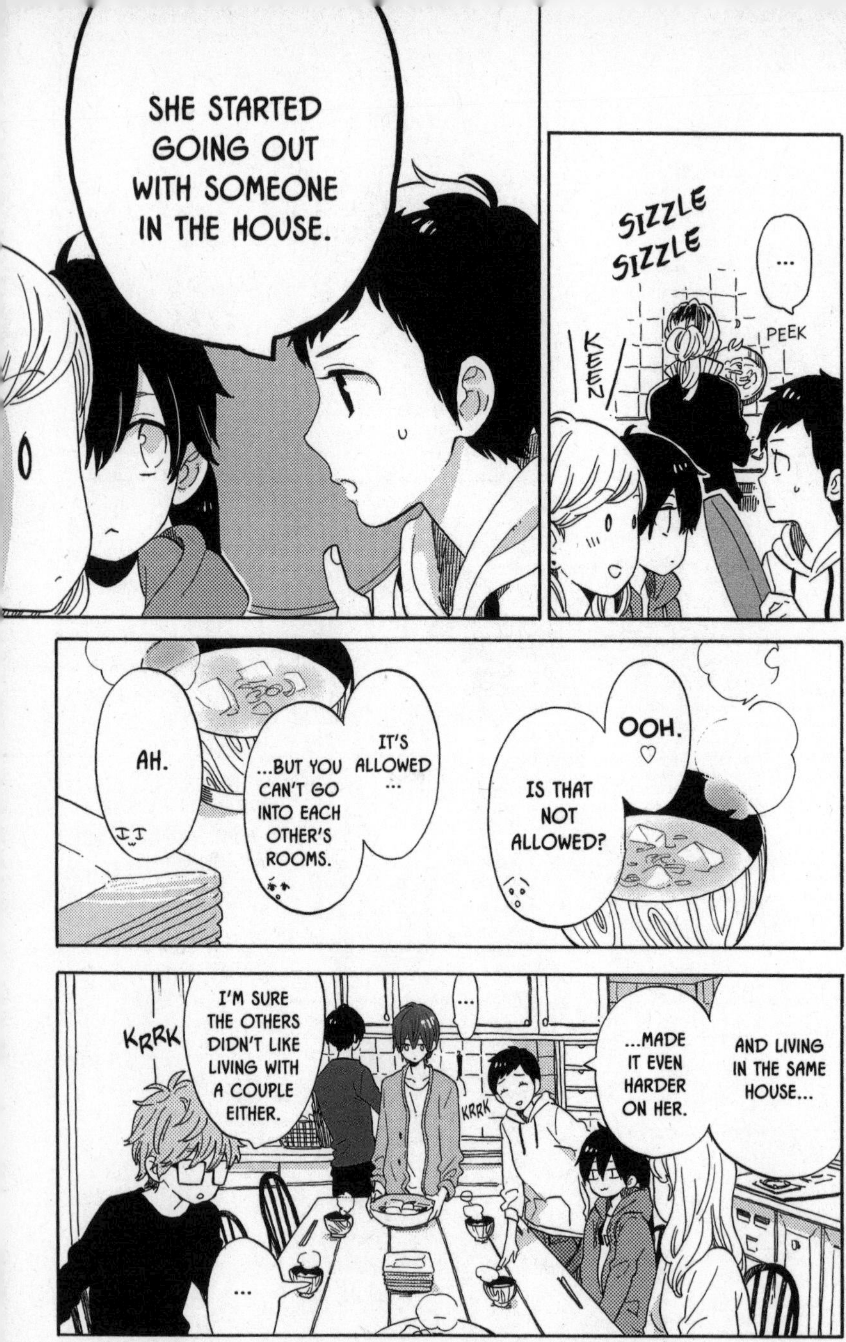
SIZZLE SIZZLE
...
PEEK
KEEN
SHE STARTED GOING OUT WITH SOMEONE IN THE HOUSE.
OOH. ♡
IS THAT NOT ALLOWED?
IT'S ALLOWED...
...BUT YOU CAN'T GO INTO EACH OTHER'S ROOMS.
AH.
AND LIVING IN THE SAME HOUSE...
...MADE IT EVEN HARDER ON HER.
KRRK
...
I'M SURE THE OTHERS DIDN'T LIKE LIVING WITH A COUPLE EITHER.
KRRK
...

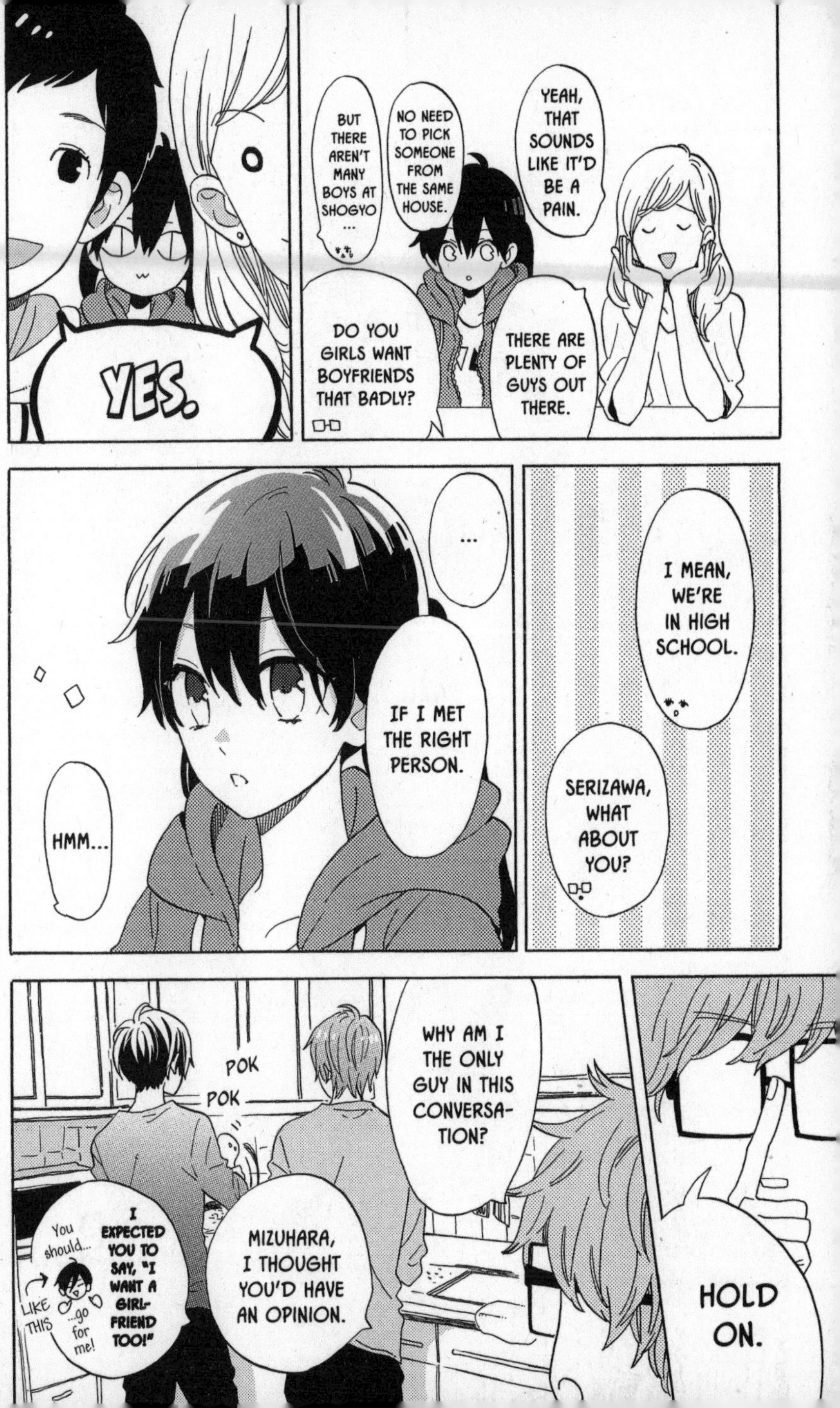
YEAH, THAT SOUNDS LIKE IT'D BE A PAIN.
NO NEED TO PICK SOMEONE FROM THE SAME HOUSE.
BUT THERE AREN'T MANY BOYS AT SHOGYO...
THERE ARE PLENTY OF GUYS OUT THERE.
DO YOU GIRLS WANT BOYFRIENDS THAT BADLY?
YES.
I MEAN, WE'RE IN HIGH SCHOOL.
SERIZAWA, WHAT ABOUT YOU?
...
IF I MET THE RIGHT PERSON.
HMM...
HOLD ON.
WHY AM I THE ONLY GUY IN THIS CONVERSA-TION?
POK POK
MIZUHARA, I THOUGHT YOU'D HAVE AN OPINION.
I EXPECTED YOU TO SAY, "I WANT A GIRL-FRIEND TOO!"
You should... ...go for me!
LIKE THIS

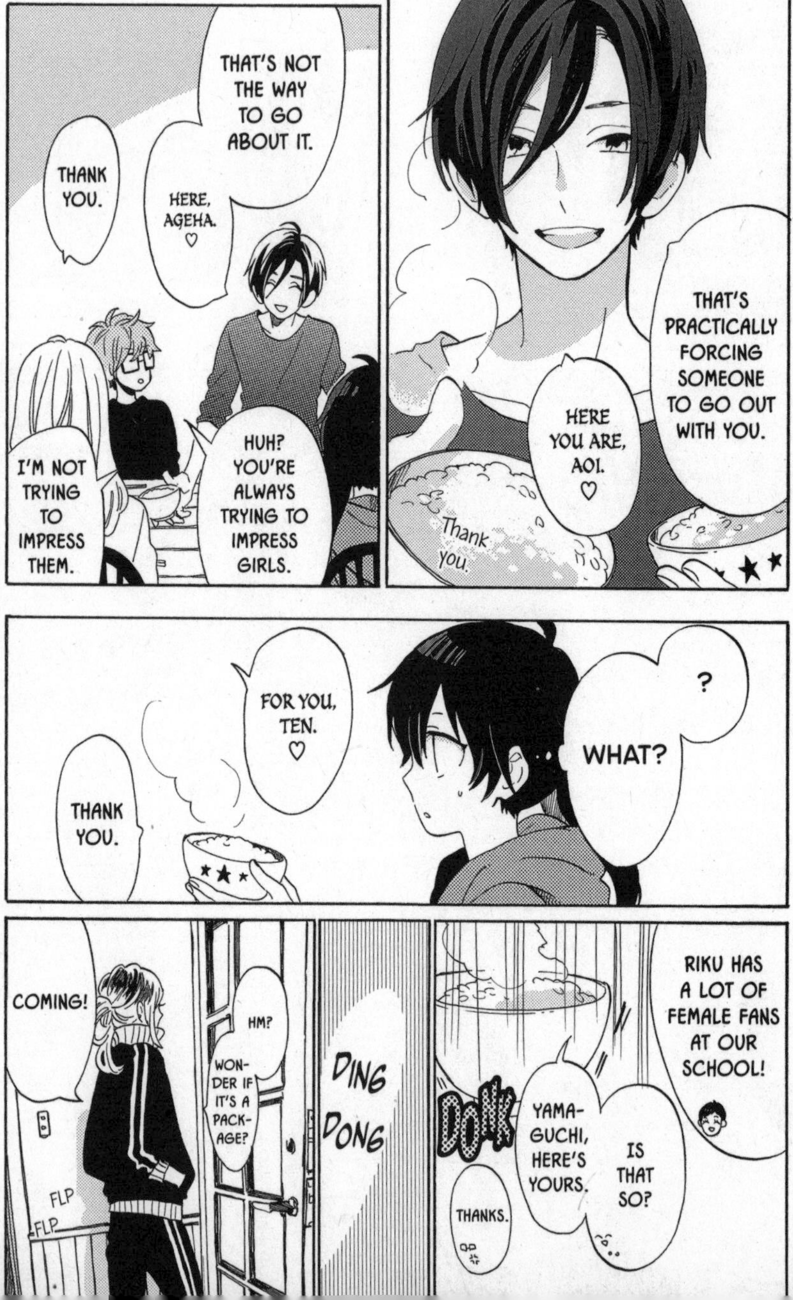
THAT'S PRACTICALLY FORCING SOMEONE TO GO OUT WITH YOU.
HERE YOU ARE, AOI. ♡
Thank you.
THAT'S NOT THE WAY TO GO ABOUT IT.
HERE, AGEHA. ♡
THANK YOU.
HUH? YOU'RE ALWAYS TRYING TO IMPRESS GIRLS.
I'M NOT TRYING TO IMPRESS THEM.
?
WHAT?
FOR YOU, TEN. ♡
THANK YOU.
RIKU HAS A LOT OF FEMALE FANS AT OUR SCHOOL!
IS THAT SO?
YAMA-GUCHI, HERE'S YOURS.
DOK
THANKS.
DING DONG
HM?
WON-DER IF IT'S A PACK-AGE?
COMING!
FLP FLP

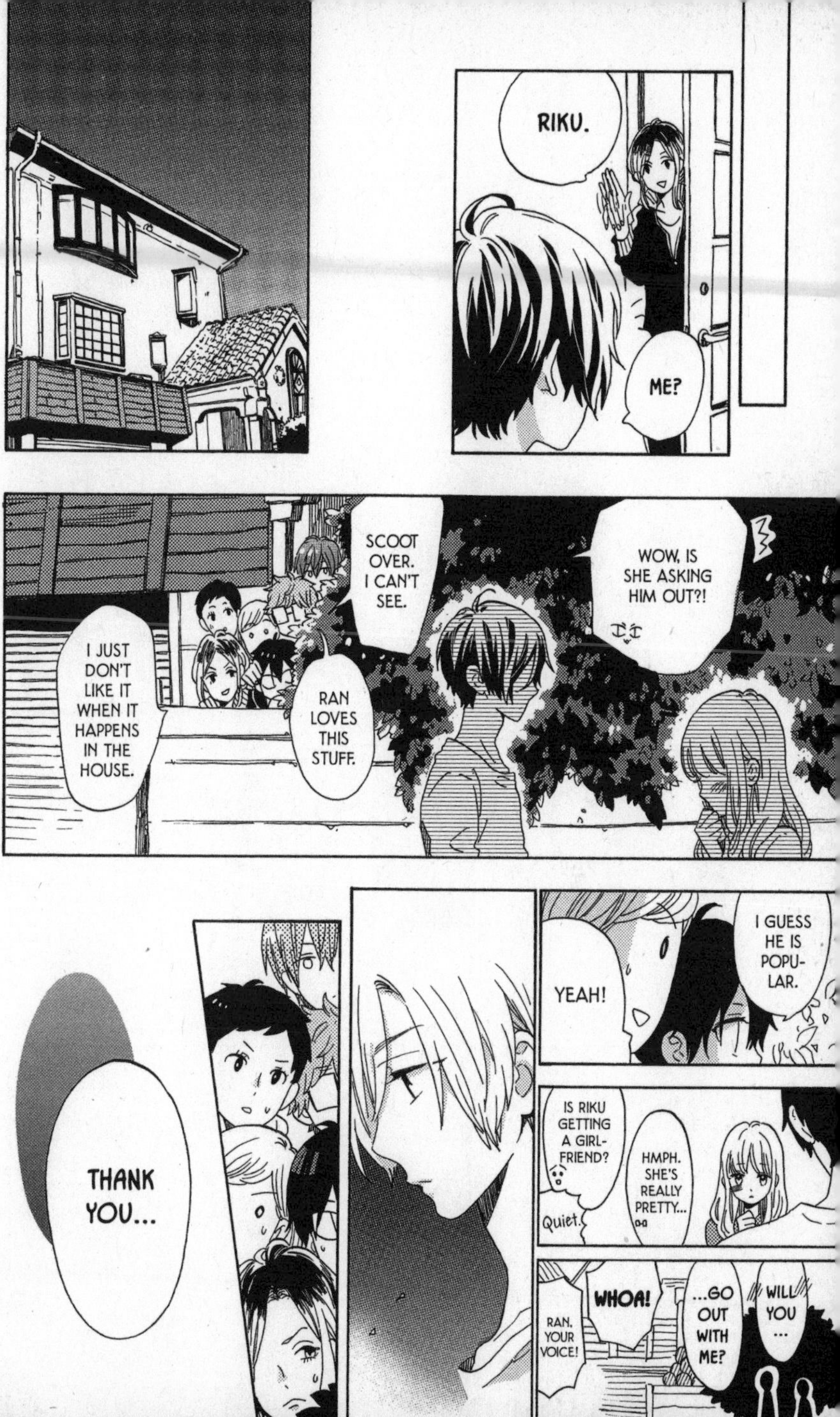
RIKU.
ME?
WOW, IS SHE ASKING HIM OUT?!
SCOOT OVER. I CAN'T SEE.
RAN LOVES THIS STUFF.
I JUST DON'T LIKE IT WHEN IT HAPPENS IN THE HOUSE.
I GUESS HE IS POPU-LAR.
YEAH!
HMPH. SHE'S REALLY PRETTY...
IS RIKU GETTING A GIRL-FRIEND?
Quiet.
WILL YOU ...
...GO OUT WITH ME?
WHOA!
RAN, YOUR VOICE!
THANK YOU...

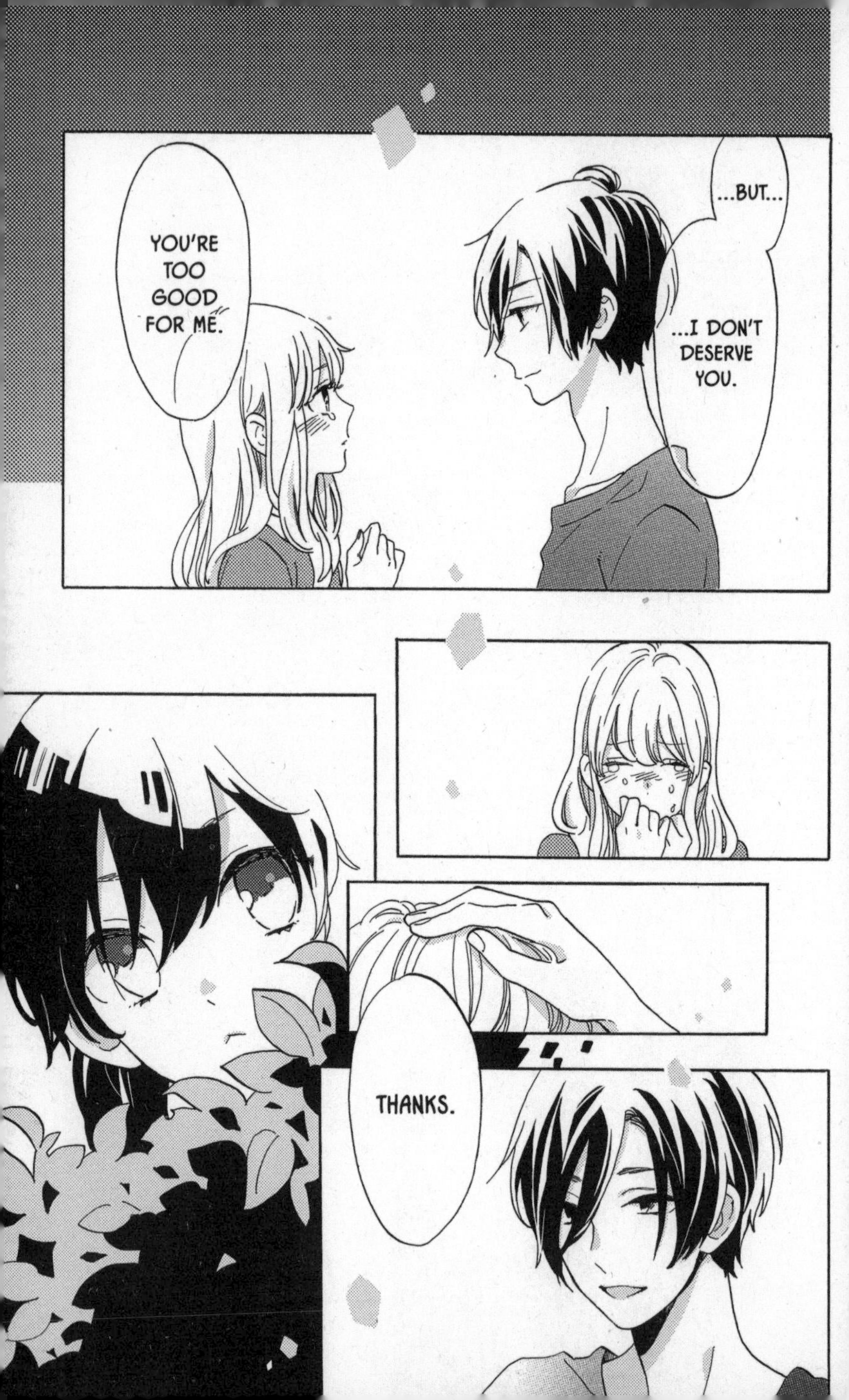

...BUT...
...I DON'T DESERVE YOU.
YOU'RE TOO GOOD FOR ME.
THANKS.

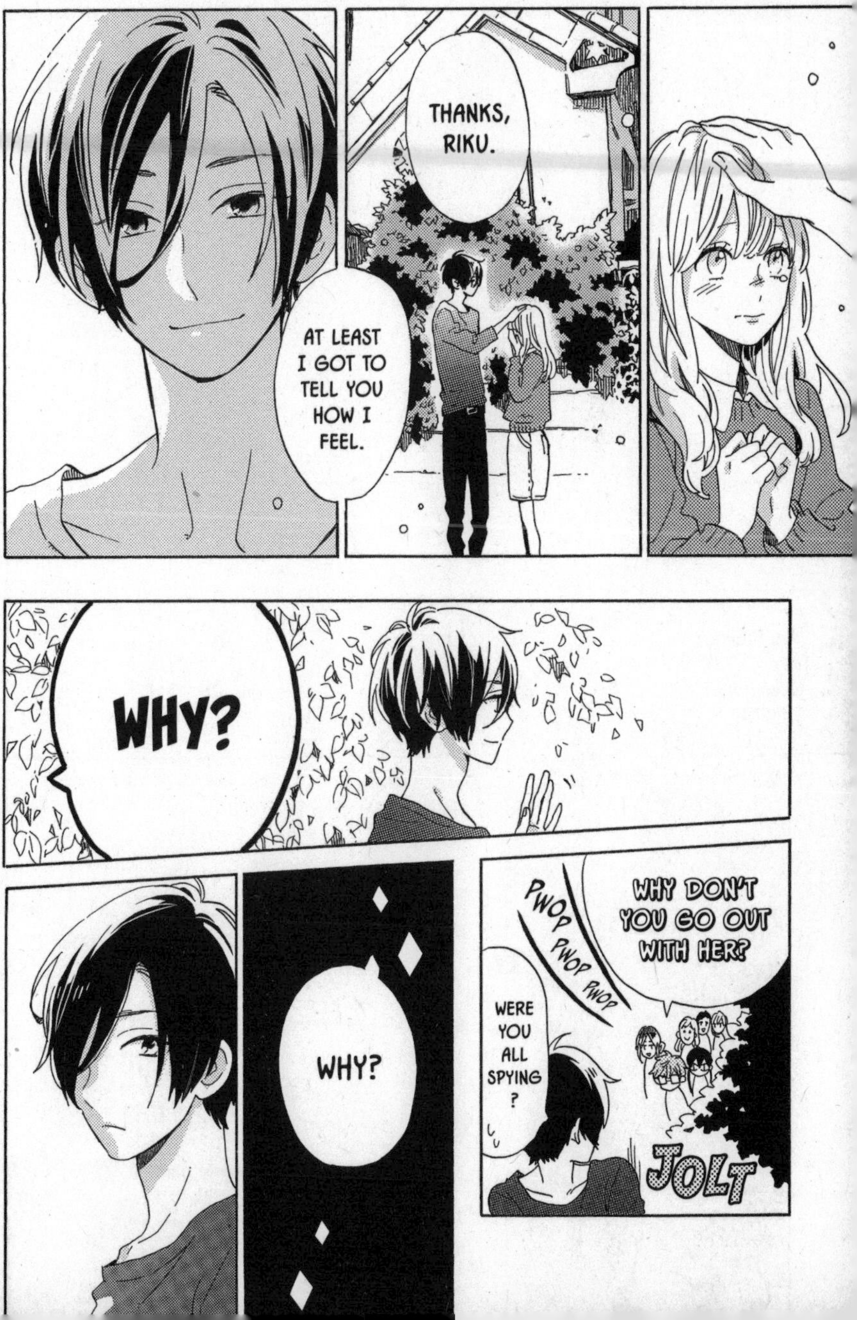
THANKS, RIKU.
AT LEAST I GOT TO TELL YOU HOW I FEEL.
WHY?
WHY DON'T YOU GO OUT WITH HER?
PWOP PWOP PWOP PWOP
WERE YOU ALL SPYING?
JOLT
WHY?

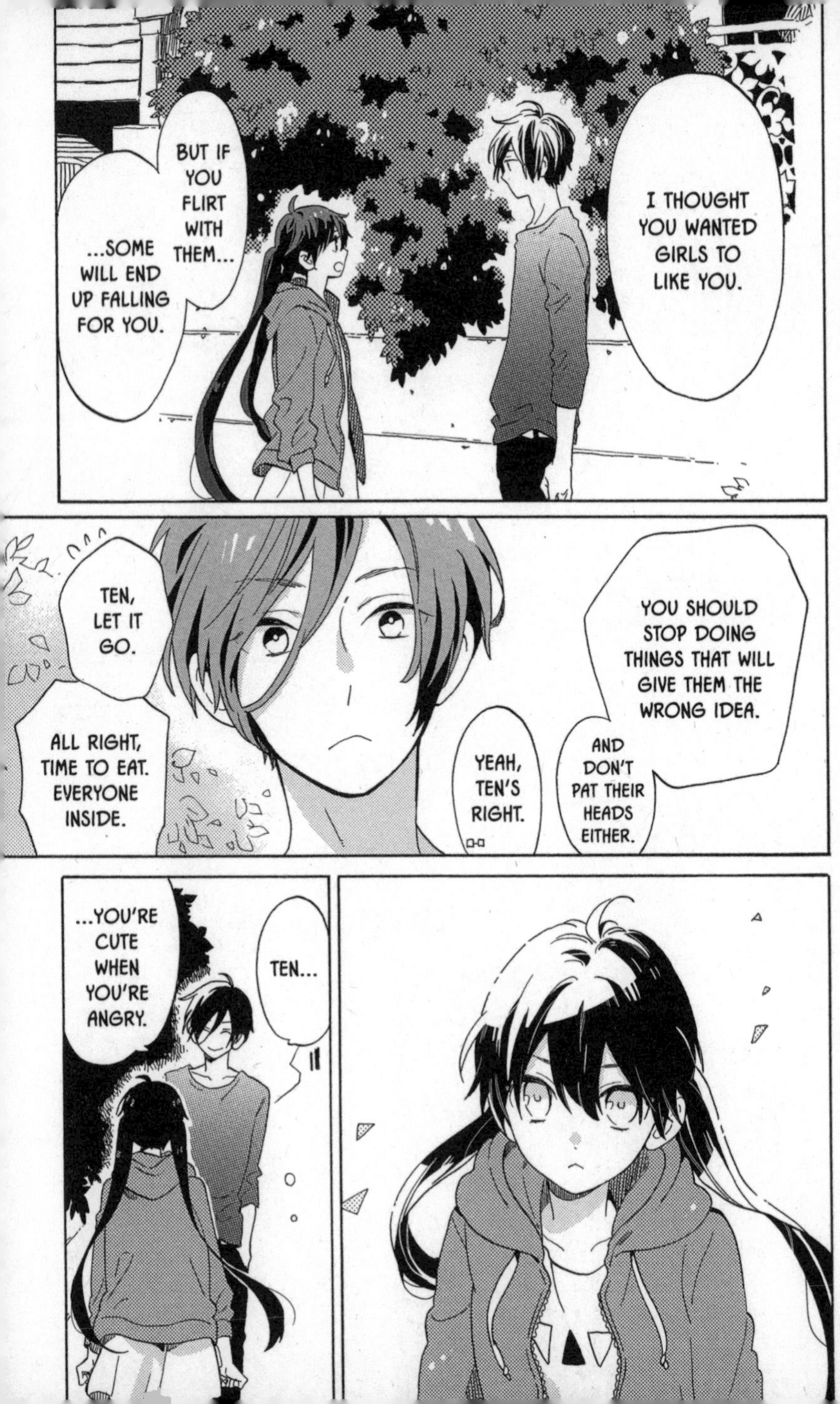
I THOUGHT YOU WANTED GIRLS TO LIKE YOU.
BUT IF YOU FLIRT WITH THEM...
...SOME WILL END UP FALLING FOR YOU.
YOU SHOULD STOP DOING THINGS THAT WILL GIVE THEM THE WRONG IDEA.
AND DON'T PAT THEIR HEADS EITHER.
YEAH, TEN'S RIGHT.
TEN, LET IT GO.
ALL RIGHT, TIME TO EAT. EVERYONE INSIDE.
TEN...
...YOU'RE CUTE WHEN YOU'RE ANGRY.

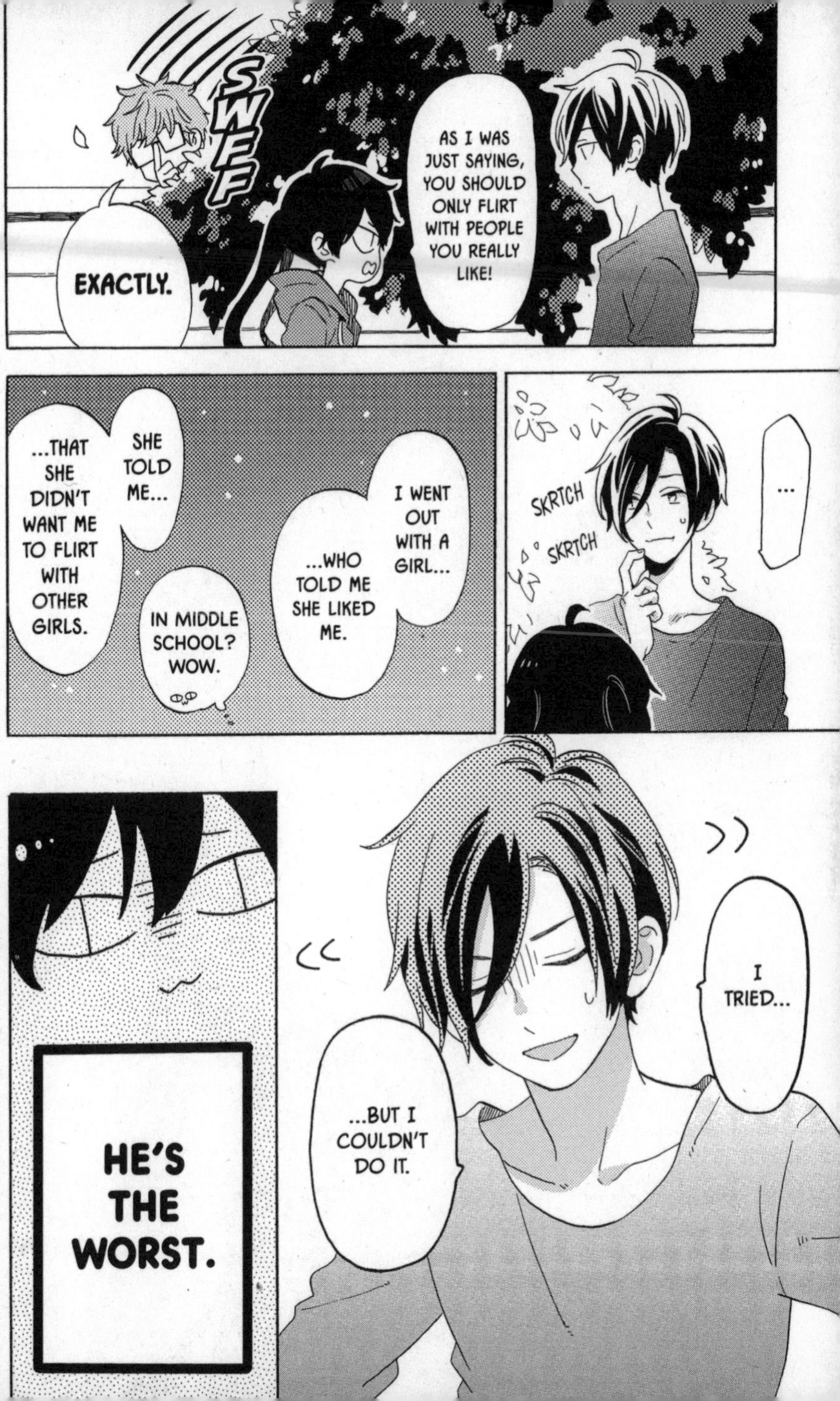
AS I WAS JUST SAYING, YOU SHOULD ONLY FLIRT WITH PEOPLE YOU REALLY LIKE!
SWFF
EXACTLY.
...
SKRTCH
SKRTCH
I WENT OUT WITH A GIRL...
...WHO TOLD ME SHE LIKED ME.
IN MIDDLE SCHOOL? WOW.
SHE TOLD ME...
...THAT SHE DIDN'T WANT ME TO FLIRT WITH OTHER GIRLS.
I TRIED...
...BUT I COULDN'T DO IT.
HE'S THE WORST.

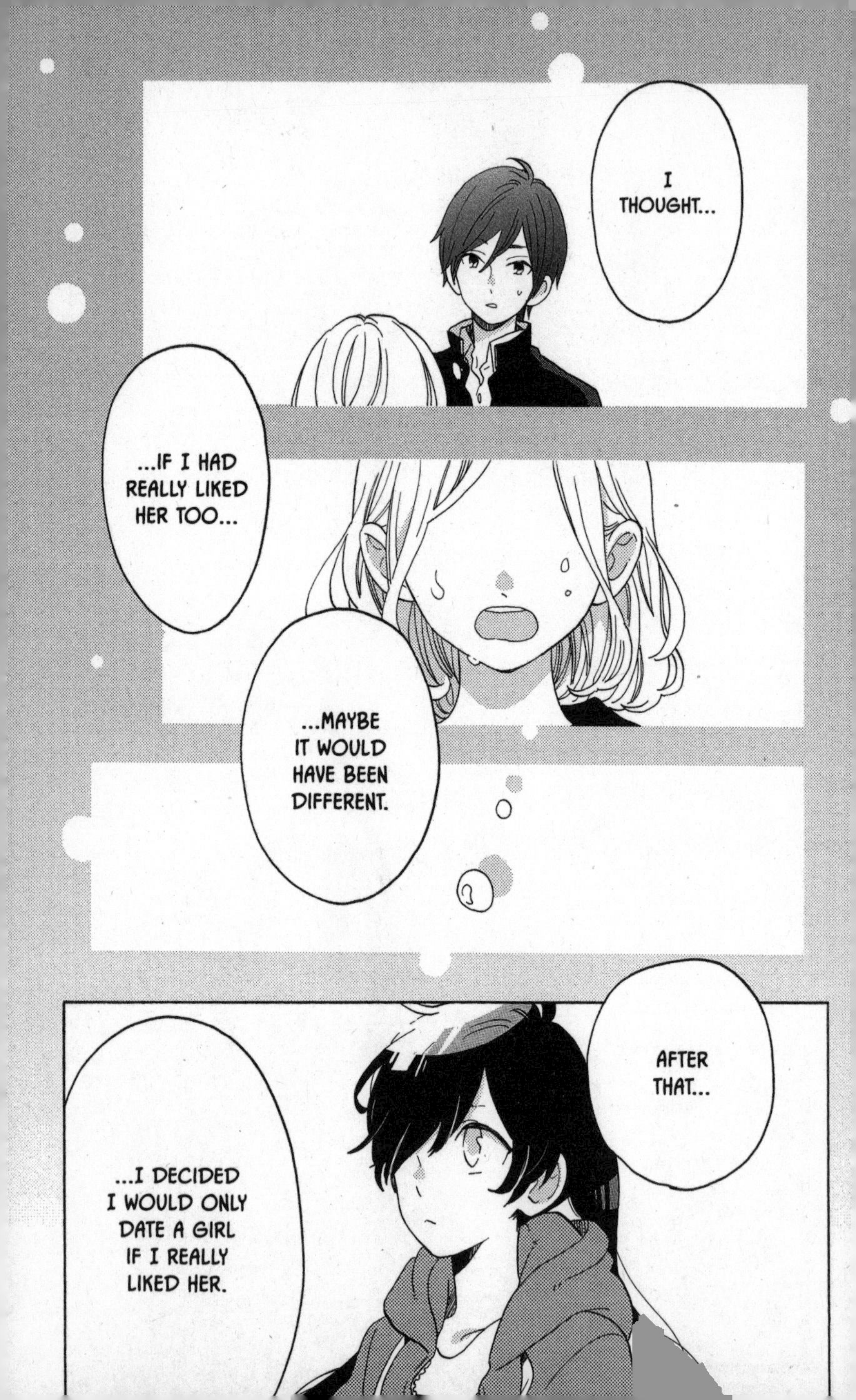
I THOUGHT...
...IF I HAD REALLY LIKED HER TOO...
...MAYBE IT WOULD HAVE BEEN DIFFERENT.
AFTER THAT...
...I DECIDED I WOULD ONLY DATE A GIRL IF I REALLY LIKED HER.

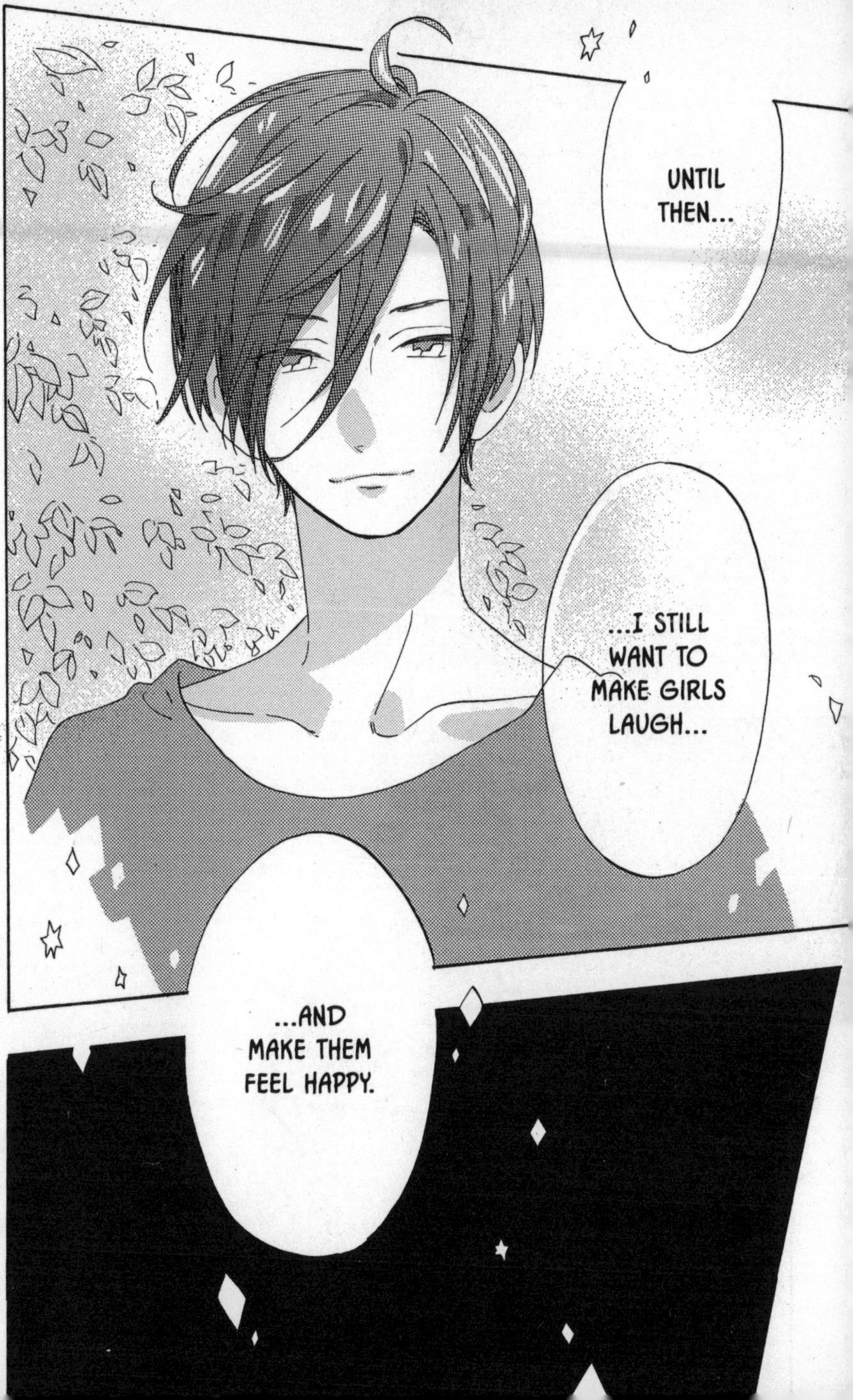
UNTIL THEN...
...I STILL WANT TO MAKE GIRLS LAUGH...
...AND MAKE THEM FEEL HAPPY.

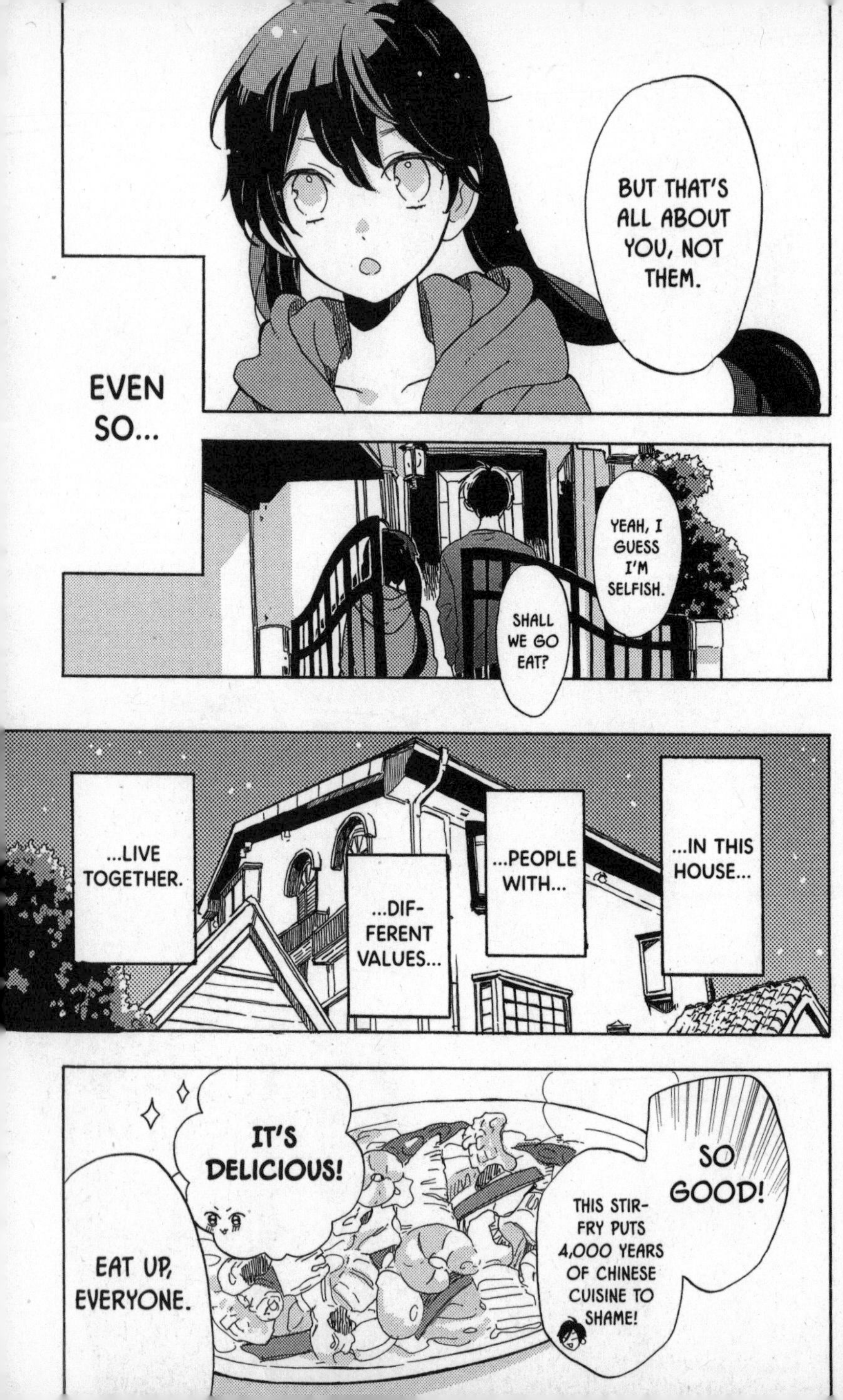
BUT THAT'S ALL ABOUT YOU, NOT THEM.
EVEN SO...
YEAH, I GUESS I'M SELFISH.
SHALL WE GO EAT?
...IN THIS HOUSE...
...PEOPLE WITH...
...DIF-FERENT VALUES...
...LIVE TOGETHER.
SO GOOD!
THIS STIR-FRY PUTS 4,000 YEARS OF CHINESE CUISINE TO SHAME!
IT'S DELICIOUS!
EAT UP, EVERYONE.

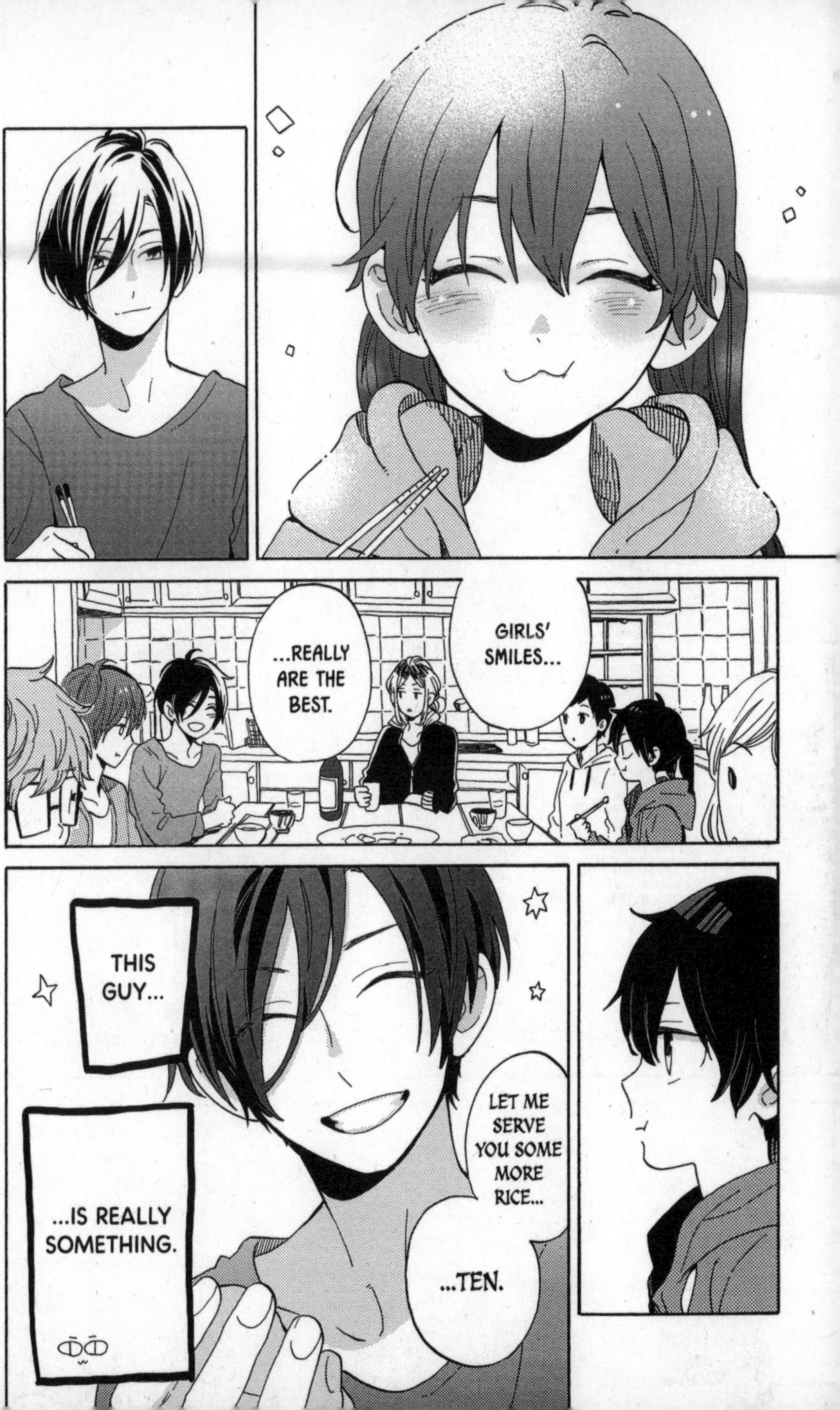
GIRLS' SMILES...
...REALLY ARE THE BEST.
LET ME SERVE YOU SOME MORE RICE...
...TEN.
THIS GUY...
...IS REALLY SOMETHING.

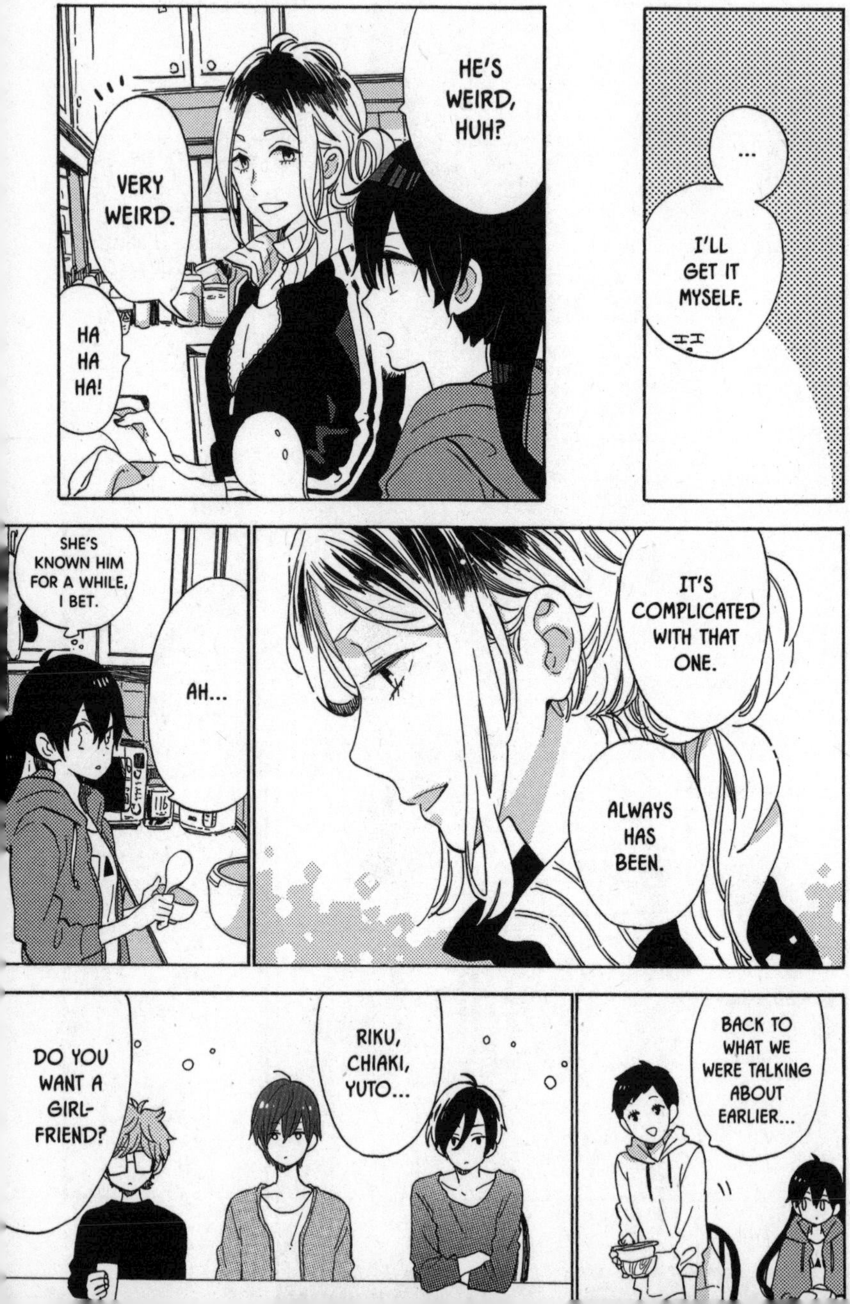
...
I'LL GET IT MYSELF.
HE'S WEIRD, HUH?
VERY WEIRD.
HA HA HA!
IT'S COMPLICATED WITH THAT ONE.
ALWAYS HAS BEEN.
SHE'S KNOWN HIM FOR A WHILE, I BET.
AH...
BACK TO WHAT WE WERE TALKING ABOUT EARLIER...
RIKU, CHIAKI, YUTO...
DO YOU WANT A GIRL-FRIEND?

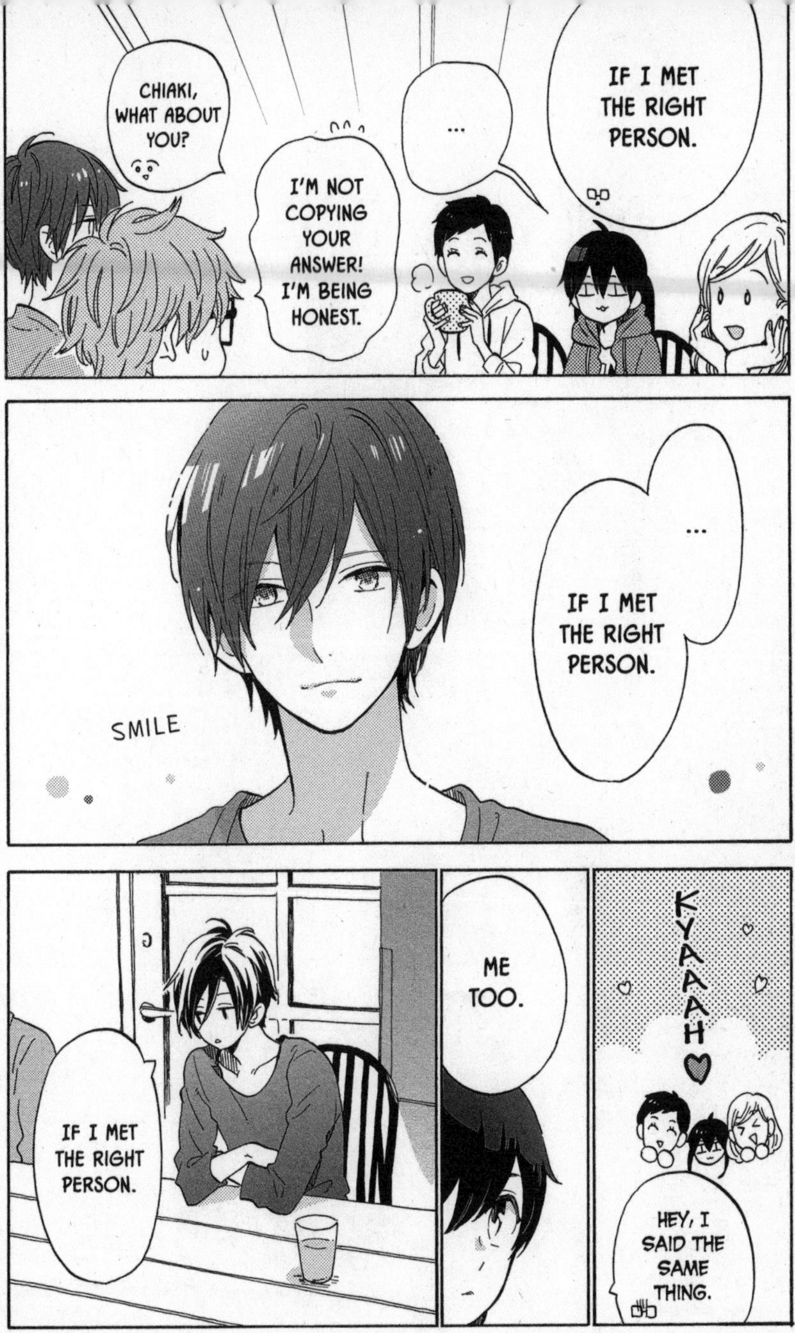
IF I MET THE RIGHT PERSON.
...
I'M NOT COPYING YOUR ANSWER! I'M BEING HONEST.
CHIAKI, WHAT ABOUT YOU?
...
IF I MET THE RIGHT PERSON.
SMILE
KYAAAH
HEY, I SAID THE SAME THING.
ME TOO.
IF I MET THE RIGHT PERSON.

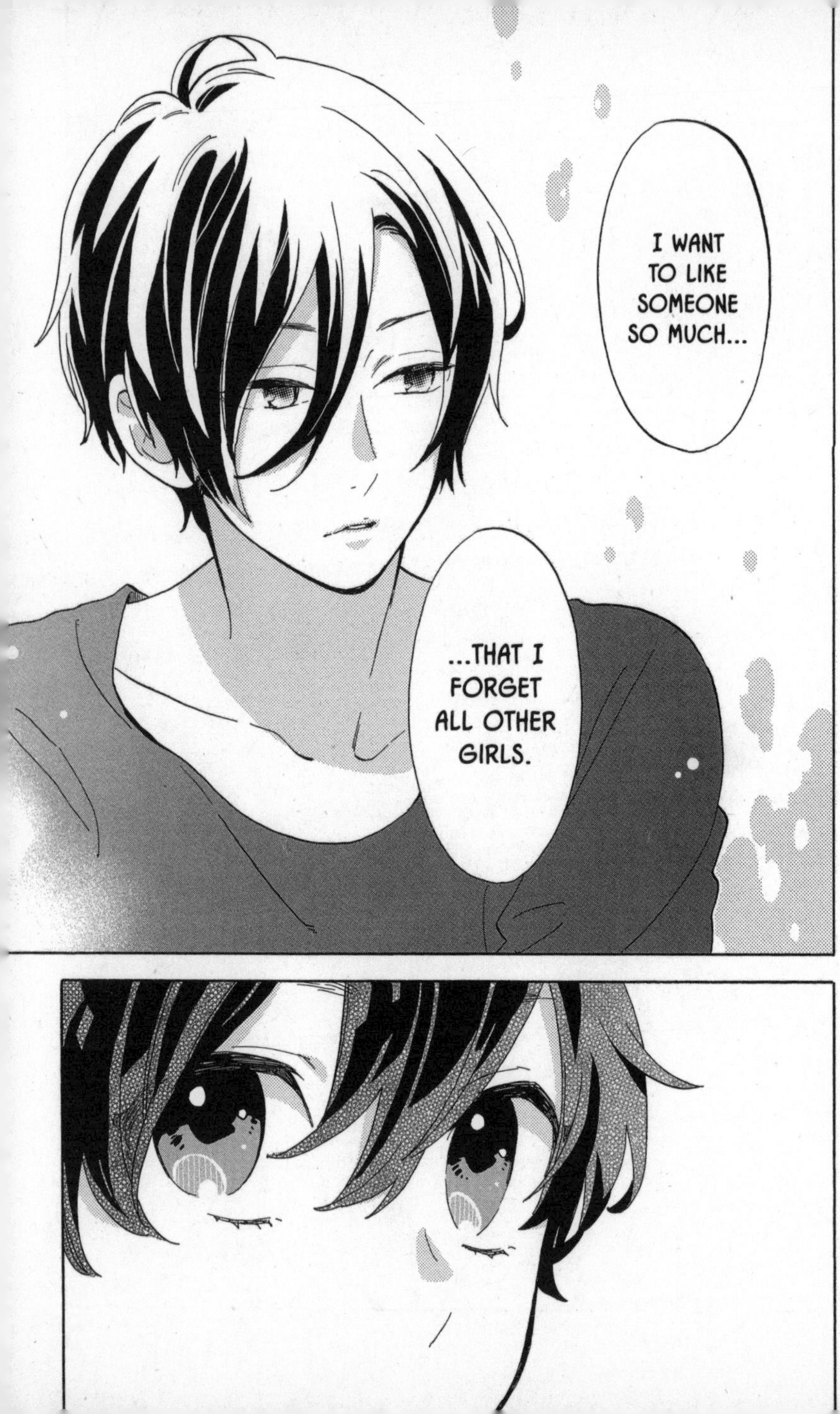
I WANT TO LIKE SOMEONE SO MUCH...
...THAT I FORGET ALL OTHER GIRLS.

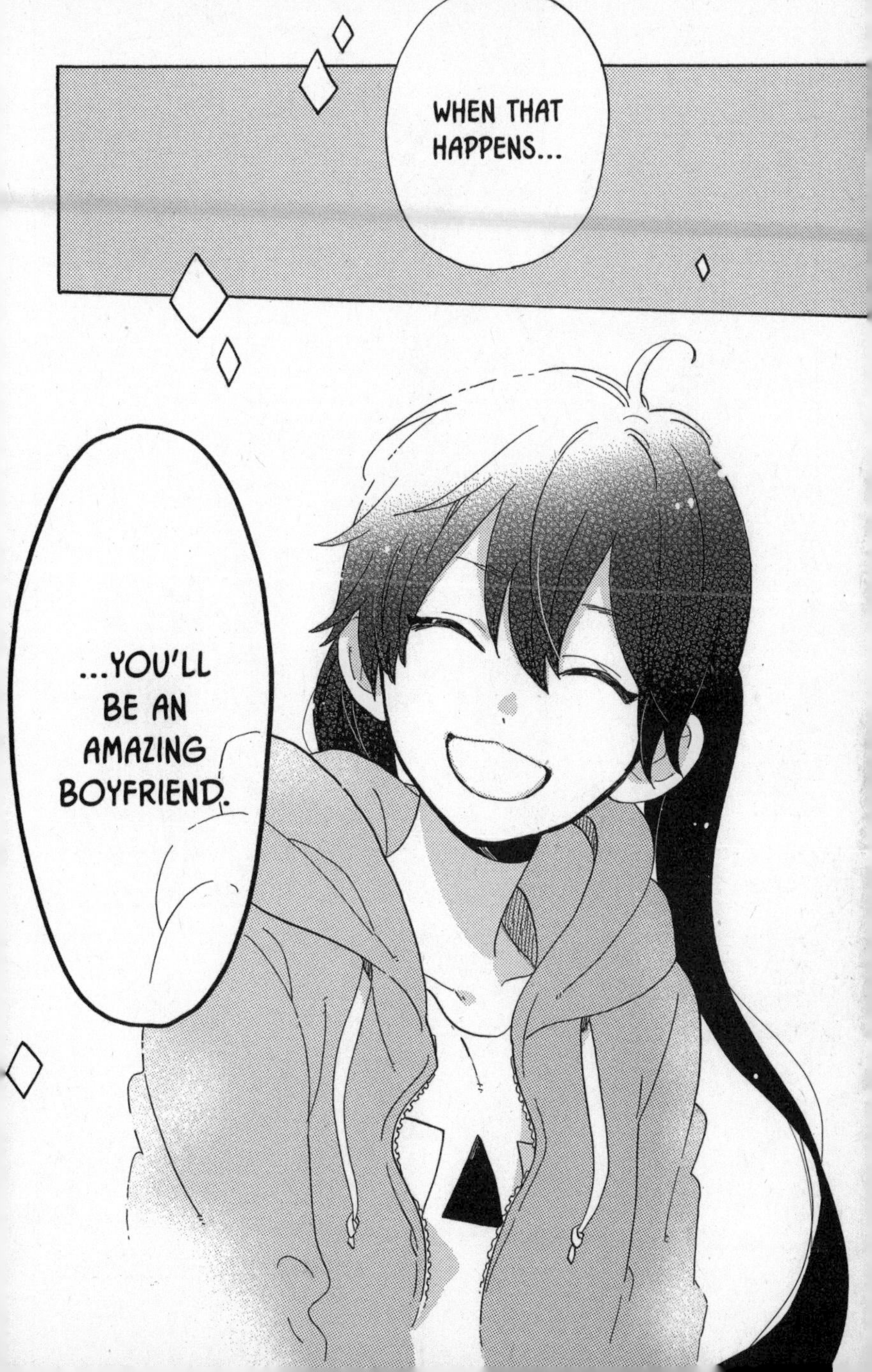
WHEN THAT HAPPENS...
...YOU'LL BE AN AMAZING BOYFRIEND.

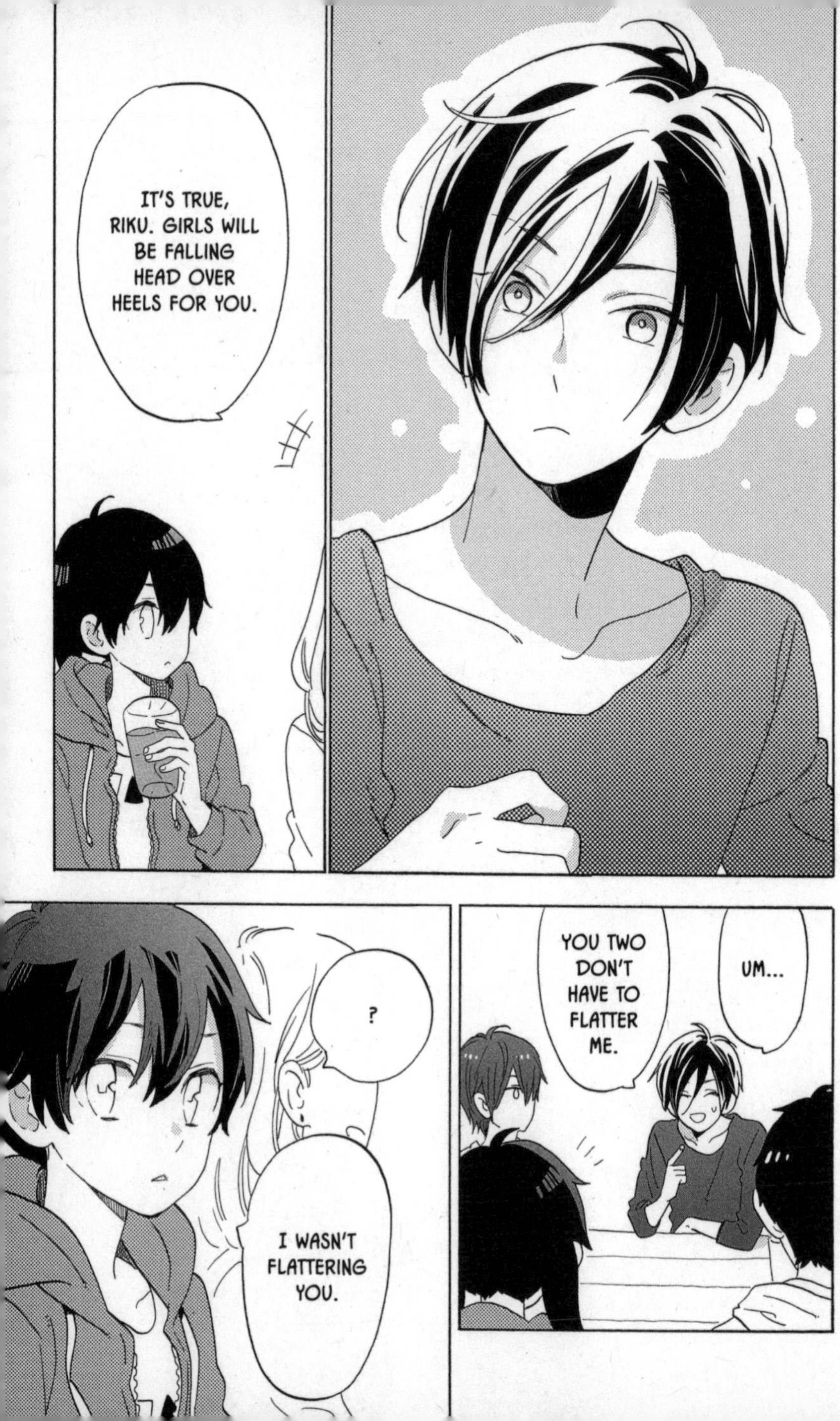
IT'S TRUE, RIKU. GIRLS WILL BE FALLING HEAD OVER HEELS FOR YOU.
UM...
YOU TWO DON'T HAVE TO FLATTER ME.
?
I WASN'T FLATTERING YOU.

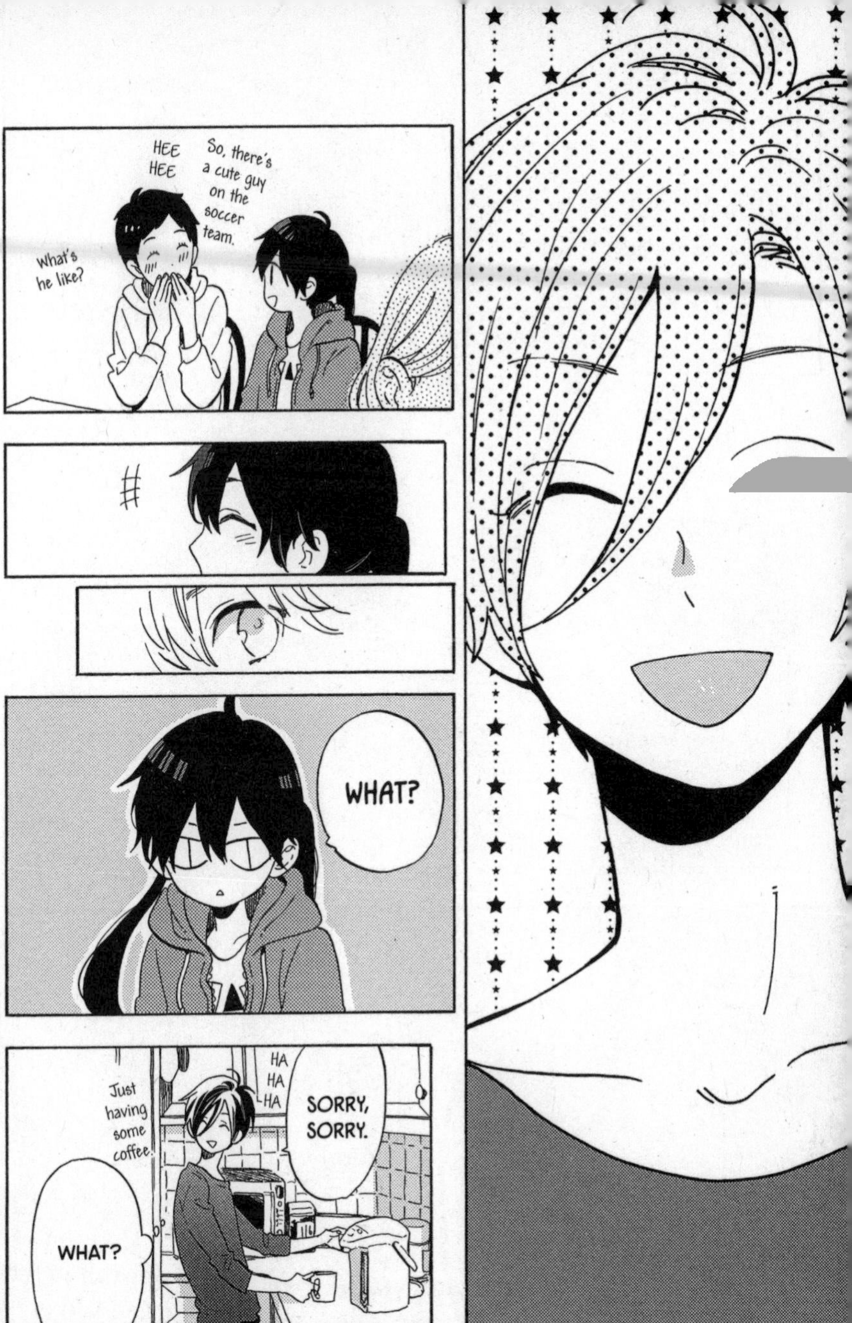
So, there's a cute guy on the soccer team.
HEE HEE
What's he like?
WHAT?
HA HA HA
SORRY, SORRY.
Just having some coffee.
WHAT?

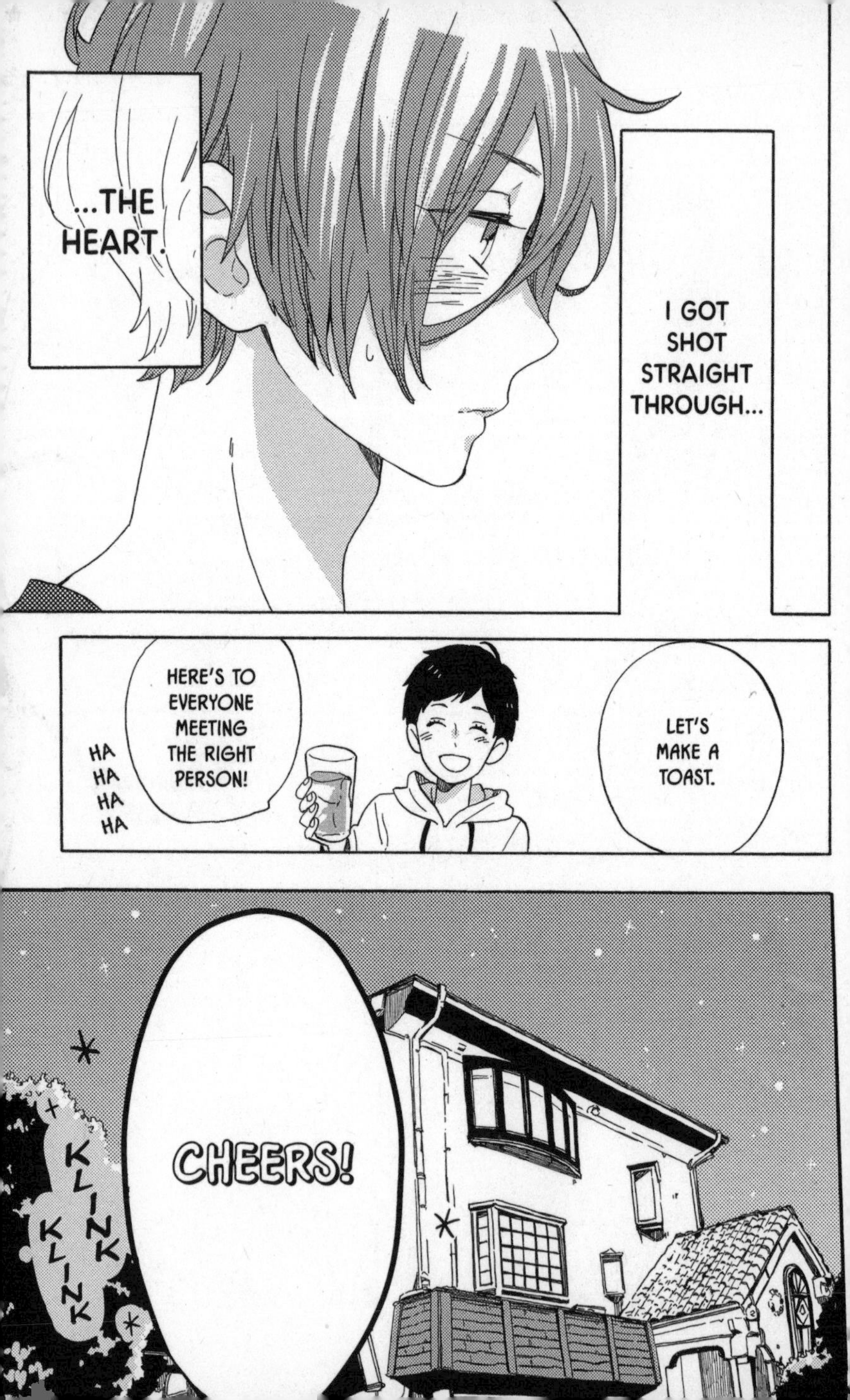
I GOT SHOT STRAIGHT THROUGH...
...THE HEART.
LET'S MAKE A TOAST.
HERE'S TO EVERYONE MEETING THE RIGHT PERSON!
HA HA HA HA
CHEERS!
KLINK KLINK

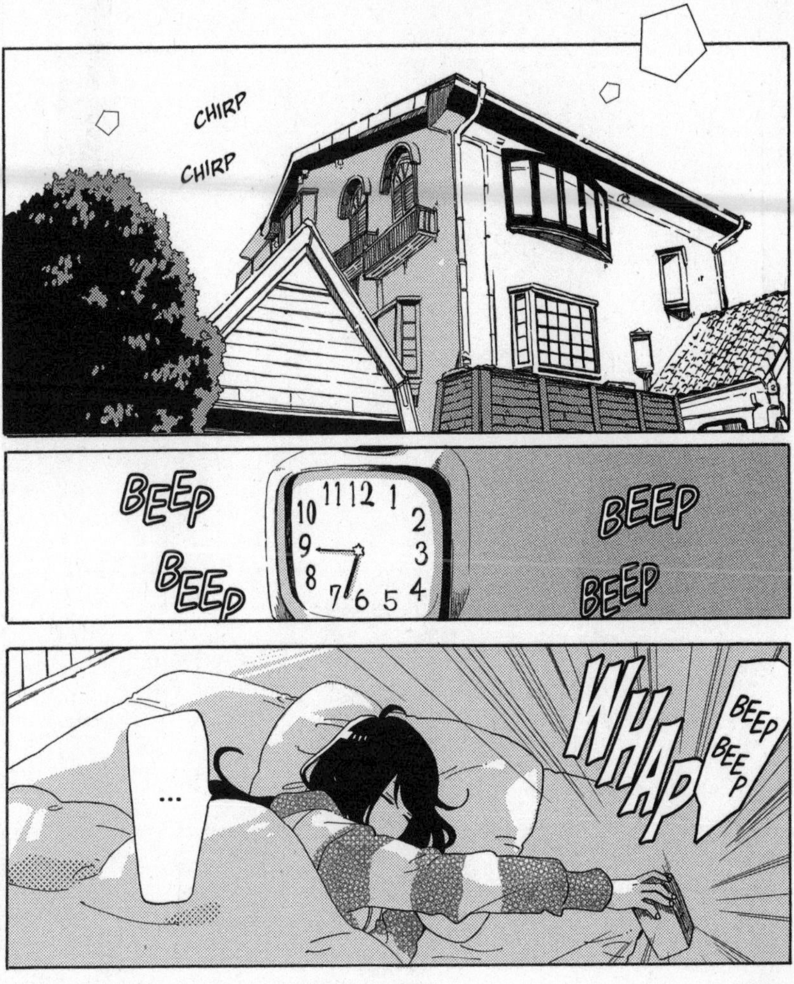
CHIRP
CHIRP
BEEP
BEEP
BEEP
BEEP
BEEP
BEEP
WHAP
...

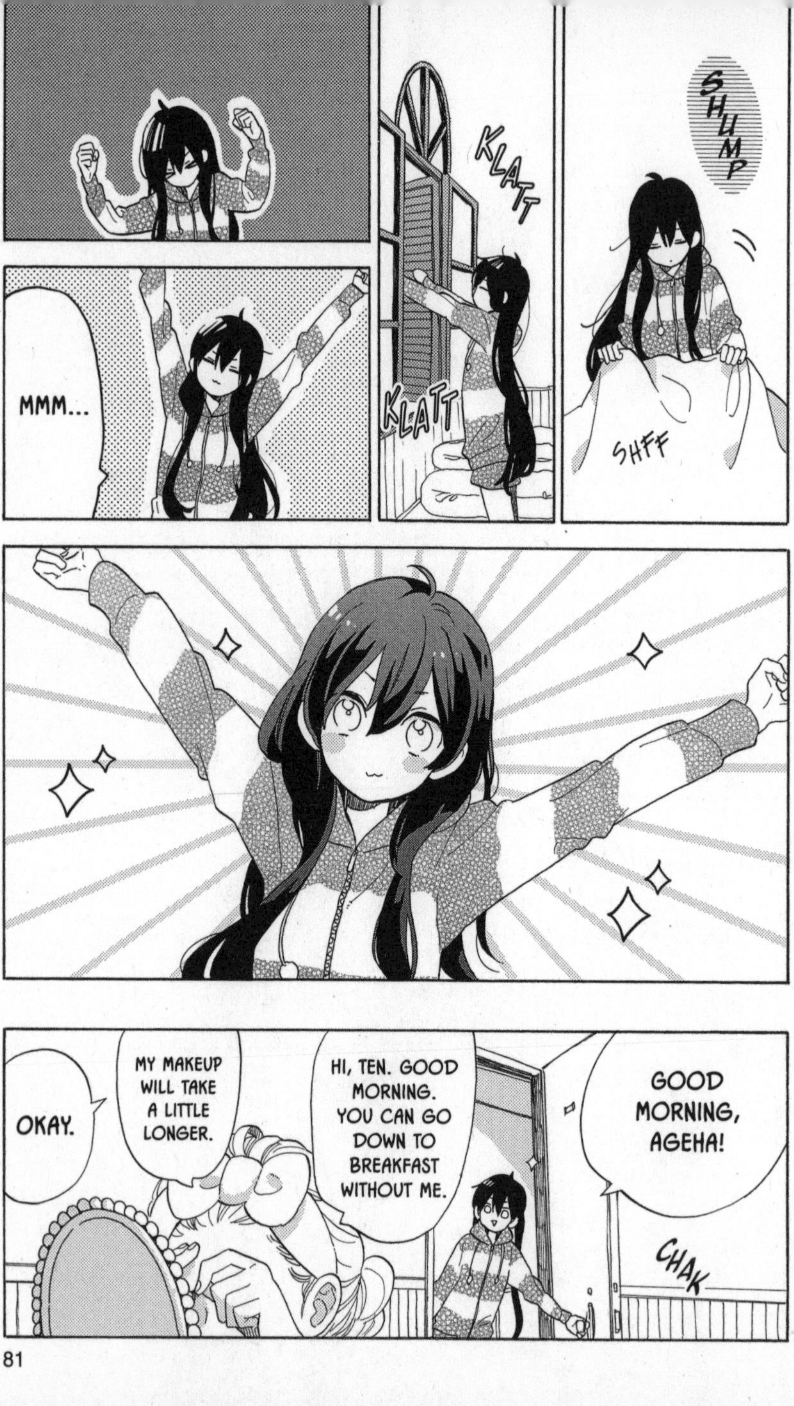
SHUMP
SHFF
KLATT
KLATT
MMM...
GOOD MORNING, AGEHA!
CHAK
HI, TEN. GOOD MORNING. YOU CAN GO DOWN TO BREAKFAST WITHOUT ME.
MY MAKEUP WILL TAKE A LITTLE LONGER.
OKAY.

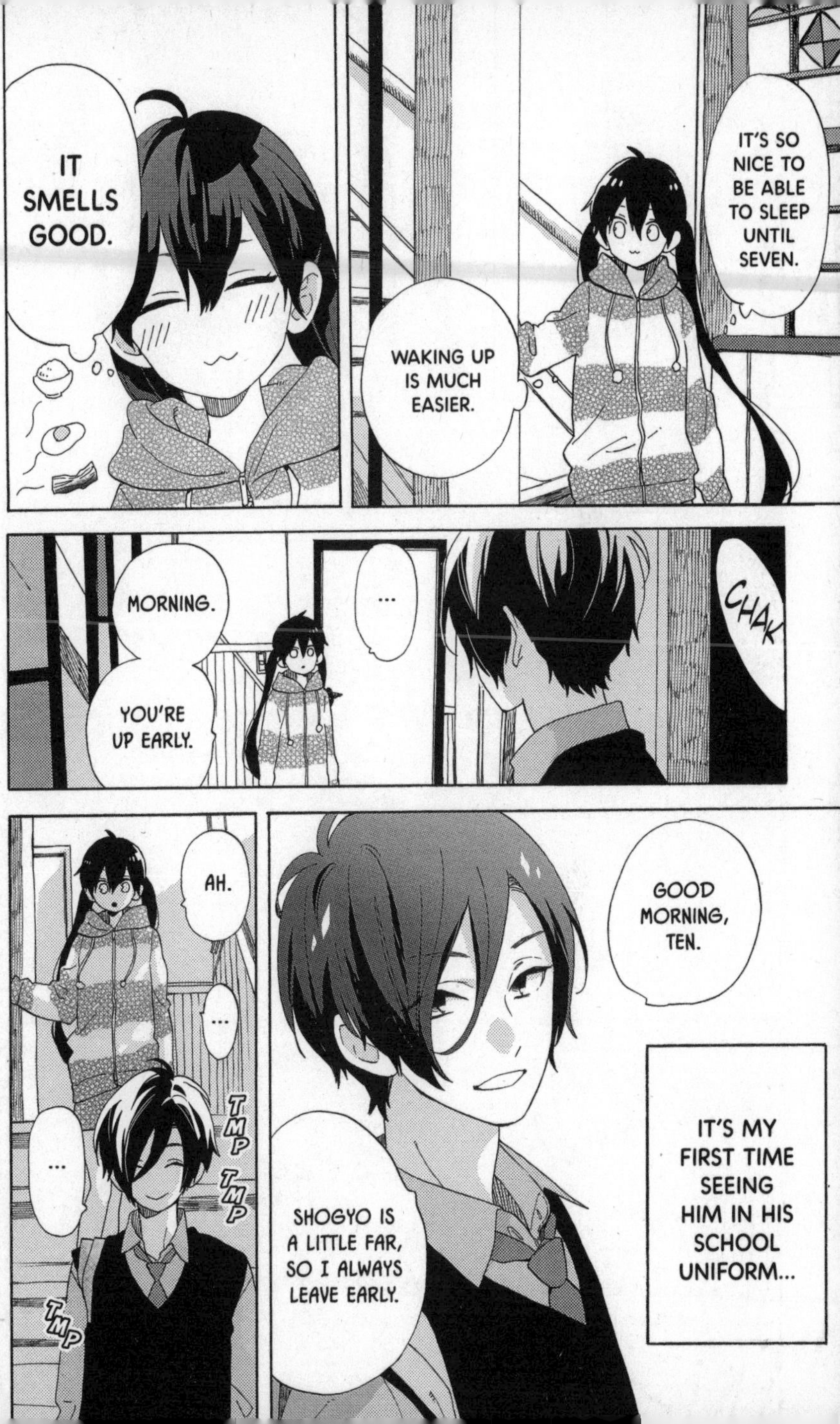
IT'S SO NICE TO BE ABLE TO SLEEP UNTIL SEVEN.
WAKING UP IS MUCH EASIER.
IT SMELLS GOOD.
CHAK
...
MORNING.
YOU'RE UP EARLY.
GOOD MORNING, TEN.
IT'S MY FIRST TIME SEEING HIM IN HIS SCHOOL UNIFORM...
SHOGYO IS A LITTLE FAR, SO I ALWAYS LEAVE EARLY.
AH.
...
TMP TMP
...
TMP

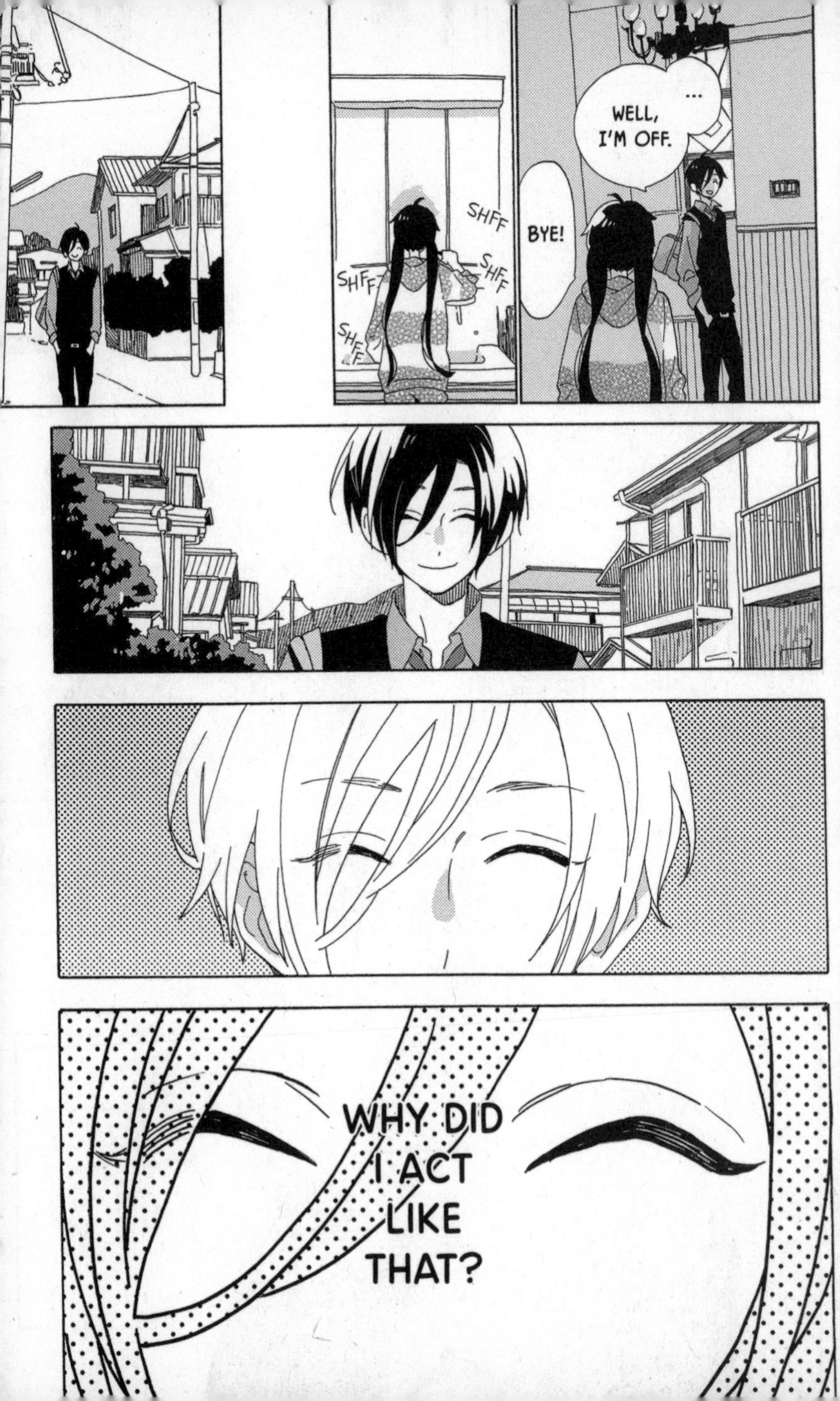
...
WELL, I'M OFF.
BYE!
SHFF
SHFF
SHFF
SHFF
WHY DID I ACT LIKE THAT?

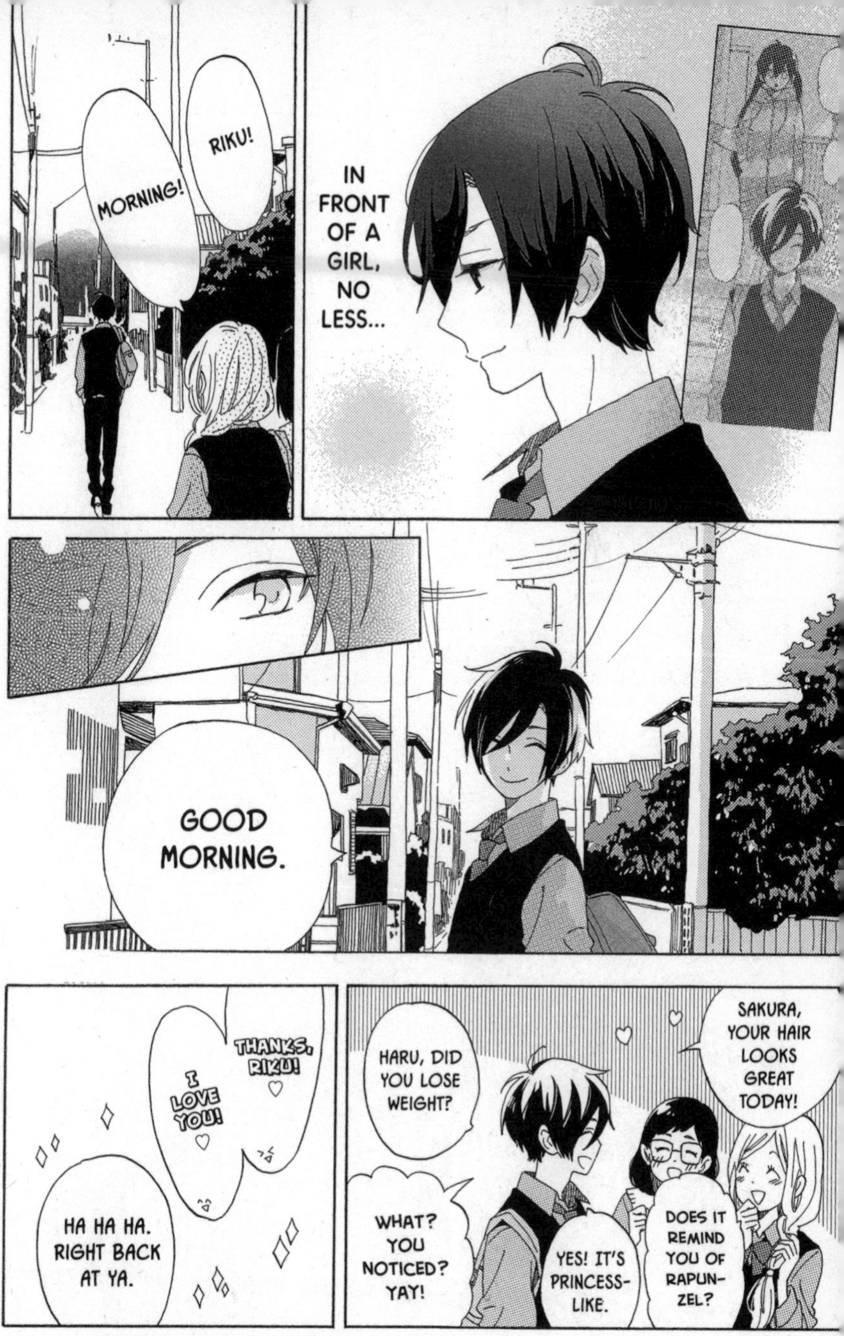
IN FRONT OF A GIRL, NO LESS...
RIKU!
MORNING!
GOOD MORNING.
SAKURA, YOUR HAIR LOOKS GREAT TODAY!
HARU, DID YOU LOSE WEIGHT?
DOES IT REMIND YOU OF RAPUN-ZEL?
YES! IT'S PRINCESS-LIKE.
WHAT? YOU NOTICED? YAY!
THANKS, RIKU! ♡
I LOVE YOU! ♡
HA HA HA. RIGHT BACK AT YA.

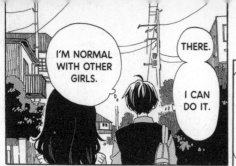

I'M NORMAL WITH OTHER GIRLS.

THERE.

I CAN DO IT.

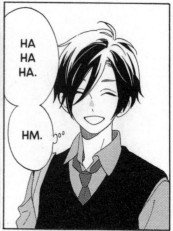

HA HA HA.

HM.

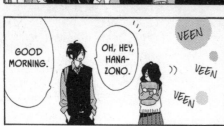

GOOD MORNING.

OH, HEY, HANA-ZONO.

VEEN

VEEN

VEEN

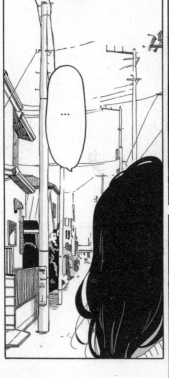

...

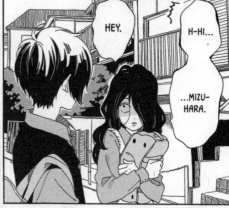

HEY.

H-HI...

...MIZU-HARA.

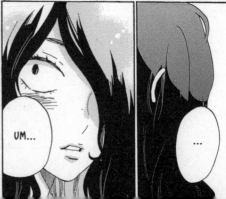

UM...

...

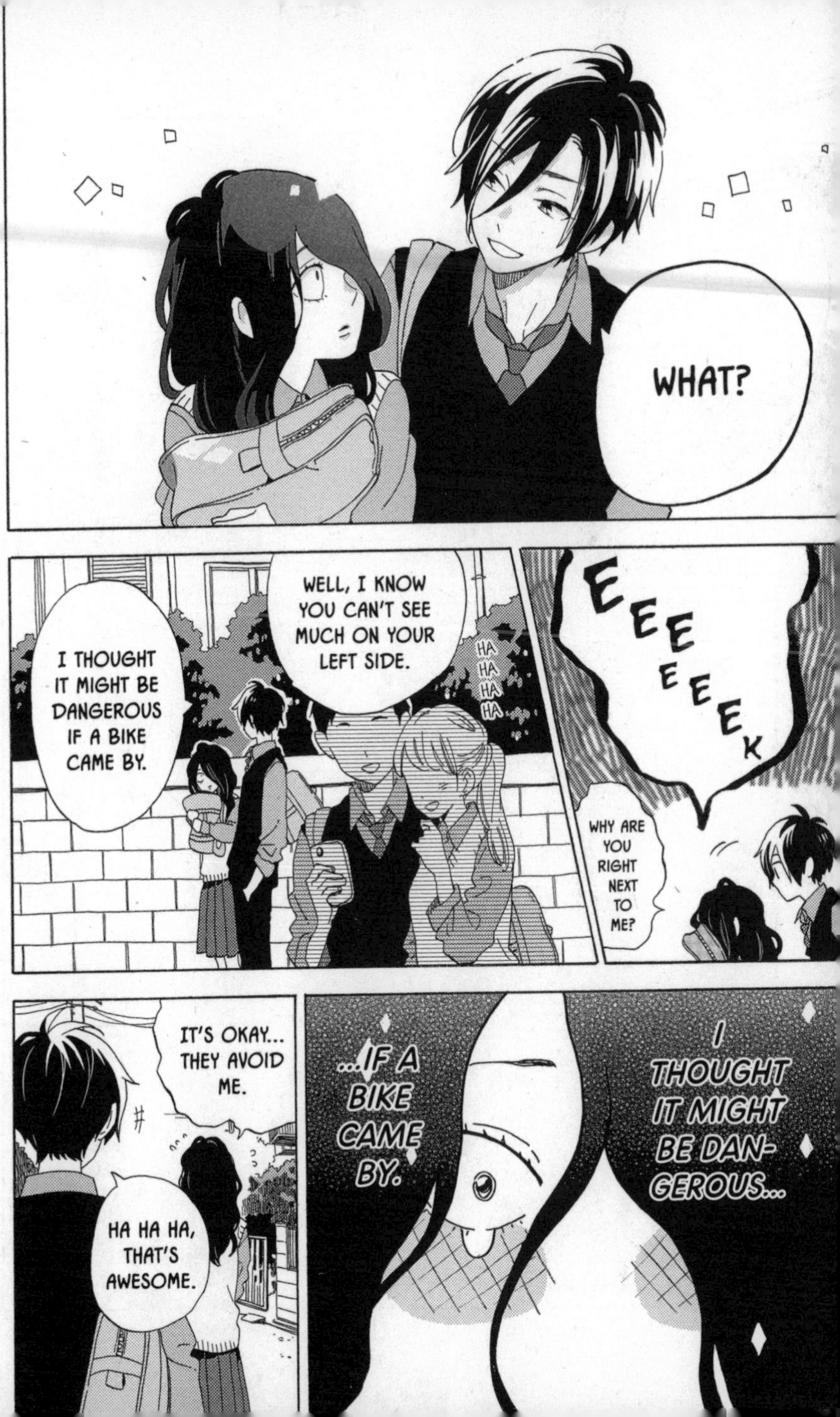
WHAT?
EEEEEEK
WHY ARE YOU RIGHT NEXT TO ME?
WELL, I KNOW YOU CAN'T SEE MUCH ON YOUR LEFT SIDE.
HA HA HA HA
I THOUGHT IT MIGHT BE DANGEROUS IF A BIKE CAME BY.
I THOUGHT IT MIGHT BE DAN-GEROUS...
...IF A BIKE CAME BY.
IT'S OKAY... THEY AVOID ME.
HA HA HA, THAT'S AWESOME.

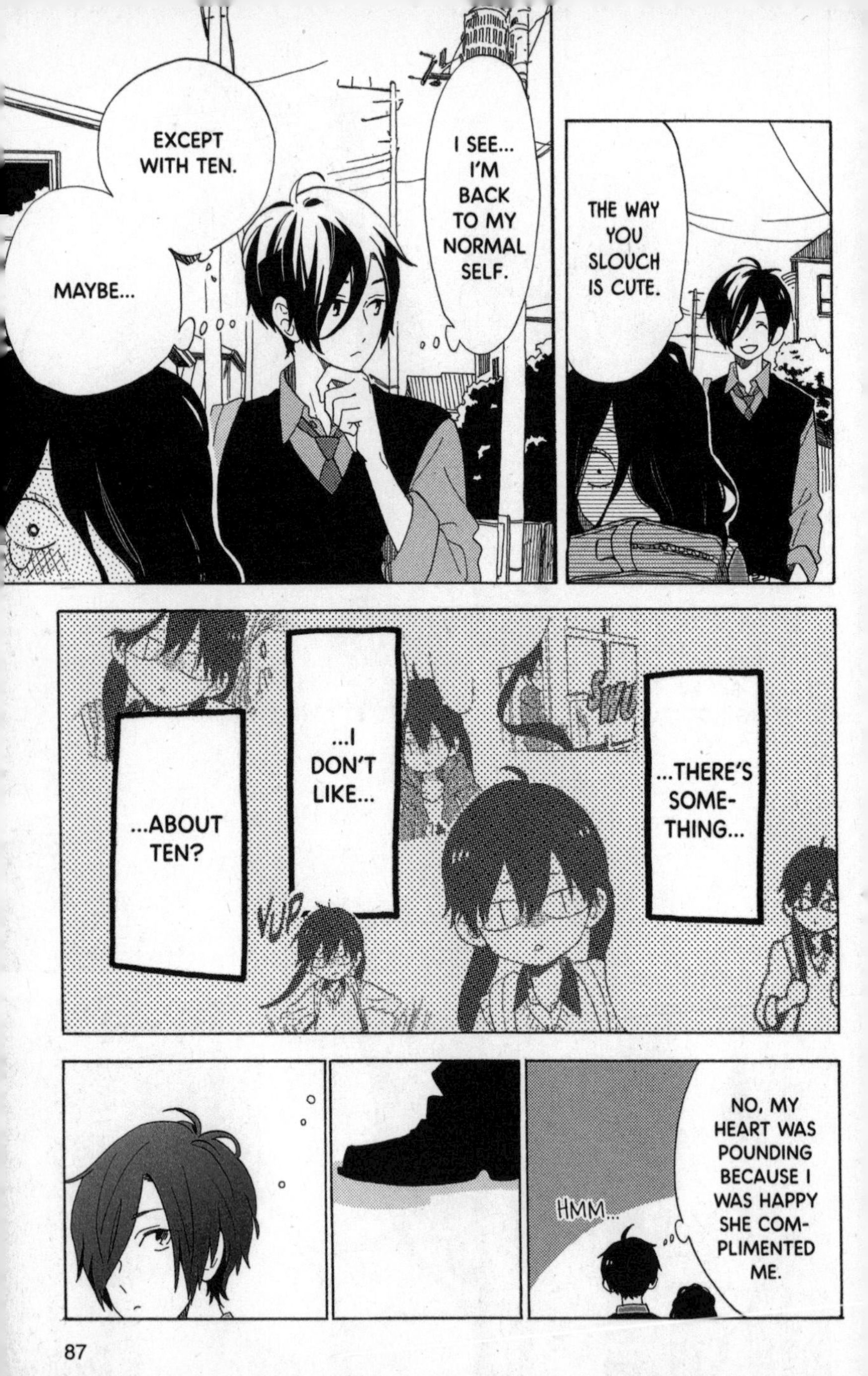
THE WAY YOU SLOUCH IS CUTE.
I SEE... I'M BACK TO MY NORMAL SELF.
EXCEPT WITH TEN.
MAYBE...
...THERE'S SOME-THING...
...I DON'T LIKE...
...ABOUT TEN?
NO, MY HEART WAS POUNDING BECAUSE I WAS HAPPY SHE COM-PLIMENTED ME.
HMM...

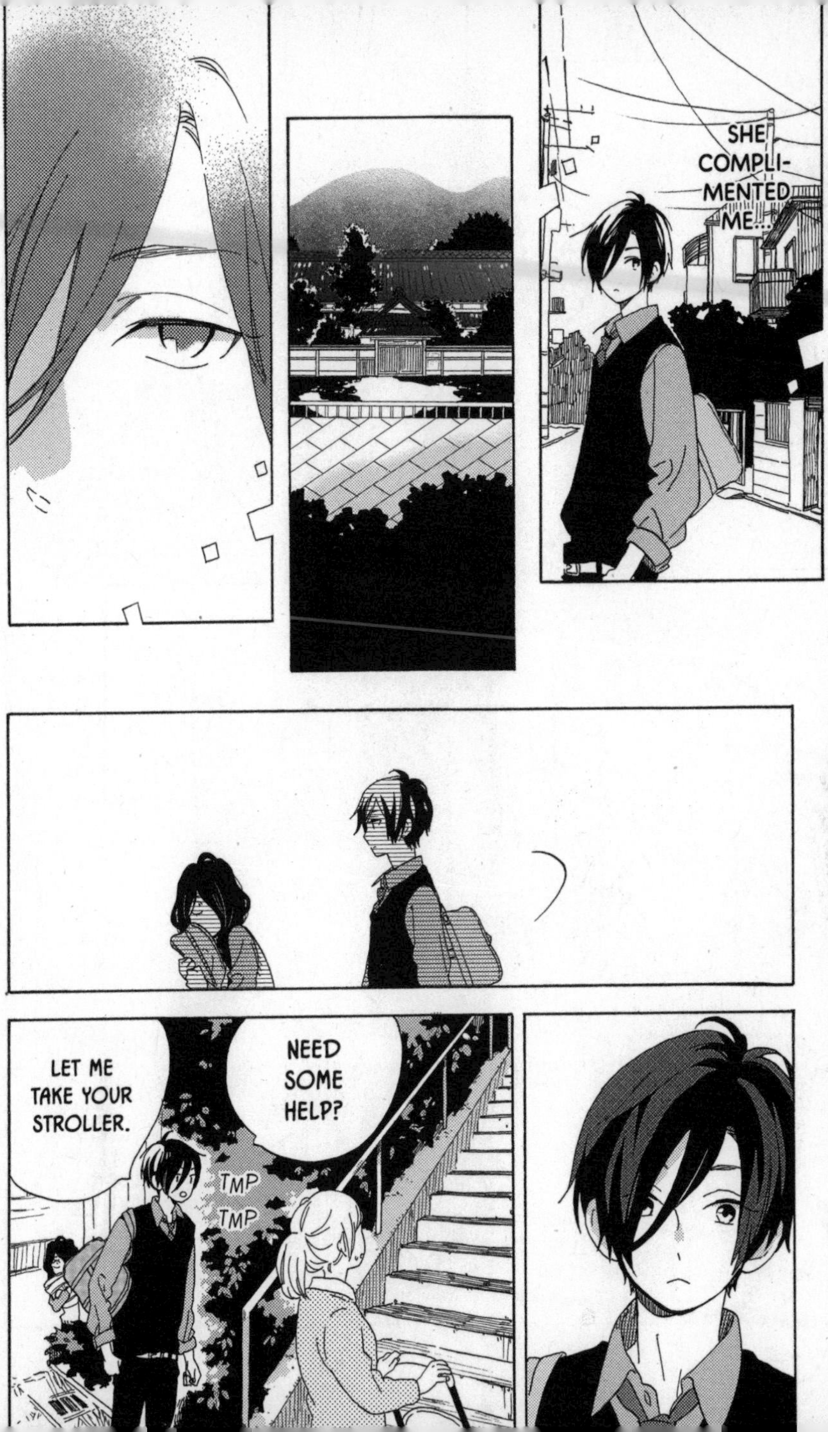
SHE COMPLI-MENTED ME...
NEED SOME HELP?
LET ME TAKE YOUR STROLLER.
TMP
TMP

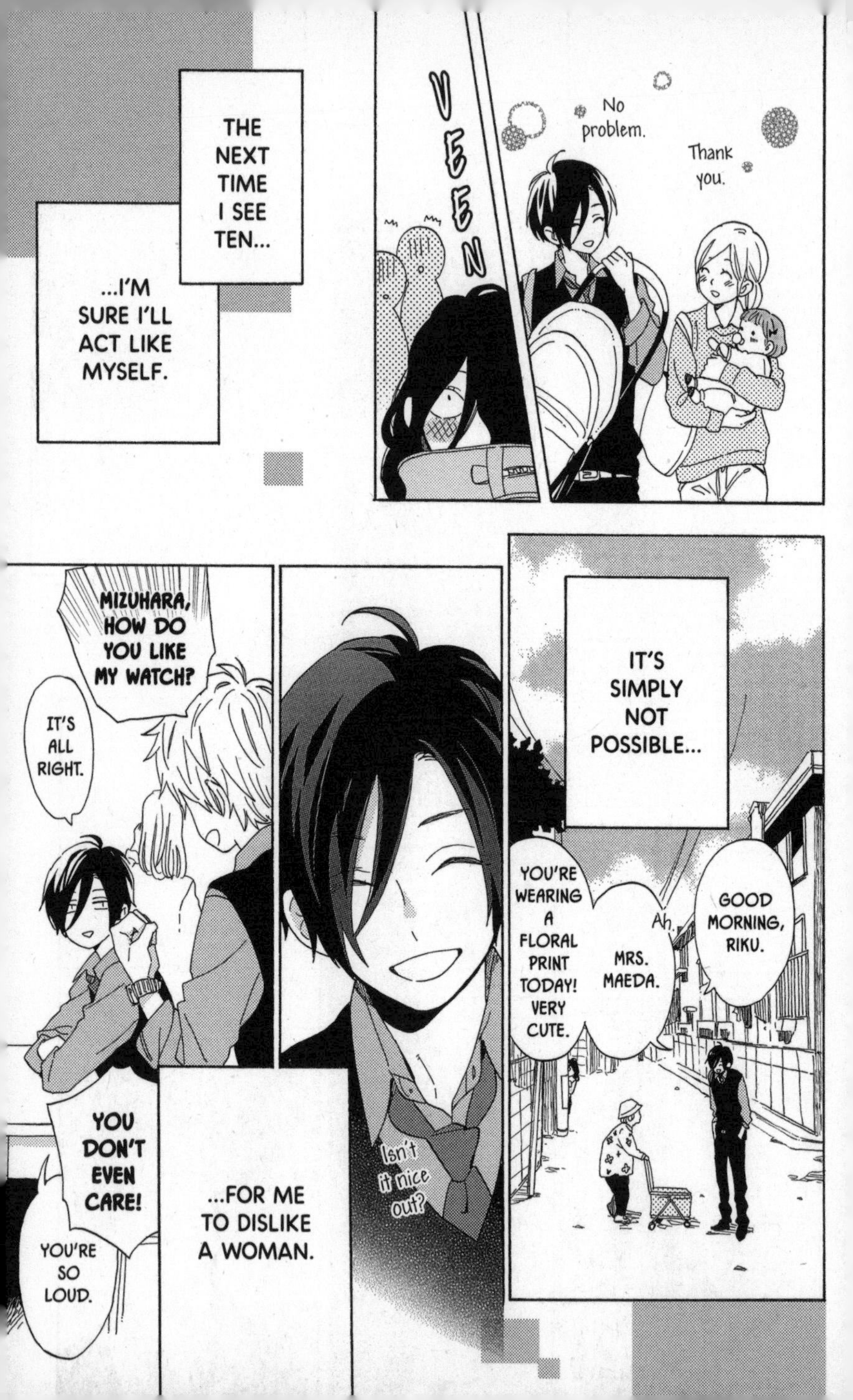
Thank you.
No problem.
VEEN
THE NEXT TIME I SEE TEN...
...I'M SURE I'LL ACT LIKE MYSELF.
IT'S SIMPLY NOT POSSIBLE...
GOOD MORNING, RIKU.
Ah.
MRS. MAEDA.
YOU'RE WEARING A FLORAL PRINT TODAY! VERY CUTE.
Isn't it nice out?
...FOR ME TO DISLIKE A WOMAN.
MIZUHARA, HOW DO YOU LIKE MY WATCH?
IT'S ALL RIGHT.
YOU DON'T EVEN CARE!
YOU'RE SO LOUD.

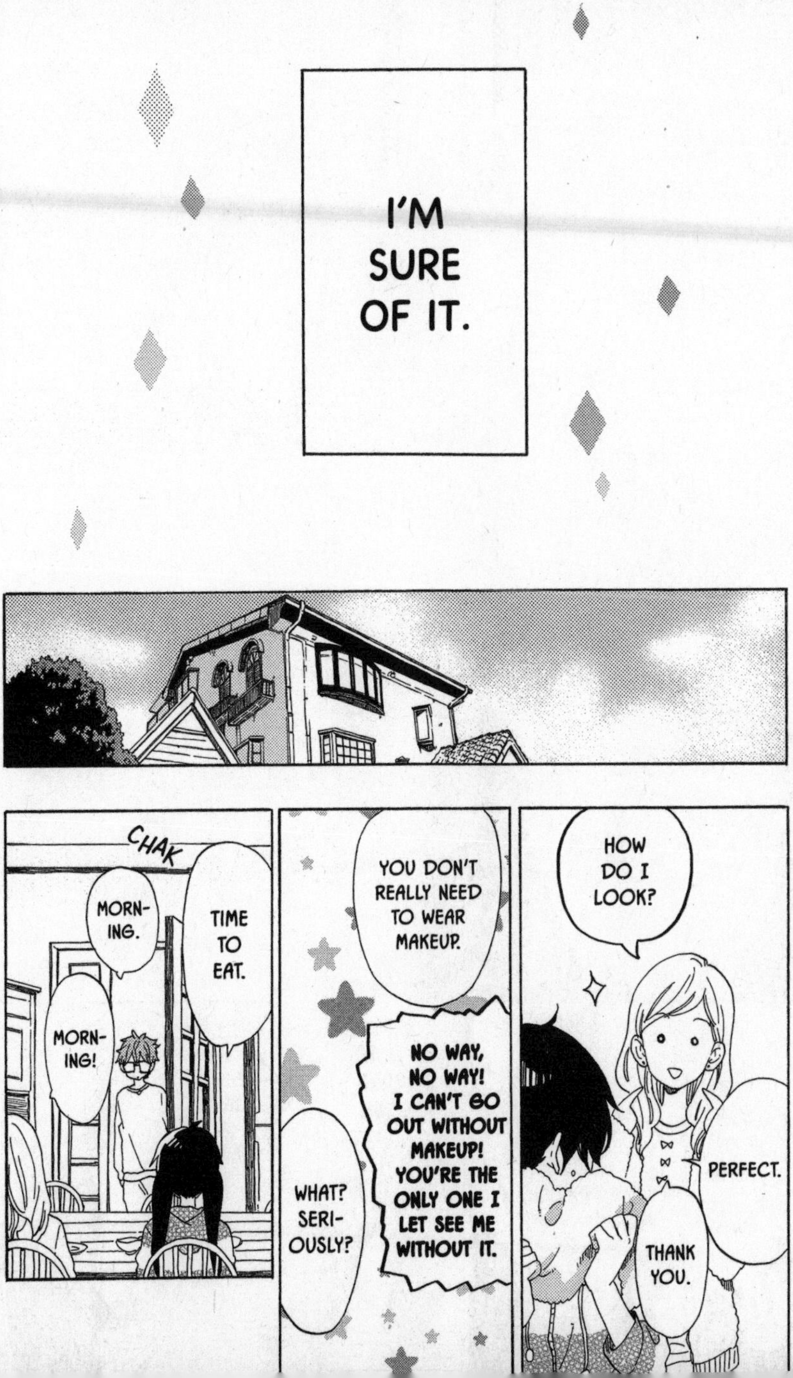
I'M SURE OF IT.
HOW DO I LOOK?
PERFECT.
THANK YOU.
YOU DON'T REALLY NEED TO WEAR MAKEUP.
NO WAY, NO WAY! I CAN'T GO OUT WITHOUT MAKEUP! YOU'RE THE ONLY ONE I LET SEE ME WITHOUT IT.
WHAT? SERIOUSLY?
CHAK
TIME TO EAT.
MORN-ING.
MORN-ING!

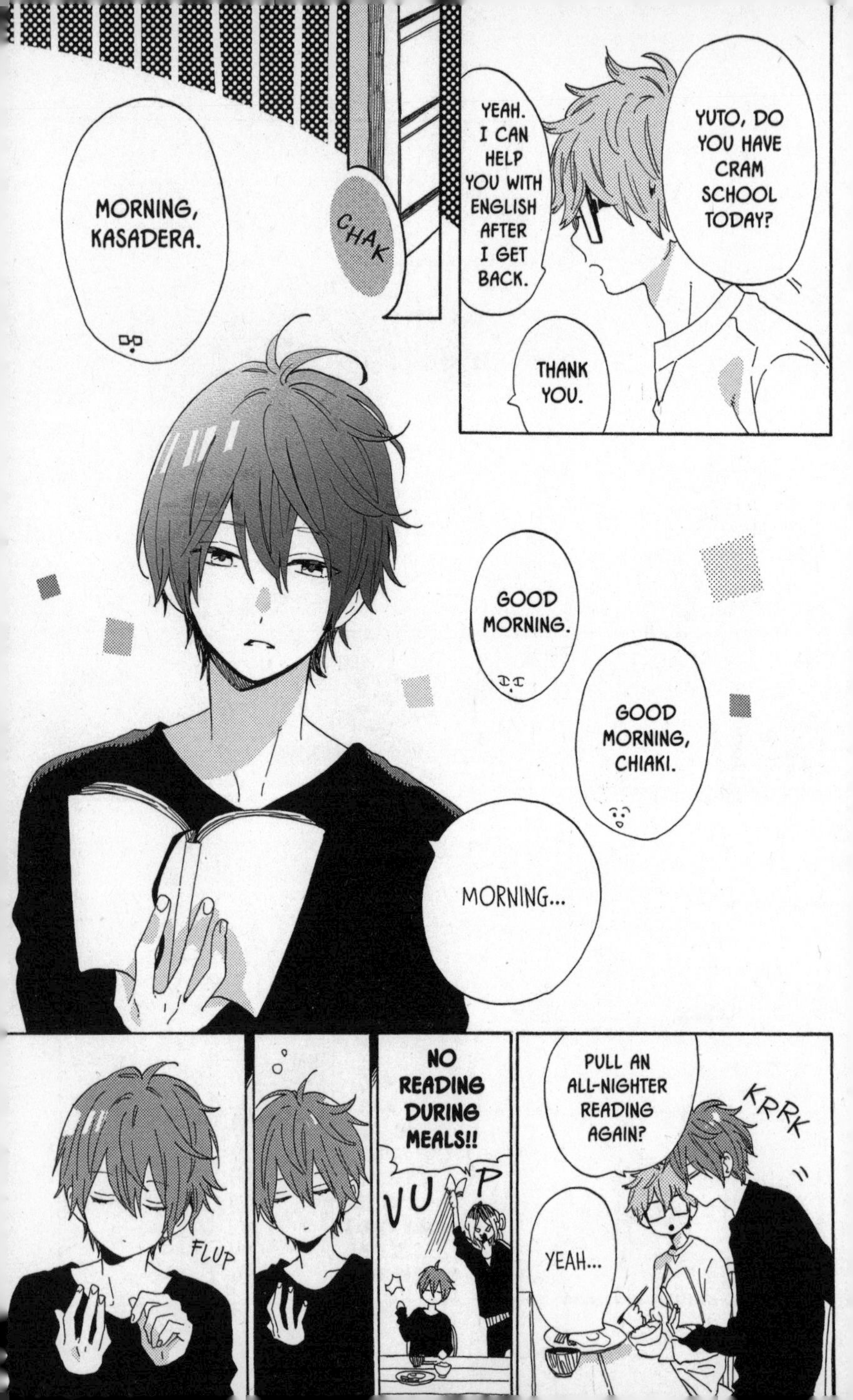
YUTO, DO YOU HAVE CRAM SCHOOL TODAY?
YEAH. I CAN HELP YOU WITH ENGLISH AFTER I GET BACK.
THANK YOU.
CHAK
MORNING, KASADERA.
GOOD MORNING.
GOOD MORNING, CHIAKI.
MORNING...
PULL AN ALL-NIGHTER READING AGAIN?
KRRK
YEAH...
NO READING DURING MEALS!!
VUP
FLUP

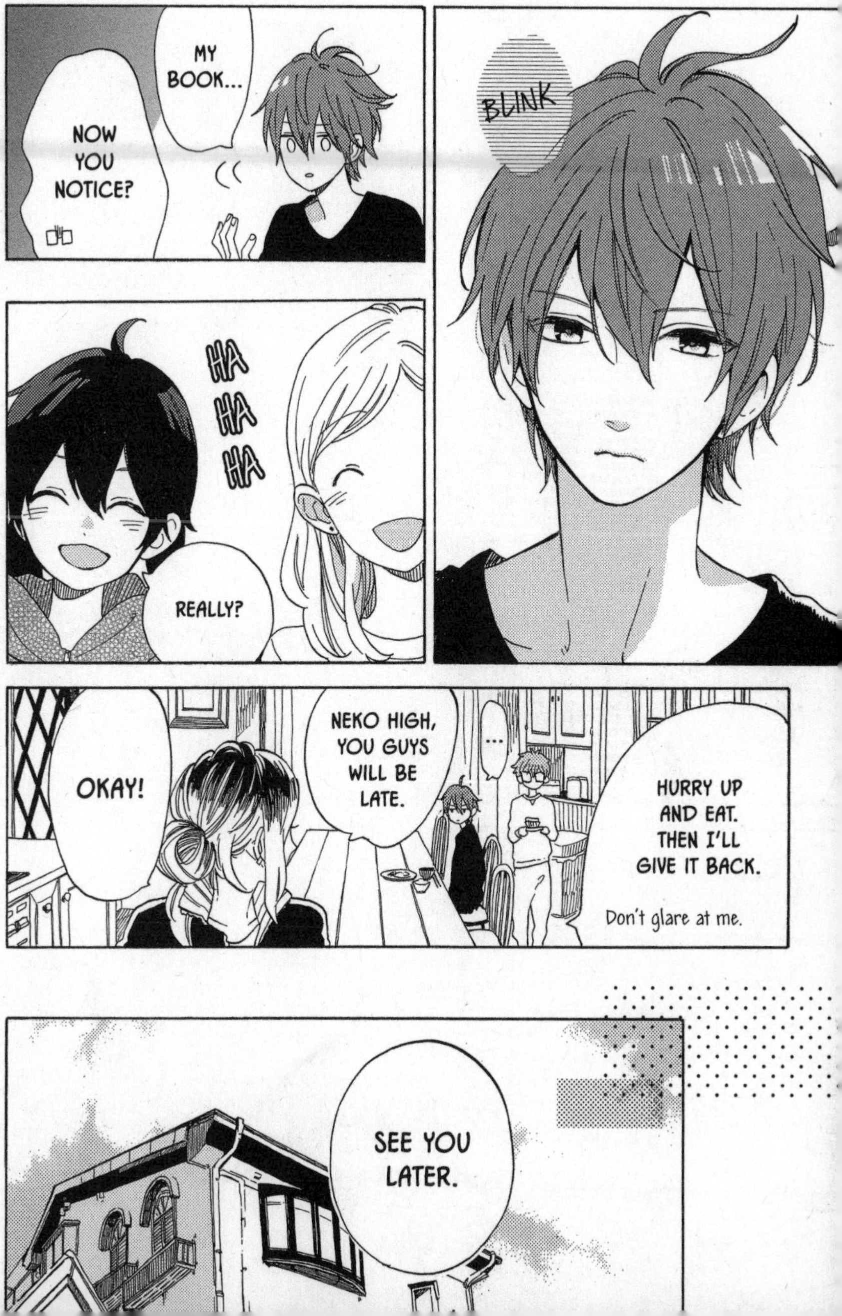
BLINK
MY BOOK...
NOW YOU NOTICE?
HA HA HA
REALLY?
HURRY UP AND EAT. THEN I'LL GIVE IT BACK.
Don't glare at me.
...
NEKO HIGH, YOU GUYS WILL BE LATE.
OKAY!
SEE YOU LATER.

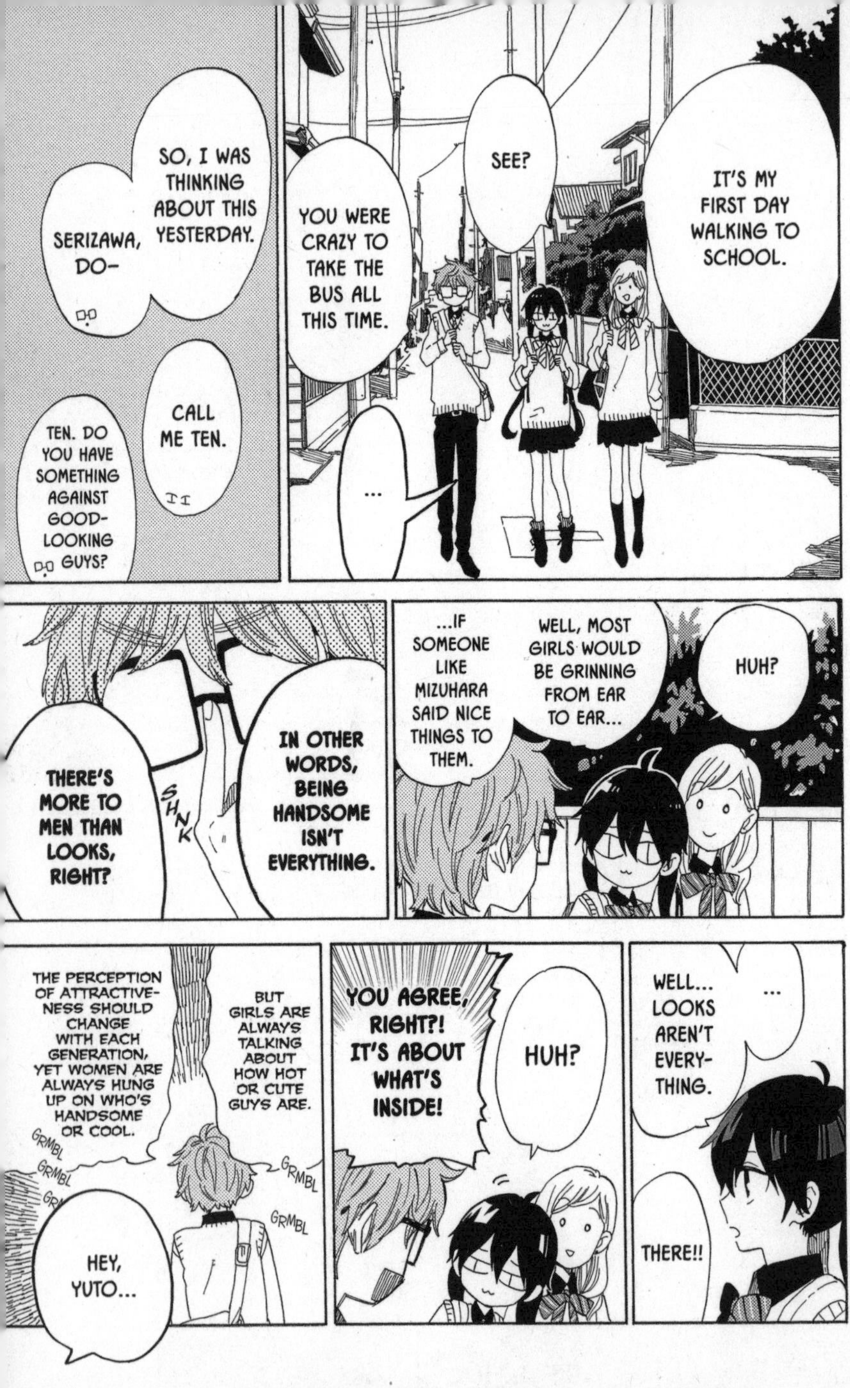
IT'S MY FIRST DAY WALKING TO SCHOOL.
SEE?
YOU WERE CRAZY TO TAKE THE BUS ALL THIS TIME.
...
SO, I WAS THINKING ABOUT THIS YESTERDAY.
SERIZAWA, DO-
CALL ME TEN.
TEN. DO YOU HAVE SOMETHING AGAINST GOOD-LOOKING GUYS?
HUH?
WELL, MOST GIRLS WOULD BE GRINNING FROM EAR TO EAR...
...IF SOMEONE LIKE MIZUHARA SAID NICE THINGS TO THEM.
IN OTHER WORDS, BEING HANDSOME ISN'T EVERYTHING.
SHNK
THERE'S MORE TO MEN THAN LOOKS, RIGHT?
...
WELL... LOOKS AREN'T EVERY-THING.
THERE!!
YOU AGREE, RIGHT?! IT'S ABOUT WHAT'S INSIDE!
HUH?
BUT GIRLS ARE ALWAYS TALKING ABOUT HOW HOT OR CUTE GUYS ARE.
THE PERCEPTION OF ATTRACTIVE-NESS SHOULD CHANGE WITH EACH GENERATION, YET WOMEN ARE ALWAYS HUNG UP ON WHO'S HANDSOME OR COOL.
GRMBL
GRMBL
GRMBL
GRMBL
HEY, YUTO...

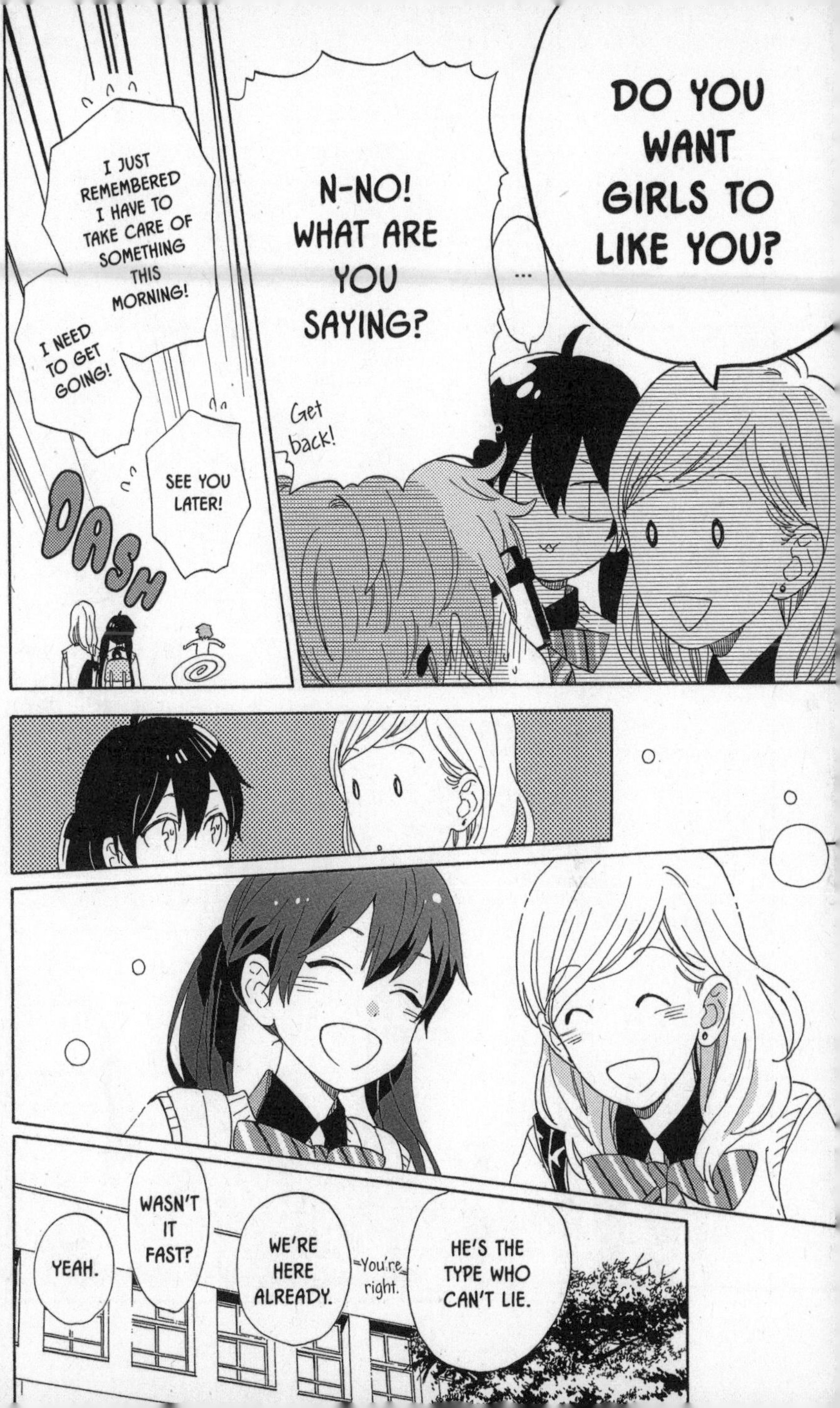
DO YOU WANT GIRLS TO LIKE YOU?
...
N-NO! WHAT ARE YOU SAYING?
Get back!
I JUST REMEMBERED I HAVE TO TAKE CARE OF SOMETHING THIS MORNING!
I NEED TO GET GOING!
SEE YOU LATER!
DASH
HE'S THE TYPE WHO CAN'T LIE.
You're right.
WE'RE HERE ALREADY.
WASN'T IT FAST?
YEAH.

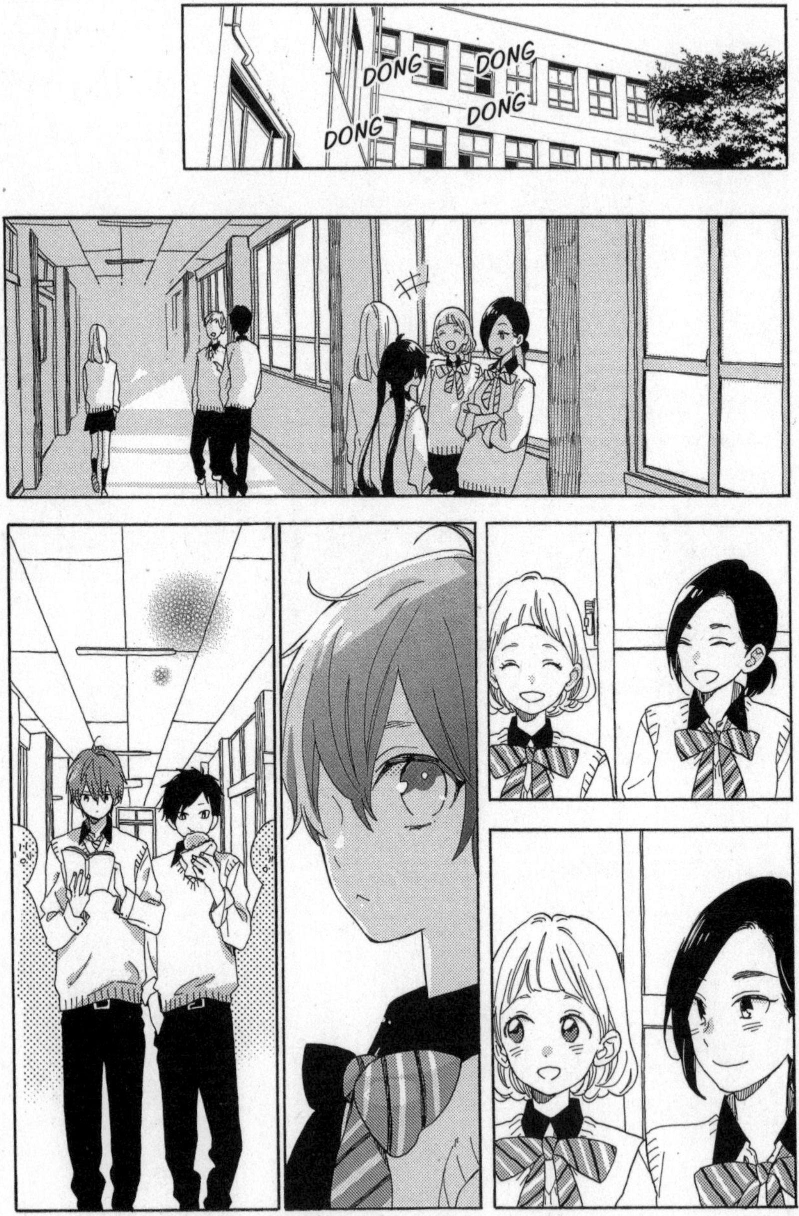
DONG
DONG
DONG
DONG

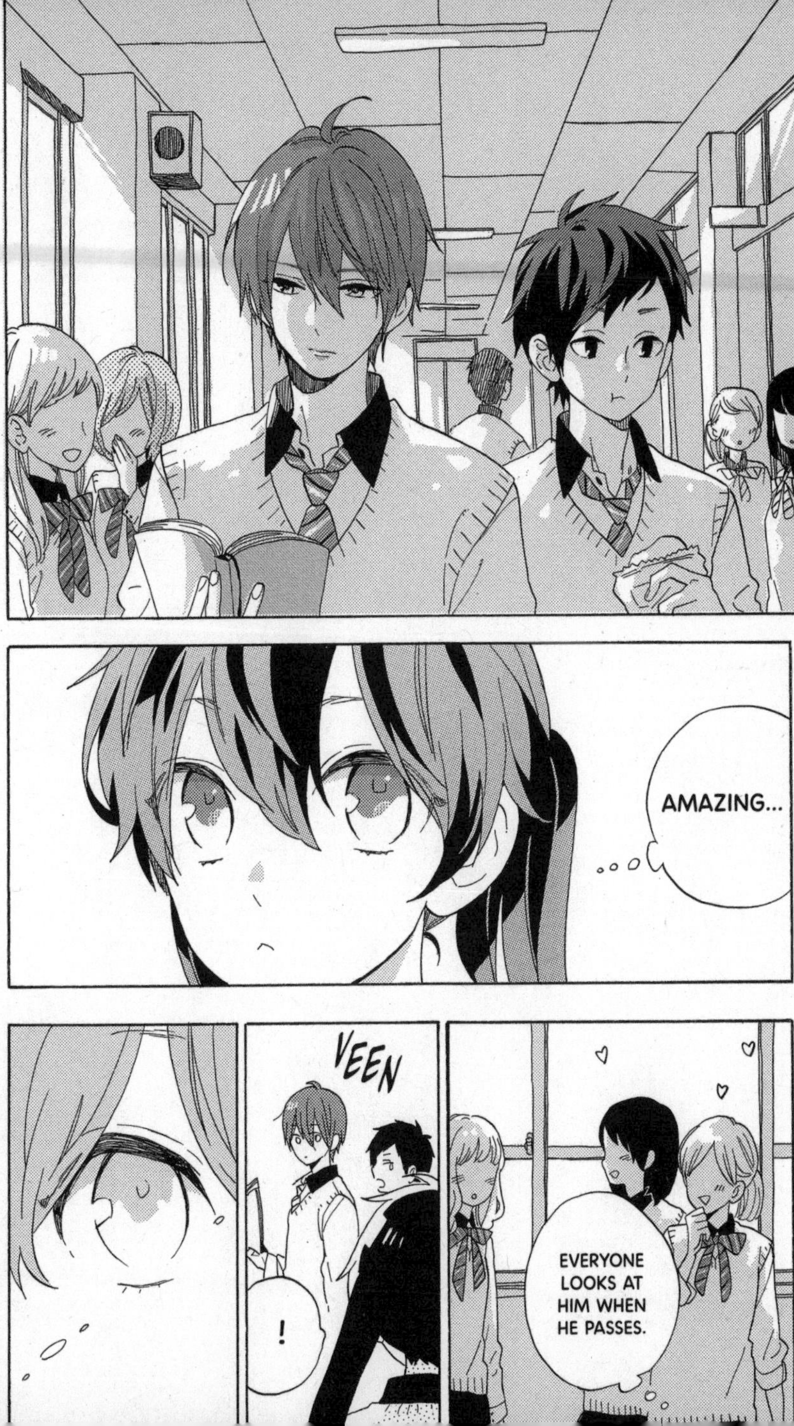
AMAZING...
EVERYONE LOOKS AT HIM WHEN HE PASSES.
VEEN
!

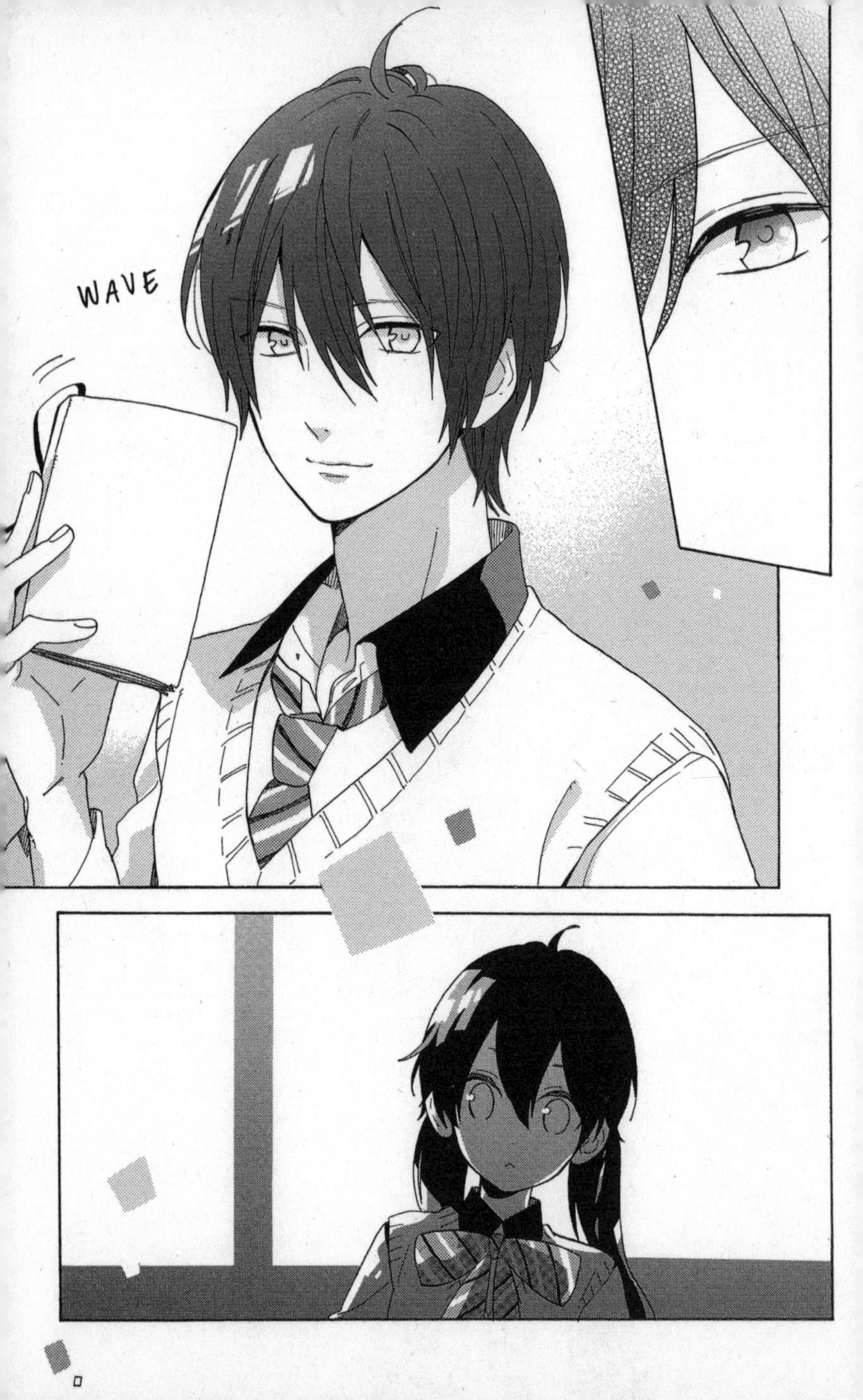
WAVE

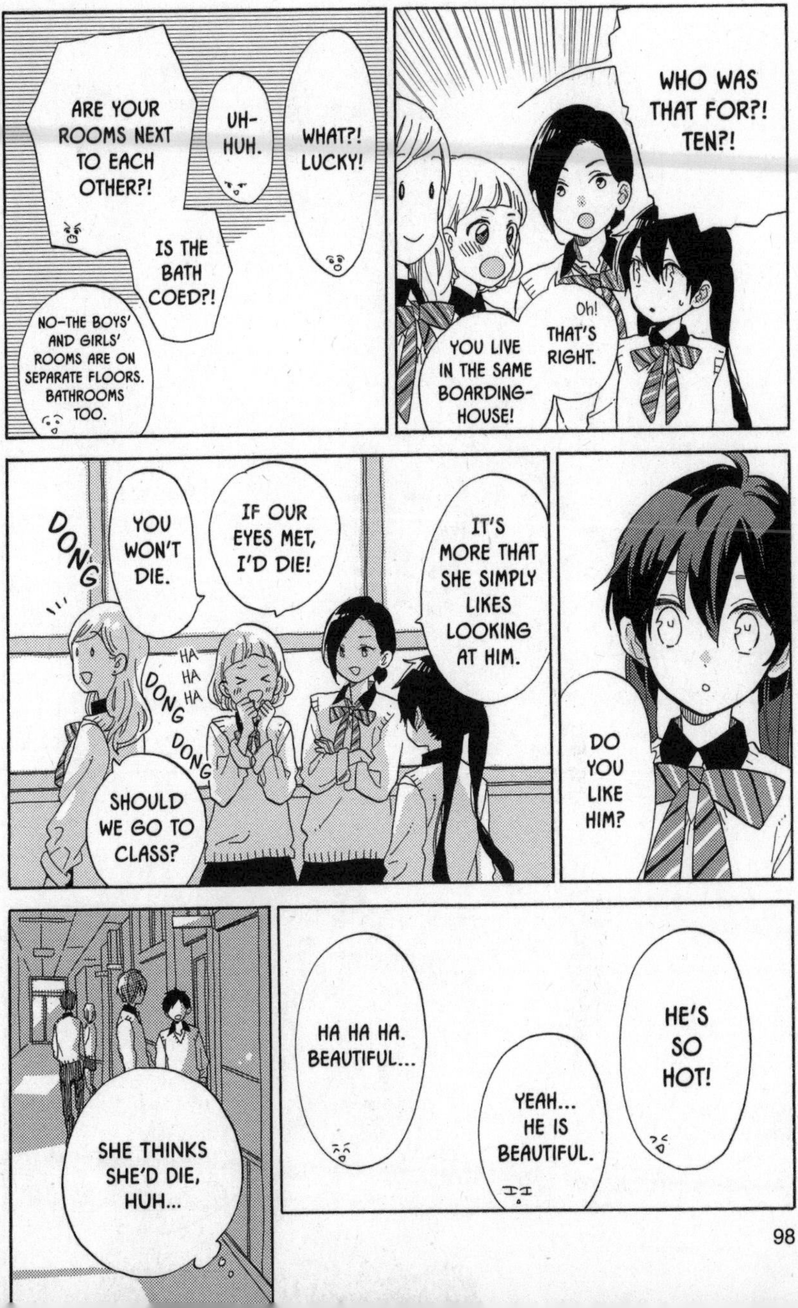
WHO WAS THAT FOR?! TEN?!
YOU LIVE IN THE SAME BOARDING-HOUSE!
Oh! THAT'S RIGHT.
WHAT?! LUCKY!
UH-HUH.
ARE YOUR ROOMS NEXT TO EACH OTHER?!
IS THE BATH COED?!
NO—THE BOYS' AND GIRLS' ROOMS ARE ON SEPARATE FLOORS. BATHROOMS TOO.
DO YOU LIKE HIM?
IT'S MORE THAT SHE SIMPLY LIKES LOOKING AT HIM.
IF OUR EYES MET, I'D DIE!
YOU WON'T DIE.
DONG
HA HA HA
DONG DONG DONG
SHOULD WE GO TO CLASS?
HE'S SO HOT!
YEAH... HE IS BEAUTIFUL.
HA HA HA. BEAUTIFUL...
SHE THINKS SHE'D DIE, HUH...

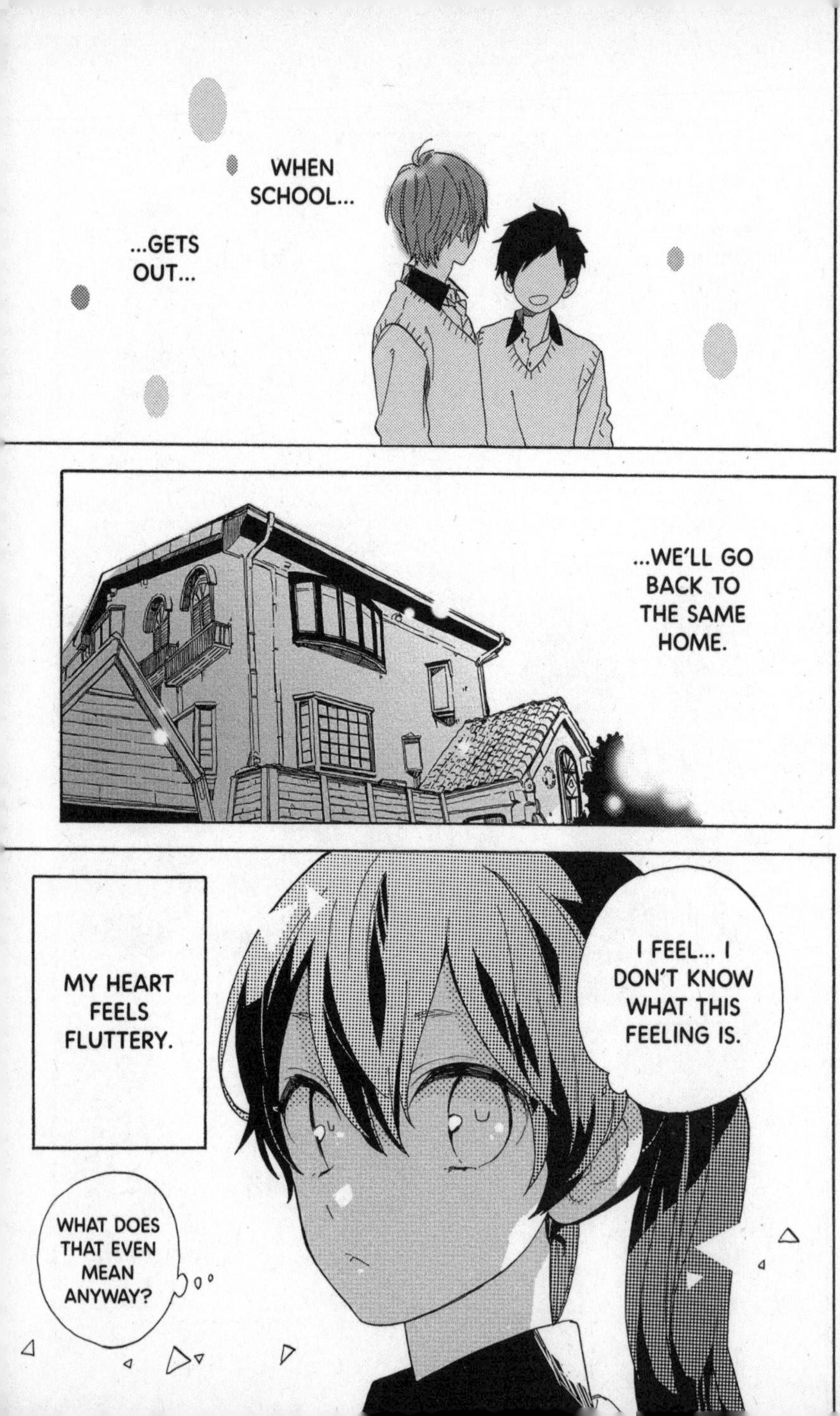
WHEN SCHOOL...
...GETS OUT...
...WE'LL GO BACK TO THE SAME HOME.
I FEEL... I DON'T KNOW WHAT THIS FEELING IS.
MY HEART FEELS FLUTTERY.
WHAT DOES THAT EVEN MEAN ANYWAY?

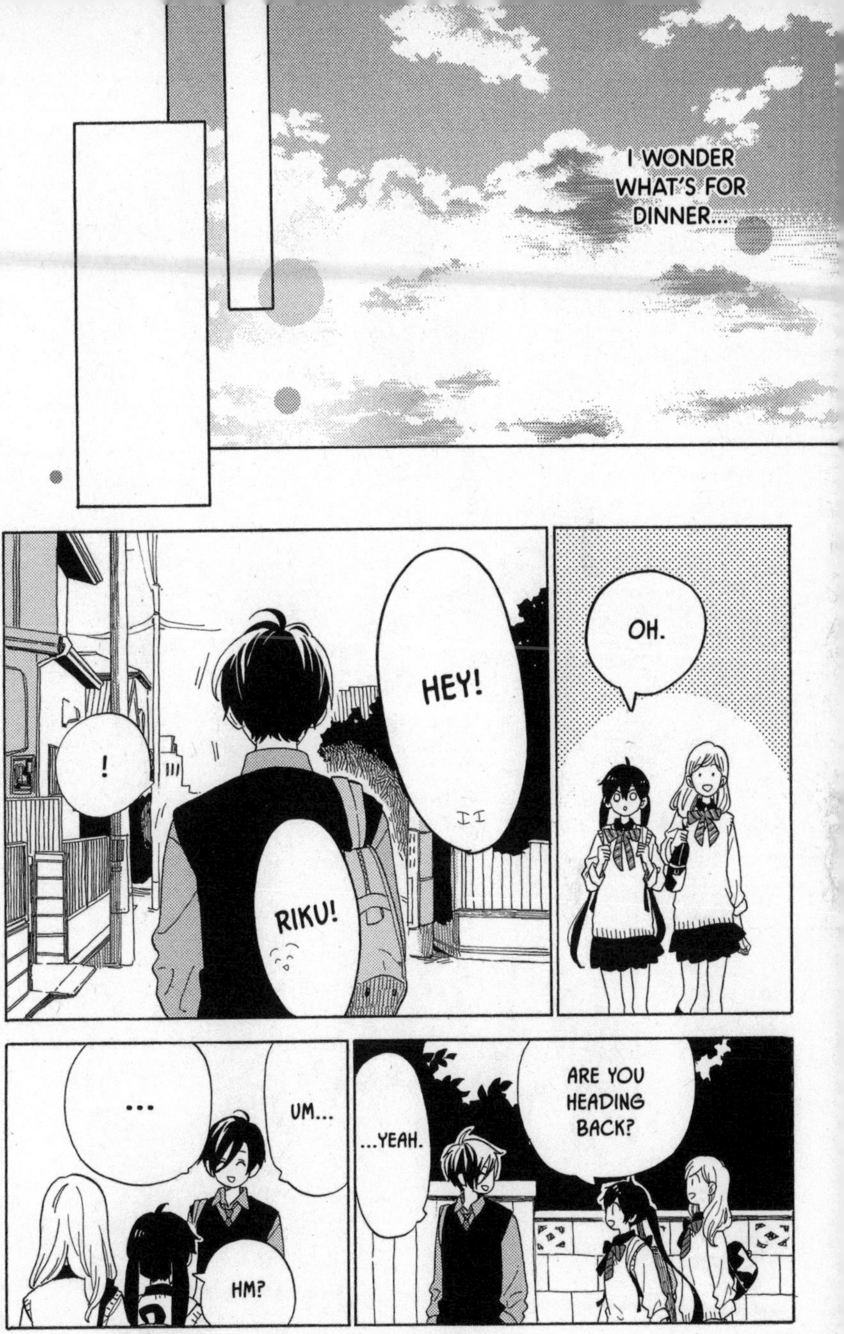
I WONDER WHAT'S FOR DINNER...
OH.
HEY!
RIKU!
!
ARE YOU HEADING BACK?
...YEAH.
UM...
...
HM?

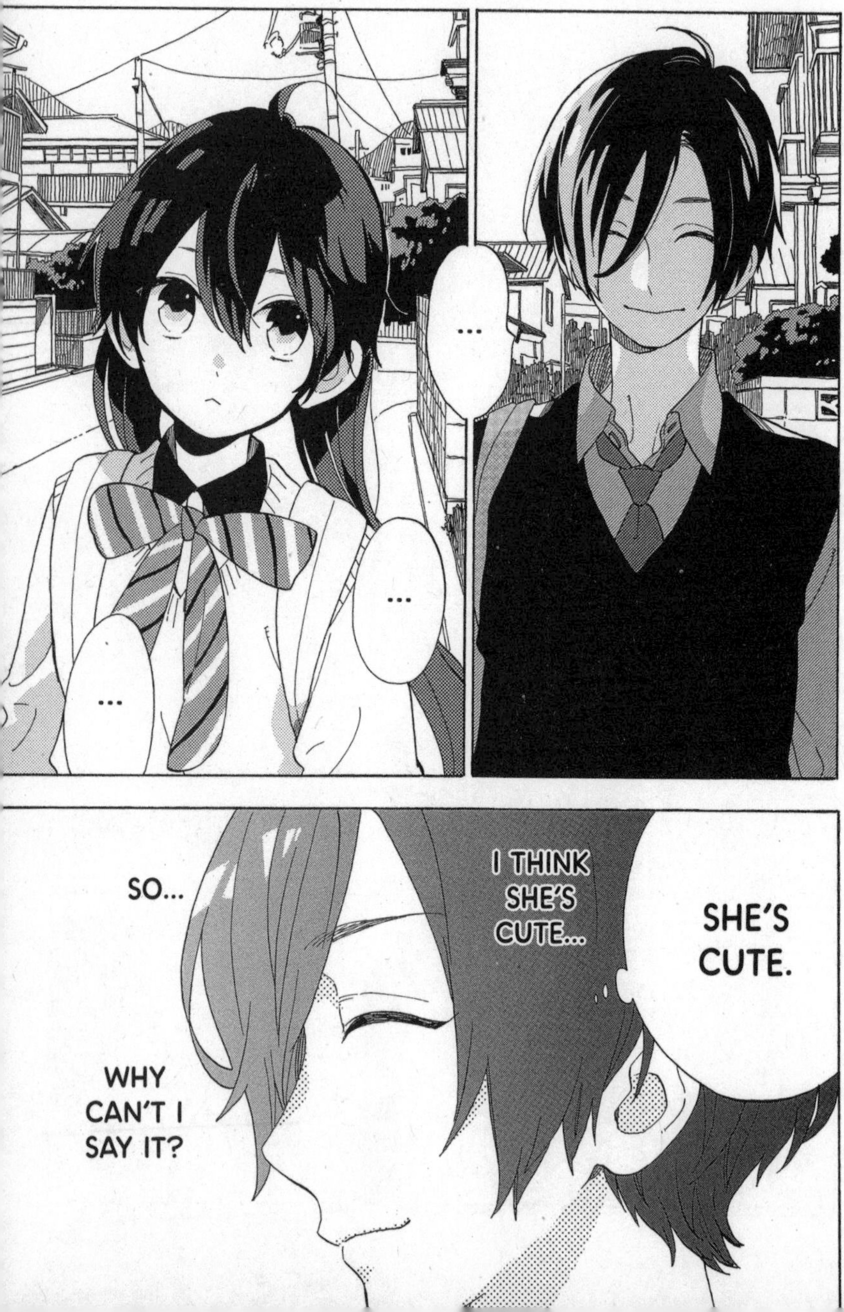
...
...
...
SHE'S CUTE.
I THINK SHE'S CUTE...
SO...
WHY CAN'T I SAY IT?

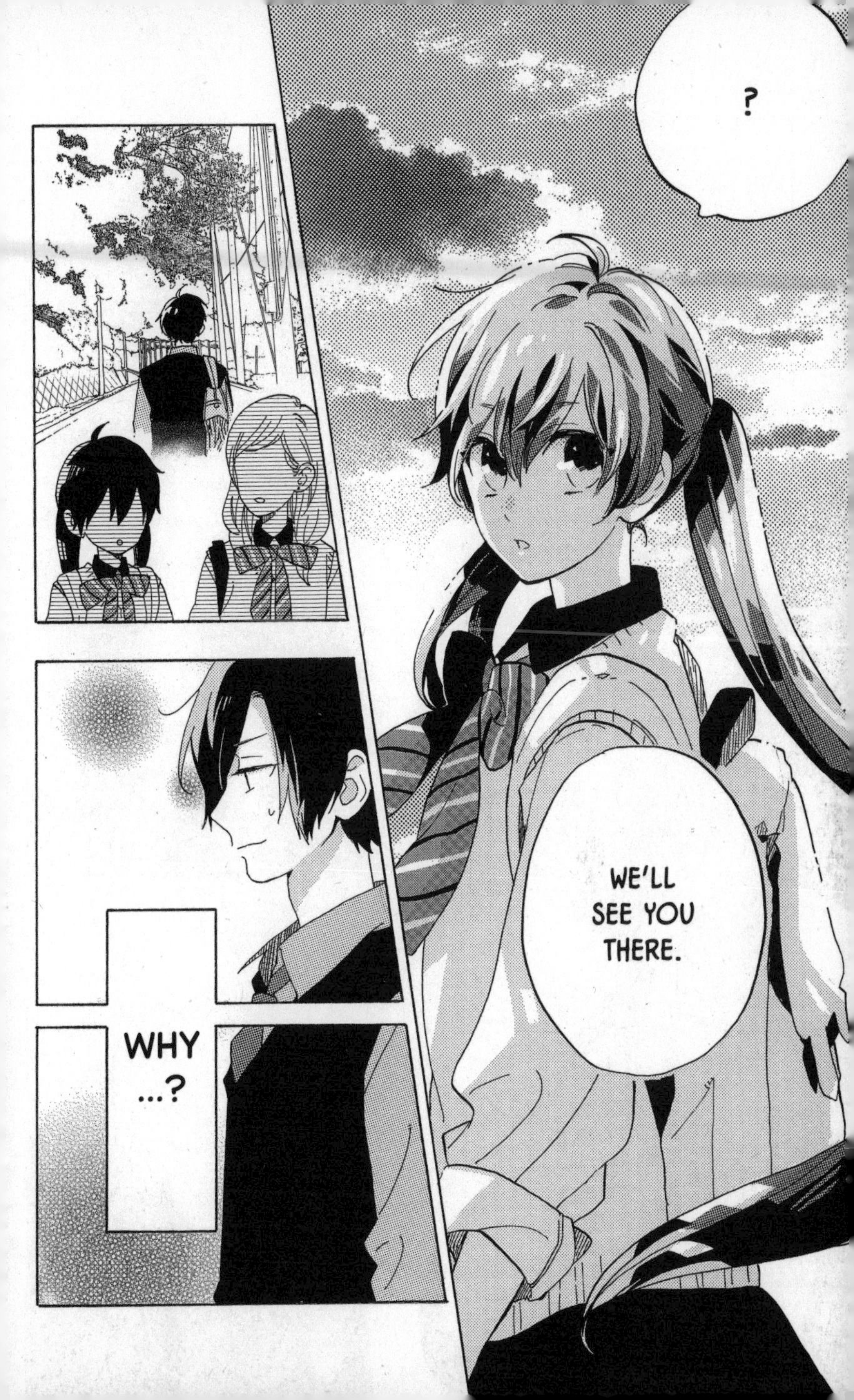
?
WE'LL SEE YOU THERE.
WHY ...?

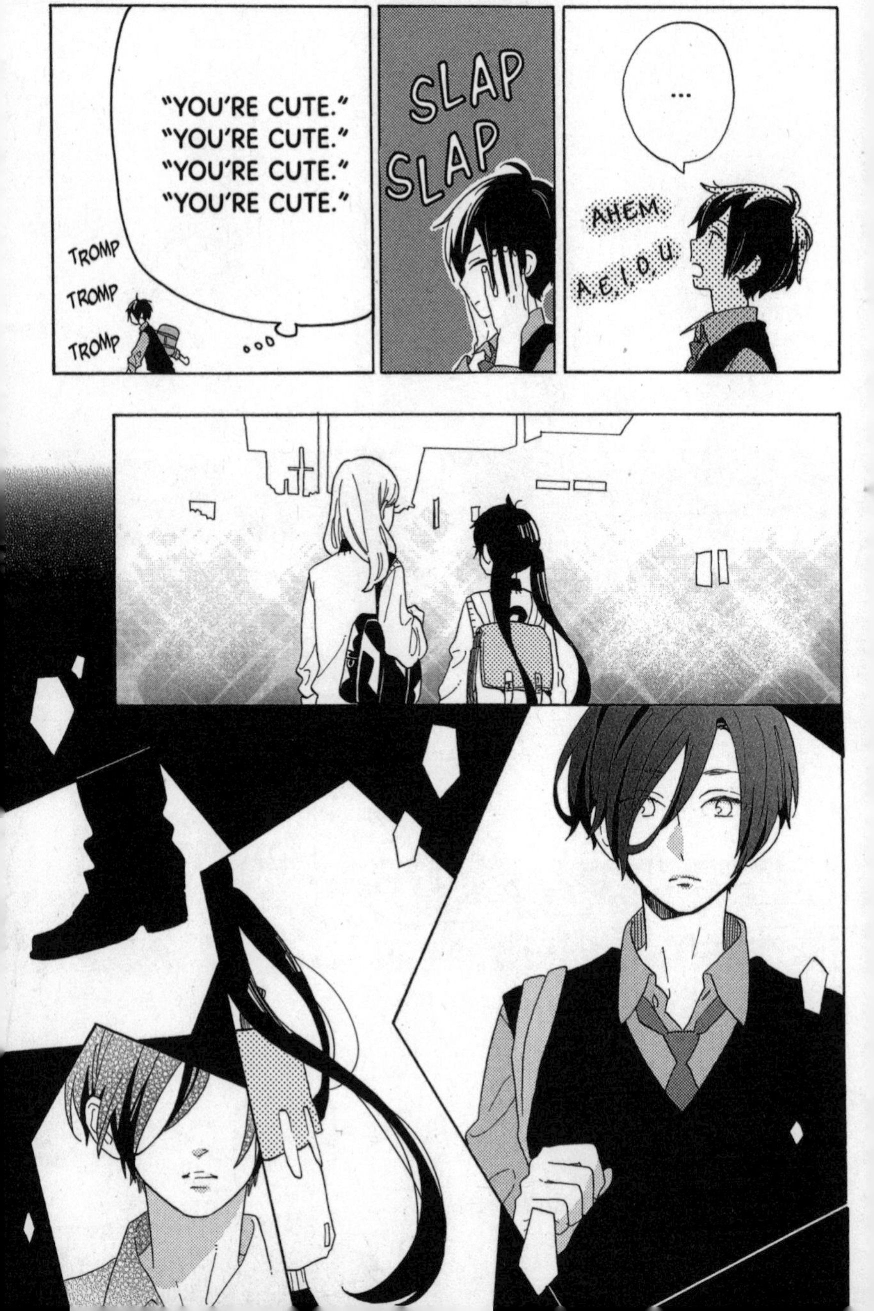
...
AHEM.
A, E, I, O, U.
SLAP
SLAP
"YOU'RE CUTE."
"YOU'RE CUTE."
"YOU'RE CUTE."
"YOU'RE CUTE."
TROMP
TROMP
TROMP

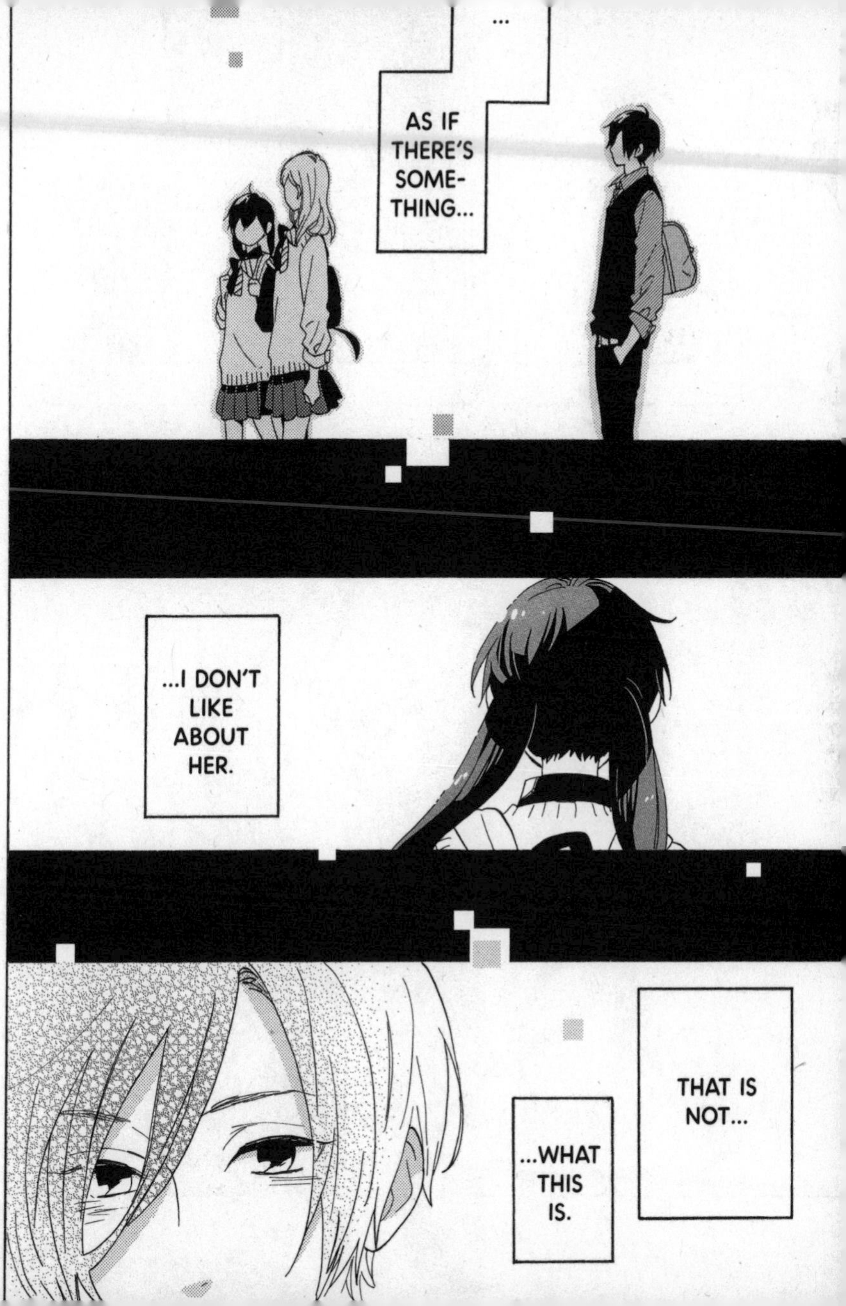
...
AS IF THERE'S SOME-THING...
...I DON'T LIKE ABOUT HER.
THAT IS NOT...
...WHAT THIS IS.

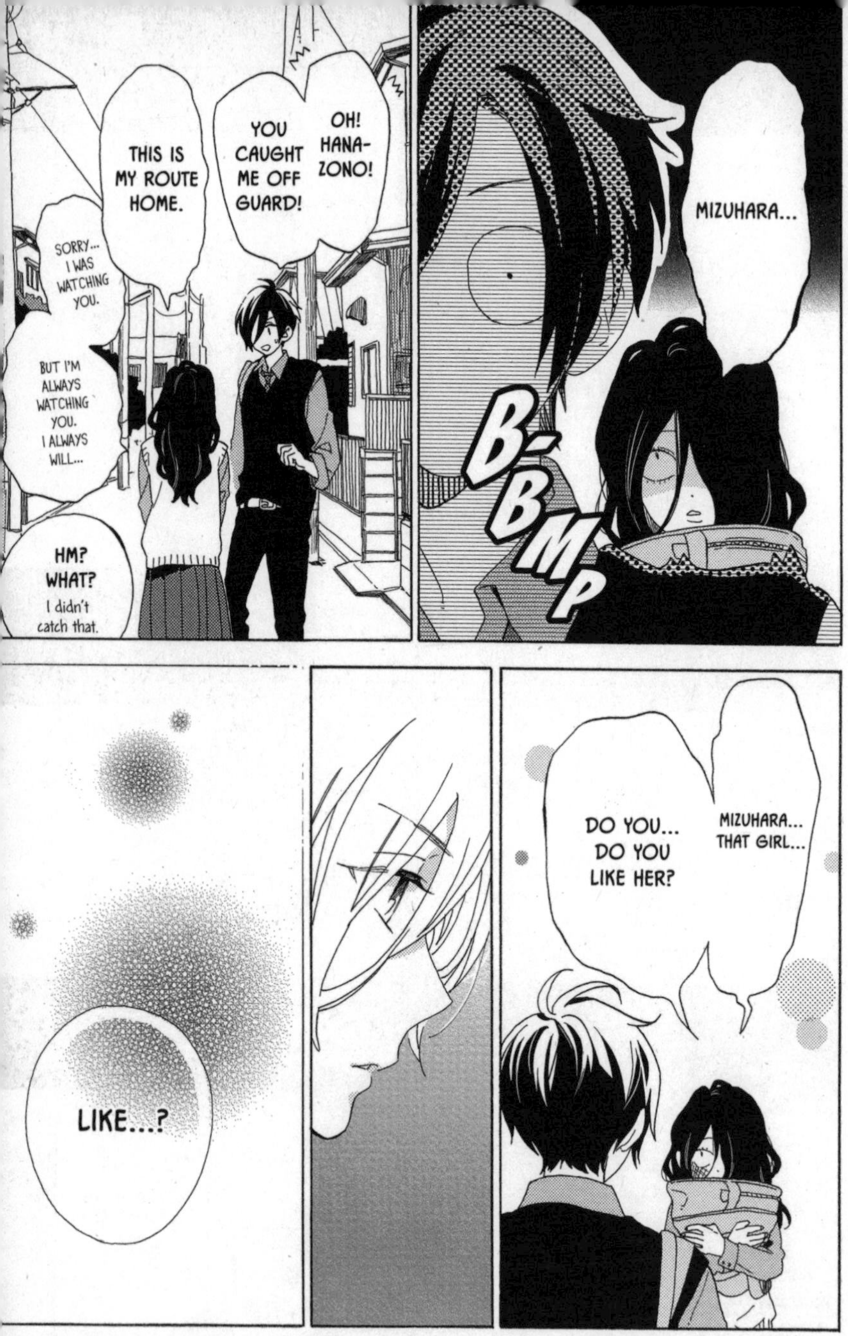
MIZUHARA...
B-BMP
OH! HANA-ZONO!
YOU CAUGHT ME OFF GUARD!
THIS IS MY ROUTE HOME.
SORRY... I WAS WATCHING YOU.
BUT I'M ALWAYS WATCHING YOU. I ALWAYS WILL...
HM? WHAT? I didn't catch that.
MIZUHARA... THAT GIRL...
DO YOU... DO YOU LIKE HER?
LIKE...?

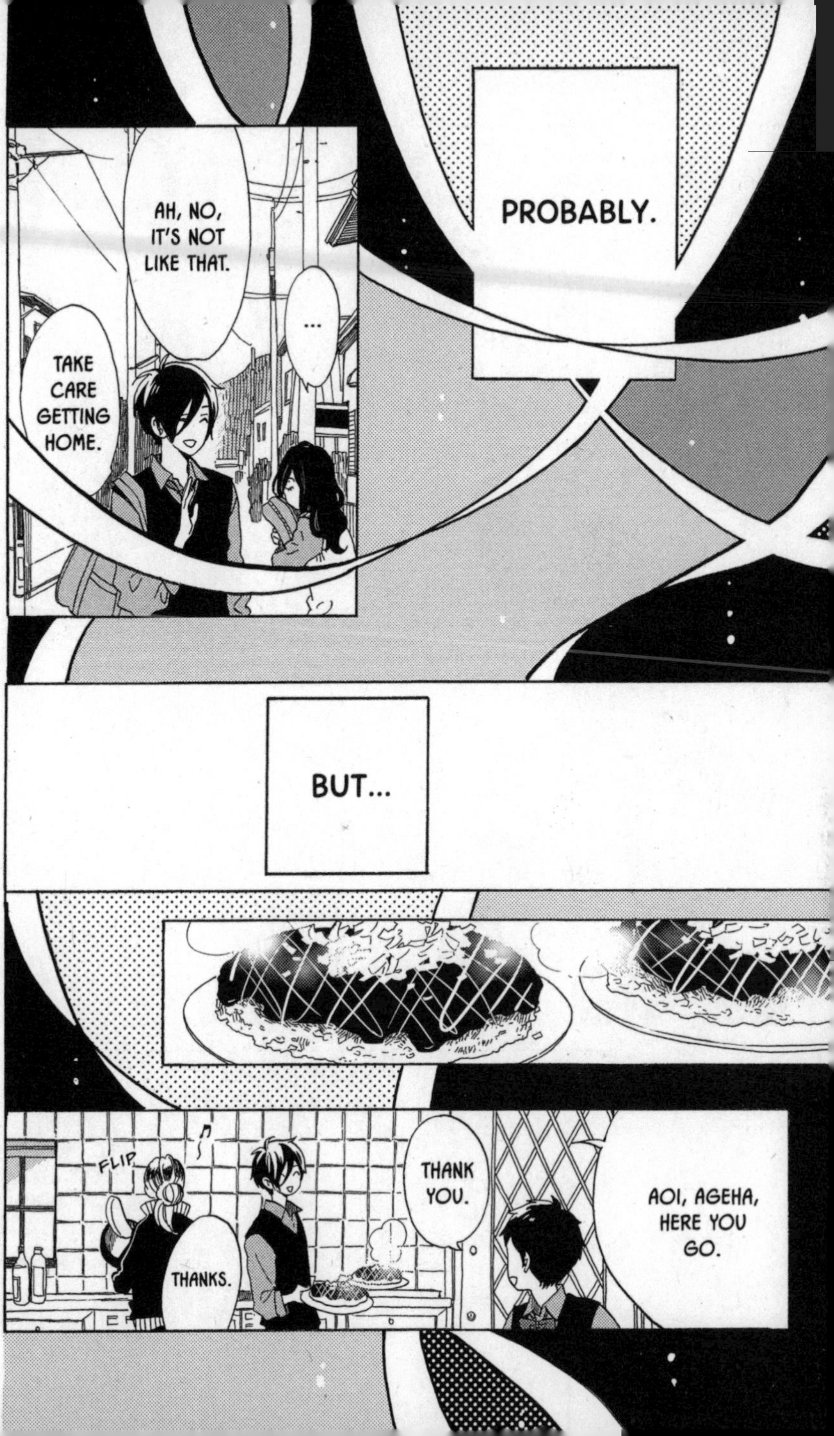
PROBABLY.
AH, NO, IT'S NOT LIKE THAT.
...
TAKE CARE GETTING HOME.
BUT...
AOI, AGEHA, HERE YOU GO.
THANK YOU.
FLIP
THANKS.

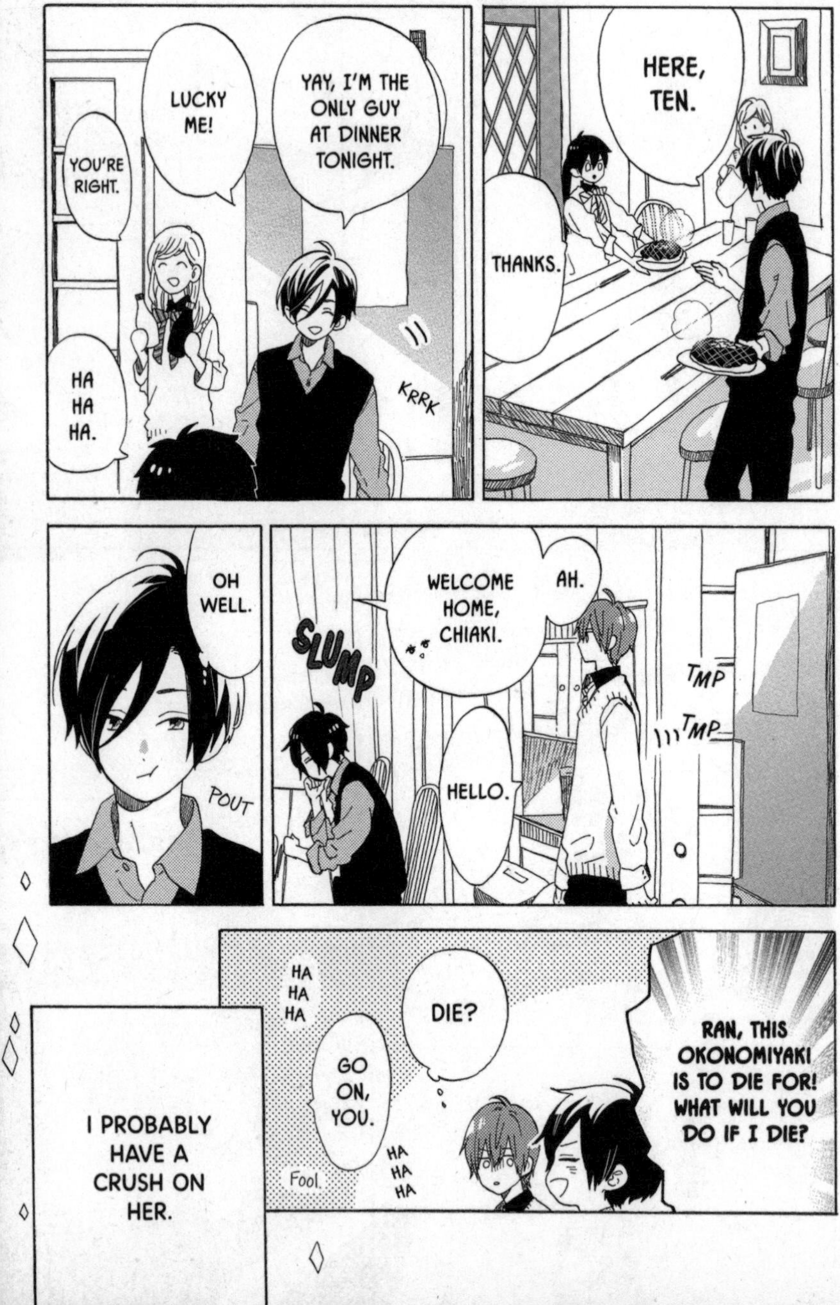
HERE, TEN.
THANKS.
YAY, I'M THE ONLY GUY AT DINNER TONIGHT.
LUCKY ME!
YOU'RE RIGHT.
HA HA HA.
KRRK
AH.
WELCOME HOME, CHIAKI.
TMP
TMP
SLUMP
HELLO.
OH WELL.
POUT
RAN, THIS OKONOMIYAKI IS TO DIE FOR! WHAT WILL YOU DO IF I DIE?
DIE?
HA HA HA
GO ON, YOU.
HA HA HA
Fool.
I PROBABLY HAVE A CRUSH ON HER.

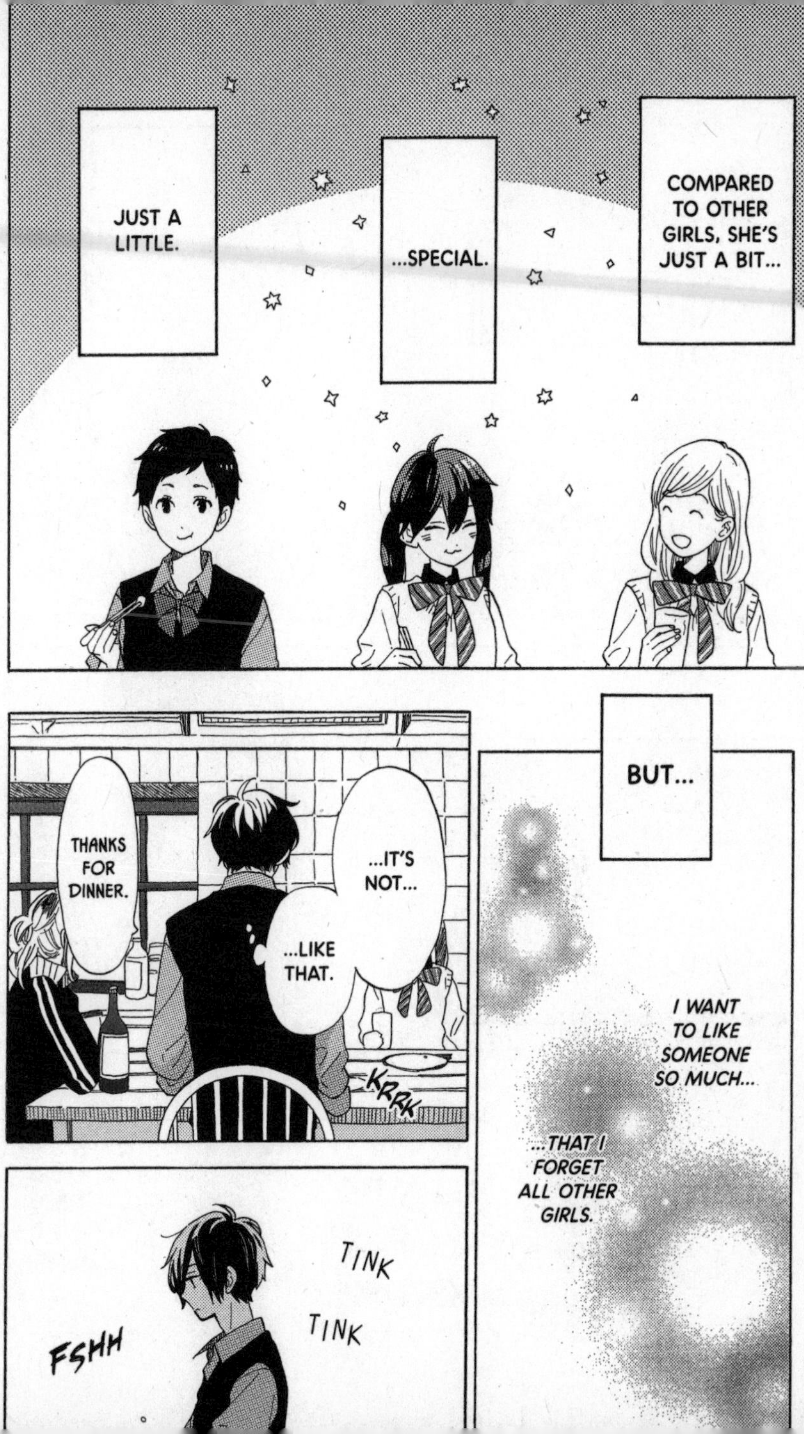
COMPARED TO OTHER GIRLS, SHE'S JUST A BIT...
...SPECIAL.
JUST A LITTLE.
BUT...
I WANT TO LIKE SOMEONE SO MUCH...
...THAT I FORGET ALL OTHER GIRLS.
...IT'S NOT...
...LIKE THAT.
THANKS FOR DINNER.
KRRK
TINK
TINK
FSHH

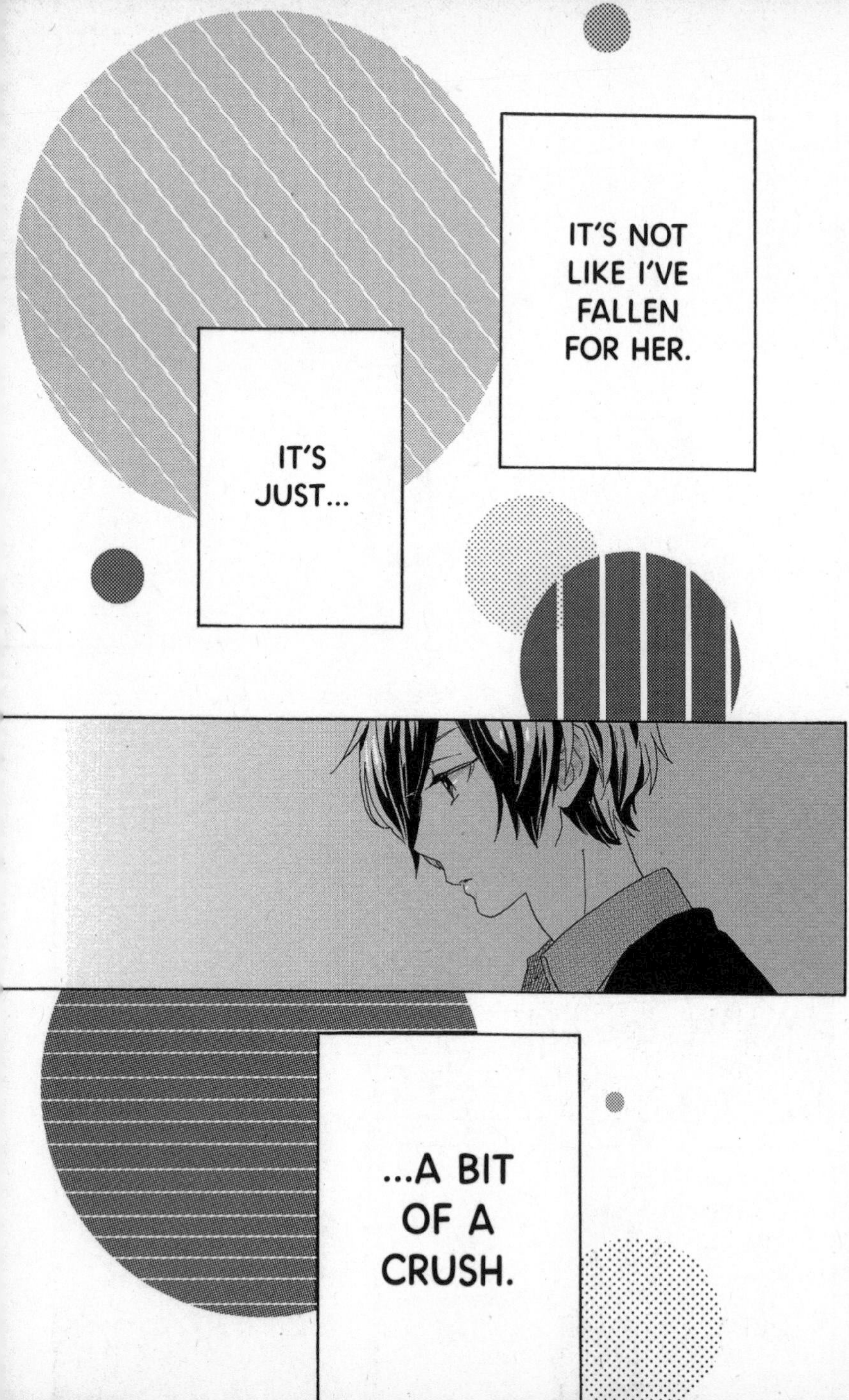
IT'S NOT LIKE I'VE FALLEN FOR HER.
IT'S JUST...
...A BIT OF A CRUSH.

SHORTCAKE CAKE
CAKE

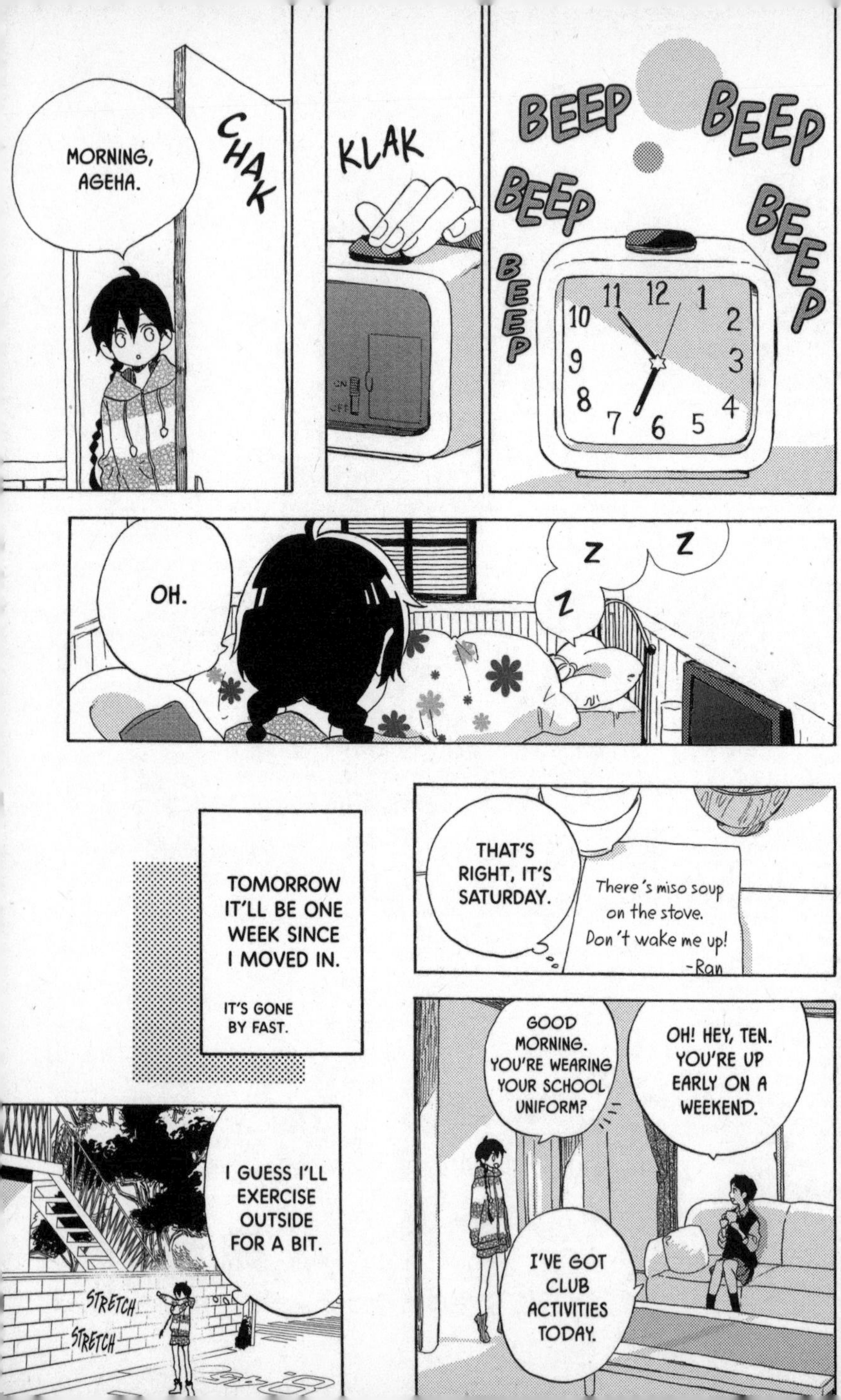

BEEP
BEEP
BEEP
BEEP
BEEP
KLAK
CHAK
MORNING, AGEHA.
Z Z Z
OH.
There's miso soup on the stove. Don't wake me up! -Ran
THAT'S RIGHT, IT'S SATURDAY.
TOMORROW IT'LL BE ONE WEEK SINCE I MOVED IN.
IT'S GONE BY FAST.
OH! HEY, TEN. YOU'RE UP EARLY ON A WEEKEND.
GOOD MORNING. YOU'RE WEARING YOUR SCHOOL UNIFORM?
I'VE GOT CLUB ACTIVITIES TODAY.
I GUESS I'LL EXERCISE OUTSIDE FOR A BIT.
STRETCH
STRETCH

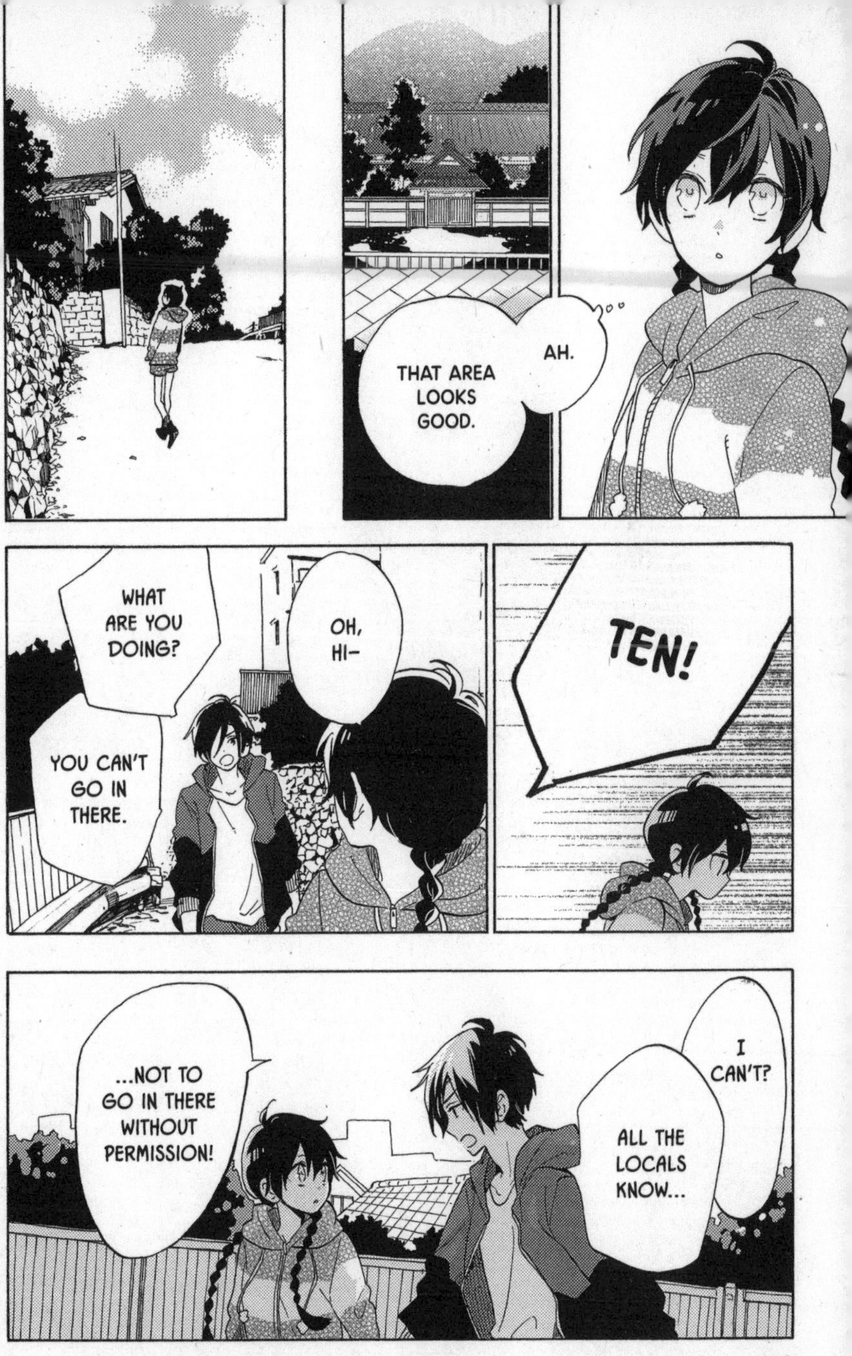
AH.
THAT AREA LOOKS GOOD.
TEN!
OH, HI-
WHAT ARE YOU DOING?
YOU CAN'T GO IN THERE.
I CAN'T?
ALL THE LOCALS KNOW...
...NOT TO GO IN THERE WITHOUT PERMISSION!

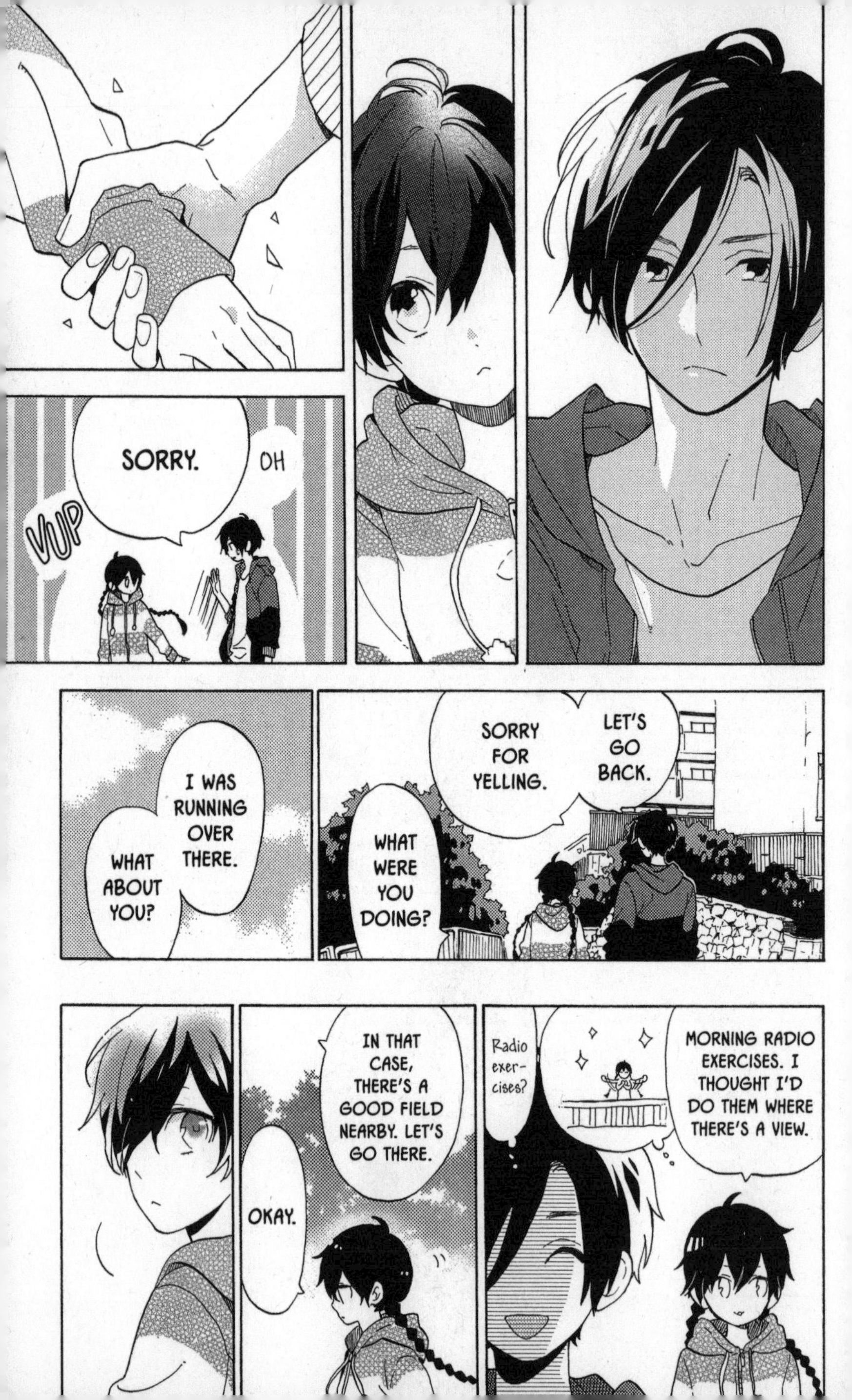
OH
SORRY.
VUP
LET'S GO BACK.
SORRY FOR YELLING.
WHAT WERE YOU DOING?
I WAS RUNNING OVER THERE.
WHAT ABOUT YOU?
MORNING RADIO EXERCISES. I THOUGHT I'D DO THEM WHERE THERE'S A VIEW.
Radio exer-cises?
IN THAT CASE, THERE'S A GOOD FIELD NEARBY. LET'S GO THERE.
OKAY.

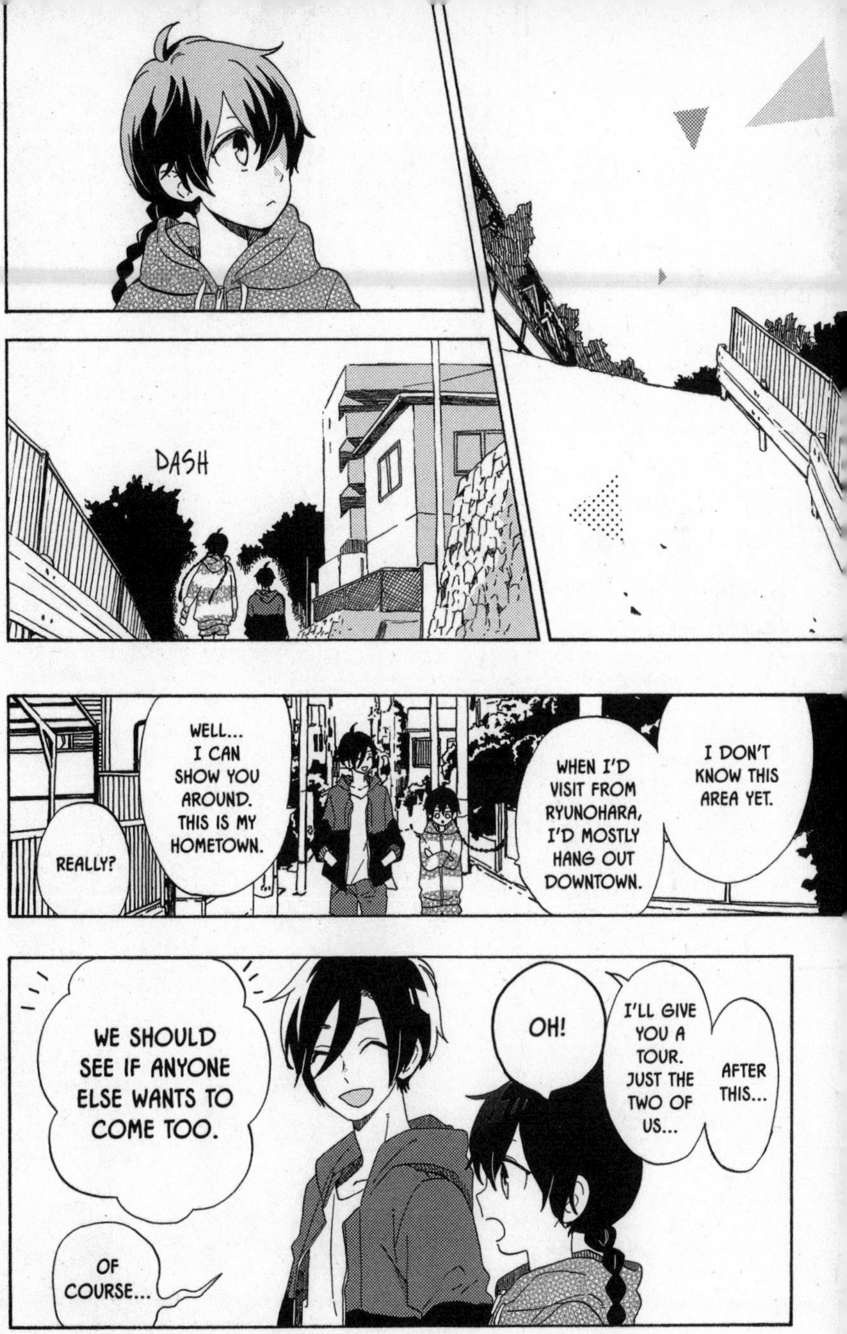
DASH
I DON'T KNOW THIS AREA YET.
WHEN I'D VISIT FROM RYUNOHARA, I'D MOSTLY HANG OUT DOWNTOWN.
WELL... I CAN SHOW YOU AROUND. THIS IS MY HOMETOWN.
REALLY?
AFTER THIS...
I'LL GIVE YOU A TOUR. JUST THE TWO OF US...
OH!
WE SHOULD SEE IF ANYONE ELSE WANTS TO COME TOO.
OF COURSE...

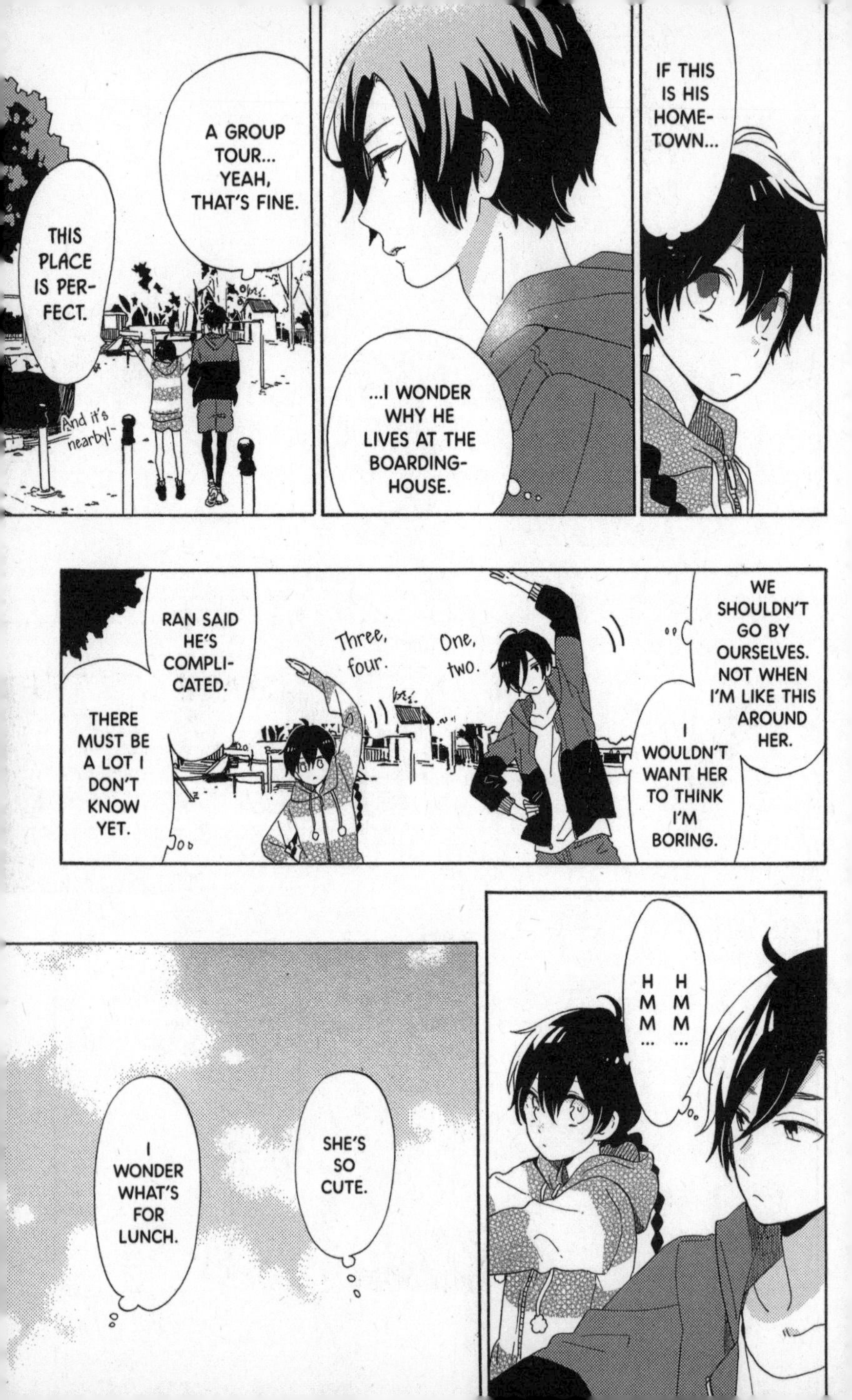
IF THIS IS HIS HOME-TOWN...
...I WONDER WHY HE LIVES AT THE BOARDING-HOUSE.
A GROUP TOUR... YEAH, THAT'S FINE.
THIS PLACE IS PER-FECT.
And it's nearby!
WE SHOULDN'T GO BY OURSELVES. NOT WHEN I'M LIKE THIS AROUND HER.
I WOULDN'T WANT HER TO THINK I'M BORING.
One, two.
Three, four.
RAN SAID HE'S COMPLI-CATED.
THERE MUST BE A LOT I DON'T KNOW YET.
HMM... HMM...
SHE'S SO CUTE.
I WONDER WHAT'S FOR LUNCH.

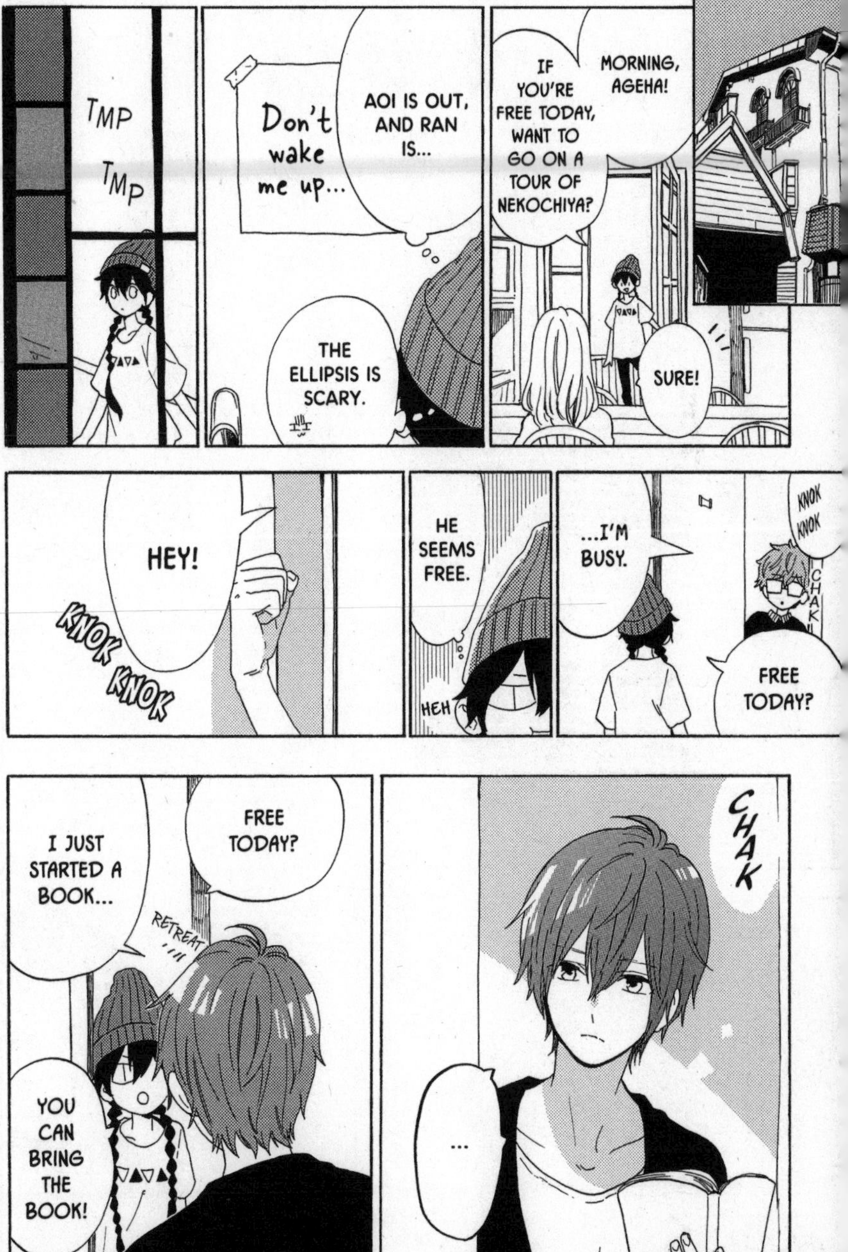
MORNING, AGEHA!
IF YOU'RE FREE TODAY, WANT TO GO ON A TOUR OF NEKOCHIYA?
SURE!
AOI IS OUT, AND RAN IS...
Don't wake me up...
THE ELLIPSIS IS SCARY.
TMP
TMP
KNOK KNOK
CHAK
FREE TODAY?
...I'M BUSY.
HE SEEMS FREE.
HEH
HEY!
KNOK KNOK
CHAK
...
FREE TODAY?
I JUST STARTED A BOOK...
RETREAT
YOU CAN BRING THE BOOK!

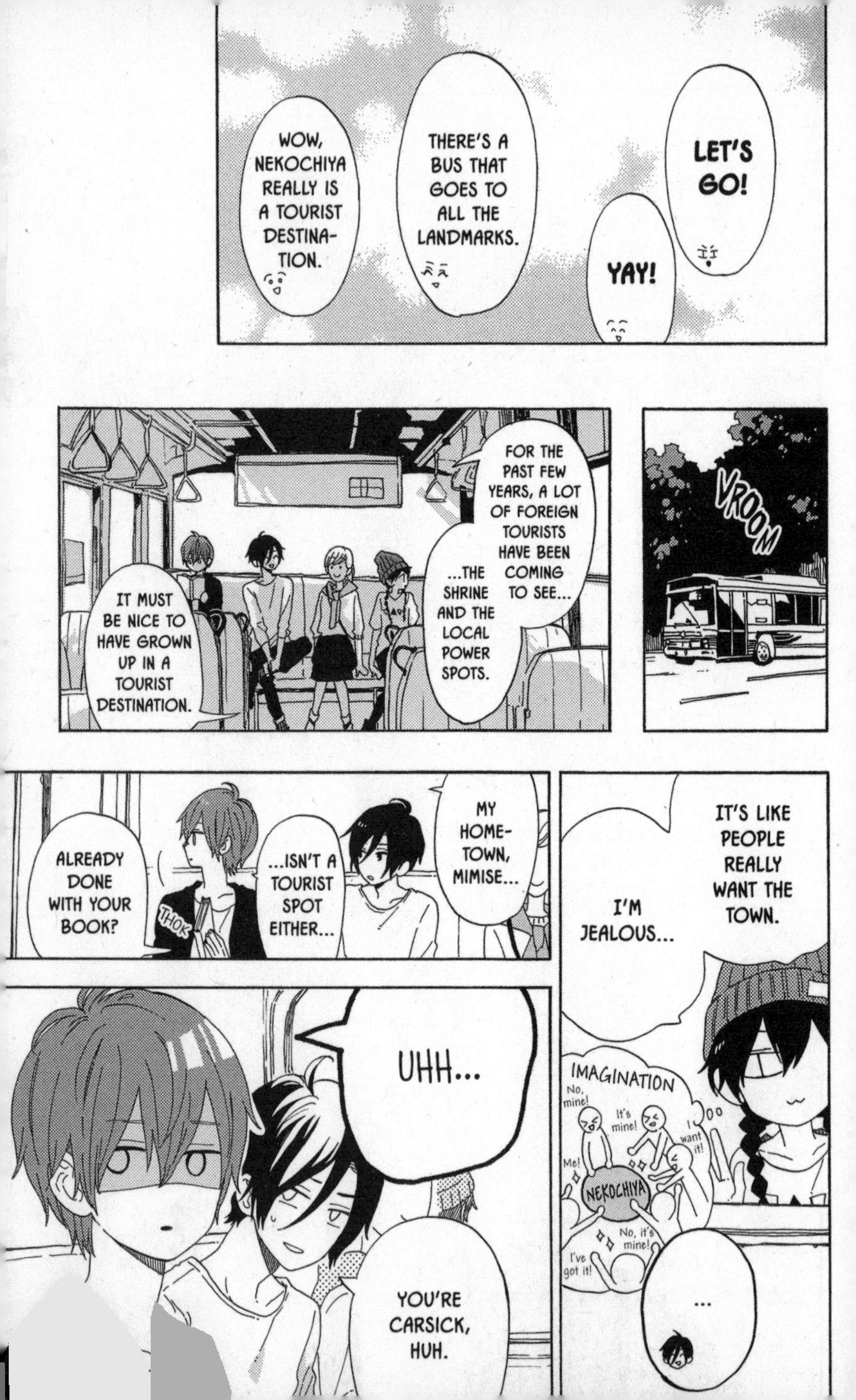
LET'S GO!
YAY!
THERE'S A BUS THAT GOES TO ALL THE LANDMARKS.
WOW, NEKOCHIYA REALLY IS A TOURIST DESTINATION.
VROOM
FOR THE PAST FEW YEARS, A LOT OF FOREIGN TOURISTS HAVE BEEN COMING TO SEE...
...THE SHRINE AND THE LOCAL POWER SPOTS.
IT MUST BE NICE TO HAVE GROWN UP IN A TOURIST DESTINATION.
IT'S LIKE PEOPLE REALLY WANT THE TOWN.
I'M JEALOUS...
IMAGINATION
No, mine!
It's mine!
I want it!
Me!
NEKOCHIYA
No, it's mine!
I've got it!
...
MY HOMETOWN, MIMISE...
...ISN'T A TOURIST SPOT EITHER...
THOK
ALREADY DONE WITH YOUR BOOK?
UHH...
YOU'RE CARSICK, HUH.

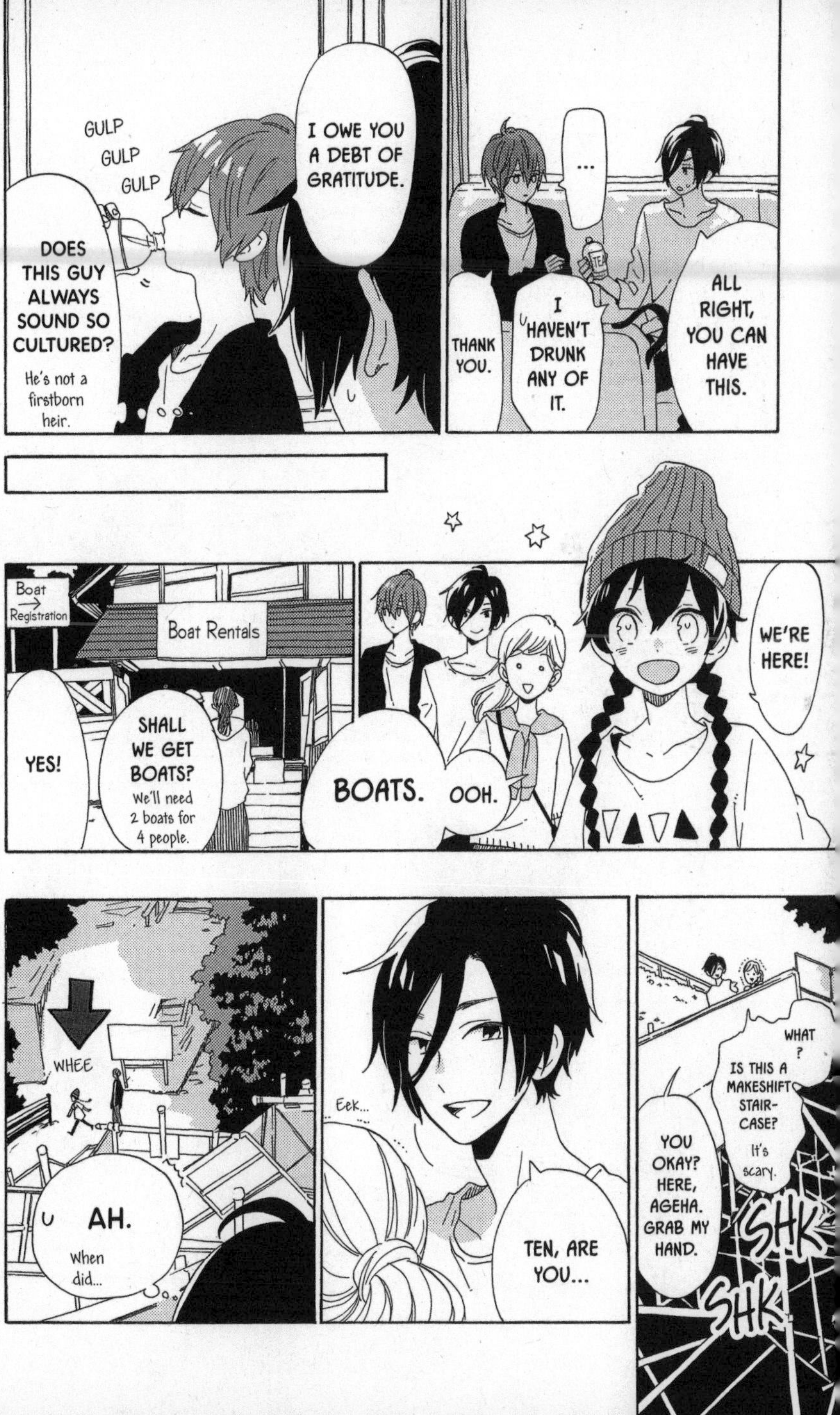
...
ALL RIGHT, YOU CAN HAVE THIS.
I HAVEN'T DRUNK ANY OF IT.
THANK YOU.
TEA
I OWE YOU A DEBT OF GRATITUDE.
GULP GULP GULP
DOES THIS GUY ALWAYS SOUND SO CULTURED?
He's not a firstborn heir.
WE'RE HERE!
OOH.
BOATS.
Boat Rentals
Boat → Registration
SHALL WE GET BOATS?
We'll need 2 boats for 4 people.
YES!
WHAT?
IS THIS A MAKESHIFT STAIRCASE?
It's scary.
YOU OKAY? HERE, AGEHA. GRAB MY HAND.
SHK
SHK
TEN, ARE YOU...
Eek...
WHEE
AH.
When did...

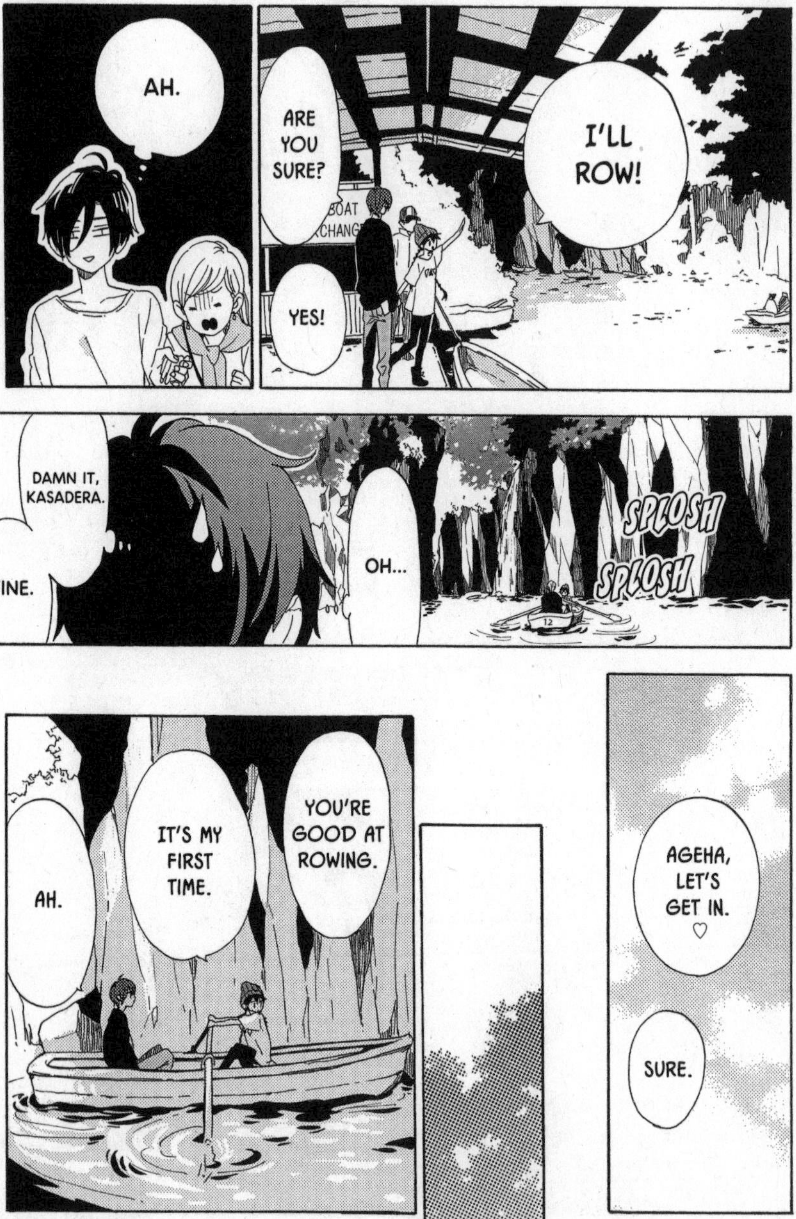
I'LL ROW!
ARE YOU SURE?
YES!
AH.
SPLOSH
SPLOSH
OH...
DAMN IT, KASADERA.
FINE.
AGEHA, LET'S GET IN. ♡
SURE.
YOU'RE GOOD AT ROWING.
IT'S MY FIRST TIME.
AH.

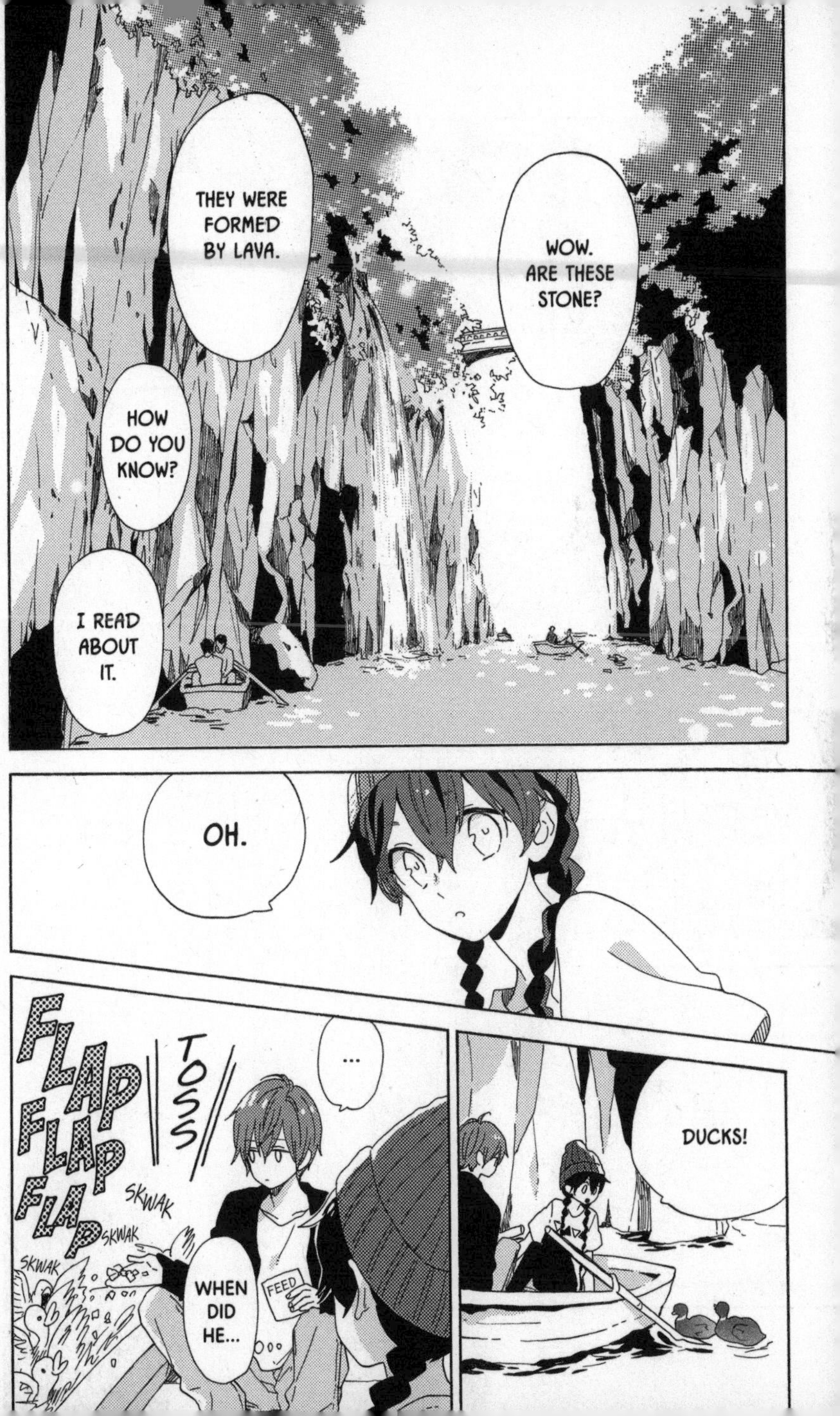
WOW. ARE THESE STONE?
THEY WERE FORMED BY LAVA.
HOW DO YOU KNOW?
I READ ABOUT IT.
OH.
DUCKS!
...
TOSS
FLAP FLAP FLAP
SKWAK
SKWAK
SKWAK
FEED
WHEN DID HE...

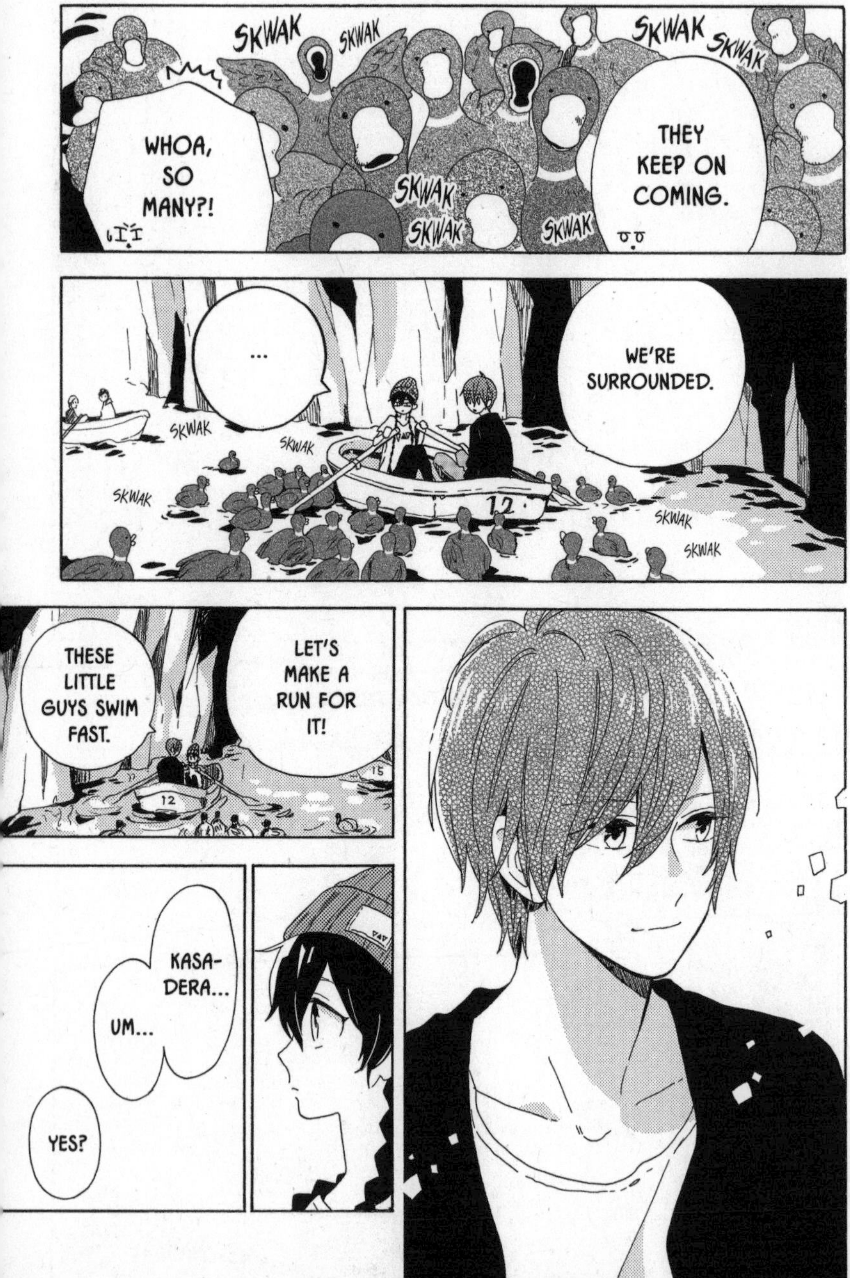
SKWAK SKWAK
THEY KEEP ON COMING.
SKWAK
SKWAK
SKWAK
SKWAK
SKWAK
WHOA, SO MANY?!
WE'RE SURROUNDED.
...
SKWAK
SKWAK
SKWAK
SKWAK
SKWAK
LET'S MAKE A RUN FOR IT!
THESE LITTLE GUYS SWIM FAST.
KASA-DERA...
UM...
YES?

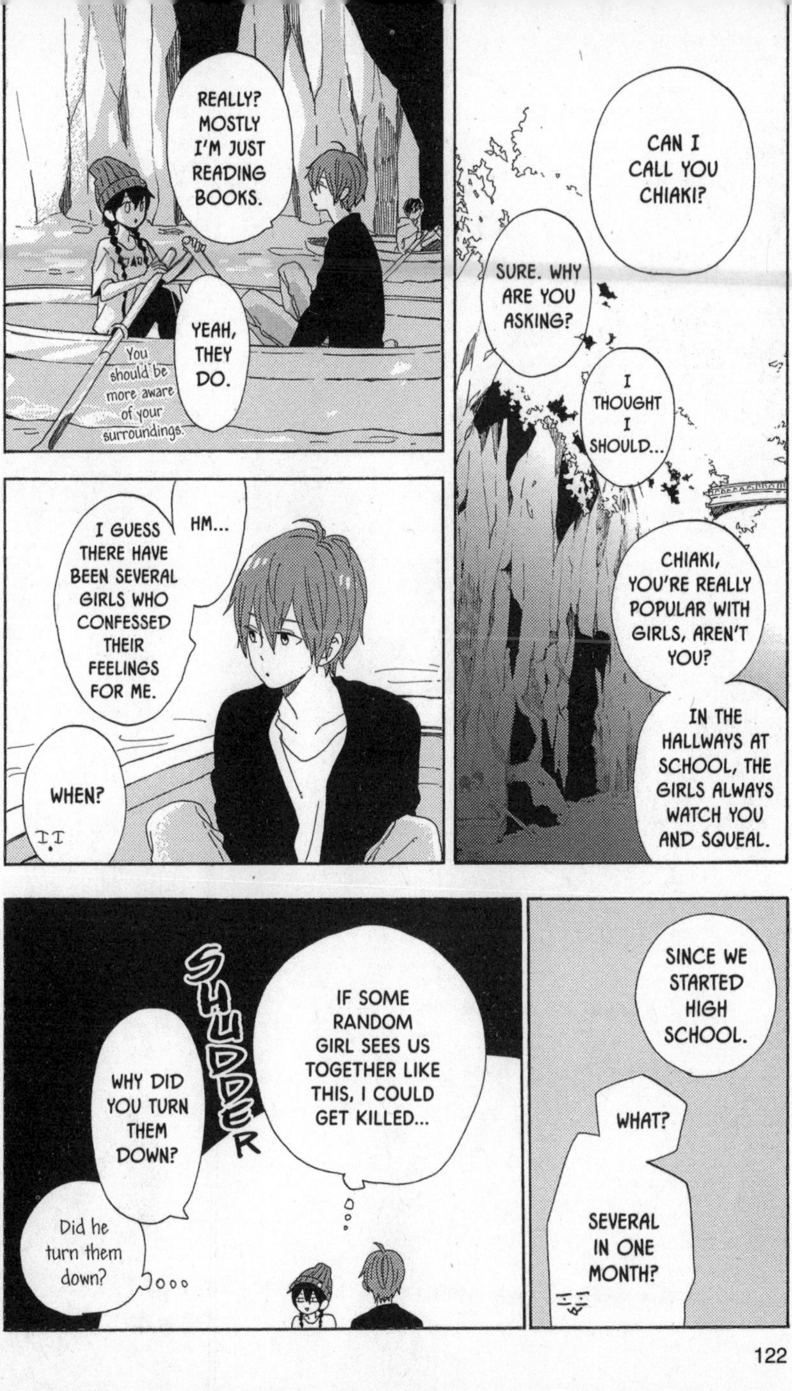
CAN I CALL YOU CHIAKI?
SURE. WHY ARE YOU ASKING?
I THOUGHT I SHOULD...
CHIAKI, YOU'RE REALLY POPULAR WITH GIRLS, AREN'T YOU?
IN THE HALLWAYS AT SCHOOL, THE GIRLS ALWAYS WATCH YOU AND SQUEAL.
REALLY? MOSTLY I'M JUST READING BOOKS.
YEAH, THEY DO.
You should be more aware of your surroundings.
HM...
I GUESS THERE HAVE BEEN SEVERAL GIRLS WHO CONFESSED THEIR FEELINGS FOR ME.
WHEN?
SINCE WE STARTED HIGH SCHOOL.
WHAT?
SEVERAL IN ONE MONTH?
IF SOME RANDOM GIRL SEES US TOGETHER LIKE THIS, I COULD GET KILLED...
SHUDDER
WHY DID YOU TURN THEM DOWN?
Did he turn them down?

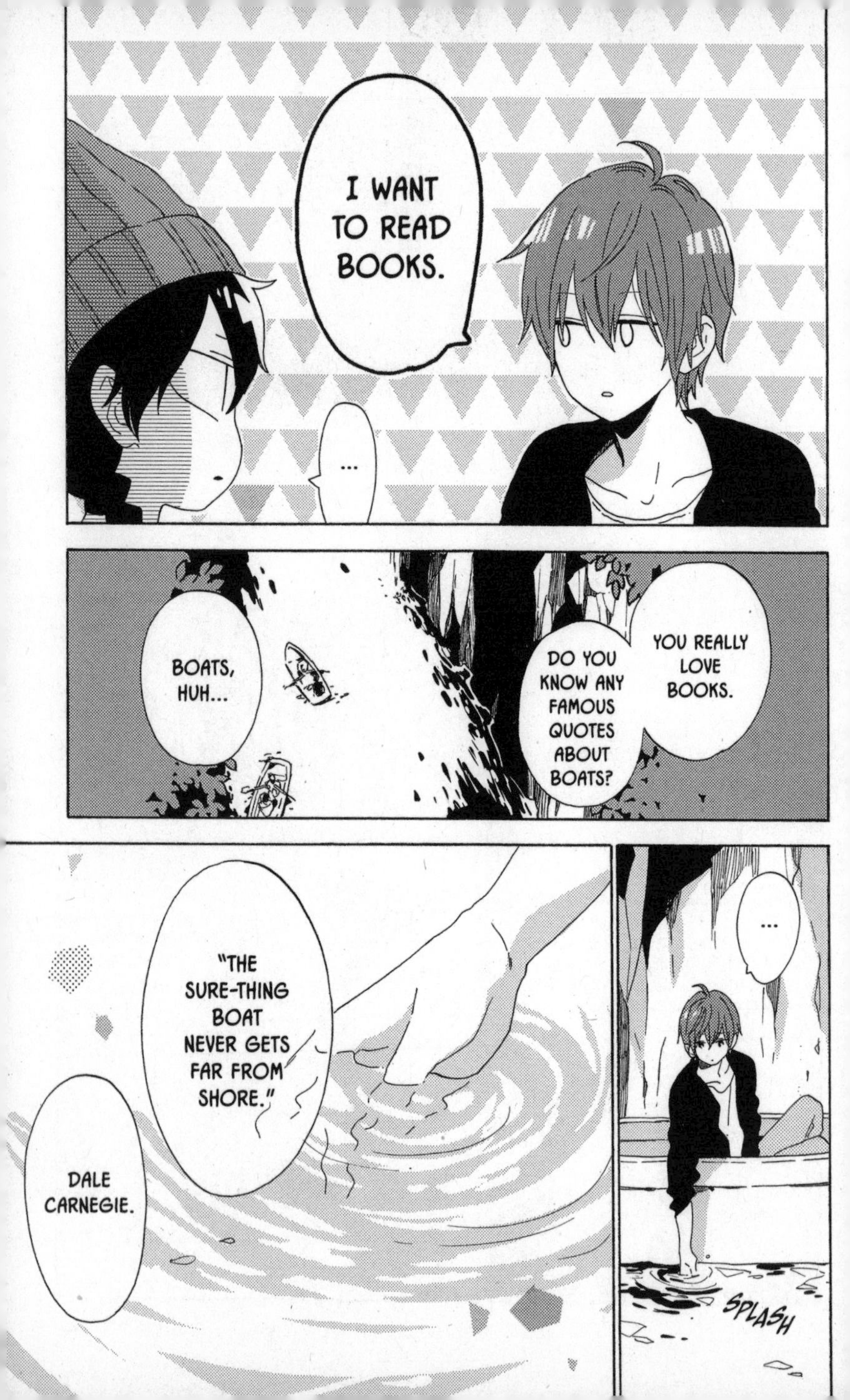
I WANT TO READ BOOKS.
...
YOU REALLY LOVE BOOKS.
DO YOU KNOW ANY FAMOUS QUOTES ABOUT BOATS?
BOATS, HUH...
...
SPLASH
"THE SURE-THING BOAT NEVER GETS FAR FROM SHORE."
DALE CARNEGIE.

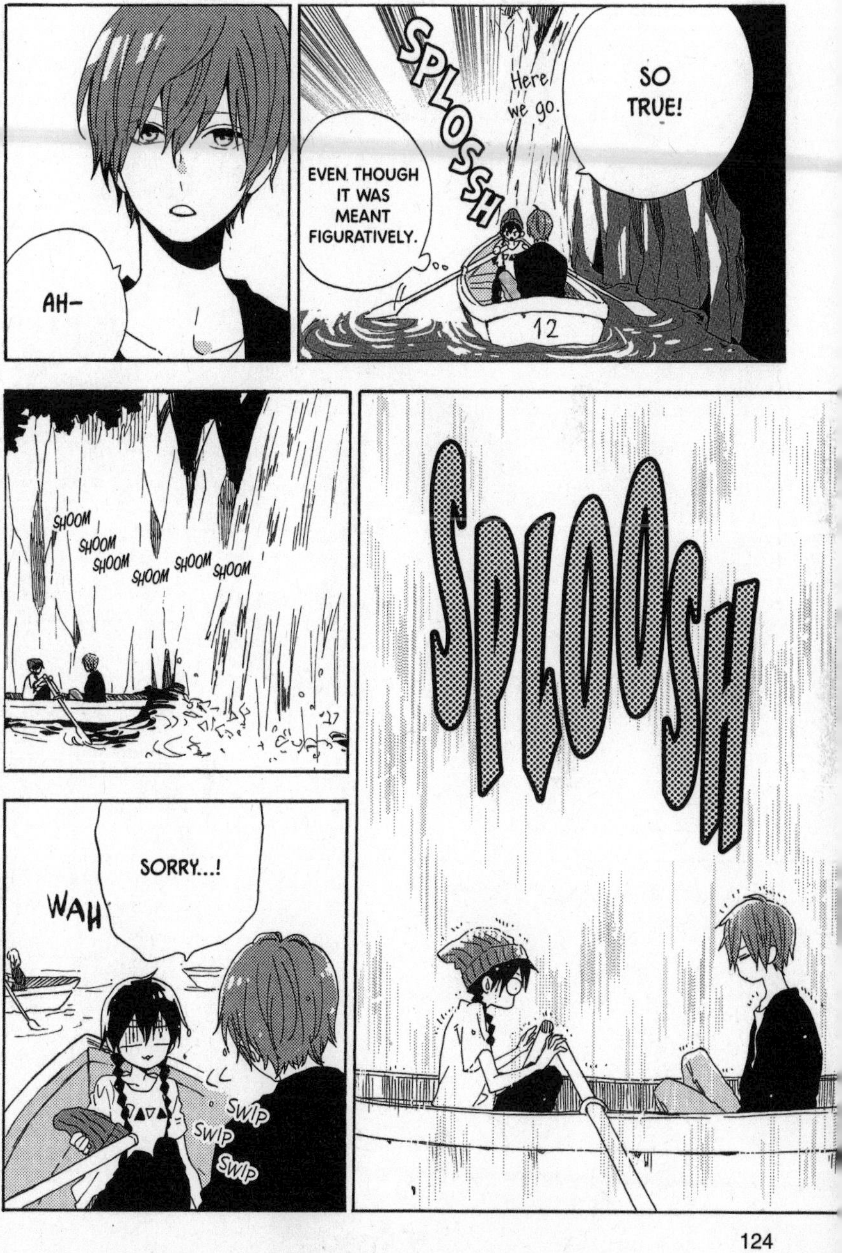
SO TRUE!
Here we go.
SPLOSH
EVEN THOUGH IT WAS MEANT FIGURATIVELY.
AH-
SPLOOSH
SHOOM SHOOM SHOOM SHOOM SHOOM SHOOM
SORRY...!
WAH
SWIP SWIP SWIP

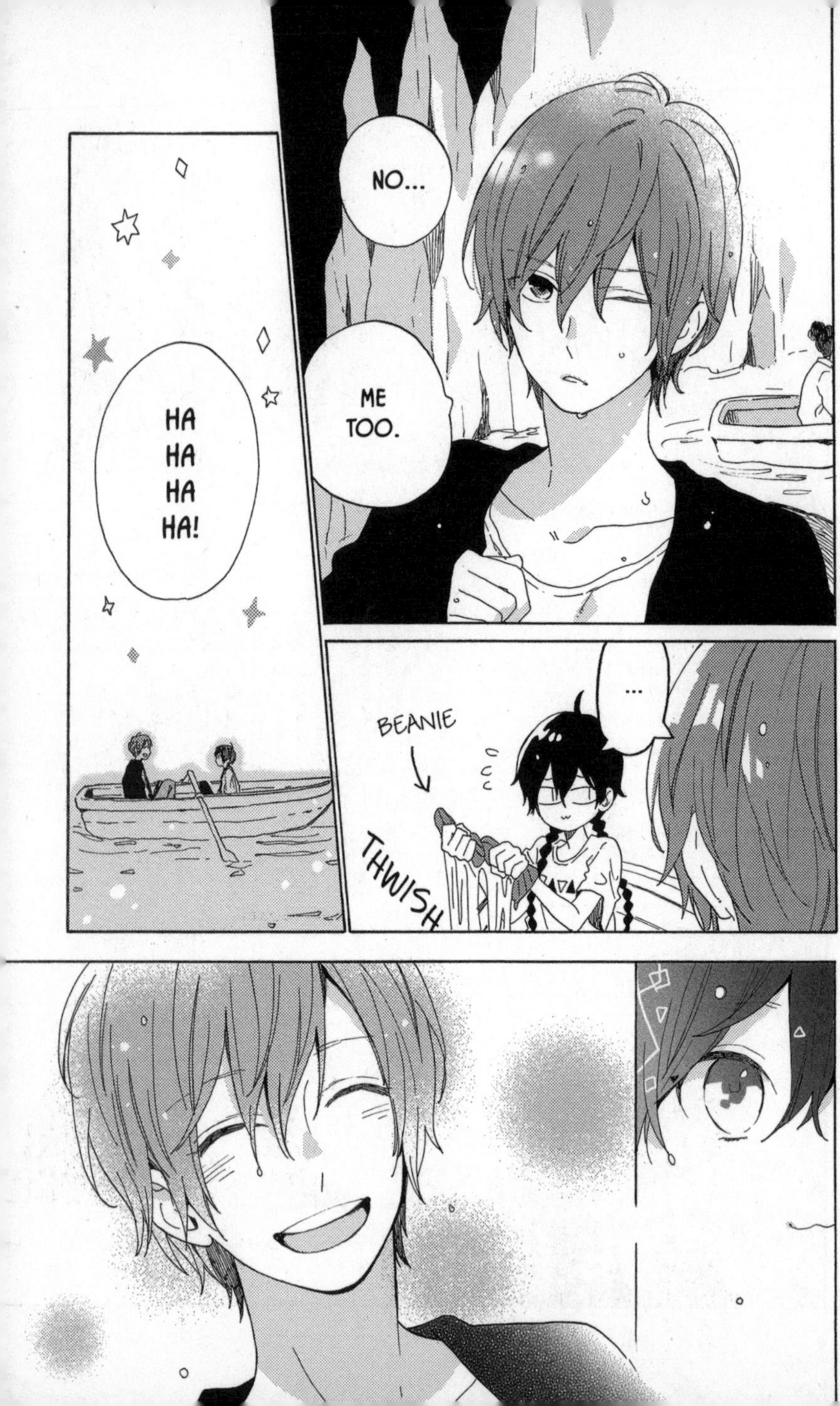
NO...
ME TOO.
...
BEANIE
THWISH
HA HA HA HA!

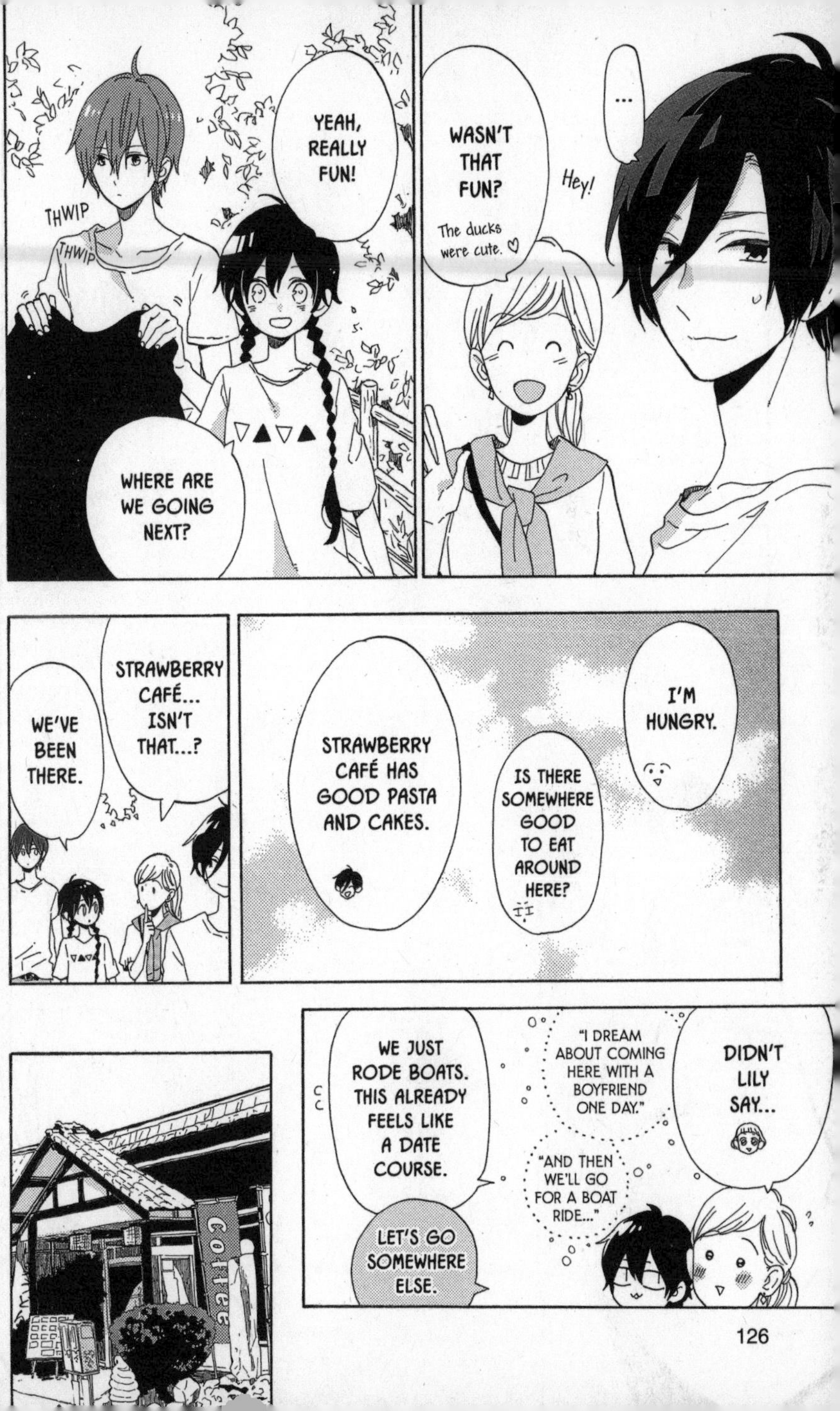
...
WASN'T THAT FUN?
The ducks were cute. ♡
Hey!
YEAH, REALLY FUN!
THWIP
THWIP
WHERE ARE WE GOING NEXT?
I'M HUNGRY.
IS THERE SOMEWHERE GOOD TO EAT AROUND HERE?
STRAWBERRY CAFÉ HAS GOOD PASTA AND CAKES.
STRAWBERRY CAFÉ... ISN'T THAT...?
WE'VE BEEN THERE.
DIDN'T LILY SAY...
"I DREAM ABOUT COMING HERE WITH A BOYFRIEND ONE DAY."
"AND THEN WE'LL GO FOR A BOAT RIDE..."
WE JUST RODE BOATS. THIS ALREADY FEELS LIKE A DATE COURSE.
LET'S GO SOMEWHERE ELSE.
coffee

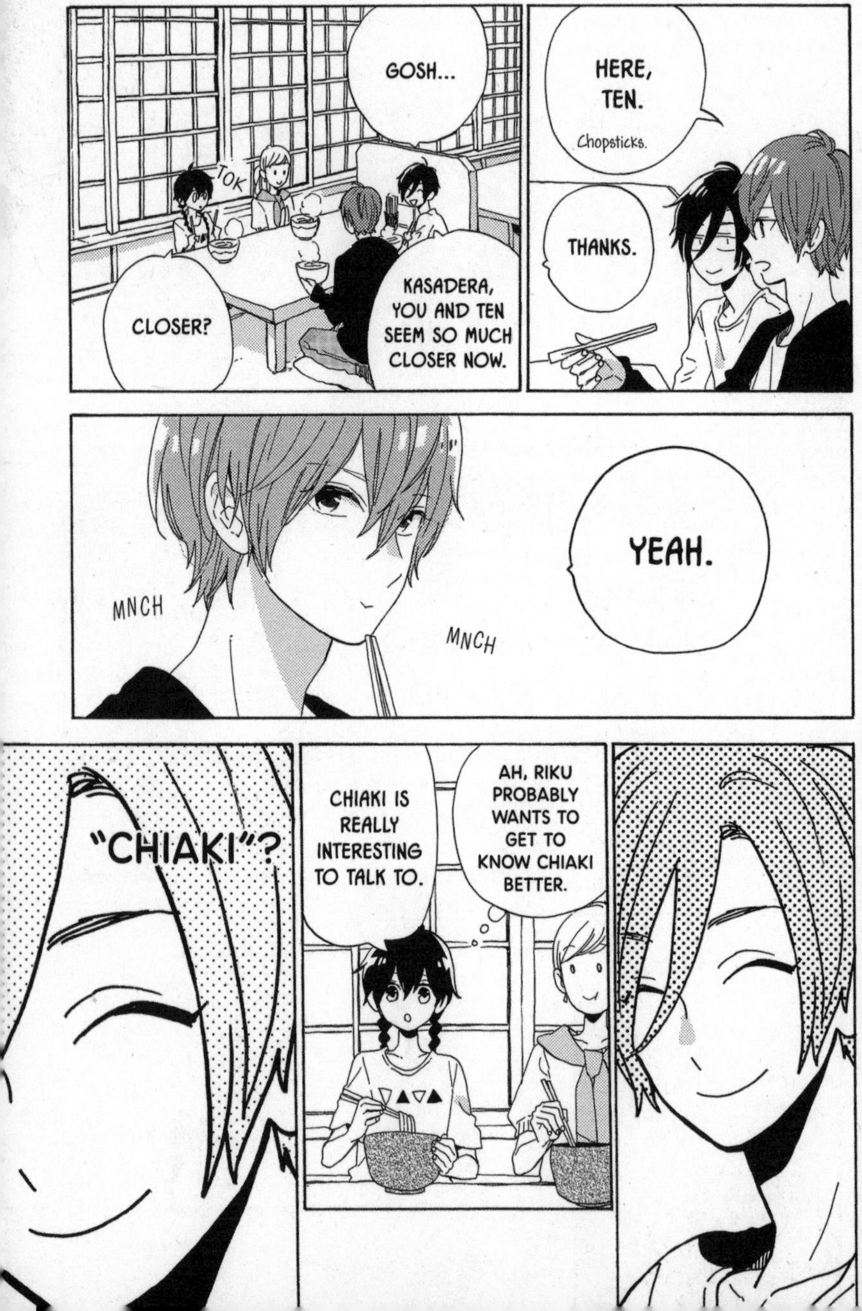
HERE, TEN.
Chopsticks.
THANKS.
GOSH...
TOK
KASADERA, YOU AND TEN SEEM SO MUCH CLOSER NOW.
CLOSER?
YEAH.
MNCH
MNCH
AH, RIKU PROBABLY WANTS TO GET TO KNOW CHIAKI BETTER.
CHIAKI IS REALLY INTERESTING TO TALK TO.
"CHIAKI"?

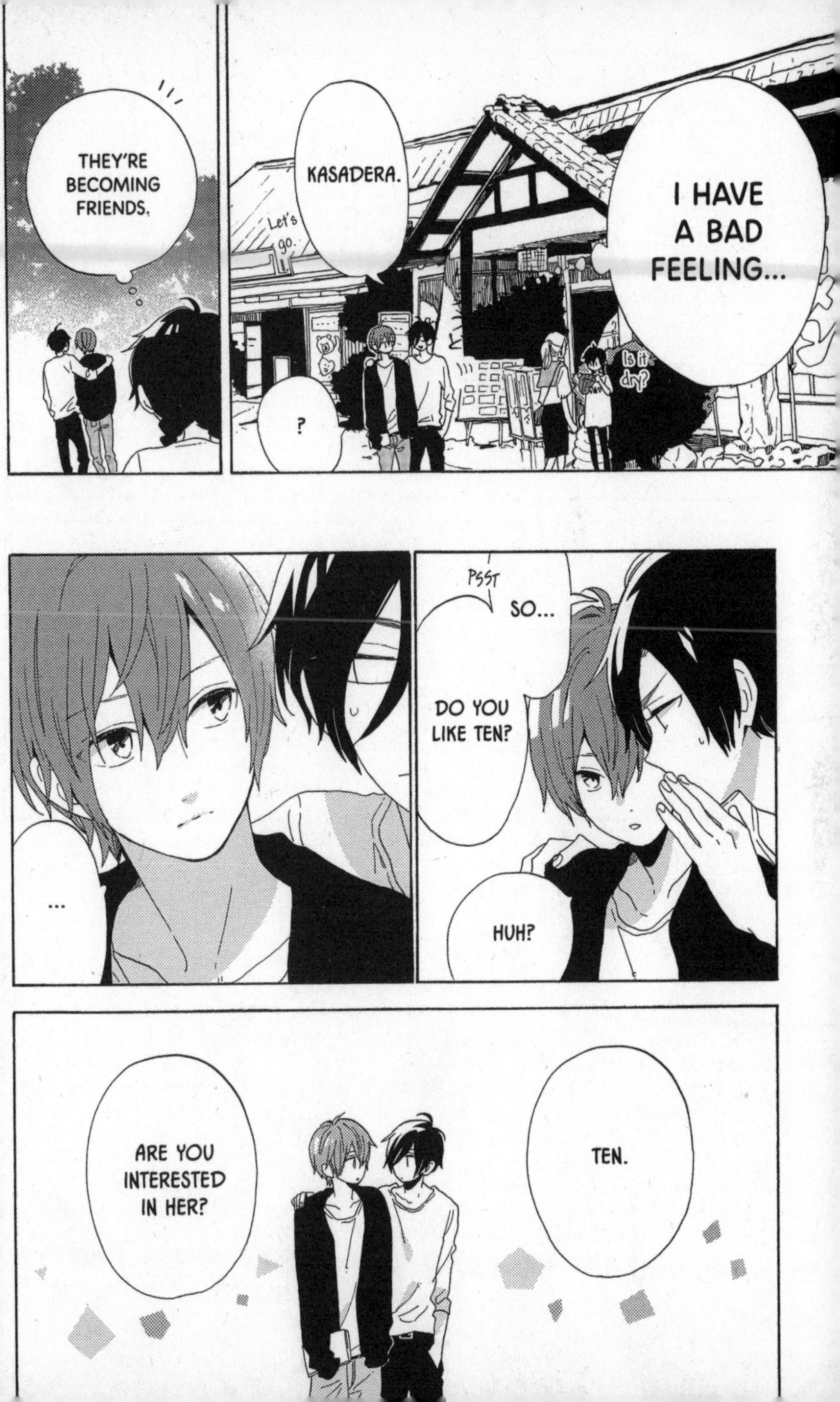
I HAVE A BAD FEELING...
KASADERA.
Let's go.
Is it dry?
?
THEY'RE BECOMING FRIENDS.
PSST
SO...
DO YOU LIKE TEN?
HUH?
...
TEN.
ARE YOU INTERESTED IN HER?

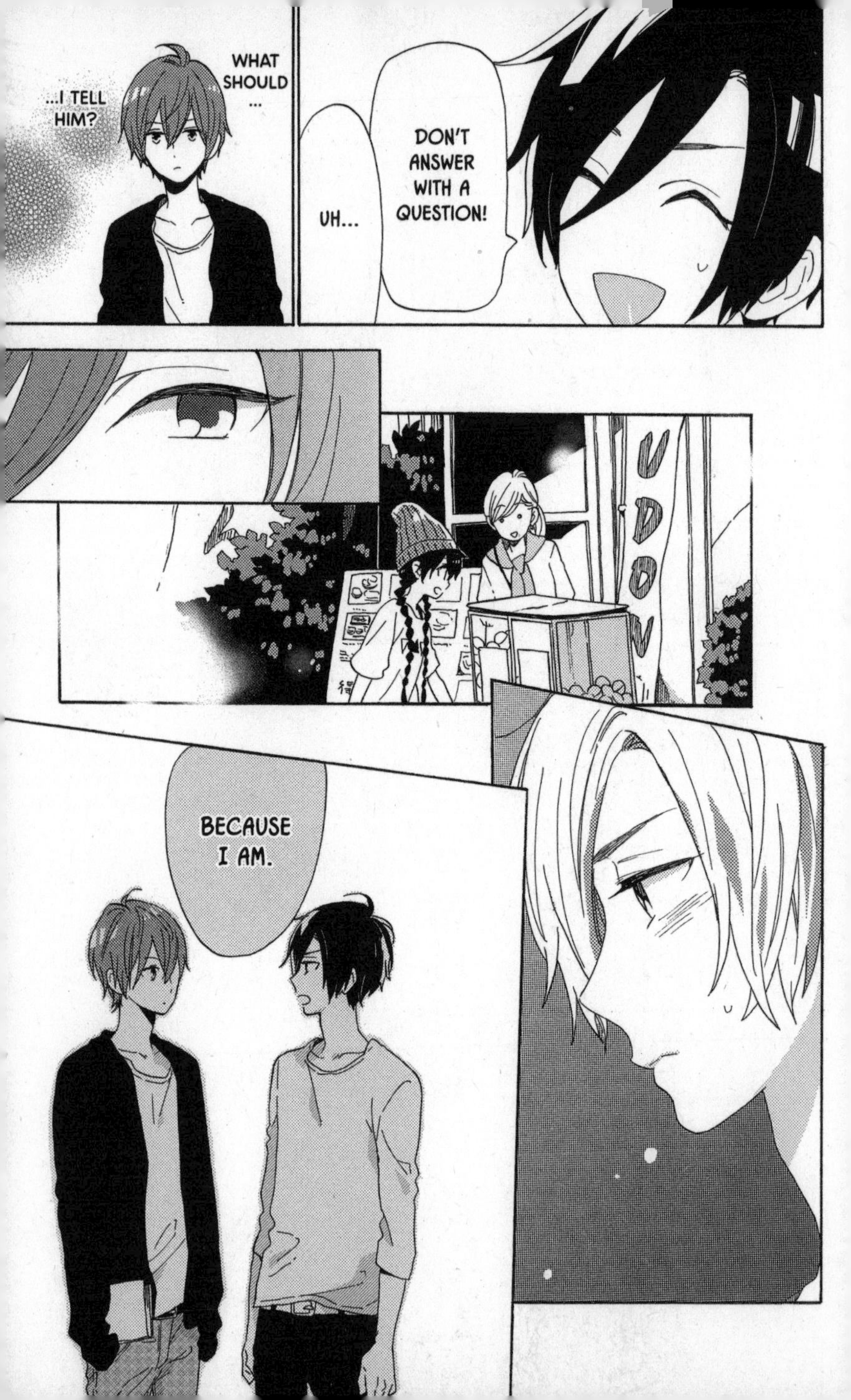
DON'T ANSWER WITH A QUESTION!
UH...
WHAT SHOULD ...
...I TELL HIM?
BECAUSE I AM.

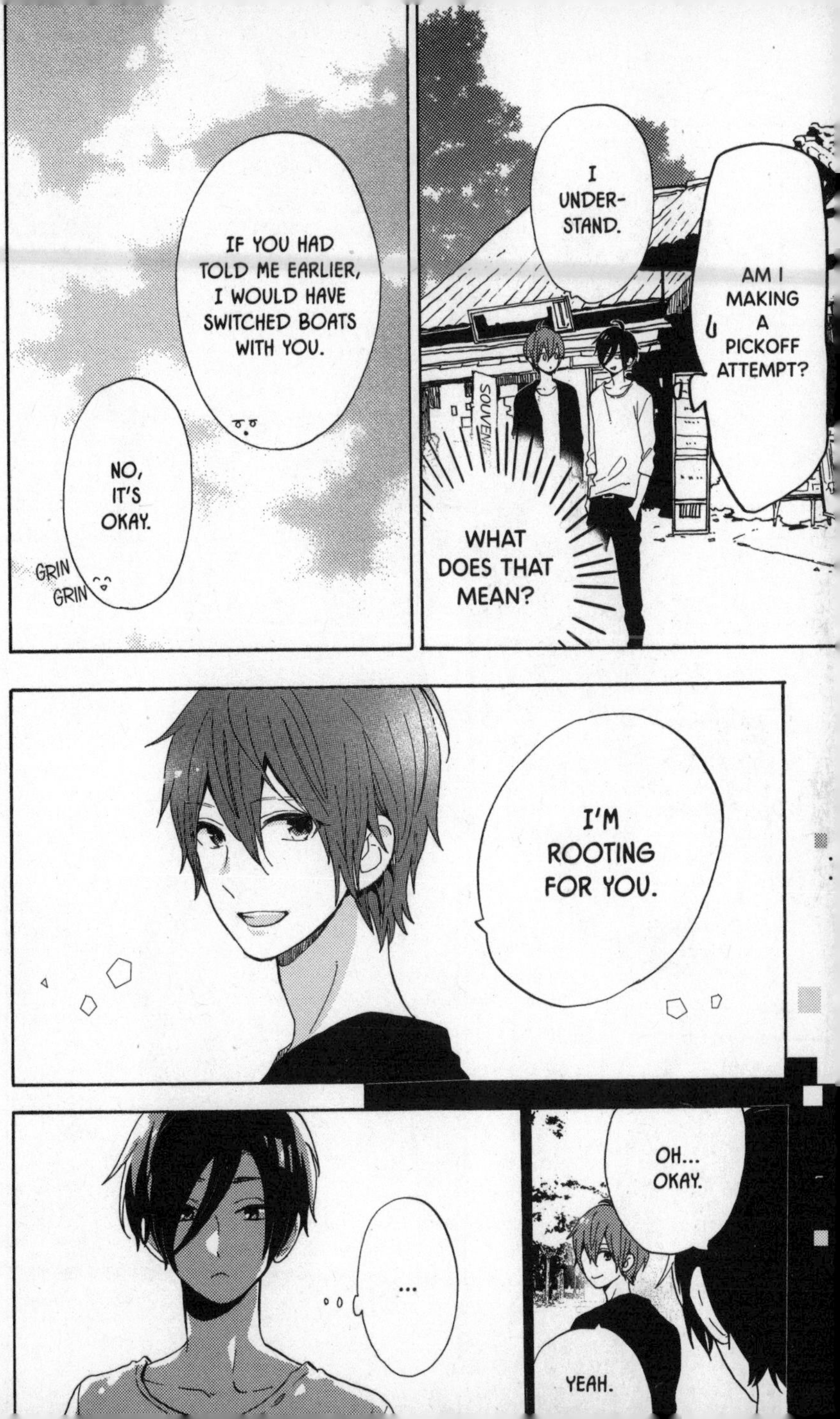
AM I MAKING A PICKOFF ATTEMPT?
I UNDER-STAND.
SOUVENI
WHAT DOES THAT MEAN?
IF YOU HAD TOLD ME EARLIER, I WOULD HAVE SWITCHED BOATS WITH YOU.
NO, IT'S OKAY.
GRIN GRIN
I'M ROOTING FOR YOU.
OH... OKAY.
YEAH.
...

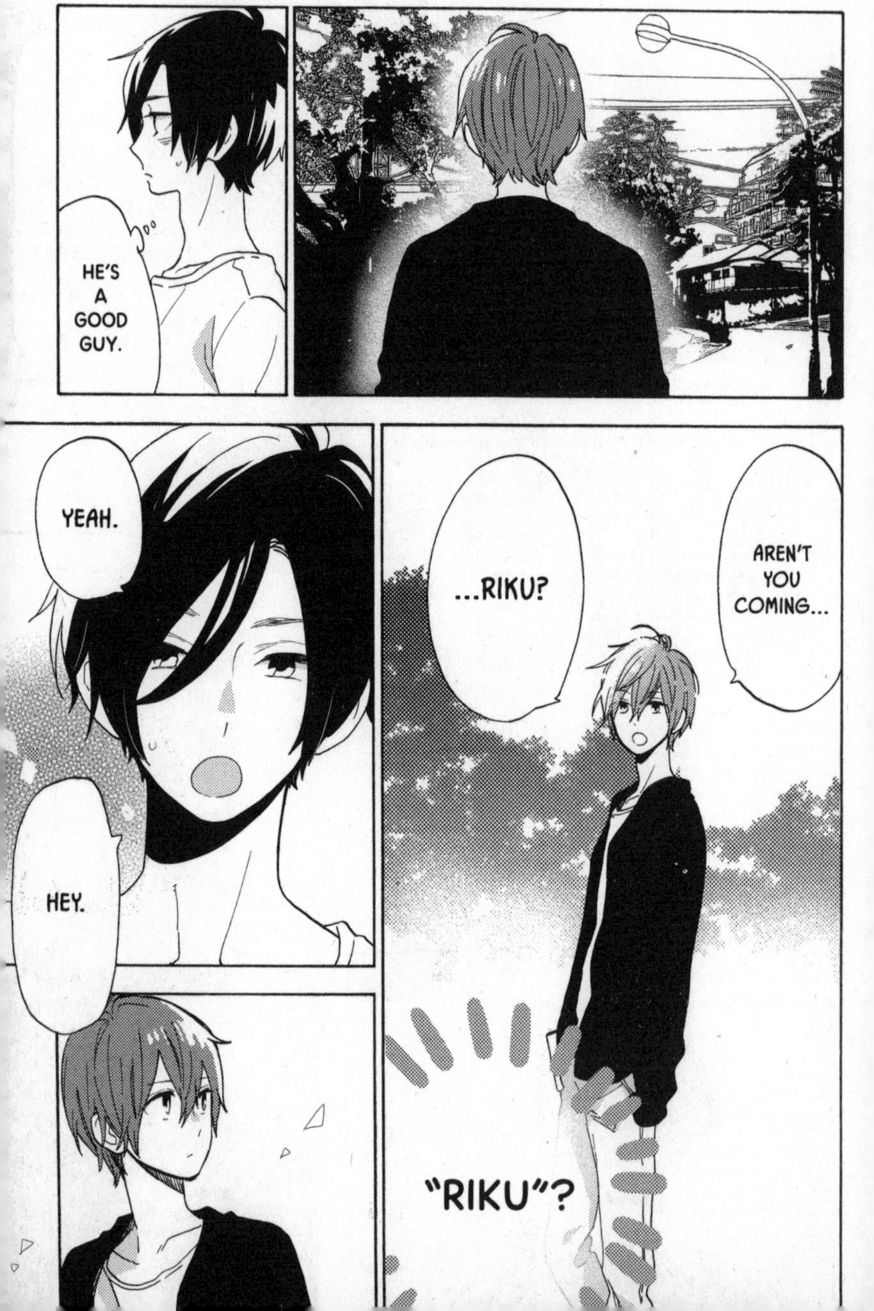
HE'S A GOOD GUY.
AREN'T YOU COMING...
...RIKU?
"RIKU"?
YEAH.
HEY.

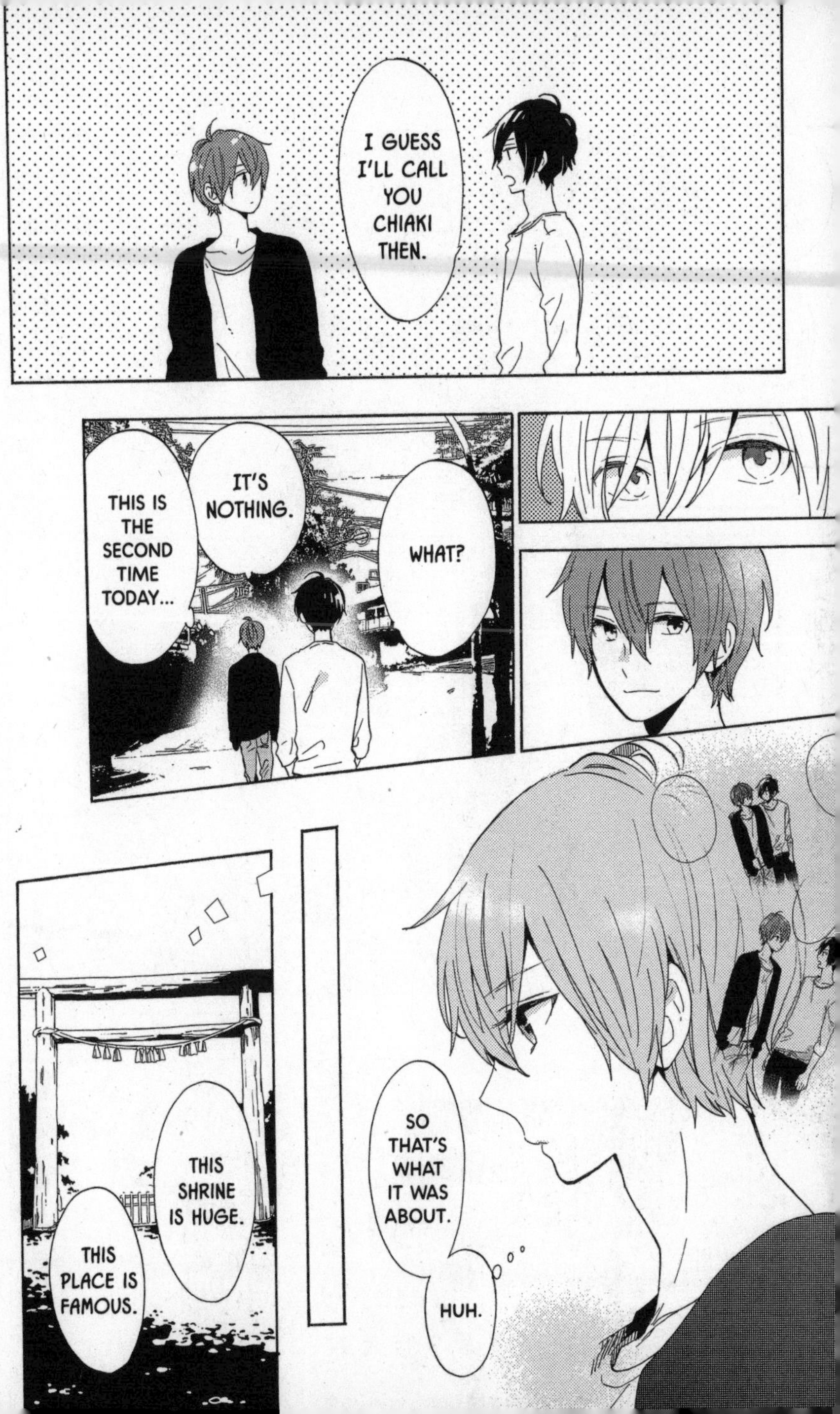
I GUESS I'LL CALL YOU CHIAKI THEN.
WHAT?
IT'S NOTHING.
THIS IS THE SECOND TIME TODAY...
SO THAT'S WHAT IT WAS ABOUT.
HUH.
THIS SHRINE IS HUGE.
THIS PLACE IS FAMOUS.

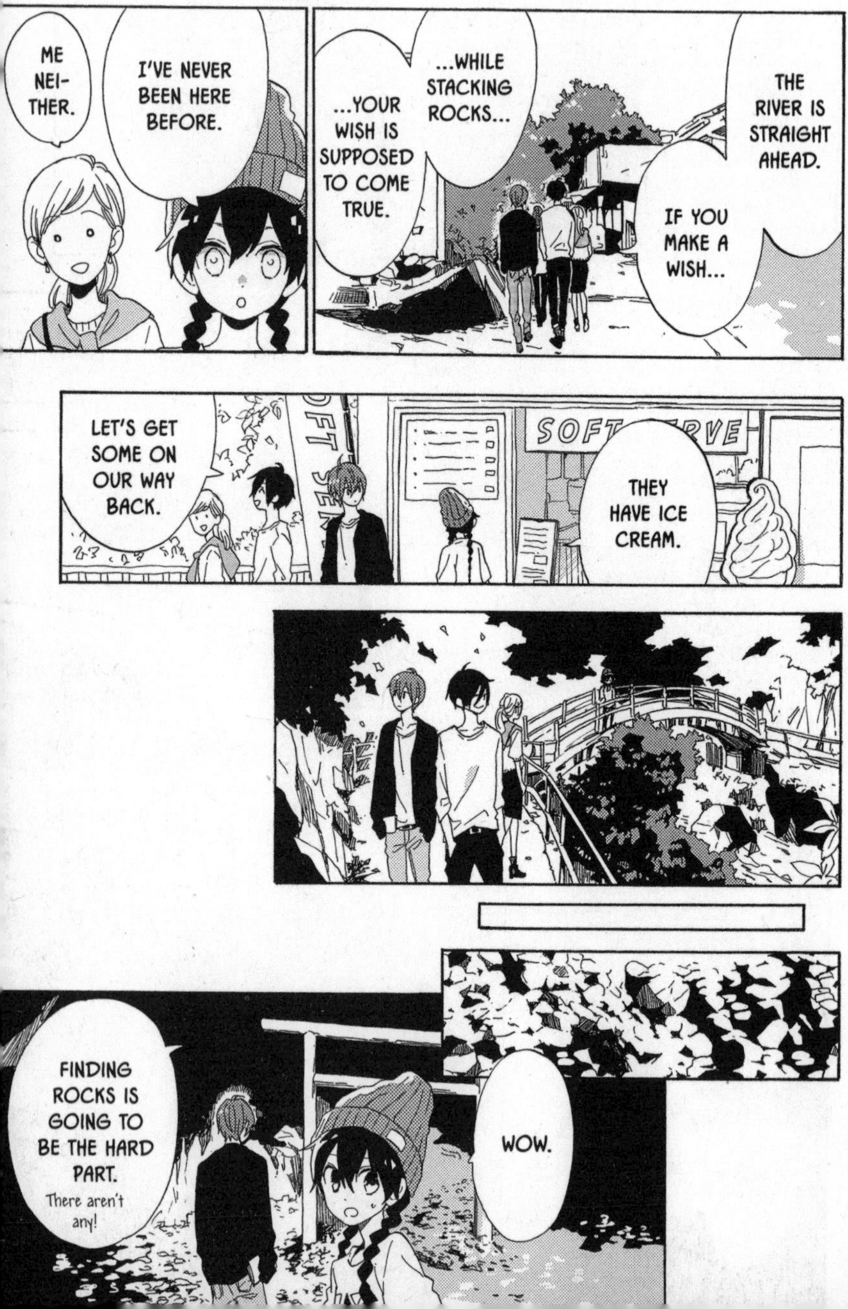
THE RIVER IS STRAIGHT AHEAD.
IF YOU MAKE A WISH...
...WHILE STACKING ROCKS...
...YOUR WISH IS SUPPOSED TO COME TRUE.
I'VE NEVER BEEN HERE BEFORE.
ME NEI-THER.
THEY HAVE ICE CREAM.
LET'S GET SOME ON OUR WAY BACK.
WOW.
FINDING ROCKS IS GOING TO BE THE HARD PART.
There aren't any!

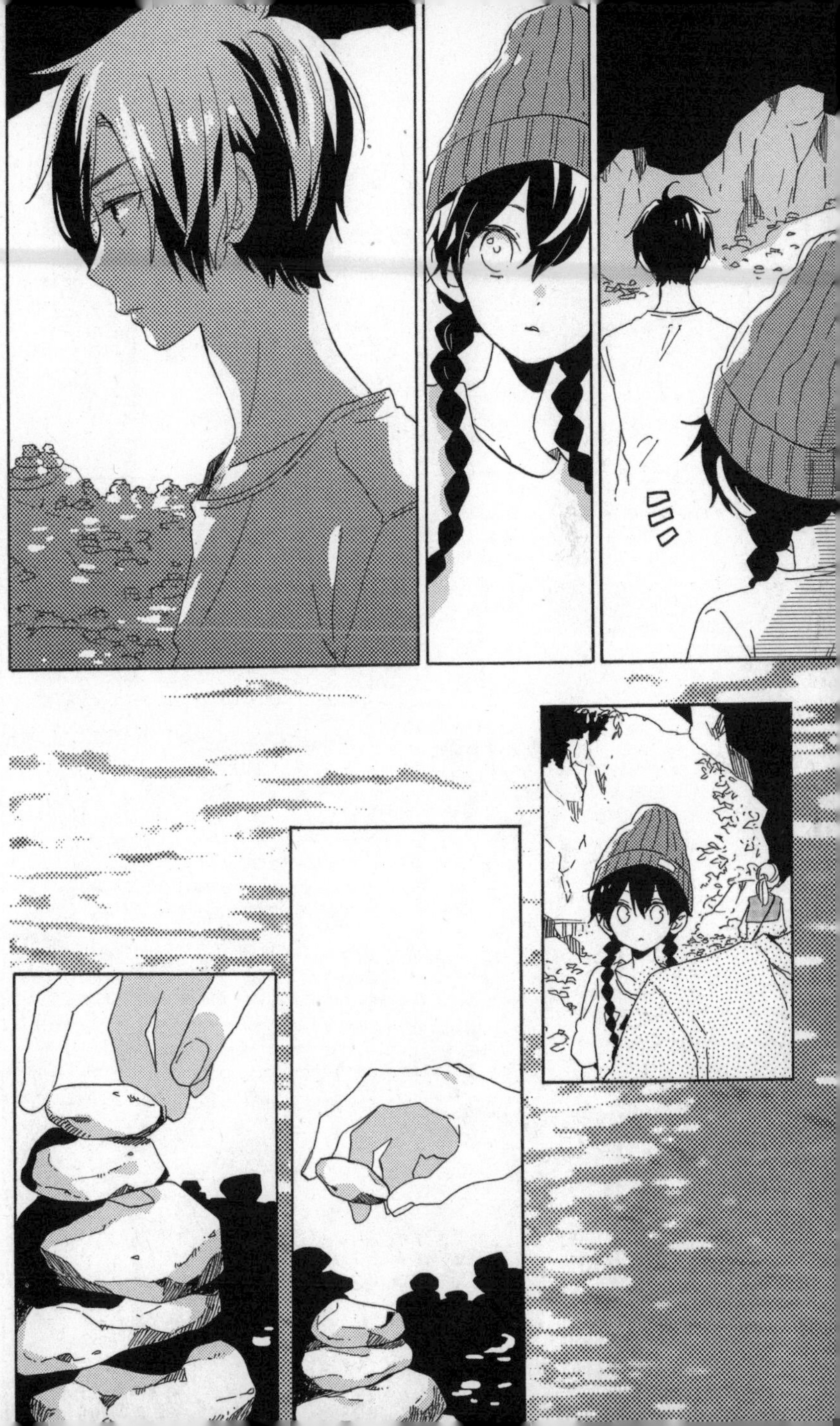

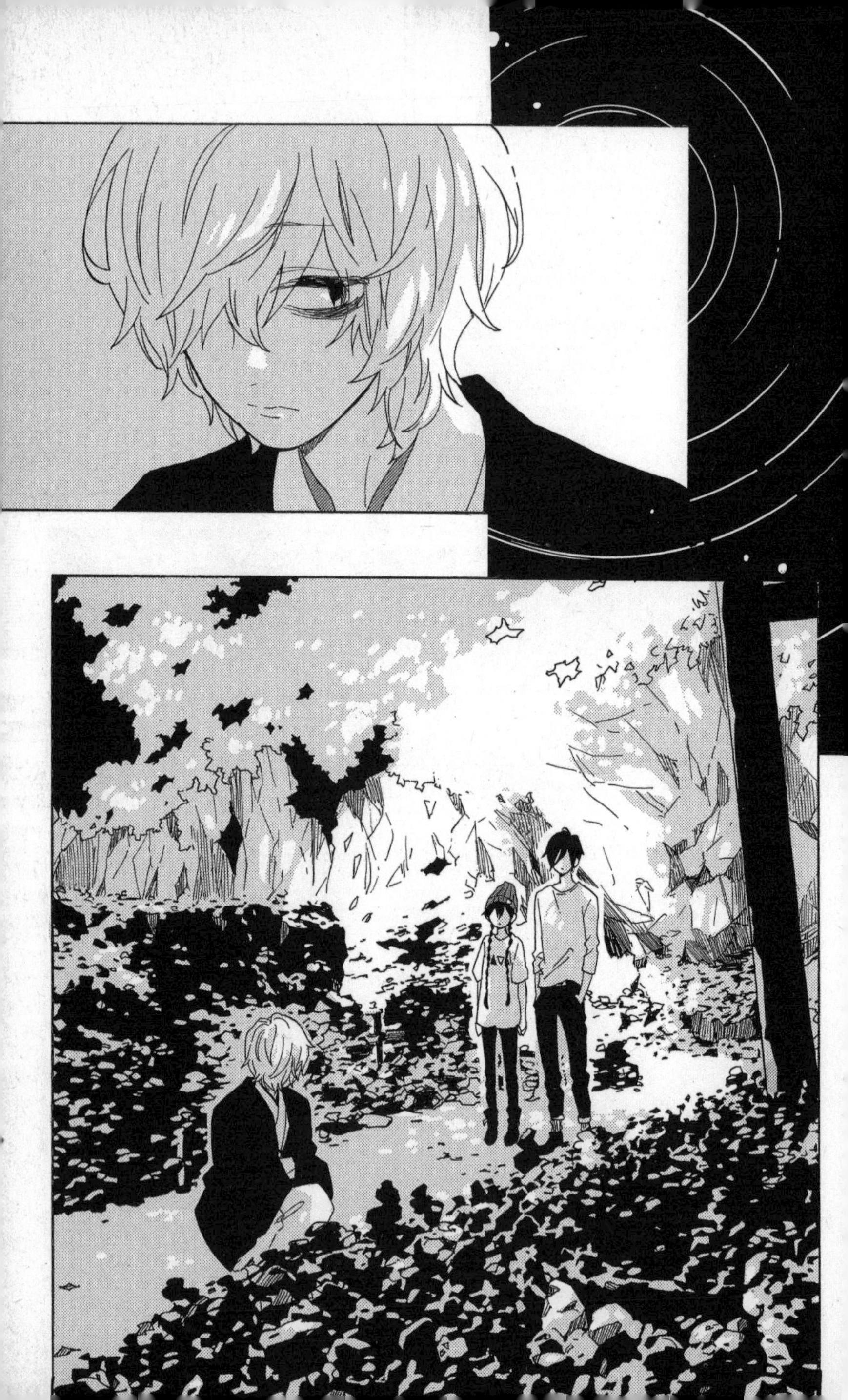

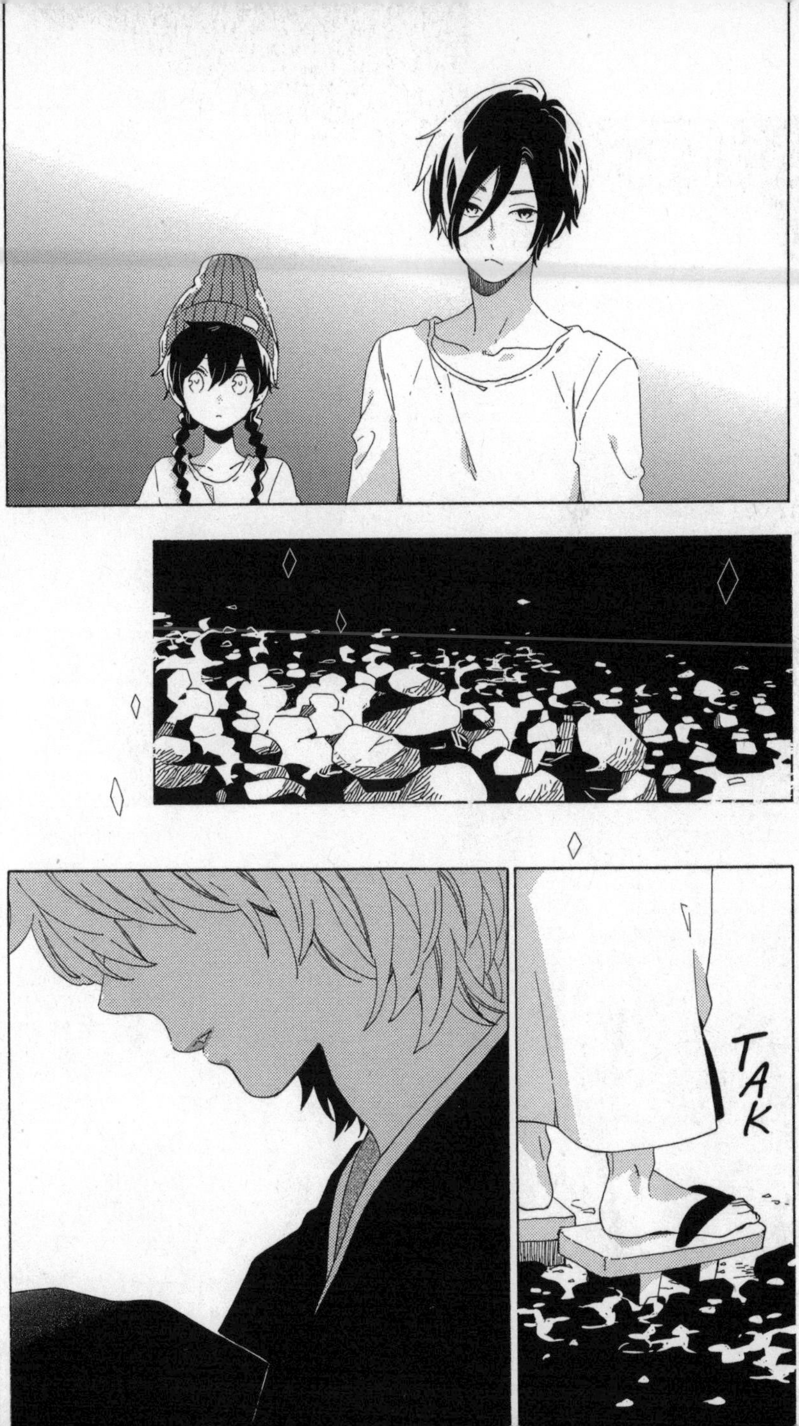
TAK

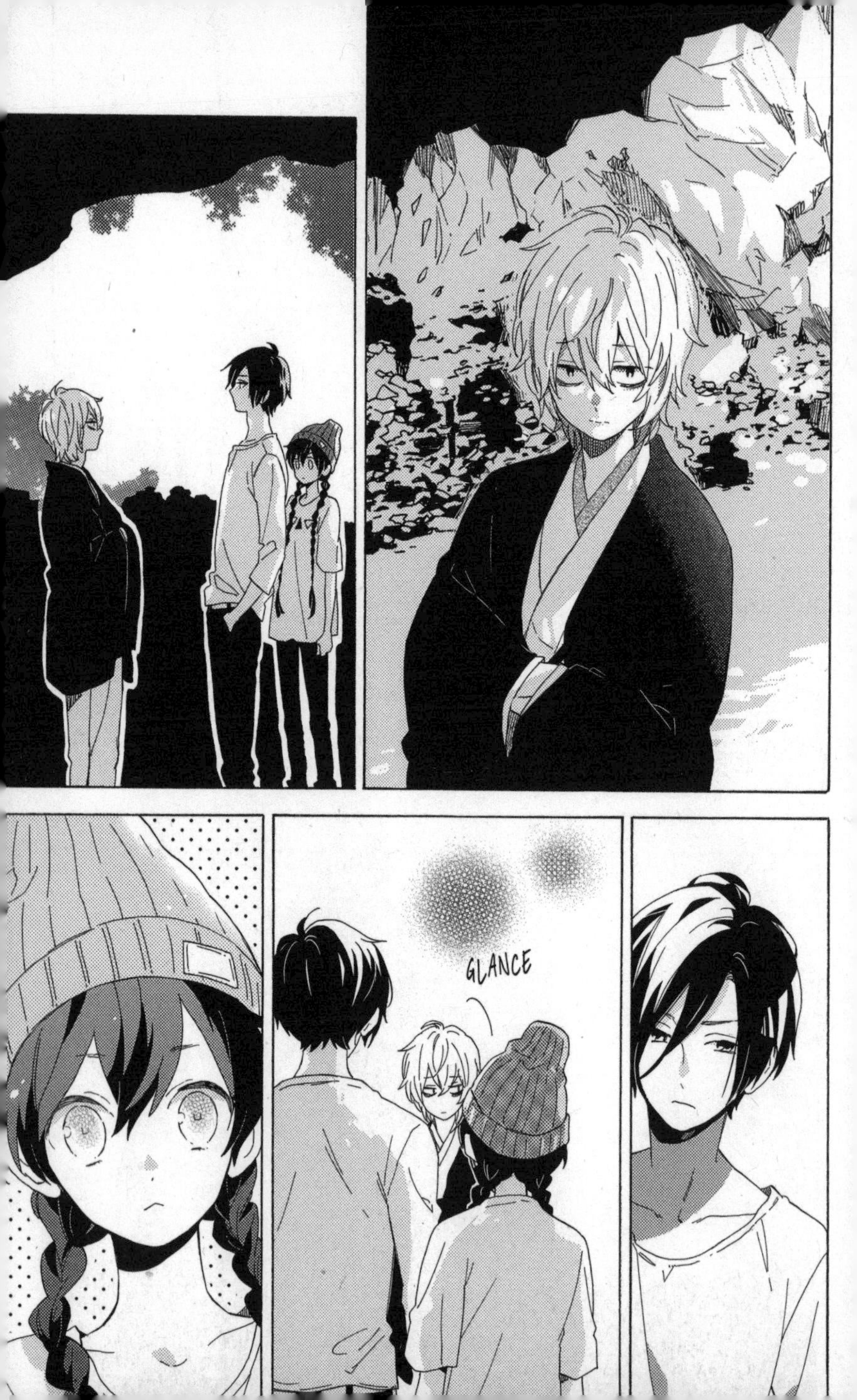
GLANCE

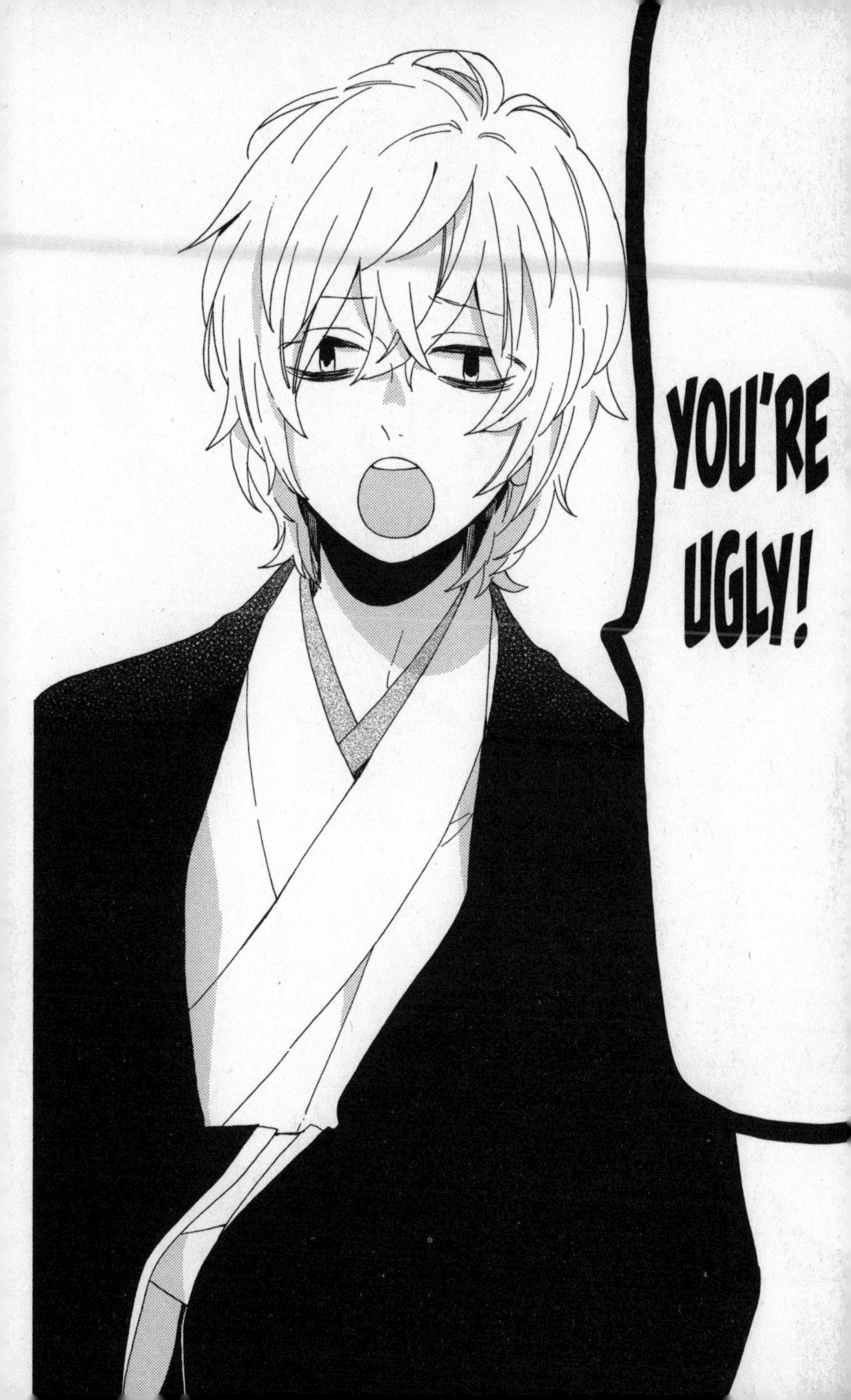
YOU'RE UGLY!

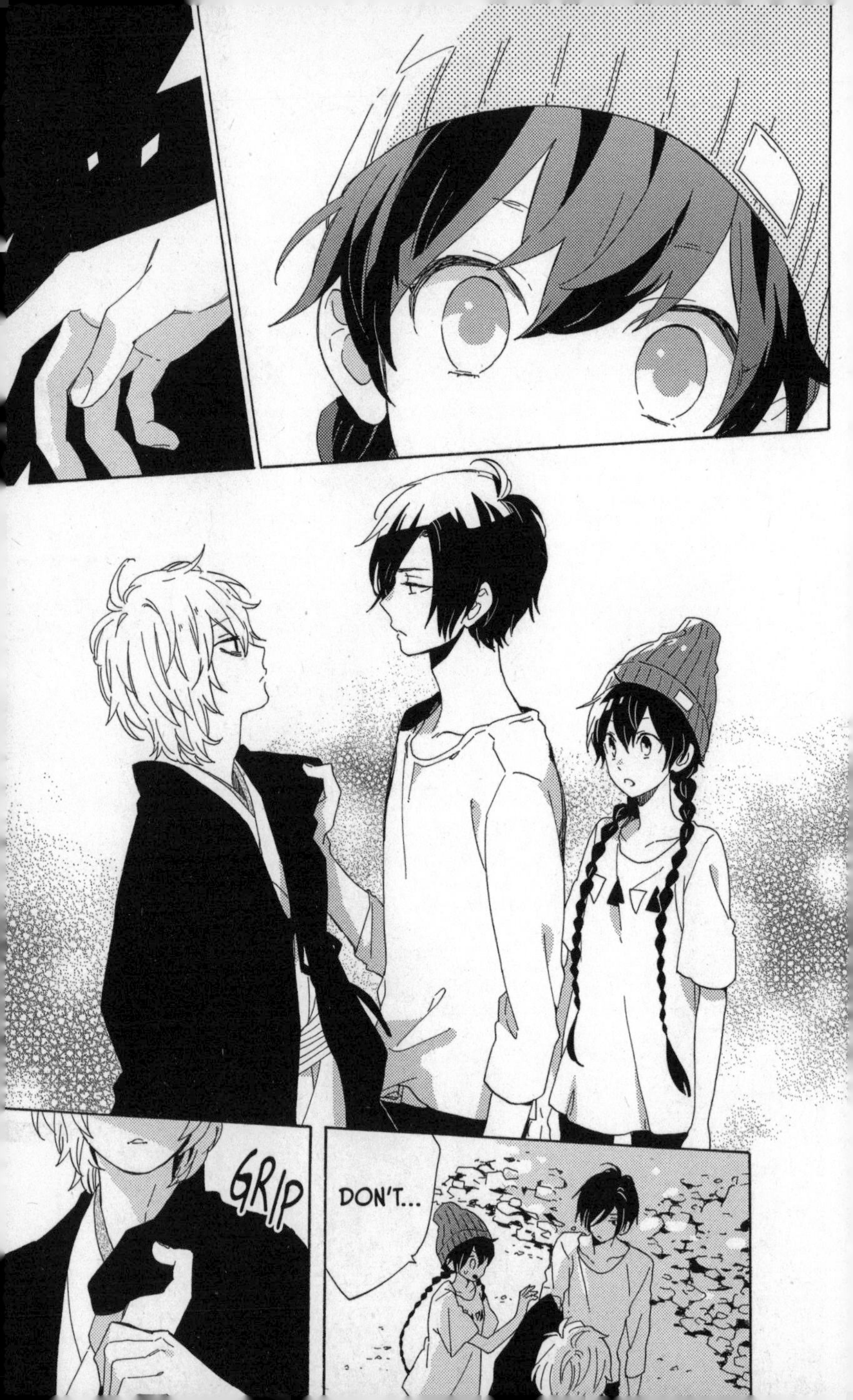
DON'T...
GRIP

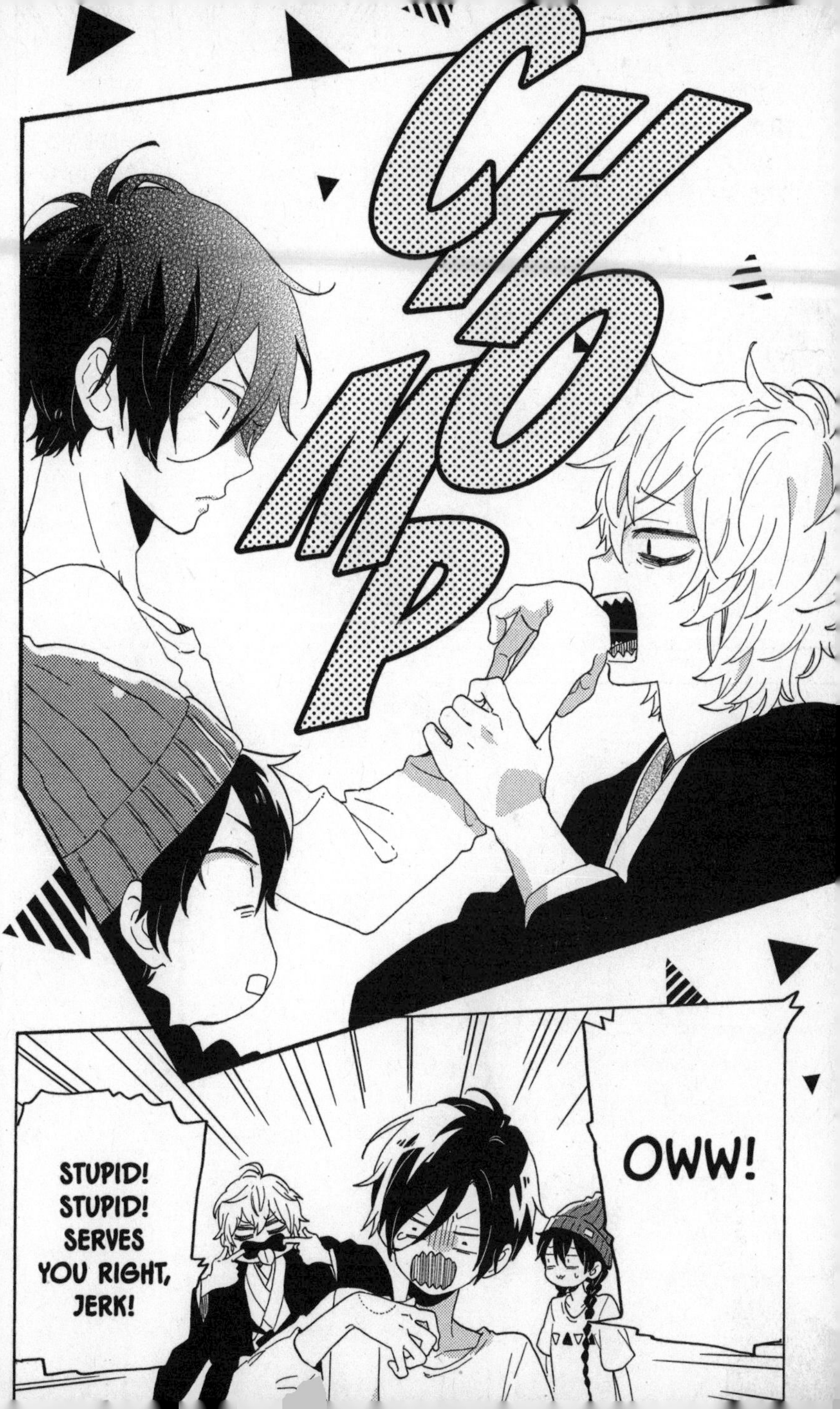
CHOMP
OWW!
STUPID! STUPID! SERVES YOU RIGHT, JERK!

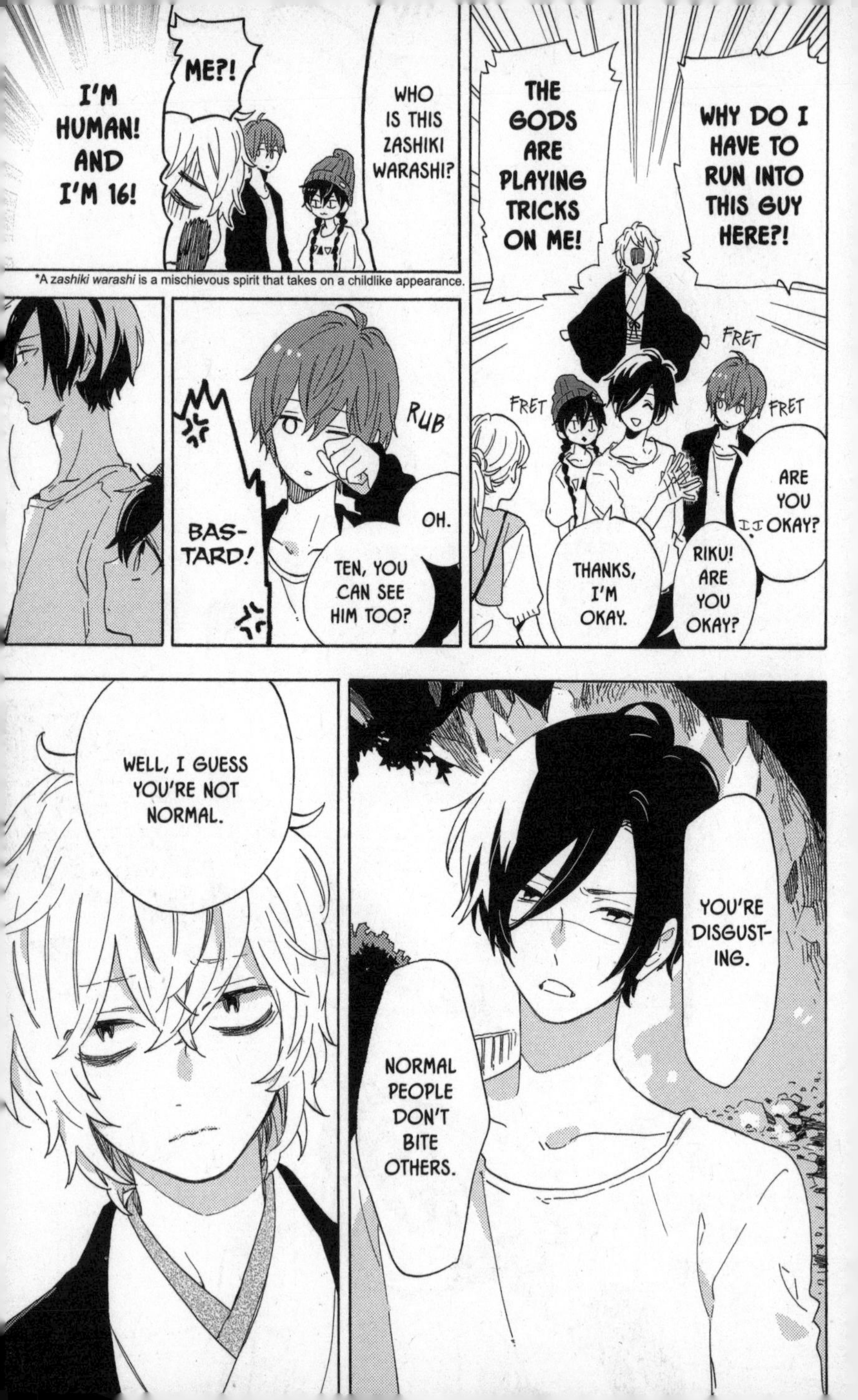
WHY DO I HAVE TO RUN INTO THIS GUY HERE?!
THE GODS ARE PLAYING TRICKS ON ME!
FRET
FRET
ARE YOU OKAY?
RIKU! ARE YOU OKAY?
FRET
THANKS, I'M OKAY.
WHO IS THIS ZASHIKI WARASHI?
ME?!
I'M HUMAN! AND I'M 16!
RUB
OH.
TEN, YOU CAN SEE HIM TOO?
BAS-TARD!
YOU'RE DISGUST-ING.
NORMAL PEOPLE DON'T BITE OTHERS.
WELL, I GUESS YOU'RE NOT NORMAL.
*A *zashiki warashi* is a mischievous spirit that takes on a childlike appearance.

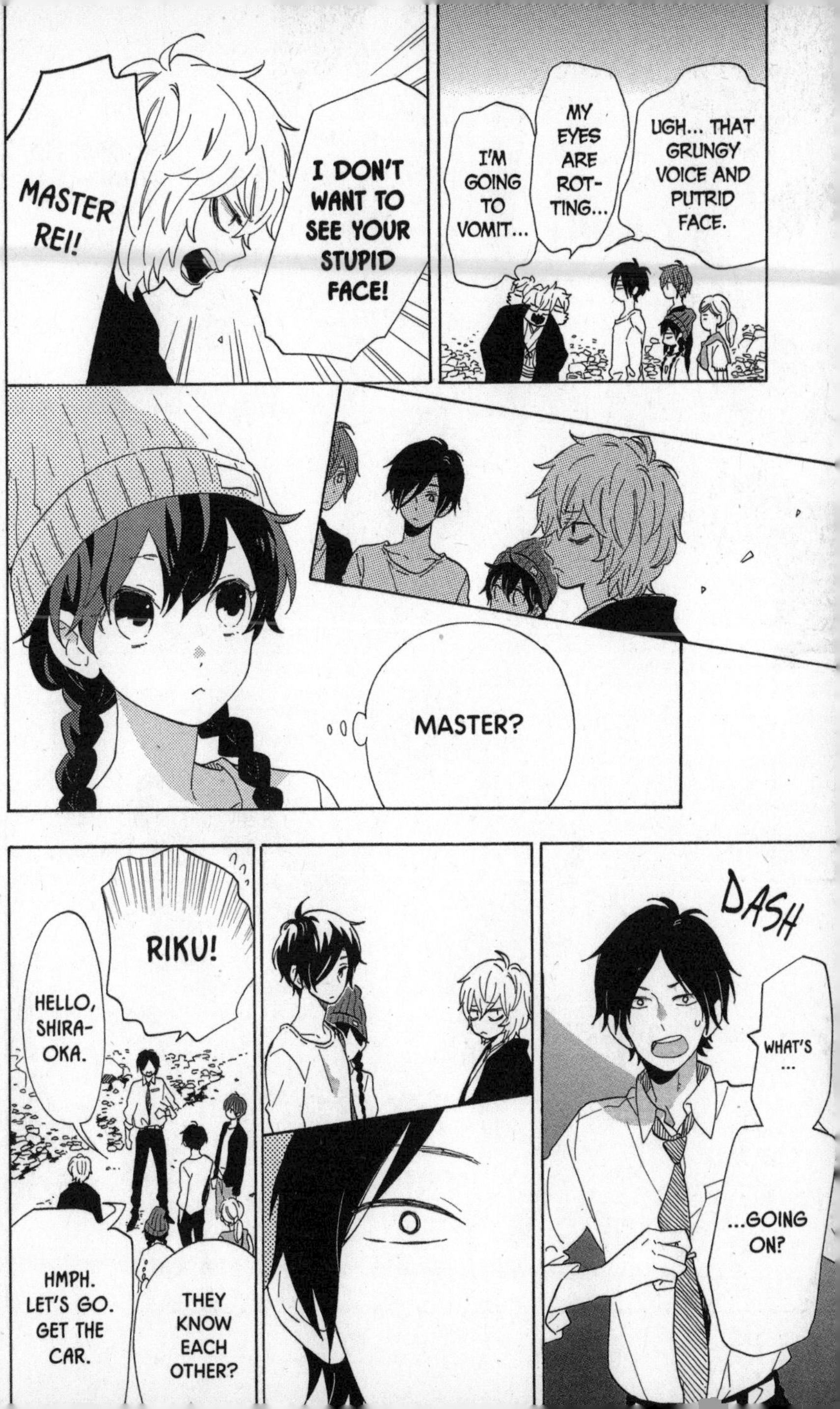
UGH... THAT GRUNGY VOICE AND PUTRID FACE.
MY EYES ARE ROT-TING...
I'M GOING TO VOMIT...
I DON'T WANT TO SEE YOUR STUPID FACE!
MASTER REI!
MASTER?
DASH
WHAT'S ...
...GOING ON?
RIKU!
HELLO, SHIRA-OKA.
THEY KNOW EACH OTHER?
HMPH. LET'S GO. GET THE CAR.

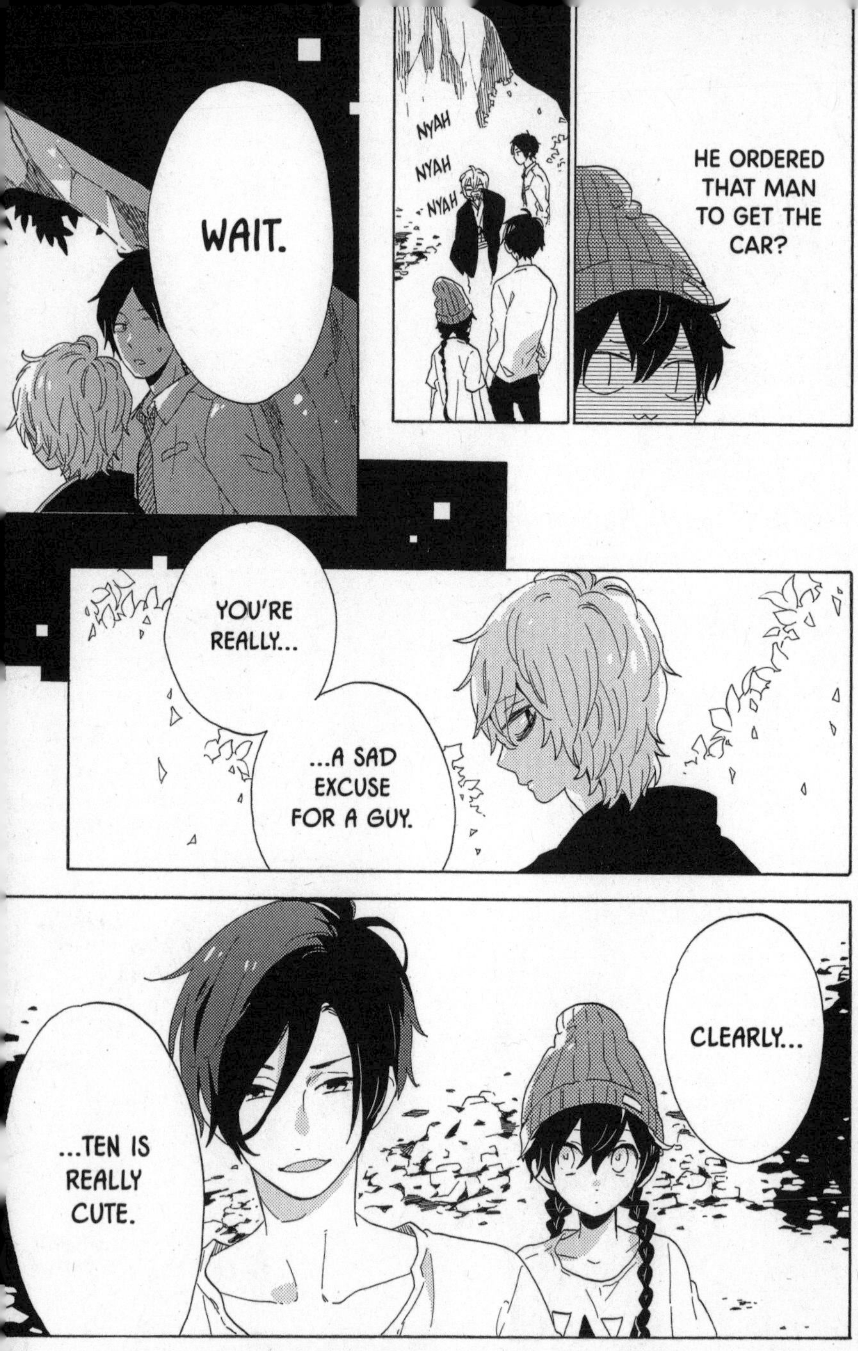
HE ORDERED THAT MAN TO GET THE CAR?
NYAH
NYAH
NYAH
WAIT.
YOU'RE REALLY...
...A SAD EXCUSE FOR A GUY.
CLEARLY...
...TEN IS REALLY CUTE.

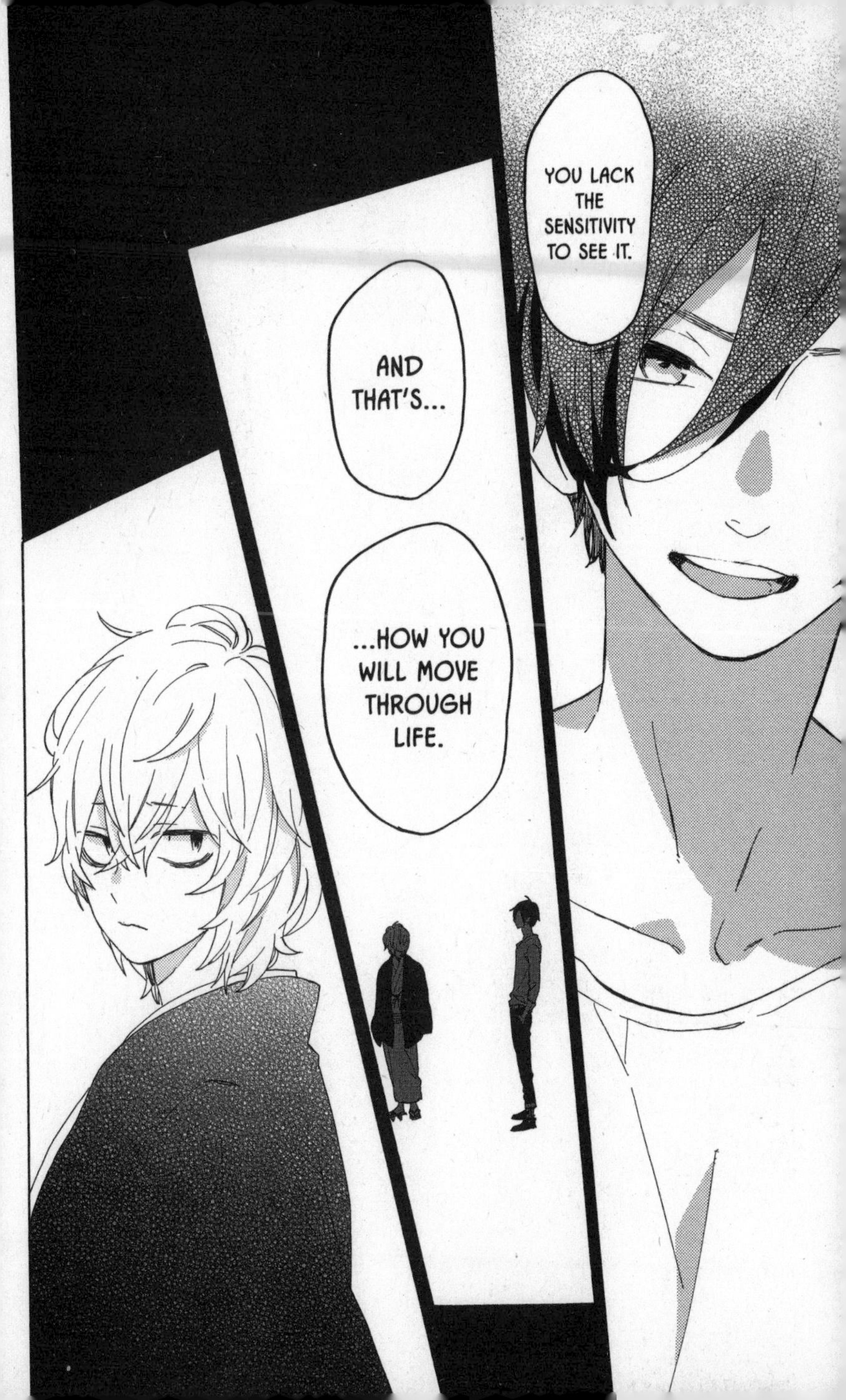
YOU LACK THE SENSITIVITY TO SEE IT.
AND THAT'S...
...HOW YOU WILL MOVE THROUGH LIFE.

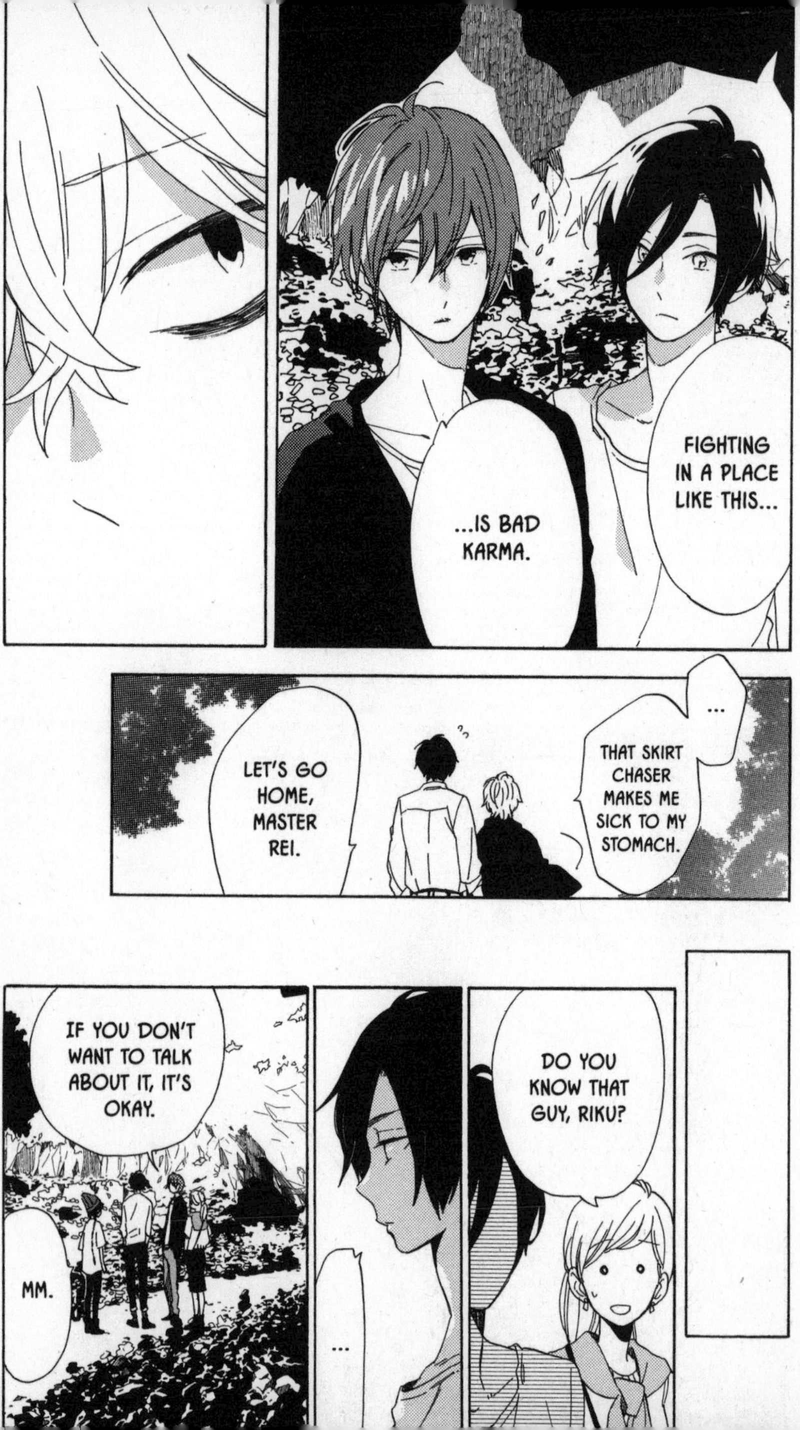
FIGHTING IN A PLACE LIKE THIS...
...IS BAD KARMA.
...
THAT SKIRT CHASER MAKES ME SICK TO MY STOMACH.
LET'S GO HOME, MASTER REI.
DO YOU KNOW THAT GUY, RIKU?
...
IF YOU DON'T WANT TO TALK ABOUT IT, IT'S OKAY.
MM.

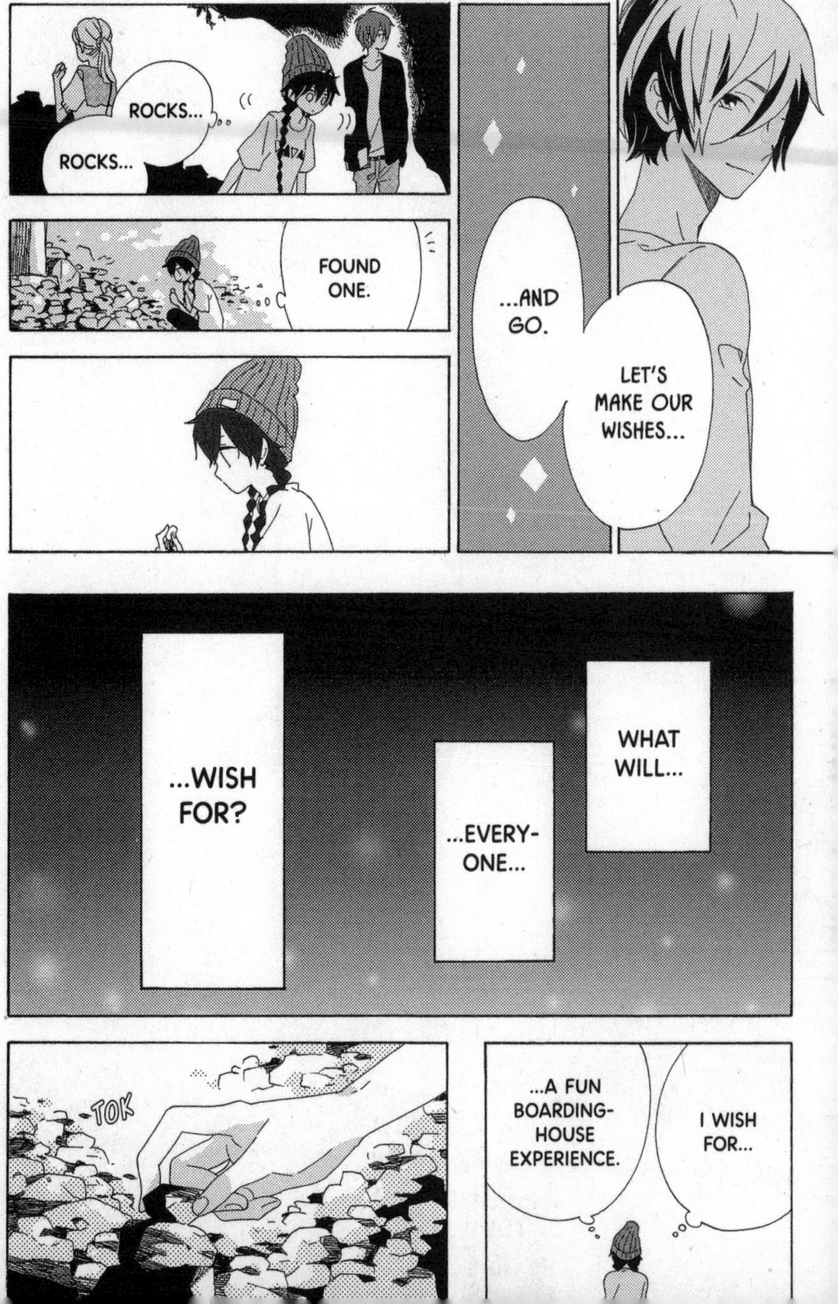
LET'S MAKE OUR WISHES...
...AND GO.
ROCKS...
ROCKS...
FOUND ONE.
WHAT WILL...
...EVERY-ONE...
...WISH FOR?
I WISH FOR...
...A FUN BOARDING-HOUSE EXPERIENCE.
TOK

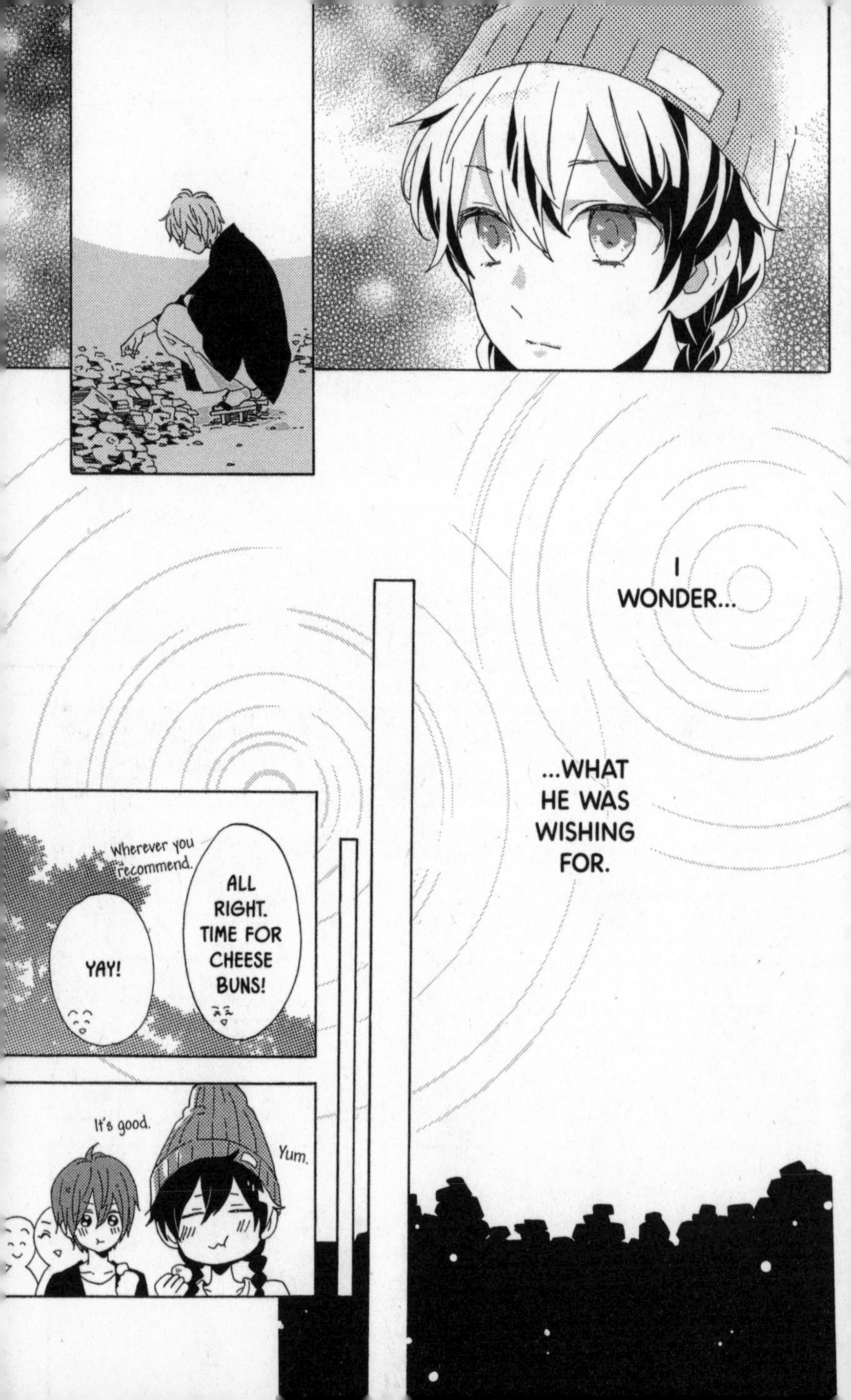
I WONDER...
...WHAT HE WAS WISHING FOR.
ALL RIGHT. TIME FOR CHEESE BUNS!
Wherever you recommend.
YAY!
Yum.
It's good.

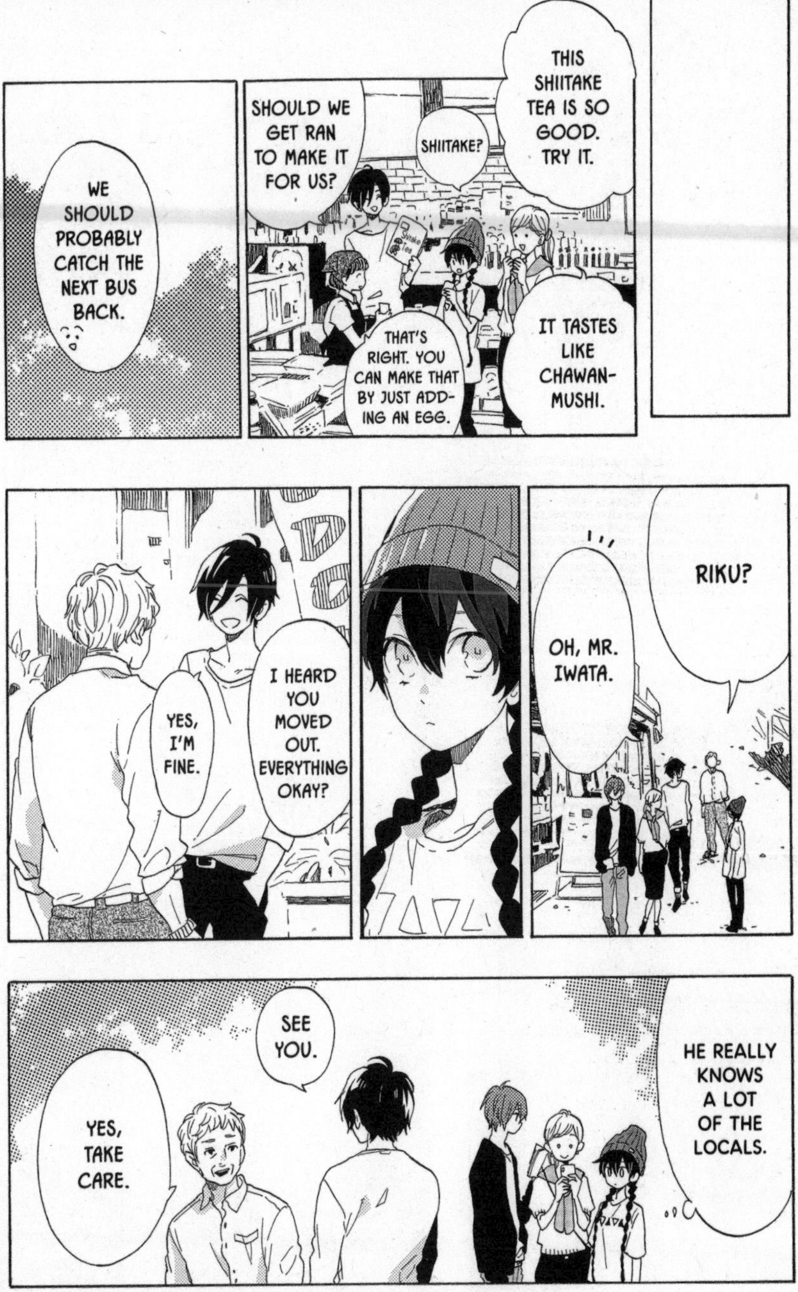
THIS SHIITAKE TEA IS SO GOOD. TRY IT.
SHIITAKE?
SHOULD WE GET RAN TO MAKE IT FOR US?
Shiitake Tea
IT TASTES LIKE CHAWAN-MUSHI.
THAT'S RIGHT. YOU CAN MAKE THAT BY JUST ADDING AN EGG.
WE SHOULD PROBABLY CATCH THE NEXT BUS BACK.
RIKU?
OH, MR. IWATA.
I HEARD YOU MOVED OUT. EVERYTHING OKAY?
YES, I'M FINE.
HE REALLY KNOWS A LOT OF THE LOCALS.
SEE YOU.
YES, TAKE CARE.

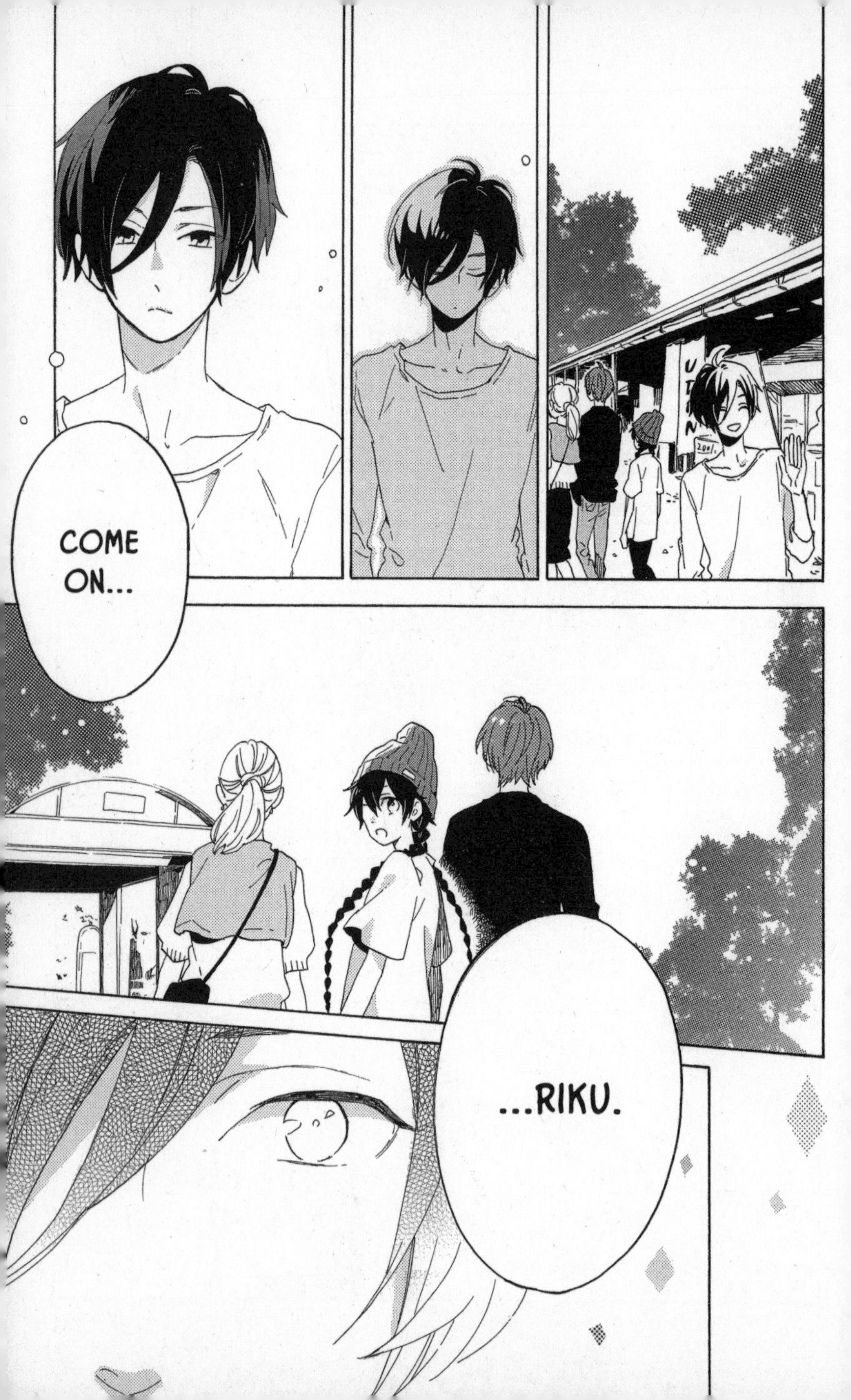
COME ON...
...RIKU.

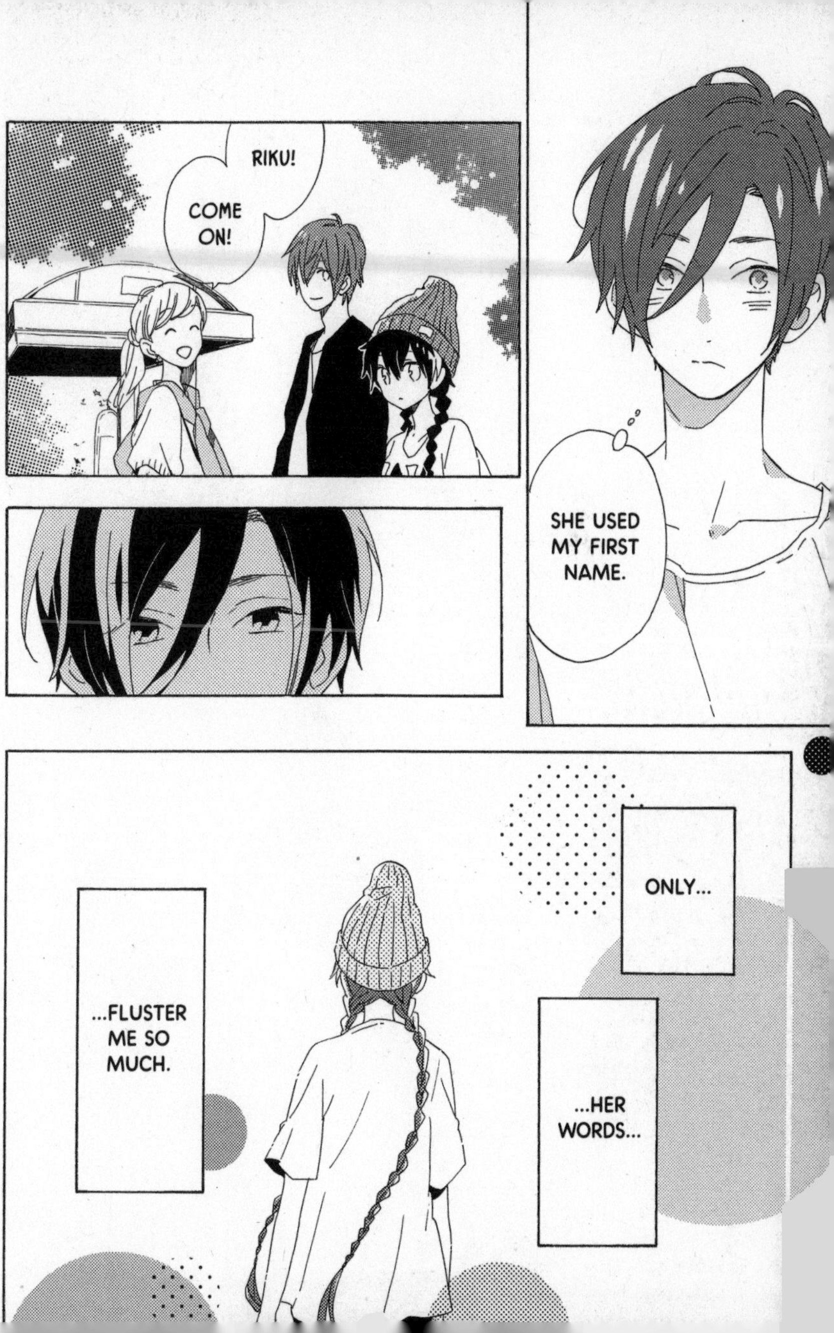
SHE USED MY FIRST NAME.
RIKU!
COME ON!
ONLY...
...HER WORDS...
...FLUSTER ME SO MUCH.

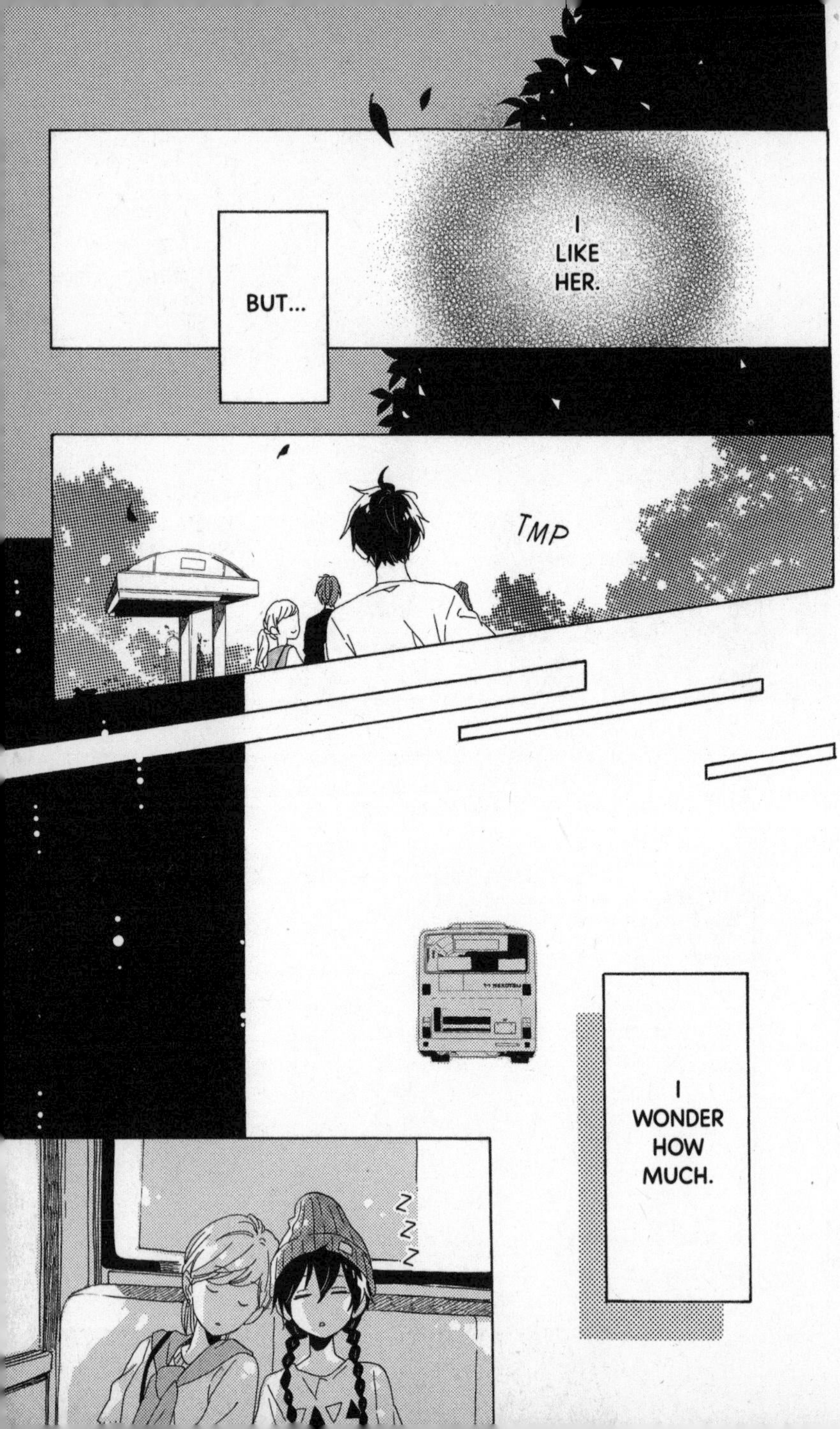
I LIKE HER.
BUT...
TMP
I WONDER HOW MUCH.
ZZZ

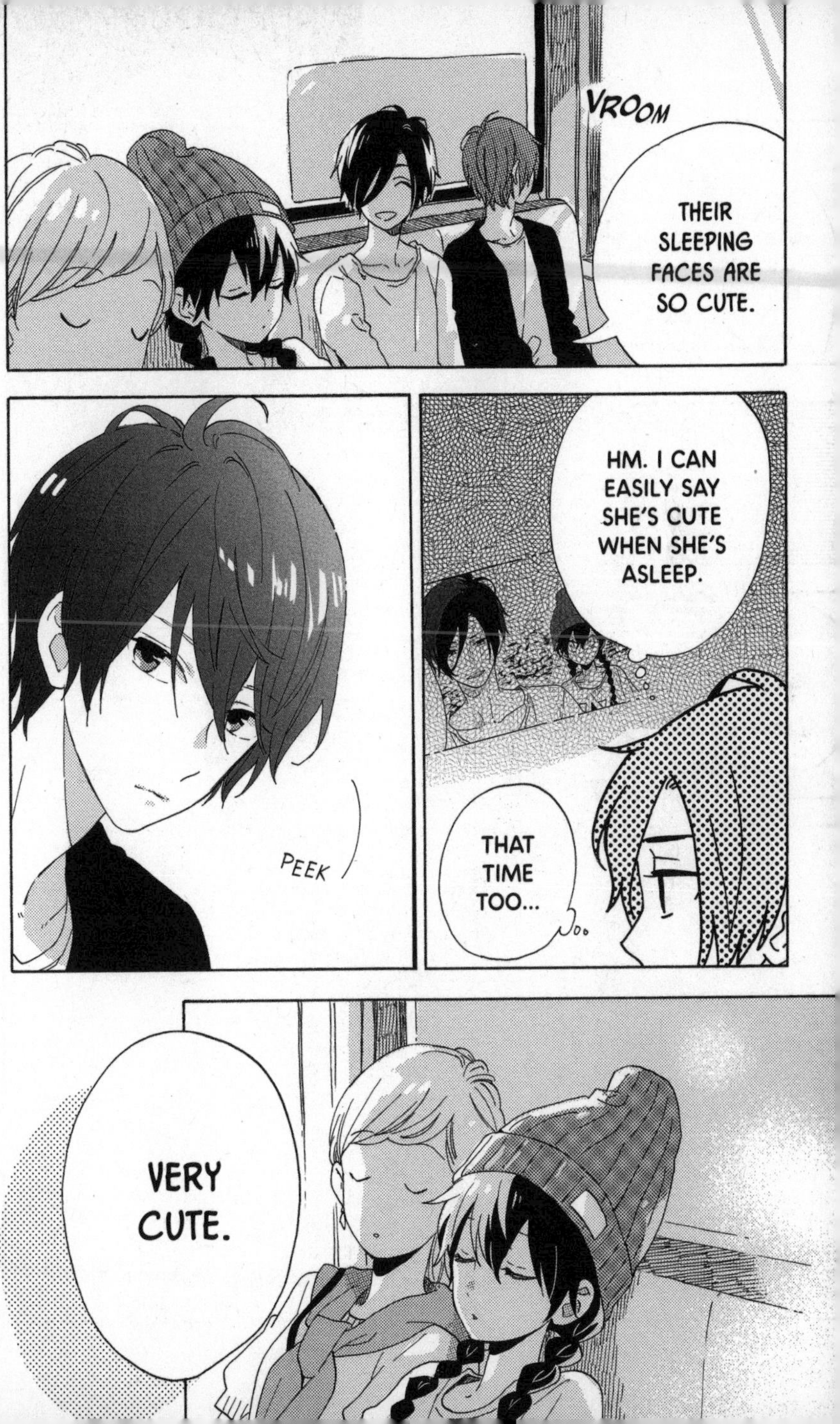
VROOM
THEIR SLEEPING FACES ARE SO CUTE.
HM. I CAN EASILY SAY SHE'S CUTE WHEN SHE'S ASLEEP.
THAT TIME TOO...
PEEK
VERY CUTE.

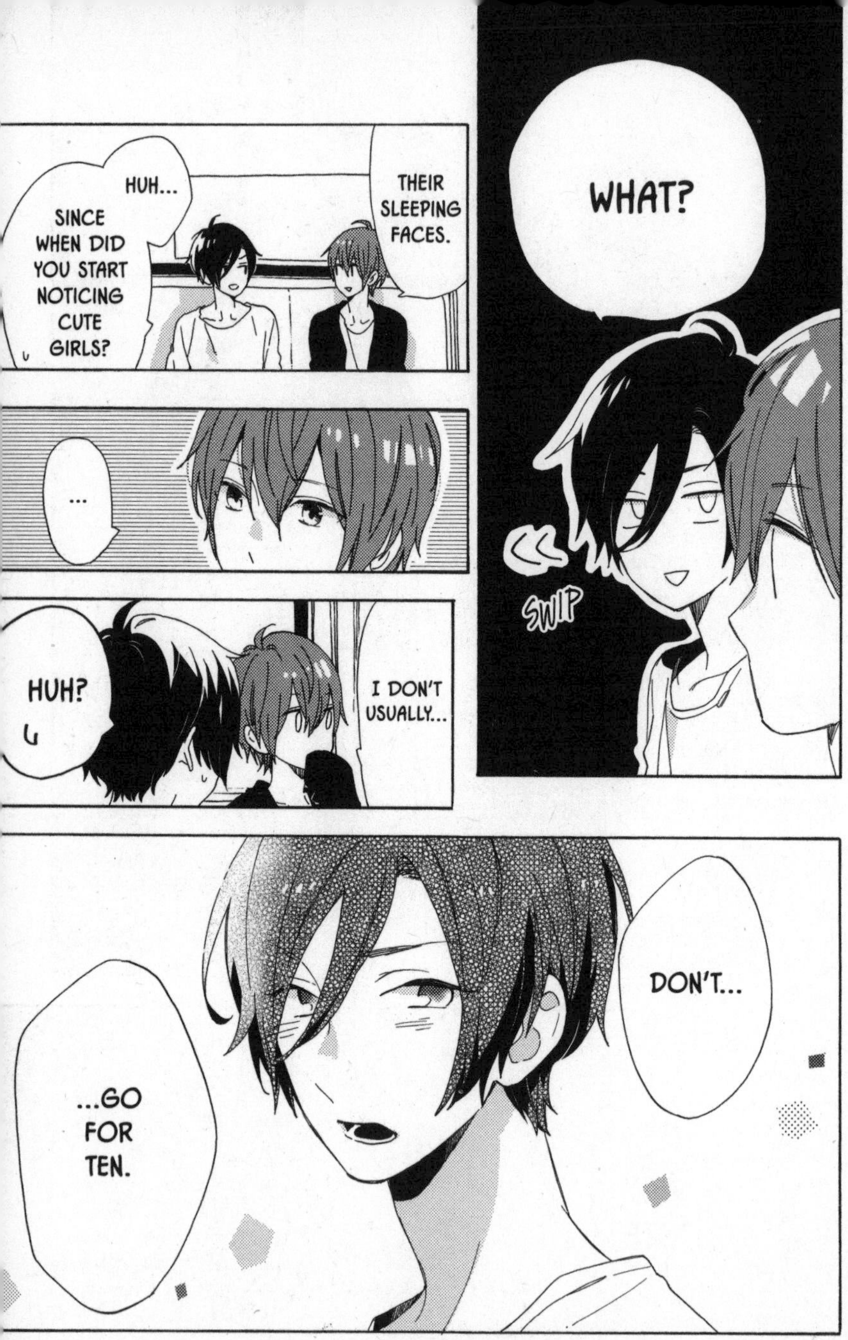
WHAT?
SWIP
THEIR SLEEPING FACES.
HUH...
SINCE WHEN DID YOU START NOTICING CUTE GIRLS?
...
I DON'T USUALLY...
HUH?
DON'T...
...GO FOR TEN.

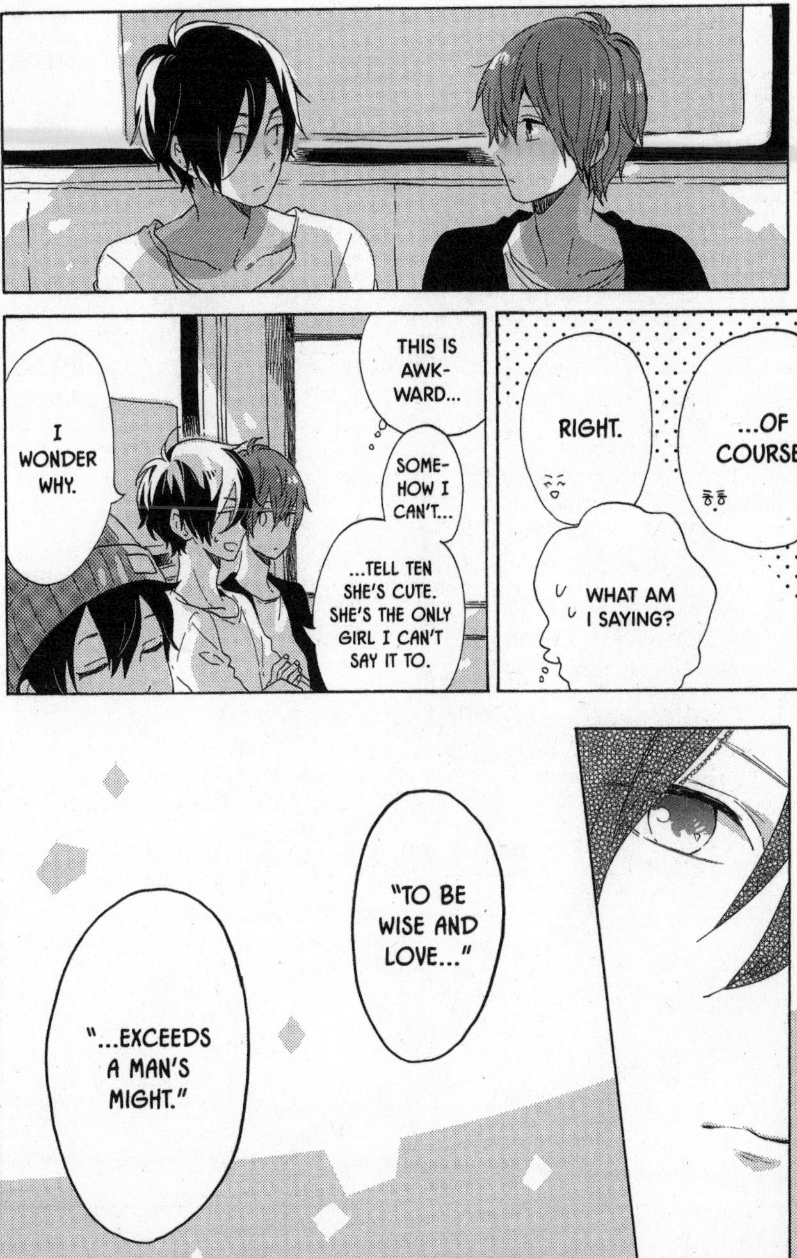
...OF COURSE.
RIGHT.
WHAT AM I SAYING?
THIS IS AWK-WARD...
SOME-HOW I CAN'T...
...TELL TEN SHE'S CUTE. SHE'S THE ONLY GIRL I CAN'T SAY IT TO.
I WONDER WHY.
"TO BE WISE AND LOVE..."
"...EXCEEDS A MAN'S MIGHT."

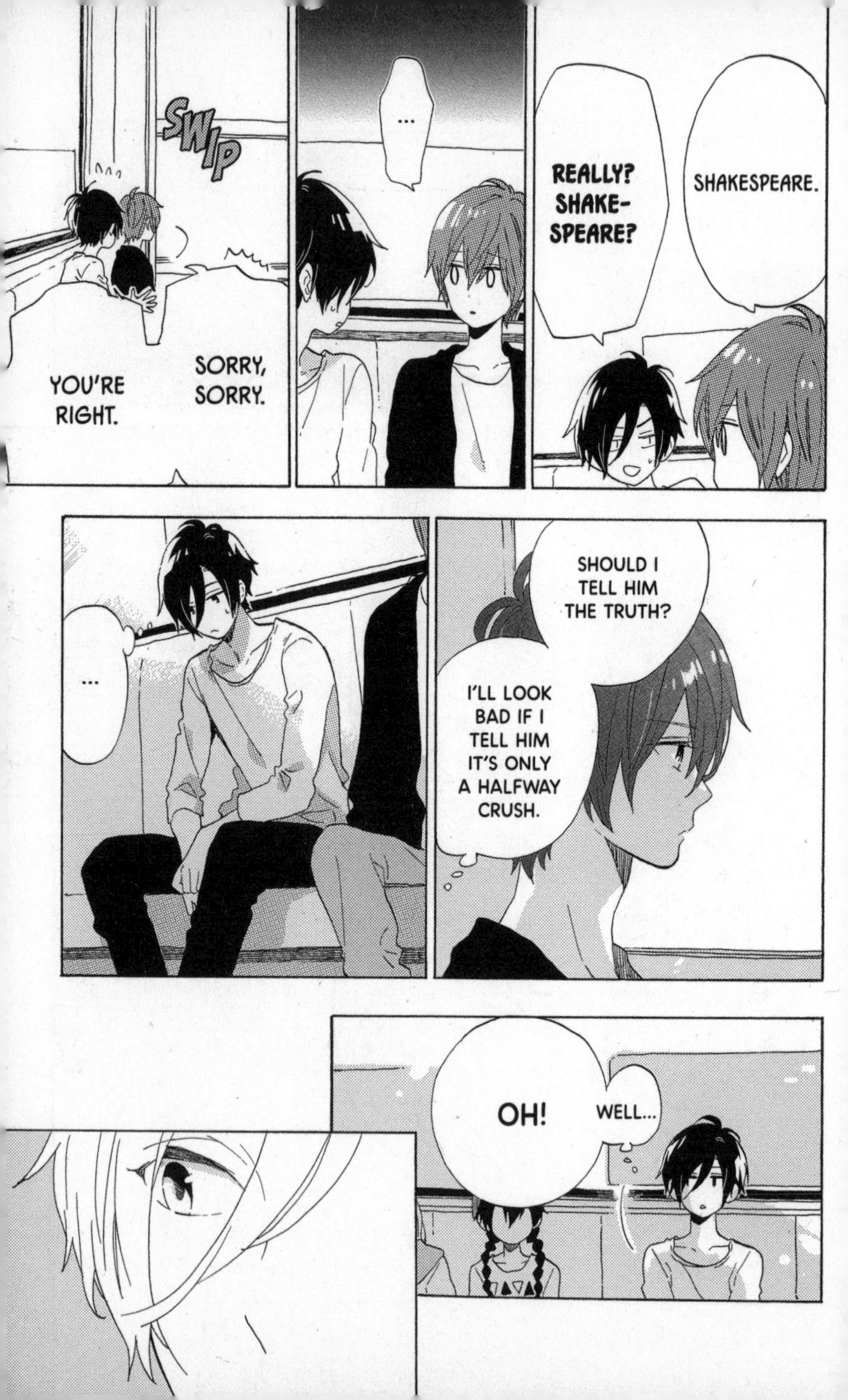
SHAKESPEARE.
REALLY? SHAKE-SPEARE?
...
SWIP
SORRY, SORRY.
YOU'RE RIGHT.
SHOULD I TELL HIM THE TRUTH?
I'LL LOOK BAD IF I TELL HIM IT'S ONLY A HALFWAY CRUSH.
...
WELL...
OH!

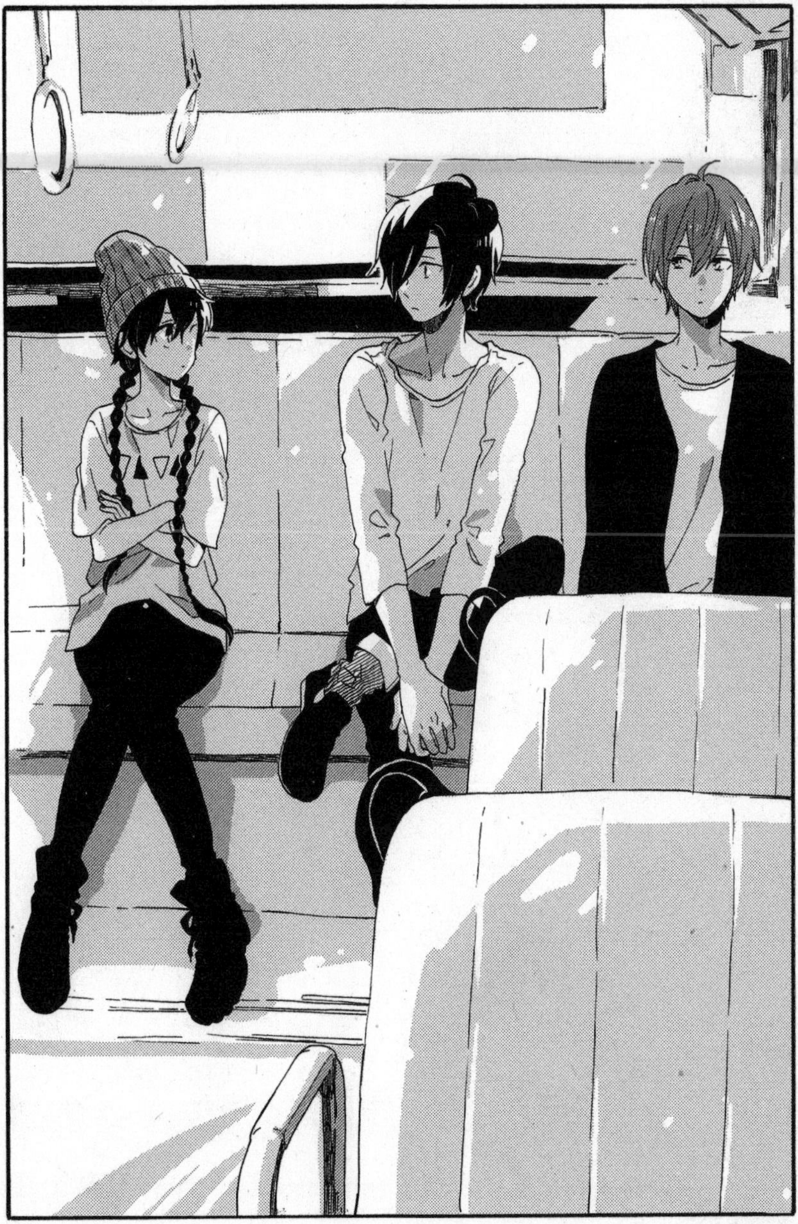

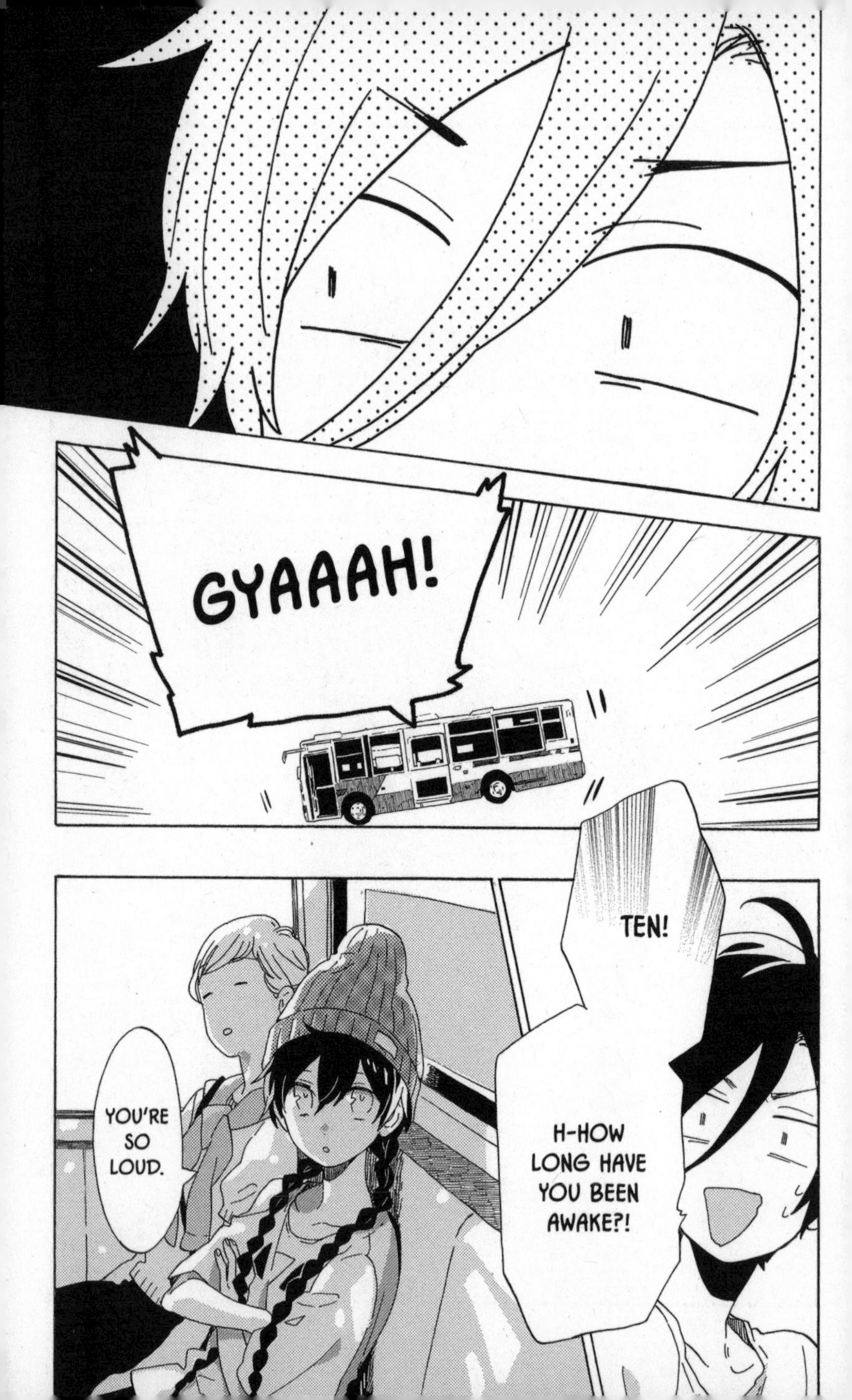
GYAAAH!
TEN!
H-HOW LONG HAVE YOU BEEN AWAKE?!
YOU'RE SO LOUD.

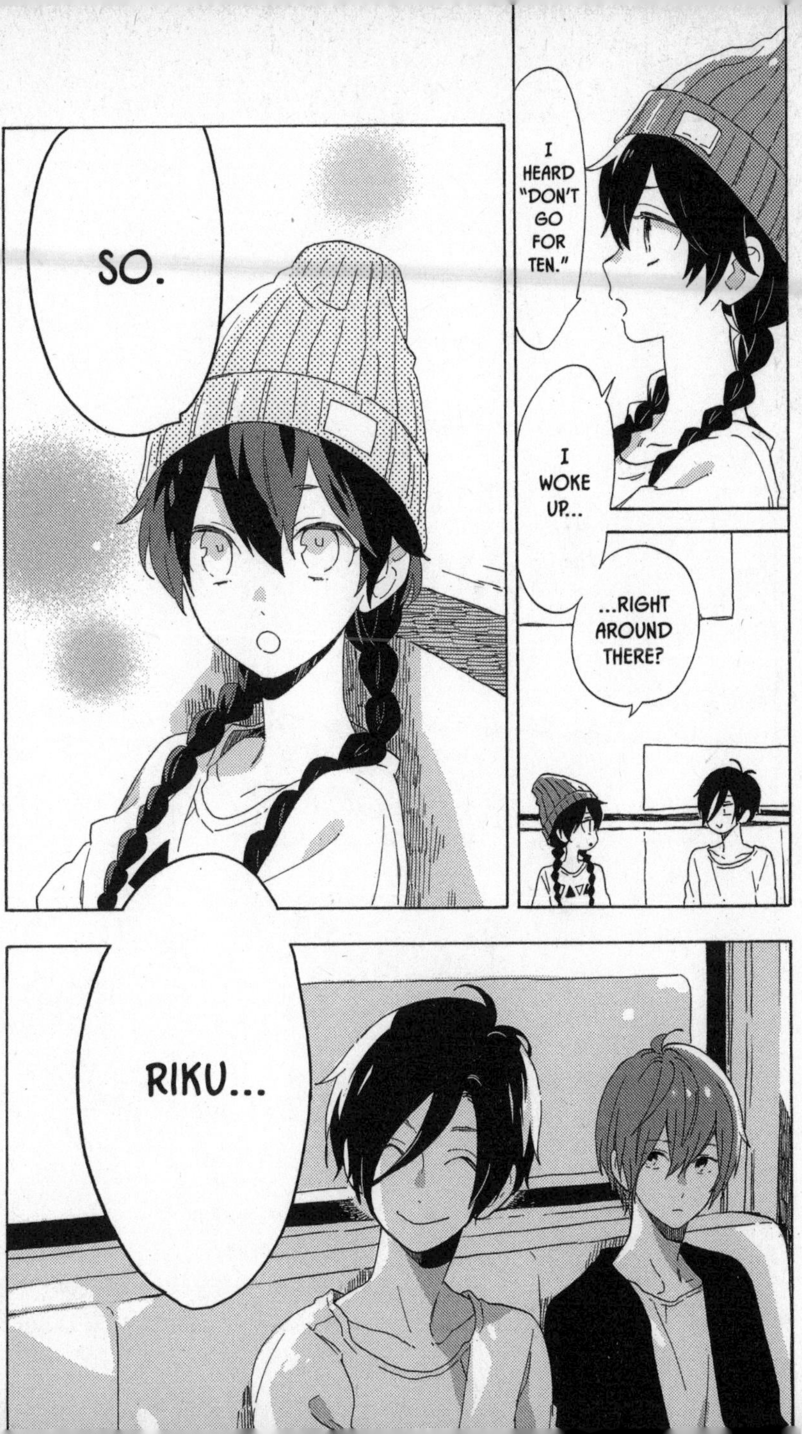
I HEARD "DON'T GO FOR TEN."
I WOKE UP...
...RIGHT AROUND THERE?
SO.
RIKU...

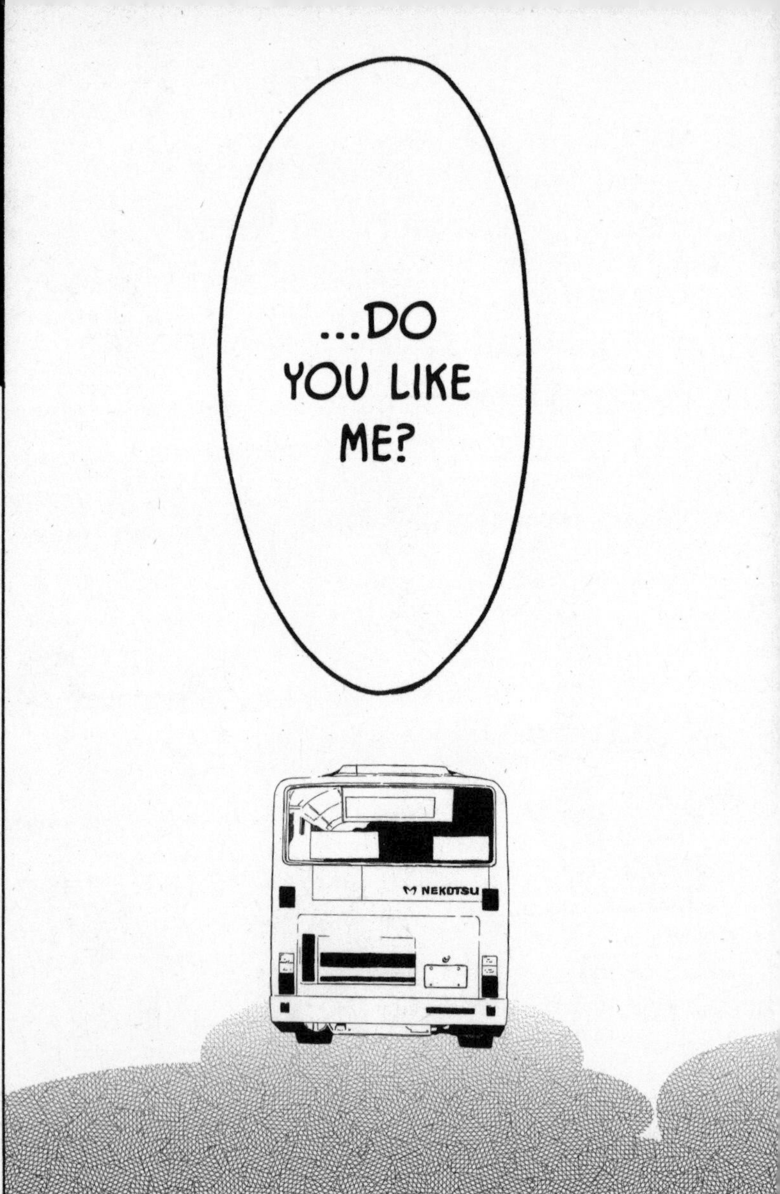
...DO YOU LIKE ME?
NEKOTSU

Vol. 1/End

Hello! Nice to meet you. It's been a while.
When we were about halfway through
Hibi Chouchou, we decided to do this series.
Shortcake Cake has a very sweet meaning.
We'll do our best to make sure you enjoy
reading it.
Thanks for your support!

Special
Thanks ♥

Nyakacchi
The *Margaret* editorial department
Our designer, Kawatani-sama
(Kawatani Design)
Our assistants, Nao Hamaguchi
and Setsuna Ousawa

Follow Shojo Beat on Twitter: @shojobeat
Send us your comments about the series!

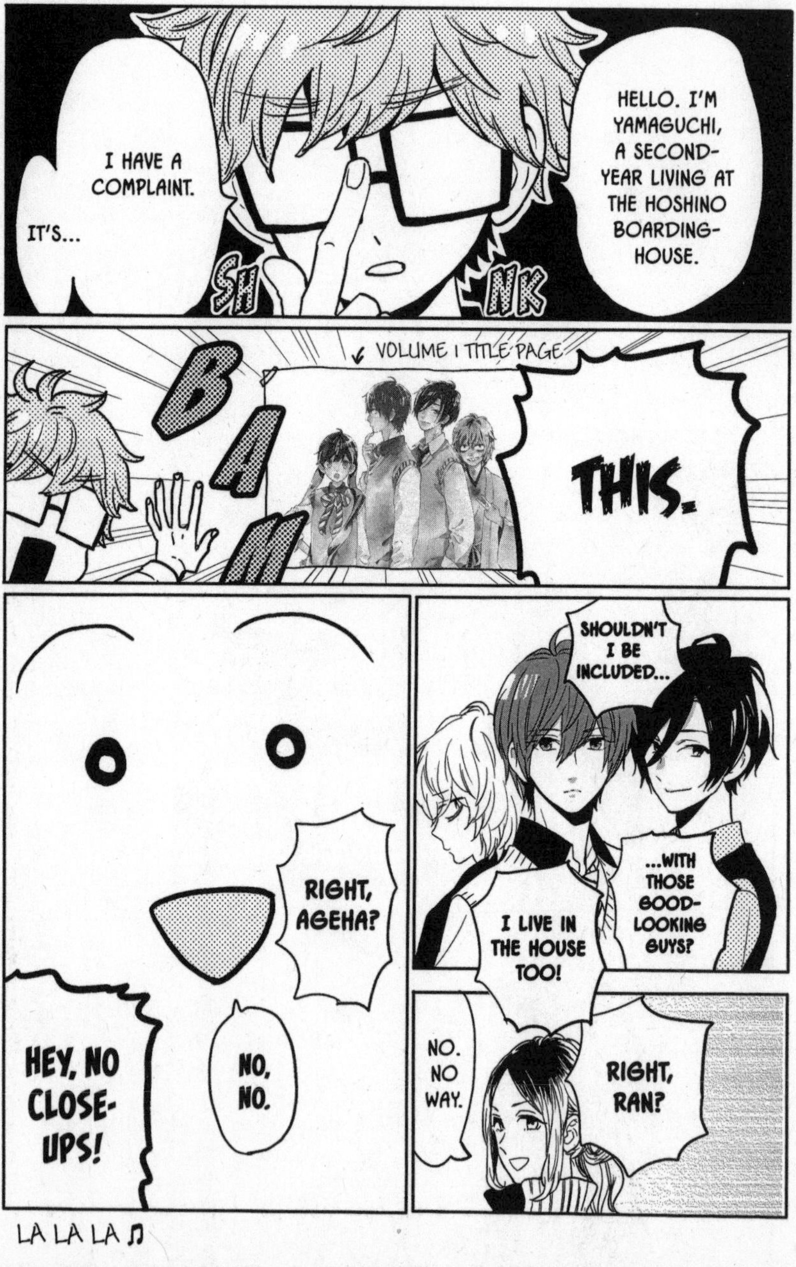
HELLO. I'M YAMAGUCHI, A SECOND-YEAR LIVING AT THE HOSHINO BOARDING-HOUSE.
SHNK
I HAVE A COMPLAINT.
IT'S...
THIS.
VOLUME 1 TITLE PAGE
BAM
SHOULDN'T I BE INCLUDED...
...WITH THOSE GOOD-LOOKING GUYS?
I LIVE IN THE HOUSE TOO!
RIGHT, RAN?
NO. NO WAY.
RIGHT, AGEHA?
NO, NO.
HEY, NO CLOSE-UPS!

LA LA LA ♫

SHORTCAKE CAKE

Title Page Collection
Preview

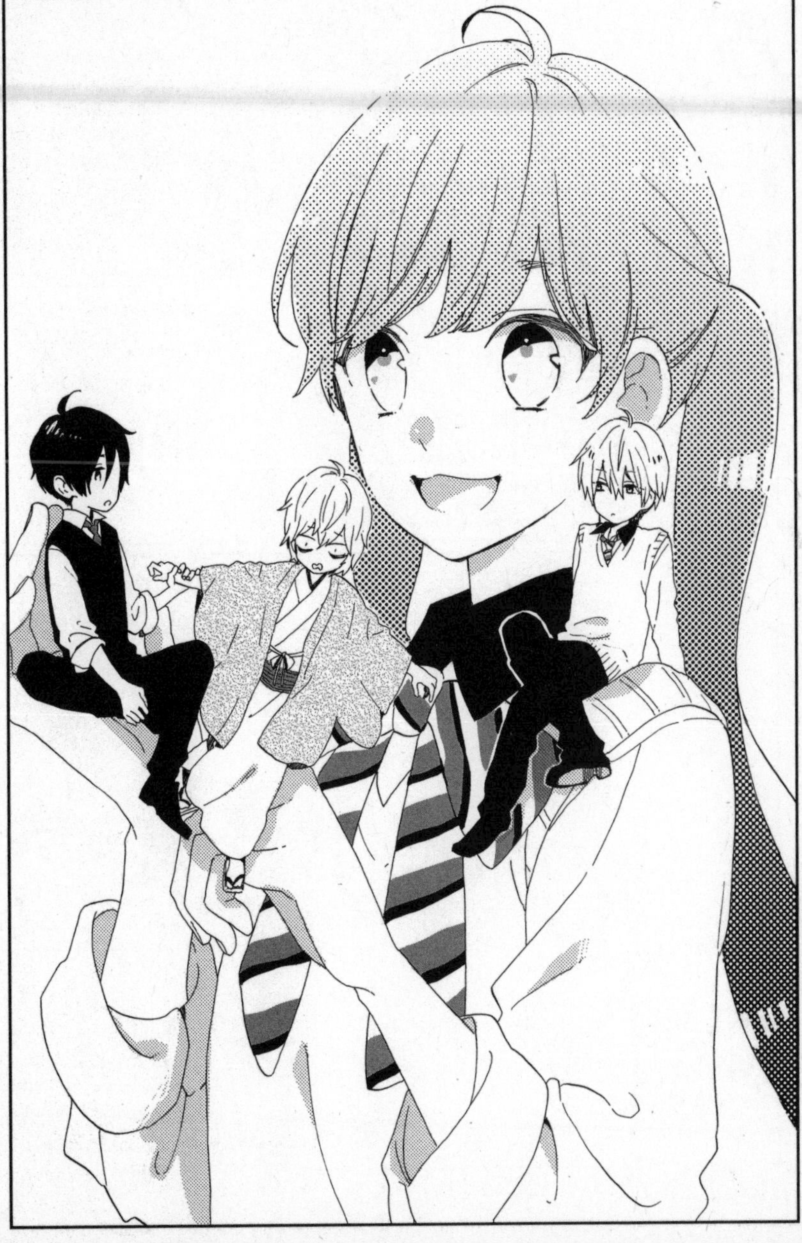

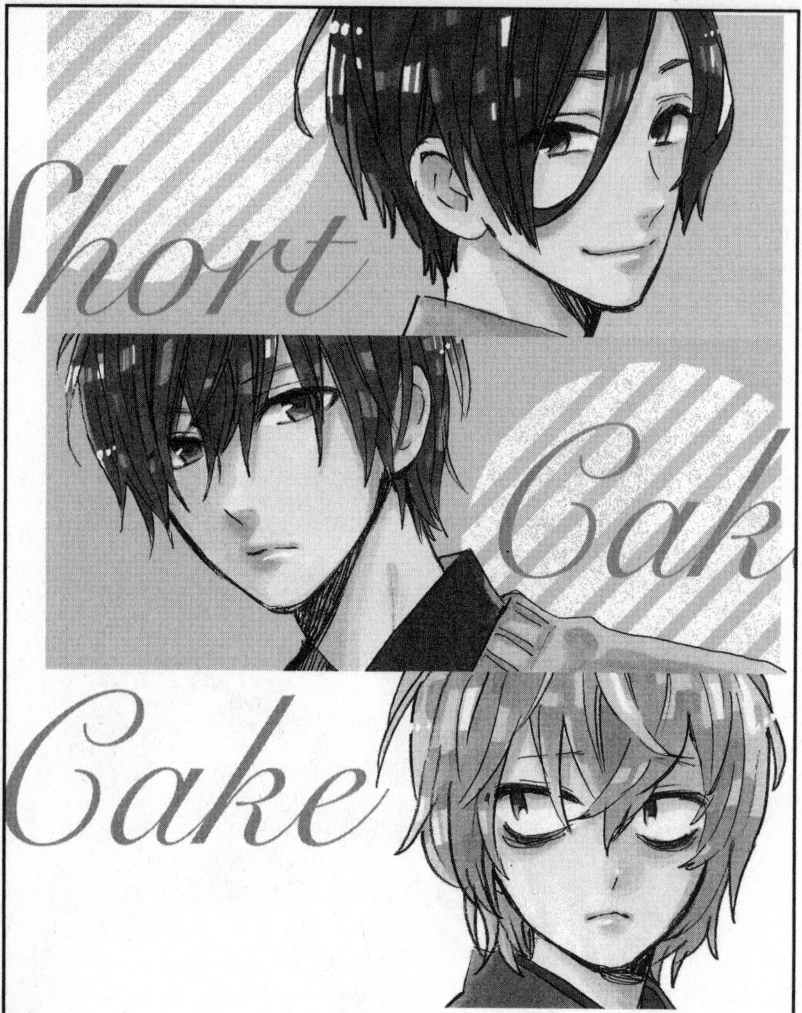
Short
Cak
Cake

SHORTCAKE CAKE

Title Page Collection

Chapter 2

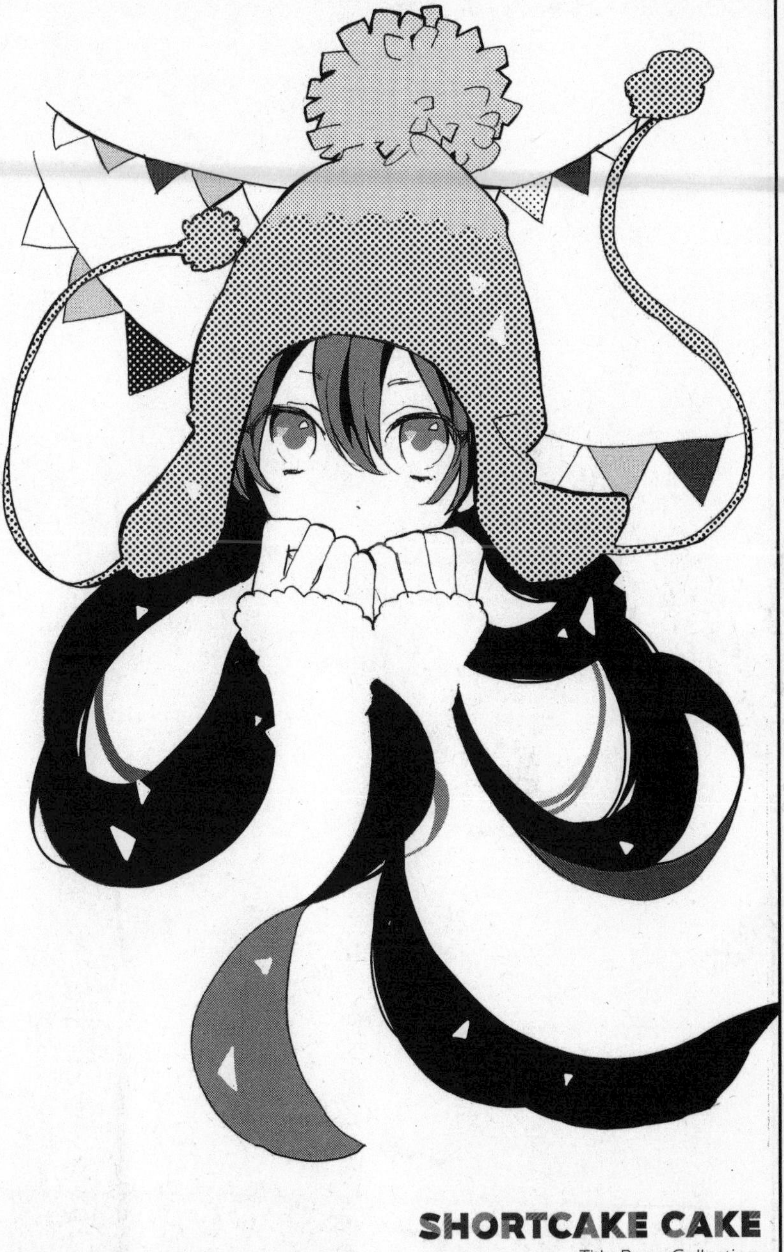

SHORTCAKE CAKE

Title Page Collection

Chapter 3

SHORTCAKE CAKE

Title Page Collection
Preview

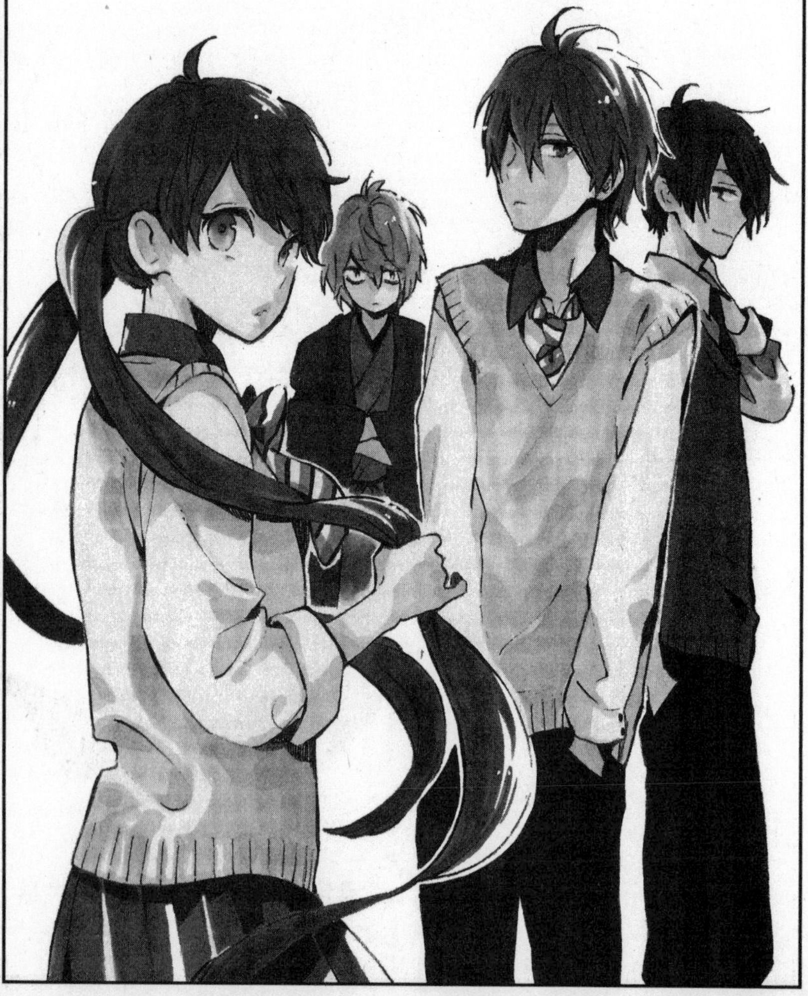

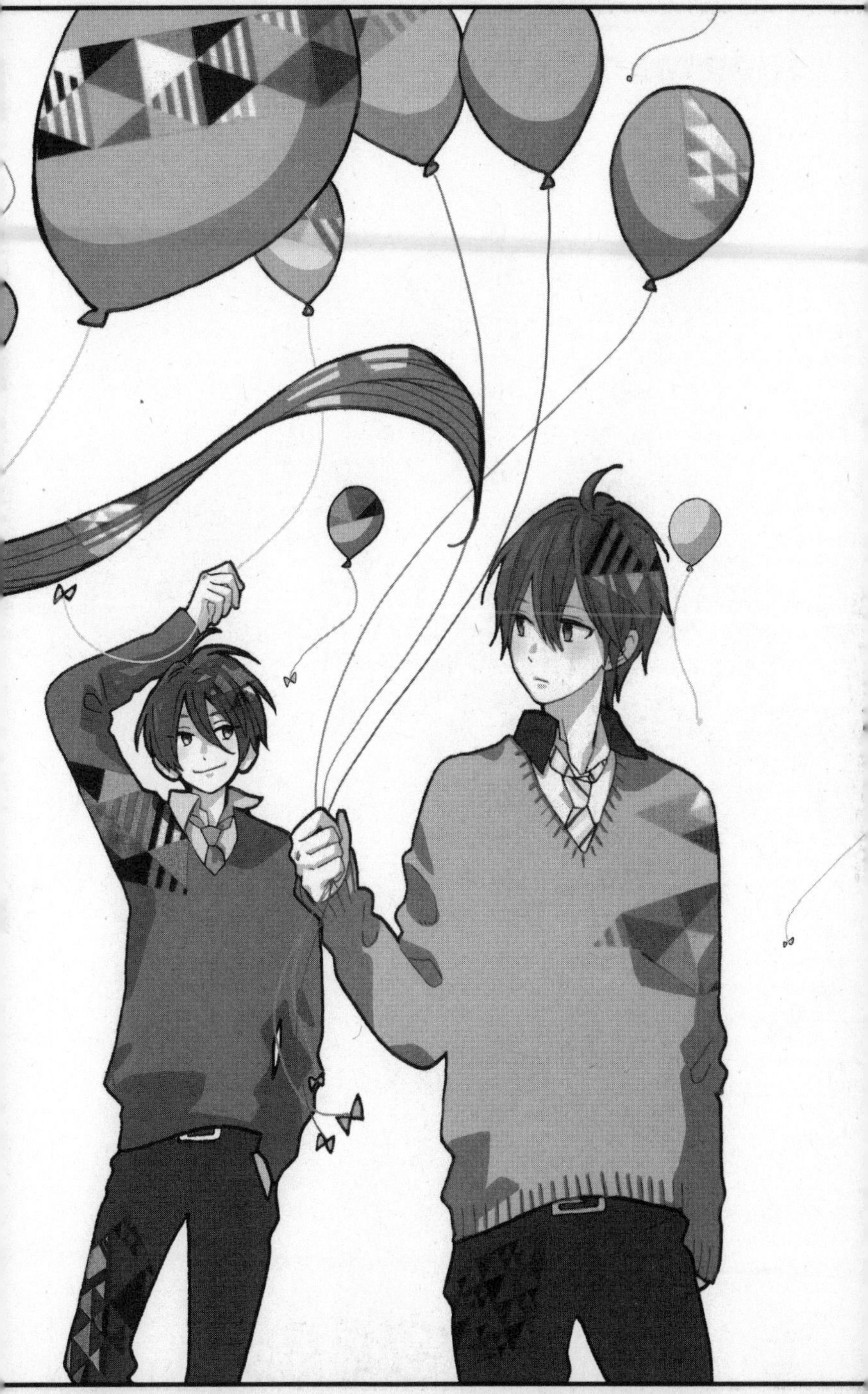

SHORTCAKE CAKE

Title Page Collection
Chapter 4

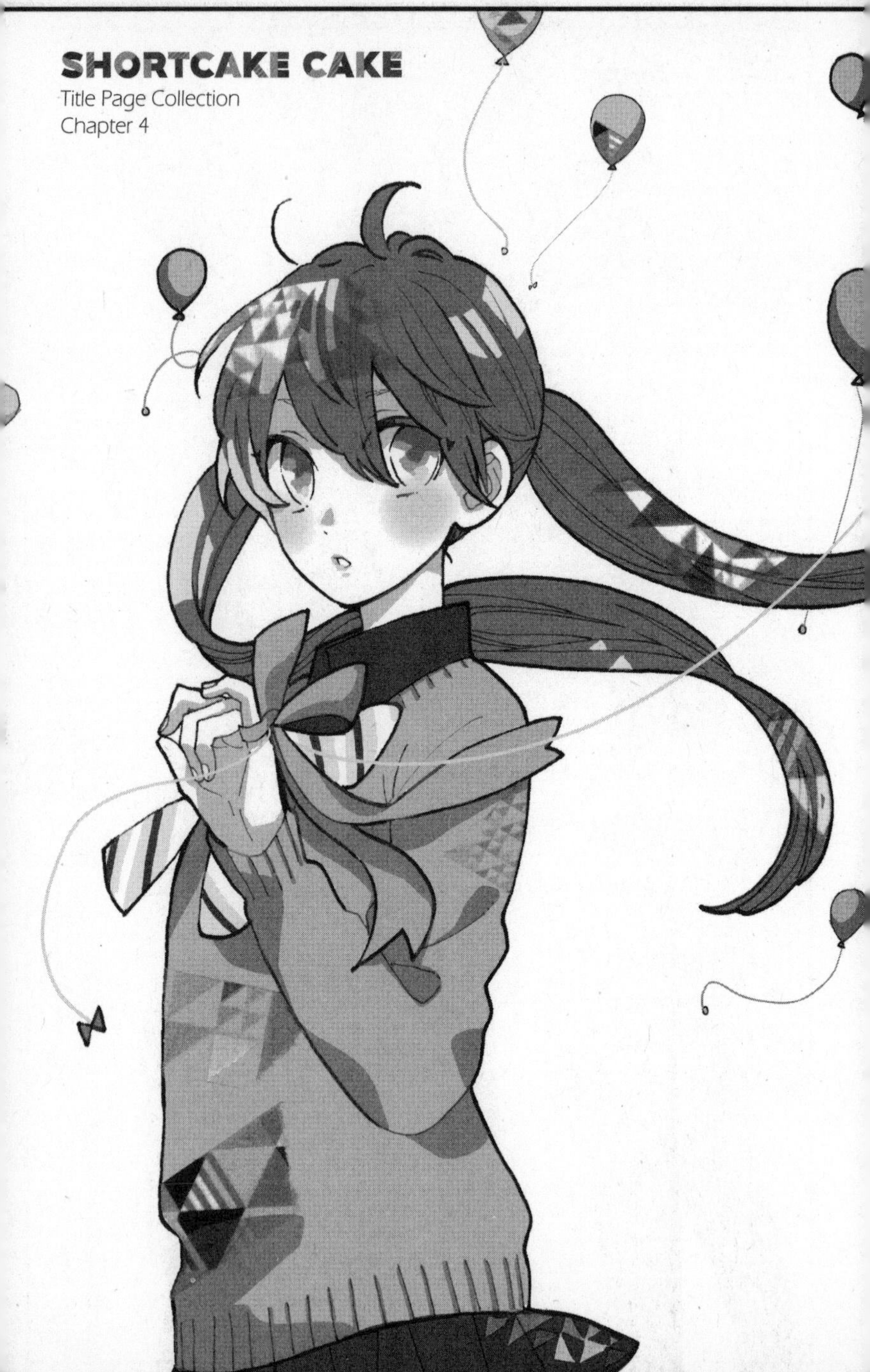

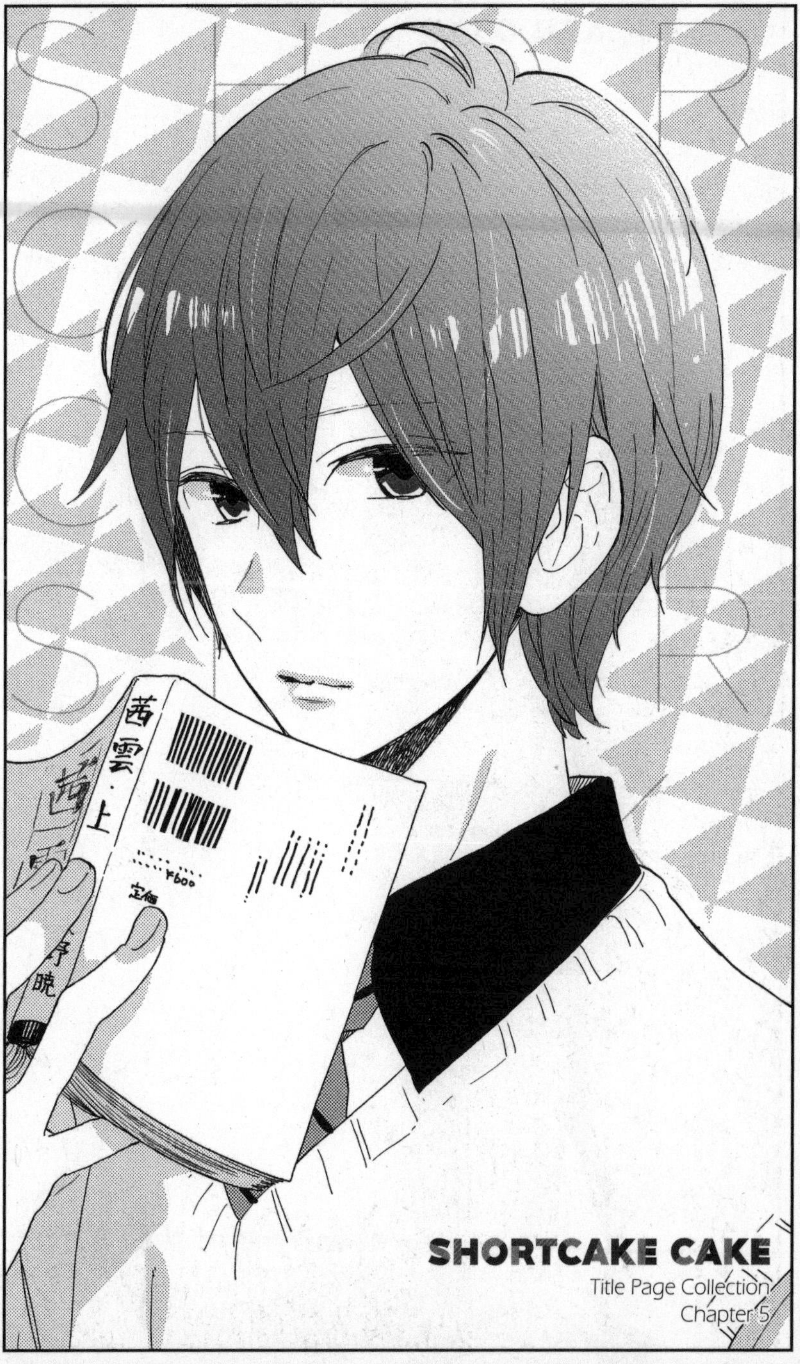
SHORTCAKE CAKE
Title Page Collection
Chapter 5

SHORTCAKE CAKE

Title Page Collection

Issue 23 Magazine Cover

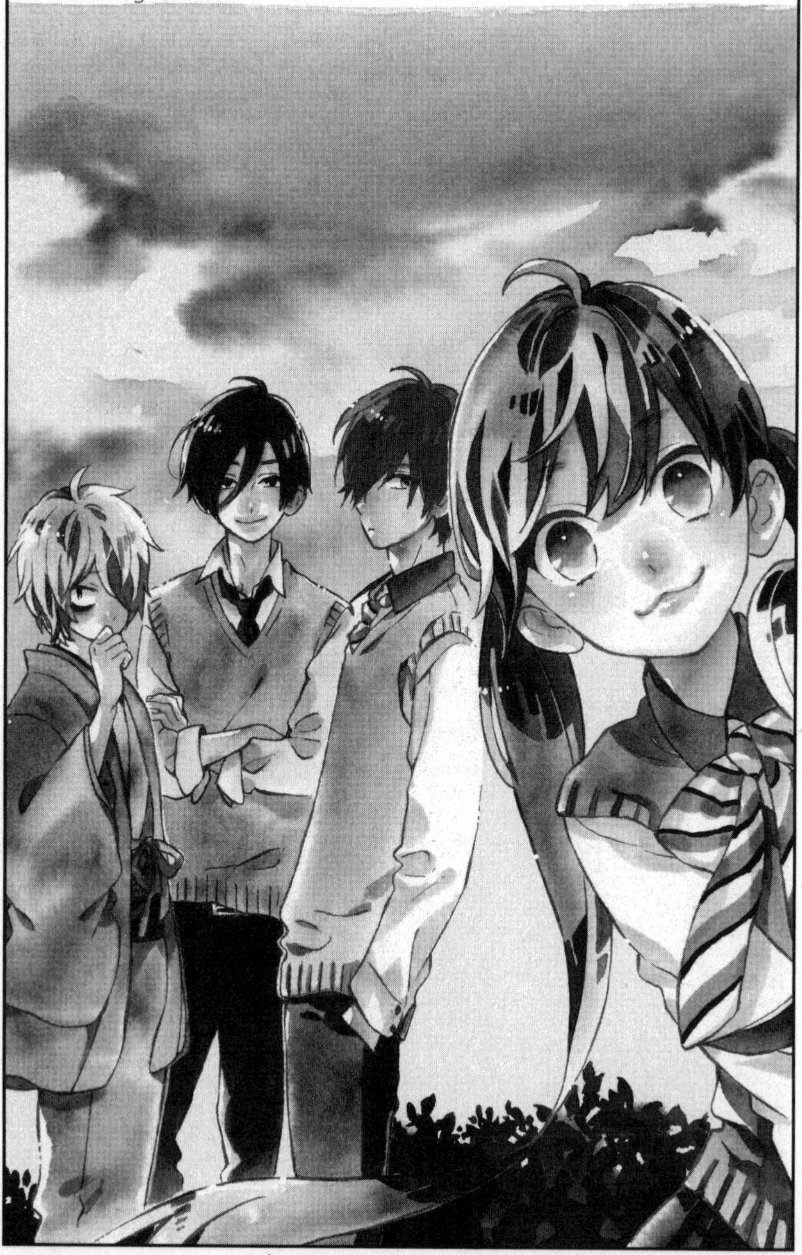

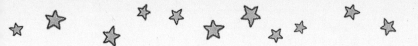

We hope you enjoy our new series.
We'll buy some shortcake to
celebrate the release of volume 1!

—suu Morishita

suu Morishita is a creator duo.
The story is by Makiro, and the art is by
Nachiyan. In 2010 they debuted with the
one-shot "Anote Konote." Their works include
Hibi Chouchou and *Shortcake Cake*.

SHORTCAKE CAKE

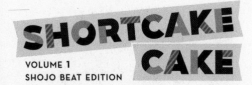

VOLUME 1
SHOJO BEAT EDITION

STORY + ART BY **suu Morishita**

TRANSLATION **Emi Louie-Nishikawa**
TOUCH-UP ART + LETTERING **Inori Fukuda Trant**
DESIGN **Shawn Carrico**
EDITOR **Nancy Thistlethwaite**

First published in Japan in 2015 by SHUEISHA Inc., Tokyo.
English translation rights arranged by SHUEISHA Inc.

Printed in the U.S.A.

Published by VIZ Media, LLC
P.O. Box 77010
San Francisco, CA 94107

10 9 8 7 6 5 4 3 2 1
First printing, August 2018

ratings.viz.com RATED T TEEN

PARENTAL ADVISORY
SHORTCAKE CAKE is rated T for Teen
and is recommended for ages 13 and up.
This volume contains mild language.

VIZ MEDIA
viz.com

Shojo Beat
shojobeat.com

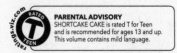

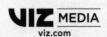

Honey
So Sweet

Story and Art by *Amu Meguro*

Little did Nao Kogure realize back in middle school that when she left an umbrella and a box of bandages in the rain for injured delinquent Taiga Onise that she would meet him again in high school. Nao wants nothing to do with the gruff and frightening Taiga, but he suddenly presents her with a huge bouquet of flowers and asks her to date him—with marriage in mind! Is Taiga really so scary, or is he a sweetheart in disguise?

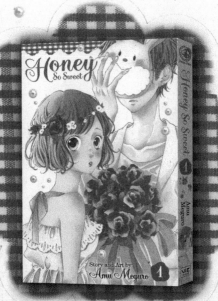

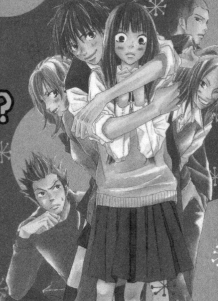
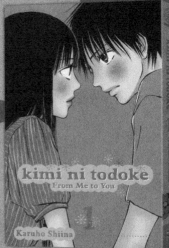
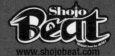

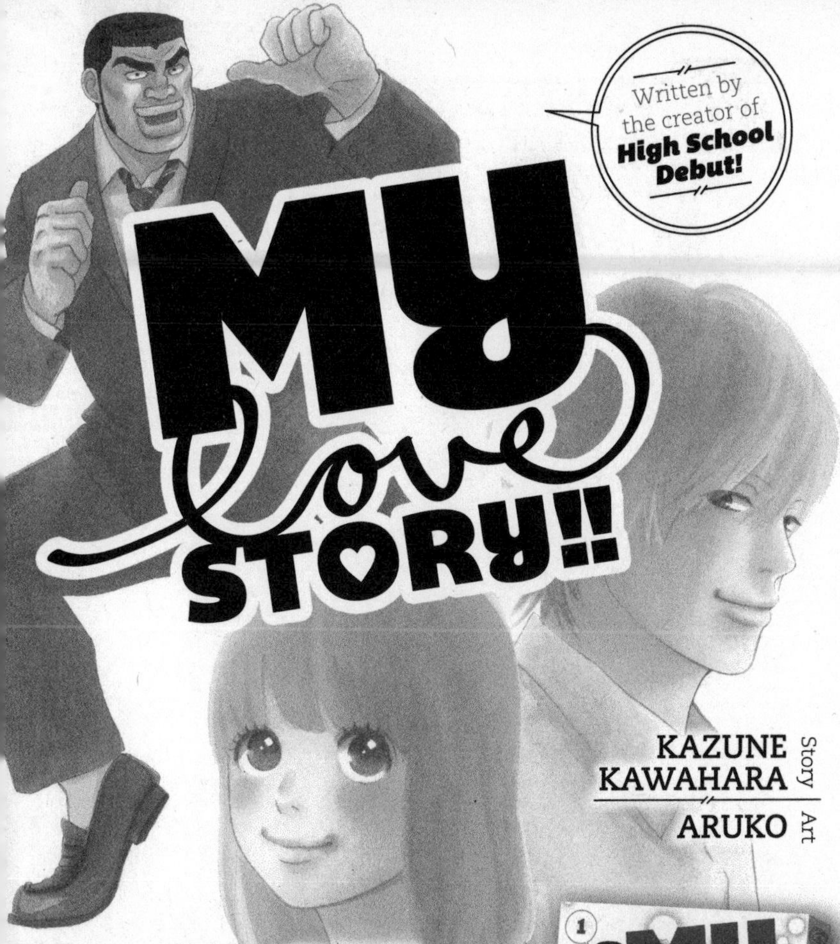
Written by the creator of High School Debut!
MY love STORY!!
KAZUNE KAWAHARA Story
ARUKO Art

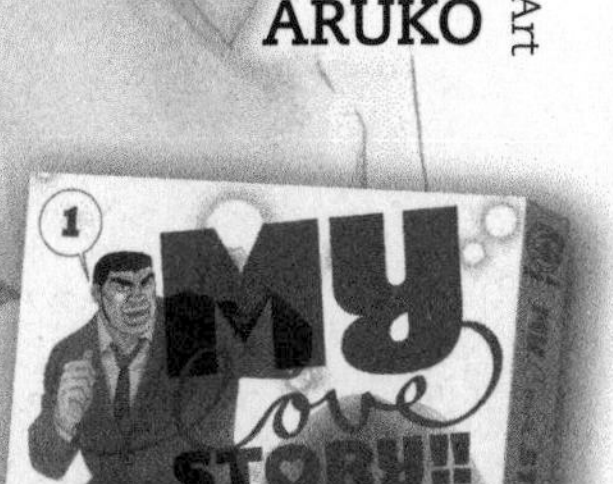
1
MY love STORY!!
KAZUNE KAWAHARA Story
ARUKO Art

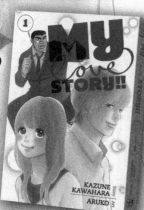

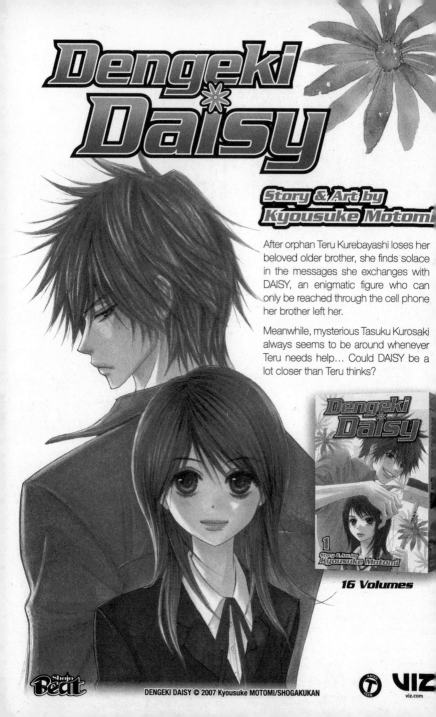

Dengeki Daisy

Story & Art by Kyousuke Motomi

After orphan Teru Kurebayashi loses her beloved older brother, she finds solace in the messages she exchanges with DAISY, an enigmatic figure who can only be reached through the cell phone her brother left her.

Meanwhile, mysterious Tasuku Kurosaki always seems to be around whenever Teru needs help... Could DAISY be a lot closer than Teru thinks?

16 Volumes

Shojo Beat

VIZ
viz.com

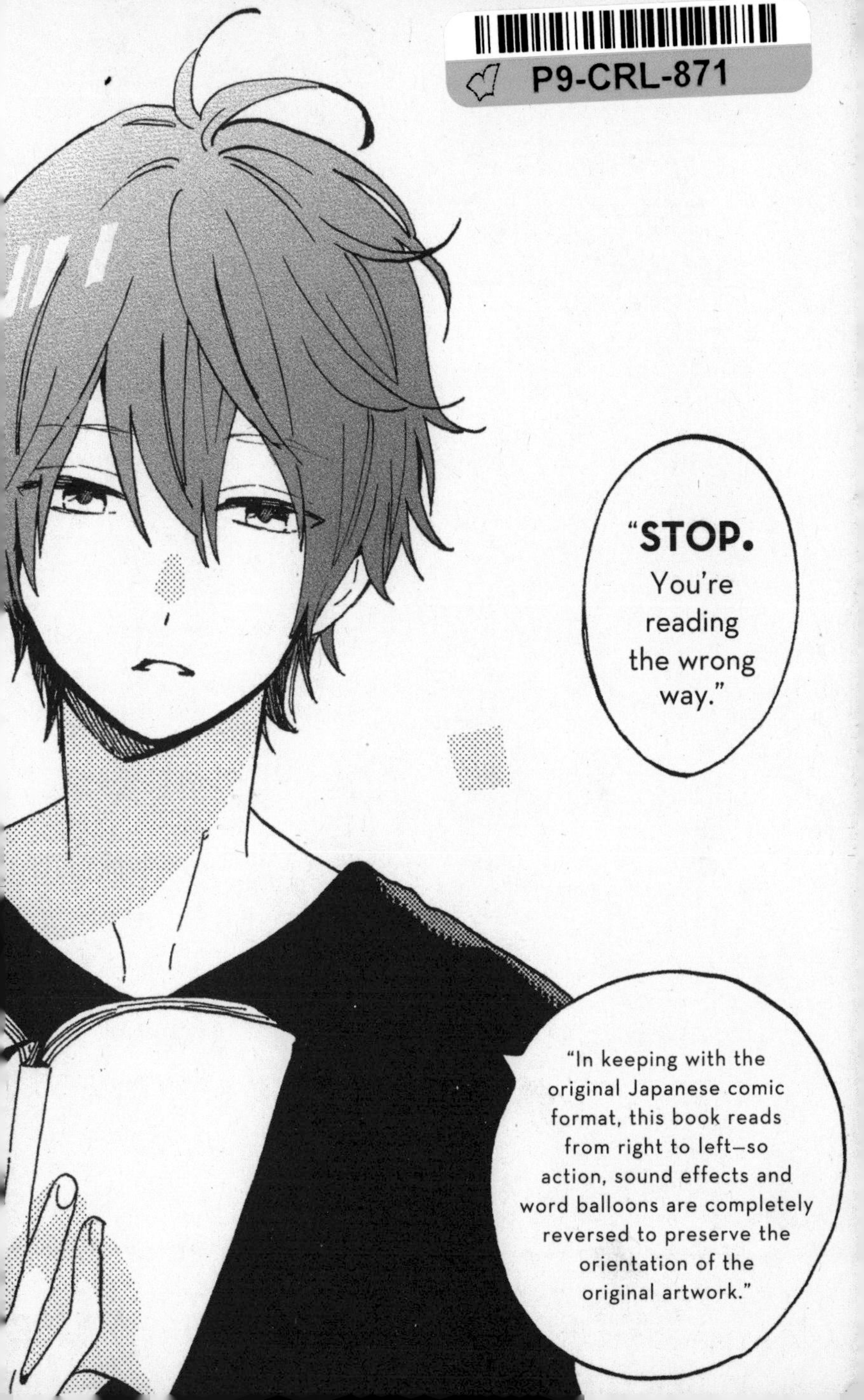
"STOP. You're reading the wrong way."
"In keeping with the original Japanese comic format, this book reads from right to left—so action, sound effects and word balloons are completely reversed to preserve the orientation of the original artwork."